WRITERS AT WORK

Fifth Series

Previously Published

WRITERS AT WORK
The *Paris Review* Interviews

Evelyn Waugh   Allen Ginsberg
Lillian Hellman   Edward Albee
William Burroughs   Harold Pinter

FOURTH SERIES

Edited by GEORGE PLIMPTON and introduced by WILFRID SHEED

Isak Dinesen   John Dos Passos
Conrad Aiken   Vladimir Nabokov
Robert Graves   Jorge Luis Borges
George Seferis   John Berryman
John Steinbeck   Anthony Burgess
Christopher Isherwood   Jack Kerouac
W. H. Auden   Anne Sexton
Eudora Welty   John Updike

Writers at Work

The *Paris Review* Interviews

FIFTH SERIES

Edited by George Plimpton
Introduction by
Francine du Plessix Gray

THE VIKING PRESS NEW YORK

First published in 1981 by The Viking Press
625 Madison Avenue, New York, N.Y. 10022

Published simultaneously in Canada by
Penguin Books Canada Limited

LIBRARY OF CONGRESS CATALOGING IN PUBLICATION DATA
Main entry under title:
Writers at work.
1. Authors—20th century—Interviews. I. Plimpton, George.
II. Paris review.
PN453.W736   809   80-18030
ISBN 0-670-79098-2

Printed in the United States of America
Set in Video Avanta

Grateful acknowledgment is made to Houghton Mifflin
Company for permission to reprint a selection from *New &
Collected Poems 1917–1976* by Archibald MacLeish. Copy-
right © 1976 by Archibald MacLeish.

Contents

Introduction

O F THE MANY CHANGES that have occurred in the United
States since World War II, few strike me as being more
alarming than our ravenous appetite for the Artist's Personality. The new vogue is as ironic as it is ominous. Americans'
traditional fear of and disdain for the artist have seldom been
equaled in the Western world. Yet artists have been vastly
glamorized in the past decades, offered a glossy media image
alongside millionaire chefs and celebrity dress designers. And
under grilling from talk-show hosts who barely know the difference between Bacon and Bakunin, they are frequently invited
to reveal to national audiences many secrets of their craft
which they might be wiser keeping to themselves.

The most dangerous of their revelations, I suspect, concerns
the nature of those elusive demons who stoke the furnace of
the creative process. My fears are admittedly based on a shamanistic, elitist view of artistic creation that centers on the art
of poetry but readily extends to all magicians of great prose.
The poet is that man considered most dangerous to Plato's
Republic precisely because his gifts are the result of divine
possession. Ralph Waldo Emerson sees him as a "liberating
God" who brings us the most concrete truths found in nature.
This traditional prophetic notion remains unaltered among

those who practice the craft in our time. Delmore Schwartz views the gifted writer as "a kind of priest" who exorcises the chaos of experience through the alchemic force of metaphor. "Fiction writing is a kind of magic," Angus Wilson says in an earlier volume of the *Paris Review* series. "If I communicate the magic spell . . . it loses its force for me." It is precisely this element of magic in both the artist and the shaman that poses a threat to them. For a great ambivalence of love and resentment lurks under the public cult of the artist's and the shaman's "magic force." On the deepest level of our fantasies and subconscious wishes—the primal urges acted out by primitive societies—we have traditionally devoured our prophets and priest-kings in order to share and absorb their mana. As surely as our desire to ingest the Godhead and its symbols is evidenced in the sacrifice of the Christian Mass, so have we always wished, however subconsciously, to feast like cannibals on the artist's sorcery.

This dialectic of love and aggression seems to have intensified in the past decade, along with that rapacious curiosity concerning artist's alcoves which lead our media to spy through their keyholes. We seem in greater need than ever to absorb their power. A general cult of "creativity" has swept the United States since the 1950s, from "creative" bread making to the plethora of "creative" writing workshops attended every summer by tens of thousands of entranced adults. The growing automatization and joylessness of twentieth-century work may lead us to covet more than ever artists' freedom to make the illicit licit, to transform through the alchemy of imagination the actuality of boredom and of death. Our adulation of them also grows apace with our secularization. As Otto Rank put it, the contemporary cult of "the immeasurably overvalued artist" has much to do with the decay of religious faith. We have moved far beyond the late Romantic view of *"l'art pour l'art"* as a redemptive force. In the age of the death of God, the artist may be the only divine substance left for us to worship and consume.

How many American magnates do we know who literally collect Artists' Presences in their homes, and hoard their confidences as if they were the incantations of some magic rites? How many authors, sandwiched between tap dancers and champions of crewel-working contests, have been invited to disclose to us—in our bedrooms, via midnight television—the sources of their inspiration? How many have performed with a prodigality of self matched only by the marked decline in the magic of their work? We curse Dick Cavett for his bewitching charm (there is also much wizardry on the part of the adversaries). We turn out the light and wonder if we'd succumb to the temptation of such quizzings if we ever became famous ourselves. We bemoan the waning of our media idols' energies and we say night-night.

Always a nation of extremes! In the past half-century we have swung from the traditional custom of letting artists famish in their garrets to the current fashion of force-feeding them into stardom for consumption in media and salon. The choice between starving and being eaten is an exotic one. Technology accelerates all acts of consumption, and threatens the artist with a very specific form of assimilation. Walter Benjamin's essays offer splendid metaphors for this novel process of devouring: true art *absorbs* the viewer (who literally "lives in" a great novel, or "walks into" the ideal painting of the Chinese parable), whereas in the contemporary media (TV, glossies) it is the viewer who *absorbs*, blotterlike, the artist's personality. The nefarious glamorization of contemporary artists thus debases their aura into another phony commodity, contaminating rather than alleviating their traditional solitude. J. D. Salinger and Thomas Pynchon said no thank you long ago. These writers' uncompromising aloofness from the press corps may be a prophetic gesture for twentieth-century artists determined to keep their powers of wizardry untouched by the devouring jaws of technology. For what the talk-show host is really asking— in between queries about sexual preference and size of legal pad —is: Where do you get your Power? What's the trick, man? Who is that private god or demon reigning over your art? SHOW ME HIS FACE.

"Hide your God," Paul Valéry warns us, "men must hide their true gods with great care."

"One should never be known by sight": advice on page 101 of this volume from the late Henry Green (designated by W. H. Auden as the finest English novelist of his generation), who preserved his anonymity almost as ritualistically as Carlos Castaneda, writing under a pen name and never allowing himself to be photographed.

Yet we should retain a sense of history and full compassion toward artists tempted by the seductive immediacy of the contemporary press. Ever since the Romantic Agony they have sacrificed themselves publicly in a variety of ways to purge us of our ambivalence toward them and to retain our love. Their anguish deepened by the growing subjectivism, arcaneness, and solitude of their work, and counting on self-destructiveness as proof of their worth and sincerity, they have acted out most of the myths we have created for them in the past two centuries: destroying themselves with drugs like Verlaine, drowning in liquor like Scott Fitzgerald and Dylan Thomas, killing themselves on the roads like Jackson Pollock and David Smith, committing public suicide like Ernest Hemingway, Sylvia Plath, John Berryman, and Anne Sexton, and, most recently, endangering great gifts—like Truman Capote—by massive television performances. (The only literary wizard excluded from my admittedly paranoid view of contemporary star mongering is Gore Vidal, a *uomo universale* unique in our time, whose talents are so varied that he can turn to his persona of gifted actor as readily as we can say Jack Paar. But how many of us have his resilience?)

The *Paris Review*'s *Writers at Work* series has made a uniquely salubrious contribution to the cult of the artist in our time. They have evolved, in four previous issues, the only technique of intimacy between author and audience that I know of which is fairly sure to leave artists' energies undiminished and their mana untainted, even in the most shamanistic view of art. The series began in 1953 with an ingenuous new literary genre that is informally called the rewritten interview. The author is sent the tape transcript of his or her conversation and has the freedom to correct, delete, annotate, expand, restructure, or even totally rewrite it. The interviewer, on the other hand, is not a reporter eager to entrap his subject into scandalous remarks on mothers, God, and orgasms. He or she has traditionally been a quietly questioning listener—usually a young writer intimately acquainted with the oeuvre at hand—who is solely interested in the craft of fiction. Authors keep the transcript of their conversation for weeks or months (a few have cradled it for years), thus retaining a control over their words that they have never had in radio, television, or even newspaper interviews. Artists, in brief, can let us into the heaven of their invention while keeping the face of their gods precisely as veiled as they wish. And I'm sure that our tour of their facilities is made all the grander by this privilege.

Is there anything more appealing than the offer of staging one's own portrait, choosing one's most advantageous expression and angle of profile? The success of *Writers at Work* is in part due to the great elasticity of its form, its remarkable hybrid of portrait and self-portrait. Its freedom is so seductive to even the most reticent authors (Henry Green's interview on page 97 is his only one on record) that *The Paris Review* may leave to posterity the richest document available on the craft of fiction in our time. And in the process it has also created a most interesting new literary genre. For the best interviews in the series—such as the astoundingly beautiful testimony of

William Gass in this newest volume—stand on their own as considerable works of art, and rank with the author's finest essays.

Those of us who have been processed through the electronic wonderland of "book tours" know that it mostly consists of lying our way across the United States to protect our privacy and powers. Do these authors lie too, or are they simply striving for the truth by exaggeration, which Oscar Wilde says is the essence of art? I trust the writer's verity in this series because most true artists are endowed with a built-in code of honor toward their own identity, if not toward that of their colleagues. Those who reveal themselves as grouches fully intend to, as James Dickey seems to intend with his shameless outburst against Allen Ginsberg, Sylvia Plath, and other poets. It is not any late-night slip on the Johnny Carson show but Dickey's evident choice, for some mysterious reason that makes the interview all the more fascinating, to go down in history sounding like a meanspirited redneck. To charm an audience is clearly John Cheever's intent; he displays a very touching pre-Modernist tenderness toward his public, stating that he writes for "all sorts of pleasant and intelligent people . . . earnest, lovable, and mysterious readers." And at the opposite end of the spectrum from Dickey's structured malice we are offered the angelic, though never sanctimonious, charity of Joyce Carol Oates, who does not tolerate any sense of competition between artists, and who states, with Flaubert, that writers "must love one another in [their] art as the mystics love one another in God."

I admit to being ambivalent, in this series, toward the more ephemeral personal gossip that these interviews share with TV talk shows and the snoopy pages of *People* magazine. Doesn't the babble concerning a writer's brand of breakfast food and of pencil sharpeners belong to that media voyeurism, to that invasion of privacy that I so deplore? Alas, as Vasari and Boswell knew, there is no absolutely clear line to be drawn between the gossip and the meat of the artist's craft. "*Blue*-black used to be an abomination to my demon," Rudyard Kipling used to say to explain that he could only compose with pitch-black ink. The presence of an Irish setter in the workroom may be as talismanic a device to conjure up the full magic of a writer's art as a certain dressing gown was to Balzac. So Joan Didion, we learn in these pages, has a maternal need to sleep in the same room as her manuscript in the second half of its gestation. Jerzy Kosinski has locked up his most recent manuscripts, which are all tape-recorded, in a bank vault. Joseph Heller writes on three-by-five-inch index cards until his last—and only —draft. The prolific Joyce Carol Oates rises at dawn and often works until two or three in the afternoon before having break-fast. Gore Vidal needs coffee and a bowel movement to get started. The poets—James Dickey and Pablo Neruda—seem to need a great deal of physical and nonverbal activity (walking, chopping wood, grooming the house) to keep their inspira-tion at peak form.

"When you're really hungry you don't try to find out the biography of the baker," Isaac Bashevis Singer recently said. Those of us hungering for artists' creations rather than for their personalities will find that the more precious material in these pages goes far beyond the wisdom of the keyhole. It concerns that highly technical material which writers have seldom confided clearly or trustfully in any other public forum: an accounting of the stages in which each fictional or poetic structure is built. One of the most poignant insights is given by Joan Didion; for her cool, glacially controlled fiction seems to grow out of a process more spontaneous and shamanistic than others recorded in this volume. She begins with no theme or plot, only a vague character and "a technical sense of what I want to do." The novel then develops from various, often deeply personal experiences and perceptions. In the case of *Play It as It Lays,* for instance, the crystallization of Maria's character came from one very brief visual flash of real-life experience: the sight of an actress walking through the lobby of a Las Vegas hotel. Didion's narrative line does not emerge until she has finished the composition of her first draft. Unlike Kosinski, who must know his last paragraph almost verbatim when he begins a novel, she has no ending in mind until she comes to it. Neither does she have a clear view of her characters until she has given them a certain amount of dialogue. She delineates the composition of *A Book of Common Prayer:* "Suddenly Charlotte says, 'He runs guns. I wish they had caviar.' When I heard Charlotte say this, I had a very clear fix on who she was." Didion is often perplexed by loose pages of descriptive prose which she needs for texture but which interrupt her narrative. She advises us to insert such fragments into the middle of our novels. "Sometimes you can get away with things in the middle of a book." The Didion interview is striking for the candid abundance of its technical insights (perhaps more precise than the male interviewees') and for the irresistible femaleness with which she describes some of her structural problems. "I promised a revolution [in *A Book of Common Prayer*]. I got within twenty pages of the end, realized I still hadn't delivered this revolution . . . putting in that revolution was like setting in a sleeve. Do you know what I mean? Do you sew? I mean I had to work that revolution in on the bias, had to ease the wrinkles out with my fingers."

Finally, I urge readers to observe the amazing optimism that these fifteen authors express concerning the future of fiction and of poetry. Their unanimous hopefulness is bracing after two decades of McLuhanesque choruses heralding the end of traditional art forms in an age of electronics. Cheever is sanguine about the future of the traditional-novel form because "the first principle of aesthetics is either interest or suspense." Green sees no problem for its survival as long as we realize that the followers of Joyce and Kafka are "like cats which have licked the plate clean"; the novel will continue to flourish as long as we can "dream up another dish." Even the most pessimistic member of this group, Jerzy Kosinski, believes that the novel's audience may be further diminished by the "ultimately deadly" technology of television, but will survive "at the edge of popular culture."

The most exuberantly sanguine forecaster is the 1978 Nobel Prize winner, Isaac Bashevis Singer. "In their despair," Mr. Singer said in his Nobel lecture, "a number of those who no longer have confidence in the leadership of our society look up to the writer, the master of words. They hope against hope that the man of talent and sensitivity can perhaps rescue civilization. Maybe there is a spark of the prophet in the artist after all." He tells the *Paris Review* interviewer, "There is no machine and no kind of reporting and no kind of film that can do for us what a Tolstoy or a Dostoyevsky or a Gogol did. Progress can never kill literature, any more than it can kill religion." In fact, Singer predicts that the pervasiveness of technology will drive humans ever more toward literature. Singer's prediction offers as optimistic a vision of the twenty-first-century artist as anyone has offered. "The more technology, the more people will be interested in what the human mind can produce *without* the help of electronics. . . . if we have people with the power to tell a story, there will always be readers."

To which one could add: but for only as long as artists can resist the siren call of media cultists and keep that "power" intact, those gods veiled.

FRANCINE DU PLESSIX GRAY

WRITERS AT WORK

Fifth Series

1. P. G. Wodehouse

P. G. Wodehouse, the celebrated master of genteel farce, was born in Guildford, England, on October 15, 1881. The son of a British judge, he spent his early years in Hong Kong, eventually returning to England to study at a prep school even though he was financially unable to go on to college. Instead, he took a job with a bank but left after two years to earn his living as a writer. In 1902 he joined the staff of the London *Globe*. During this time Wodehouse also wrote a series of stories for a boys' magazine, and it was in one of these pieces that Psmith made his initial appearance. The first of his ninety books, *Love Among the Chickens*, was published in 1906.

Wodehouse became best known to U.S. readers through his long association with the *Saturday Evening Post*, in which dozens of his novels were serialized. He also wrote some sixteen plays and eighteen musical comedies, collaborating with such composers as Jerome Kern and George Gershwin.

In France in 1940, he was taken into custody as an enemy alien by the invading Germans. Held under house arrest in Berlin, Wodehouse innocently agreed to a suggestion that he make a series of humorous broadcasts to the American radio public regarding his experiences during the war. The result was disastrous: Britain was under Nazi siege, and his reputation there was seriously damaged.

Wodehouse returned to the United States after the war and became an American citizen in 1955. His postwar publications include *Spring Fever* (1948), *The Mating Season* (1949), *French Leave* (1959), and *The Girl in Blue* (1971). Oxford University awarded him an honorary doctorate in 1959, and the process of reconciliation with his native England was completed in 1975, when he was knighted.

Married for sixty-one years to the former Ethel Rowley, Wodehouse died on St. Valentine's Day, 1975.

Al's first scene with Ld E. P. stayed in dark to clear up
As pal when P.'s husband. They tell, & his hardness   V-Good

Bringing In Florence's Husband

1. He might be spoken of in Gally's scene with Beach in Ch 2 No
   1A: Ad Vosby mentions him in her first scene with Gally? No
2. Also in Gally's first scene with Florence (P. c/ reproach
   her with being hard on husband. Yes
3. On p.31. Piper c/ leave and Gally story on to Trump more beer.
   Enter husband (~~and lawby say~~). He c/ ask Gally about
   how Florence is and how to get reconciliation.
   Gally c/ Go in to castle and tell F. husband wants
   reconciliation - F. obdurate;
4. The big scene w/ be when Ld E finds Claude escorting Jeff's
   bedroom (Get corr reason why Ld E comes to Jeff's room). Claude
   says I suspect Jeff & Neff. Ld E furious, rushes off, abuses F.
   Get some reason why husband is there (It ust be from
   G's abroad. Husband stands up for J, tells Ld E he is a bully, & Exit Ld E
   urges J to come back to him and J. says she will.

Problems.
   A. Who is husband? Is he old pal of Gally's?
   B. How does he come to be in J's room? (G. ought to have
      told him to hide and spring out at her. Or 3. He has given
      husband some method in her use; who Murdling)
5. It looks as if husband ought not to be rich or he w/
   give V. money. Try this. Make Florence widow of American
   millionaire who has married a careless now a alarming
   penniless man.

4 c/f. F. husband reconciled. They are lovey. Gally begs F.
        to give V money to marry on, She refuses and leaves.
        Then we come to Piper - Murchison stuff.
        No, Before that Ld E must find jewel. Then the P.M stuff.
        P grateful to Gally who suggests going & Jeff the
        architectural job.

A page from P. G. Wodehouse's notes plotting a book about Blandings Castle, on which he was at work at the time of his death.

P. G. Wodehouse

When I first went to see him, I telephoned P. G. Wodehouse and asked for directions from New York to his house on Long Island. He merely chuckled, as if I had asked him to compare Euclid with Einstein or attempted some other laughably impossible task. "Oh, I can't tell you that," he said. "I don't have a clue." I learned the route anyway, and my arrival for lunch, only ten minutes late, seemed to astonish him. "You had no trouble? Oh, that is good. That's wonderful!" His face beaming at having in his house such a certified problem-solver, a junior Jeeves almost, he led me without further to-do to a telephone, which he had been dialing all morning in a futile effort to reach a number in New York. He had, of course, done everything right but dial the area code, an addition to the Bell system that had somehow escaped his attention since he had last attempted long distance. He was intensely pleased when New York answered, and I sunned myself in the warm glow of his gratitude for the rest of the day. All of which is by way of saying that Wodehouse, who lived four months past his ninety-third birthday, had discovered his own secret of long life: he simply ignored what was worrisome, bothersome, or confusing in the world around him.

His wife, Ethel, or his sister-in-law Helen did the worrying for him. On my three visits Ethel would hover around him at the beginning of our conversation to plump his pillow or fill his sherry glass, then discreetly disappear to tend to an ailing dog or cat. They had about a half dozen of each, most of them strays that had come begging to the door. Wodehouse himself had not found it necessary to carry money in twenty years, and though he had spent most of his adult life in America, he still reckoned such things as book prices in pounds and shillings. His accent, like his arithmetic, remained pure English. Aside from his writing, his two passions were the New York Mets and a soap opera called The Edge of Night. *On those extremely rare occasions when he had to leave the house for the day, Ethel was assigned to watch the program and write down exactly what had happened. "I understand that you're going to watch* The Edge of Night *with me," he said on one of my visits. "That's splendid!"*

Wodehouse lived on twelve acres in Remsenburg, a pretty, quiet little town in eastern Long Island, and from his glass-enclosed study, and most of the rest of the house, all that he could see was greenery. He was as happily isolated there as if he were living in Blandings Castle itself. He enjoyed all the hoopla that surrounded him in his old age, but he also found the attention very tiring. "Everything more or less quiet here now," he wrote me a week after he had been dubbed Sir Pelham, "but it has been hell with all the interviewers." A month after that he died, as peacefully and as quietly as he had lived, according to all accounts.

INTERVIEWER: The last time I saw you was at your ninetieth birthday party in 1971.

WODEHOUSE: Oh, yes. All that ninetieth-birthday thing gave me not exactly a heart attack. But I had to have treatment, you know. I'm always taking pills and things. One good effect of the treatment, however, is that I lost about twenty pounds. I feel frightfully fit now, except my legs are a bit wobbly.

INTERVIEWER: You're ninety-one now, aren't you?

WODEHOUSE: Ninety-one and a half! Ninety-two in October.

INTERVIEWER: You don't have any trouble reading now, do you?

WODEHOUSE: Oh, no!

INTERVIEWER: How about writing?

WODEHOUSE: Oh, as far as the brain goes, I'm fine. I've just finished another novel, in fact. I've got a wonderful title for it, *Bachelors Anonymous*. Don't you think that's good. Yes, everybody likes that title. Peter Schwed, my editor at Simon and Schuster, nearly always alters my titles, but he raved over that one. I think the book is so much better than my usual stuff that I don't know how I can top it. It really is funny. It's worked out awfully well. I'm rather worried about the next one. It will be a letdown almost. I don't want to be like Bernard Shaw. He turned out some awfully bad stuff in his nineties. He said he knew the stuff was bad but he couldn't stop writing.

INTERVIEWER: What is your working schedule these days?

WODEHOUSE: I still start the day off at seven-thirty. I do my daily dozen exercises, have breakfast, and then go into my study. When I am between books, as I am now, I sit in an armchair and think and make notes. Before I start a book I've usually got four hundred pages of notes. Most of them are almost incoherent. But there's always a moment when you feel you've got a novel started. You can more or less see how it's going to work out. After that it's just a question of detail.

INTERVIEWER: You block everything out in advance, then?

WODEHOUSE: Yes. For a humorous novel you've got to have a scenario, and you've got to test it so that you know where the comedy comes in, where the situations come in . . . splitting it up into scenes (you can make a scene of almost anything) and have as little stuff in between as possible.

INTERVIEWER: Is it really possible to know in a scenario where something funny is going to be?

WODEHOUSE: Yes, you can do that. Still, it's curious how a scenario gets lost as you go along. I don't think I've ever actually kept completely to one. If I've got a plot for a novel worked out and I can really get going on it, I work all the time. I work in the morning, and then I probably go for a walk or something, and then I have another go at the novel. I find that from four to seven is a particularly good time for working. I never work after dinner. It's the plots that I find so hard to work out. It takes such a long time to work one out. I like to think of some scene, it doesn't matter how crazy, and work backward and forward from it until eventually it becomes quite plausible and fits neatly into the story.

INTERVIEWER: How many words do you usually turn out on a good day?

WODEHOUSE: Well, I've slowed up a good deal now. I used to write about two thousand words. Now I suppose I do about one thousand.

INTERVIEWER: Do you work seven days a week?

WODEHOUSE: Oh, yes, rather. Always.

INTERVIEWER: Do you type or do you write in longhand?

WODEHOUSE: I used to work entirely on the typewriter. But this last book I did sitting in a lawn chair and writing by hand. Then I typed it out. Much slower, of course. But I think it's a pretty good method; it does pretty well.

INTERVIEWER: Do you go back and revise very much?

WODEHOUSE: Yes. And I very often find that I've got something which ought to come in another place, a scene which originally I put in chapter two and then when I get to chapter ten, I feel it would come in much better there. I'm sort of molding the whole time.

INTERVIEWER: How long does it take you to write a novel?

WODEHOUSE: Well, in the old days I used to rely on it being about three months, but now it might take any length of time. I forget exactly how long *Bachelors Anonymous* took, but it must have been six or seven months.

INTERVIEWER: That still seems very fast to me.

WODEHOUSE: It's still good, yes.

INTERVIEWER: If you were asked to give advice to somebody who wanted to write humorous fiction, what would you tell him?

WODEHOUSE: I'd give him practical advice, and that is always get to the dialogue as soon as possible. I always feel the thing to go for is speed. Nothing puts the reader off more than a great slab of prose at the start. I think the success of every novel—if it's a novel of action—depends on the high spots. The thing to do is to say to yourself, "Which are my big scenes?" and then get every drop of juice out of them. The principle I always go on in writing a novel is to think of the characters in terms of actors in a play. I say to myself, if a big name were playing this part, and if he found that after a strong first act he had practically nothing to do in the second act, he would walk out. Now, then, can I twist the story so as to give him plenty to do all the way through? I believe the only way a writer can keep himself up to the mark is by examining each story quite coldly before he starts writing it and asking himself if it is all right *as a story.* I mean, once you go saying to yourself, "This is a pretty weak plot as it stands, but I'm such a hell of a writer that my magic touch will make it OK," you're sunk. If they aren't in interesting situations, characters can't be major characters, not even if you have the rest of the troop talk their heads off about them.

INTERVIEWER: What do you think makes a story funny?

WODEHOUSE: I think character mostly. You know instinctively what's funny and what isn't if you're a humorous writer. I don't think a man can deliberately sit down to write a funny story unless he has got a sort of slant on life that leads to funny stories. If you take life fairly easily, then you take a humorous view of things. It's probably because you were born that way. Lord Emsworth and his pig—I *know* they're funny.

INTERVIEWER: Did you ever know anyone who was actually like Lord Emsworth?

WODEHOUSE: No. Psmith is the only one of my characters who is drawn from life. He started in a boys' story, and then I did a grown-up story about him in the *Saturday Evening Post*. People sometimes want to know why I didn't go on with Psmith. But I don't think that the things that made him funny as a very young man would be funny in an older man. He had a very boring sort of way of expressing himself. Called everybody comrade and all that sort of thing. I couldn't go on with him. I don't think he'd have worked as a maturer character. In a way my character Galahad is really Psmith grown up.

INTERVIEWER: But Galahad works very well as a character.

WODEHOUSE: Yes, Galahad is fine.

INTERVIEWER: How old is he supposed to be?

WODEHOUSE: How old all those characters are I don't know. The first short story I wrote about Lord Emsworth said that he had been to Eton in 1864, which would make him a hundred-and-something now!

INTERVIEWER: What period are the books set in?

WODEHOUSE: Well, between the wars, rather. I try not to date them at all, but it's rather difficult. I'm bad at remembering things, like when flying really became fashionable. The critics keep saying that the world I write about never existed. But of course it did. It was going strong between the wars. In a way it is hard to write the sort of stuff I do now because it really is so out-of-date. The character of Jeeves is practically unknown in England now, though I believe someone told me the butler was creeping back. Bertie Wooster and Oofie Proster have more or less vanished too. I suppose a typical member of the Drones Club now is someone with a job and very earnest about it. Those rather hit-or-miss days have passed away. But thank God, that doesn't seem to matter!

INTERVIEWER: I suppose that the world has gone the way of spats. You were very fond of spats, weren't you? Tell me a little about them.

WODEHOUSE: I don't know why spats went out! The actual name was spatterdashers, and you fastened them over your ankles, you see, to prevent the spatter dashing you. They certainly lent tone to your appearance, and they were awfully comfortable, especially when you wore them in cold weather. I've written articles, which were rather funny, about how I used to go about London. I would borrow my brother's frock coat and my uncle's hat, but my spats were always new and impeccable. The butler would open the door and take in my old topcoat and hat and sniff as if to say, "Hardly the sort of thing we are accustomed to." And then he would look down at the spats and everything would be all right. It's a *shame* when things like spats go out.

INTERVIEWER: Did you ever have a butler like Jeeves?

WODEHOUSE: No, never like Jeeves. My butlers were quite different, though I believe J. M. Barrie had one just like Jeeves.

INTERVIEWER: How did you create Jeeves, then?

WODEHOUSE: I only intended to use him once. His first entrance was: "Mrs. Gregson to see you, sir," in a story called "Extricating Young Gussie." He only had one other line, "Very good, sir. Which suit will you wear?" But then I was writing a story, "The Artistic Career of Corky," about two young men, Bertie Wooster and his friend Corky, getting into a lot of trouble, and neither of them had brains enough to get out of the trouble. I thought: Well, how can I get them out? And I thought: Suppose one of them had an omniscient valet? I wrote a short story about him, then another short story, then several more short stories and novels. That's how a character grows. I think I've written nine Jeeves novels now and about thirty short stories.

INTERVIEWER: I like Jeeves, but my favorite character of yours is really Lord Emsworth.

WODEHOUSE: Oh, yes. He's about my favorite character, too. Well, now, he must be entirely out-of-date. I don't suppose anybody in England is living in a castle like that anymore.

INTERVIEWER: Maybe not, but I suspect that there are still some woolly-headed English aristocrats around.

WODEHOUSE: Oh, yes?

INTERVIEWER: Will you write any more Lord Emsworth stories?

WODEHOUSE: I don't know if I shall. I've got him in such a pleasant position now. He's free of both his sisters. He's got his pig, and he's living alone and loving it. He's comfortable by himself. It seems rather unkind to disturb him. . . . I do think I'd like to have a try, though. You see, *that's* the problem. I'd love to do a Lord Emsworth story, but what could it be about? I mean, what could happen? The trouble is, you see, that I've so featured the pig that I couldn't leave her out. And yet, what could happen to a pig? It is difficult to find plots when you have written so much. The ideas don't seem to come to me now. I suppose it's temporary. I've always felt like this in between books. But I have used up every possible situation. If I do get a good idea, I find it is something I wrote in the thirties.

INTERVIEWER: I think the closest you have come to sex in your novels is a kiss on the cheek. Have you ever been tempted to put anything spicier into them?

WODEHOUSE: No. No, I don't think the framework of the novel would stand it. Sex, of course, can be awfully funny, but you have to know how to handle it. And I don't think I can handle it properly.

INTERVIEWER: Sex aside, have you ever thought of writing anything more serious?

WODEHOUSE: No. I don't think I'm capable of writing anything but the sort of thing I do write. I couldn't write a serious book.

INTERVIEWER: Did you always know you would be a writer?

WODEHOUSE: Yes, always. I know I was writing stories when I was five. I don't remember what I did before that. Just loafed, I suppose. I was about twenty when I sold my first story, and I've been a full-time writer since 1902. I can't think of myself as anything but a writer.

INTERVIEWER: Did you ever have another career?

WODEHOUSE: When I left school. I was first working for scholarship at Oxford when my father's finances took rather a nasty jar and I wasn't able to go up to Oxford, and instead was put in the bank, the Hong Kong and Shanghai Bank, which I hated at first but later got to like. The bank had branches all over the East. After two years in the London branch you'd get your orders to go out there, which of course appalled me because in my two years I never learned a thing about banking. The idea of going out to Bombay or somewhere and being a branch manager and being paid in rupees scared me stiff.

All this time I was writing and getting rejections. Because the trouble is when you start writing, you write awful stuff. And I was writing on banking hours too. My second year I got into the cash department and my job was to enter the deposits on the ledger. After a while a new ledger was provided and I sat down and suddenly thought of a wonderful idea—to write *in* the new ledger an account of the Great Opening of the New Ledger, with the King coming and all that. And I did this and, having done it, repented and thought this was going to get me into trouble, and I got a knife and I cut the first page of the ledger out. It so happened that the chief cashier had got a long feud on with the stationers and he'd been trying to catch them out for years and when he saw this ledger with the front page missing, he thought, Ah, this is my chance, and he went and cursed them for giving us an imperfect ledger. But I didn't get the sack for it.

I left the bank after that second year, however, to go to the [London] *Globe.* I had been doing occasional day jobs for an old master of mine who'd become a journalist and ran the comic column at the *Globe.* I'd pretend I'd sprained my back lifting a ledger or something, and I'd do my work for the *Globe.* Then when he went on summer holiday, I took his place and eventually got on the staff in 1902 when he resigned. In those days the pay was three pounds a week (about fifteen dollars) and I could live on that very well.

INTERVIEWER: From those days to now, have you continued to read criticism of your own work?

WODEHOUSE: Yes. I get a lot of reviews sent to me. They are invariably favorable. And somehow I always read them really carefully. You do get tips from them. Now, that last Jeeves book of mine, *Jeeves and the Tie That Binds,* I forget which critic it was, but he said that the book was dangerously near to self-parody. I know what he meant. I had exaggerated Jeeves and Bertie. Jeeves always reciting some poetry or something. I'll correct that in the next one. I do think one can learn from criticism. In fact, I'm a pretty good critic of my own work. I know when it isn't as good as it ought to be.

INTERVIEWER: Do you ever feel angry at critics? Do you ever feel they are unfair?

WODEHOUSE: No, I don't think so. You always feel that you can't please everybody.

INTERVIEWER: Some critics, going beyond any particular book, think that your short stories are better than your novels. What do you think?

WODEHOUSE: Yes, I think I'd sooner write short stories than novels. I feel really happy with a short story. I like the sense of completing something. The only trouble is that if I do get a good idea, I rather want to work it into a novel. I mean, I'm rather wasting a novel if I write a short story.

INTERVIEWER: Who are your own favorite humorists?

WODEHOUSE: The ones I like most are all dead—James

Thurber, Robert Benchley, Wolcott Gibbs, George S. Kaufman.

INTERVIEWER: Do you like S. J. Perelman?

WODEHOUSE: Oh, yes, yes, yes. He's quite a favorite of mine. But there are very few writers like that now, just writing funny stuff, not like in the twenties and thirties. When I first came over here all the evening papers, the evening *World* and the others, all had funny poems and columns in them. I liked FPA's column very much. But I don't think people buy funny books nowadays. I never have had a big sale over here. Where I get my money is England, Sweden, Italy, France, and Germany.

INTERVIEWER: Do you think there are more humorous writers in England than America?

WODEHOUSE: They haven't got any in England either.

INTERVIEWER: Do you like Peter DeVries?

WODEHOUSE: I'm not frightfully keen on him. I haven't read very much of his stuff. But I'll tell you who is awfully good is Jean Kerr. Ooooh, she's wonderful. *Mary, Mary* was one of the best plays I've ever read. Anthony Powell is also a good writer. It's extraordinary how interesting his stuff is, you know. And it just goes on and on, with nothing much in the way of scenes or anything. You wouldn't call it funny stuff, though, would you?

INTERVIEWER: No, I don't suppose so. What have you been reading most recently?

WODEHOUSE: I've been reading the old books, books that I've read before. The first time you read a book, you don't read it at all carefully; you just read it for the story. You have to keep rereading. Every year or so I read Shakespeare straight through. But then I go to the latest by Agatha Christie or Rex Stout. I read every book of theirs. I do like a book with an elaborate plot. But I haven't any definite plan of reading. I read almost everything, and I like anything that's good. I've just reread a book of A. A. Milne's called *Two People,* which I had read several times before. His novel is simply a novel of character. It's not the sort of thing I can write myself, but as a reader I enjoy it thoroughly.

INTERVIEWER: Do you read any contemporary novels?

WODEHOUSE: I've read some of Norman Mailer.

INTERVIEWER: Do you like his writing?

WODEHOUSE: I don't like his novels very much, but he writes very interesting nonfiction stuff. I liked *Advertisements for Myself* very much.

INTERVIEWER: How about the Beats? Someone like Jack Kerouac, for instance, who died a few years ago?

WODEHOUSE: Jack Kerouac died! Did he?

INTERVIEWER: Yes.

WODEHOUSE: Oh . . . Gosh, they do die off, don't they?

INTERVIEWER: Do you ever go back and reread your own books?

WODEHOUSE: Oh, yes.

INTERVIEWER: Are you ever surprised by them?

WODEHOUSE: I'm rather surprised that they're so good.

INTERVIEWER: Of all the books you've written, do you have any favorites?

WODEHOUSE: Oh, I'm very fond of a book called *Quick Service* and another called *Sam in the Suburbs,* a very old one. But I really like them all. There are very few exceptions.

INTERVIEWER: Have you ever been envious of another writer?

WODEHOUSE: No, never. I'm really such a voracious reader that I'm only too grateful to get some stuff I can read.

INTERVIEWER: Have any other writers ever been envious of you?

WODEHOUSE: Well, I always thought A. A. Milne was rather. We were supposed to be quite good friends, but, you know, in a sort of way I think he was a pretty jealous chap. I think he was probably jealous of all other writers. But I loved his stuff. That's one thing I'm very grateful for: I don't have to like an awful person to like his stuff. I like Somerset Maugham's stuff tremendously, for example, but I should think he was unhappy all the time, wouldn't you? He was an unpleasant man.

INTERVIEWER: Was he unpleasant to you?

WODEHOUSE: No. He was all right to me. We got along on just sort of "how do you do" terms. I remember walking back from a cricket match at Lords in London, and Maugham came along on the other side. He looked at me and I looked at him, and we were thinking the same thing: Oh, my God, shall we have to stop and talk? Fortunately, we didn't.

INTERVIEWER: I don't think writers get along very well with one another.

WODEHOUSE: No, I don't think they do, really. I think they're jealous of each other. I do get along with them superficially, if everything's all right. But you feel they're resenting you, rather. . . . What do you imagine the standing of a writer like Arnold Bennett is now?

INTERVIEWER: I don't think anybody reads him.

WODEHOUSE: That's what I think, too. But when he was alive, he was very much a sort of great literary man.

INTERVIEWER: Let's switch to your own life for a minute. You and Ethel were living in France when the Germans invaded in 1940. You were interned for about a year in Germany and Ethel had to live in Berlin. Why didn't you escape to England when you had a chance?

WODEHOUSE: Oh, everything happened so suddenly. Until the Germans arrived there didn't seem to be any danger at all. I suppose really the whole thing was that we had two dogs we were very fond of, and because of the English quarantine laws we couldn't take them into England. We aren't very good at organizing a thing like that.

INTERVIEWER: You later made some broadcasts from Berlin for CBS radio describing your life in the camp. Those broadcasts caused great controversy in Britain, and for a time you were rather savagely denounced there. Do you regret making them?

WODEHOUSE: Oh, yes. Oh, rather. I wish I hadn't. It never occurred to me that there was anything wrong in the broadcasts. They altered my whole life. I suppose I would have gone back to England and so on if it hadn't been for them. Yet they were so perfectly harmless, just a comic description of my adventures in camp. Of course, nobody ever published them.

INTERVIEWER: Do you resent the way you were treated by the English?

WODEHOUSE: Oh, no, no, no. Nothing of that sort. The whole thing seems to have blown over now.

INTERVIEWER: Would you ever like to go back to England?

WODEHOUSE: I'd certainly like to, but at my age it's awfully difficult to get a move on. But I'd like to go back for a visit in the spring. They all seem to want me to go back. The trouble is that I've never flown. I suppose that would solve everything.

INTERVIEWER: I imagine most people think that you live in England even now. But you are an American citizen, and you have spent most of your life here.

WODEHOUSE: Yes, that is true. I have always been awfully fond of America. It always seemed like my own country. I don't know why. I'd much sooner live here than in England, I think. I can't think of any place in England I prefer to this. I used to like London, but I don't think I'd like it now. I had always wanted to go to America, and when I got a holiday from the *Globe,* in 1904, I came over for about three weeks. Indeed, I saw more of New York then than I've ever seen since, and having been in America gave my reputation in London a tremendous boost. I was suddenly someone who counted to editors who threw me out before. Then I came back in 1909 for another visit and lived in Greenwich Village. It was a quiet sort of place, all of us young writers trying to get on. I was going to return to England when I sold two short stories to *Cosmopolitan* and *Collier's* for a total of $500—much more than I had ever earned before. So I resigned from the *Globe* and stayed. But the wolf was always at the door. I used to think I was being followed about by little men with black beards. If it hadn't been for Frank Crowninshield, the editor of *Vanity Fair*, taking all the articles I could do, I should have been in real trouble. When Ethel and I got married in September ·1914, she had $75 and I had $50.

The *Saturday Evening Post* gave me my first break. I wrote a novel called *Something New* and they bought it for $3500 and serialized it. They then bought *Uneasy Money*, *Piccadilly Jim*, and *A Damsel in Distress* and gave me a raise with each one, $5000, $7500, and $10,000.

Just about that time I started writing musical comedies— eighteen in all—with Guy Bolton and Jerry Kern. I did the lyrics to Jerry's melodies. Our terrific smash was *Oh Boy!* So it all came in a rush. Guy is one of the best fellows I ever met. He lives a mile from here; that's why we came down here. We were spending the weekend with him, and Ethel went out and came back for lunch and said, "I've bought a house."

INTERVIEWER: You once told me that when you worked with Ziegfeld, he said that he envied your happy temperament.

WODEHOUSE: Yes, he always used to say that.

INTERVIEWER: To what do you attribute your good nature? Was it a happy childhood?

WODEHOUSE: I certainly had a very happy childhood. My position was the same as Rudyard Kipling's. His parents were in India and boarded him out with a family in England. My parents were in Hong Kong, and I was also boarded out in England. Yet Kipling had one hell of a time, and I got on marvelously with the people I was with and I loved them. What *can* you attribute a good nature to, I wonder. Do you think you're born with it? I suppose you are.

INTERVIEWER: There must have been some bad times for you, even so.

WODEHOUSE: Do you know, I don't think I've had any really bad times. I disliked the bank I had to work in when I was young very much my first month or so. But once I got used to it, I became very fond of it.

INTERVIEWER: How about the war years, particularly the year in the German internment camp? That must have been pretty bad.

WODEHOUSE: I don't know. Looking back to it, it wasn't at all unpleasant. Everybody seems to think a German internment camp must be a sort of torture chamber. It was really perfectly normal and ordinary. The camp had an extraordinarily nice commander, and we did all sorts of things, you know. We played cricket, that sort of thing. Of course, I was writing all the time. Most writers would have gotten fifty novels out of the experience—the men they met there—but I have never written a word about it, except those broadcasts.

INTERVIEWER: It sounds as if you've never had any worries at all.

WODEHOUSE: I'm rather blessed in a way. I really don't worry about anything much. I can adjust myself to things pretty well.

INTERVIEWER: Do you think it is essential for a writer to have a happy home life?

WODEHOUSE: Well, I think it's a *tremendous* help, yes. Ethel has always been wonderful in that way. You've got to be alone quite a bit when you're writing. She doesn't mind that at all. I've always had great luck with the things that really matter in life. I should imagine an unhappy marriage would simply kill a man.

INTERVIEWER: Do you think you would have been so happy if you had not been a writer?

WODEHOUSE: No. I think a writer's life is the ideal life. I can never understand these fellows like Evelyn Waugh who did not always have the idea of being a writer. I *always* wanted to be a writer.

INTERVIEWER: Do you always enjoy writing?

WODEHOUSE: Oh, yes. I love writing. I never feel really comfortable unless I am either actually writing or have a story going. I could not stop writing.

GERALD CLARKE
Winter 1975

2. Archibald MacLeish

Archibald MacLeish has been, at different times, a soldier, lawyer, staff writer on *Fortune* magazine, librarian of Congress (1939–44), assistant secretary of state (1944–45), cofounder of UNESCO, and Boylston Professor of Rhetoric and Oratory at Harvard University. To him all this has had one meaning—the practice of poetry.

He was born in Glencoe, Illinois, on May 7, 1892, and was educated at Yale and the Harvard Law School. His collegiate career at Yale was a varied one: he was editor of the literary magazine and a member of both the football and swimming teams. In 1916, at the end of his first year at the Harvard Law School, he married Ada Hitchcock and at the end of his second year he went off to France and the First World War.

After the war and his graduation from law school in 1919, MacLeish briefly taught constitutional law at Harvard College but moved to France in 1923 to pursue his writing career. One year later his first book of poems, *The Happy Marriage,* was published. Through the rest of the decade he concentrated on writing poetry while his wife began an illustrious career as a singer.

His many works include *The Pot of Earth* (1925), *The Hamlet of A. MacLeish* (1928), and *Conquistador* (1932), winner of that year's Pulitzer Prize in poetry. For his *Collected Poems 1917–1952* MacLeish was awarded a second Pulitzer Prize as well as the Bollingen Prize and the National Book Award in 1953, and *J. B.,* a verse play, won both the Pulitzer Prize in drama and the Antoinette Perry Award for best play in 1959. His latest book of verse is *New and Collected Poems 1917 to 1976,* and his newest prose collection is *Riders on the Earth* (1978).

A passionate civil libertarian, MacLeish's life has been marked by distinguished public service. He lives with his wife in Conway, Massachusetts.

Whistler in the Dark

George Barker, British poet,
writes a eulogy on Dylan Thomas,
calls him whistler in the dark
and great because the dark is getting darker.

Is it? Was the dark not always darker?
Have we not always had their silver whistlers
Listen! ...   (?
        That's Chaucer like a bobolink.

I think it's not the darkness, Mr. Barker
makes for whistling well. I think
perhaps it's knowing how to whistle.
Listen! ...
        That's Dylan trilling like a lark

                        Archibald

Dear George,
    Will this do as a manuscript? It doesn't show corrections but it shows me
up as a pencil man and, worse still, a slave to the eraser. (Black Wing pencils
have erasers which eradicate clean as time.)
    As for the lies themselves—they went into a notebook and never came out
again because Dylan's death was too great a loss and George Barker's piece
was too deeply felt to fool with in a tone like this one.
    But that's all in the past now. People die too absolutely these days—
disappear like pencil marks to an eraser—black wing.

                                            Yours ever,
                                            Archie

Archibald MacLeish

Archibald MacLeish winters in Antigua, but the bearable portion of the year finds him at Uphill Farm, a country place in Conway, Massachusetts, bought in the twenties on the Mac-Leishes' return from Europe. The region has meaning for him because his Connecticut Yankee mother's family, the Hillards, "knew these hills well." His Hillard grandfather was a Congregational minister who worked his way north up the Connecticut River in the years of the Civil War, fighting with his deacons —many of whom were copperheads—and finally ending his journey in the 1880s when he crossed the Massachusetts state line and eventually settled in Conway itself. The poet greets his guests in countryman clothes—fine confident head, a manner of kindly command—and leads the way to the pool. The impression everywhere—sharpest in MacLeish's style of talk, but no less evident in the domestic arrangements—is of a world well managed. MacLeish is a short man with bearing—powerful shoulders give good drive to his crawl in the pool. There are drinks outside, soufflé, salad, and Riesling in a dining room with a mountain view, and some jokes with Mrs. MacLeish, whose voice Joyce praised, about certain of her husband's poems making her out to be U.S. Champion Homemaker and Breadbaker and omitting she sings Poulenc. MacLeish laughs hardest at himself and his wife takes back her complaint charmingly: "I never minded at all." Thereafter a descent down stone stairs to the music room—past a wall of framed honorary degrees, pictures of treasured friends (Felix Frankfurter, for one), a huge photo of the moon. The poet speaks graciously of his hope that someday there'll be a conversation, not just a tape, and then it's time to work.

INTERVIEWER: Can we start outside the gates and work in? You're seen as a writer with unusual experience of the public world—perhaps as a "public man." Is A. MacLeish as a public man recognizable to you?

MACLEISH: No, but I've had him pointed out to me. I suppose all writers have that experience sooner or later—the double personality—the "other" you're supposed to be and can't remember ever having met. Except that in this case the problem is complicated by the fact that those who see me as a "public man" don't always mean it kindly. There are those on the fringes of the art who think that poetry and the public world should be mutually exclusive—as though poets were the internists of the profession and should stick to their bowels. I've been hearing from them for some time. After my tour of public duty during the Second World War, I published a poem called "Actfive," which was a kind of report on the look and feel of things "out there." Random House published it, and before it appeared Bob Linscott, then an editor at Random House, warned me that I was to be disciplined as a renegade. I didn't believe him, but so it turned out. There were no reviews. There

were even letters to the *Times about* there being no reviews.
INTERVIEWER: The silence meant somebody thought the
"public man" thing had violated the poet?
MACLEISH: Something like that. Though the poem itself, if
they had read it, wouldn't have given them much comfort. I
suppose it is now the most frequently reprinted—quoted from
—of my books. No, it was the usual ideological nonsense: the
usual nonsense to which ideology leads unthinking men—even
unthinking critics. I don't know how it was with Terence, to
whom nothing human was indifferent, but I do know how it
is with the practice of the art of poetry. You can't cut off a part
of human life by critical fiat and expect your poets to be whole.
Poetry is the art of understanding what it is to be alive and a
poet isn't alive by quarter-acres or front-feet. He's alive as a
man. With a world to live in. No poet down to very recent
times—not even the privatest, the most confessional—ever
doubted that. And the greatest of recent poets is the most
convincing proof that the old poets were right. It was when
Yeats broke through the fences around the Lake Isle of Innis-
free and took to ranging the public world of Ireland that he
became what he became. Discovering his time he discovered
himself. And what was true for Yeats in 1914 is even truer for
us in the angry and bewildered world we live in. Take away a
poet's public life by critical edict in a time like ours and what
do you leave him? Not, certainly, himself.
INTERVIEWER: But staying in touch with the whole self is
tough work, isn't it, if you're trying to make reasonable words
in the media about Apollo Eight or the Pentagon Papers? You
don't feel squeezed?
MACLEISH: Tougher, you mean, than keeping in touch with
the *whole* self when you're writing about a private part of your
experience? It isn't the subject that betrays a writer, but the
way he takes the subject. Rhetoric, in the bad sense of that
abused word, is just as bad in confessional writing as it is out
in the open air. What matters in either case is the truth of the

feeling—the feel of the truth. If you can break through the confusion of words about a political crisis like the Pentagon Papers to the human fact—such as the human reality of an attorney general's behavior—you have *written* the experience. And the fact that the writing appears in *The New York Times* won't change that fact for better or worse. Journalism also has its uses—and to poets as well as to journalists. You spoke of the Apollo flight—the first circumnavigation of the moon—the one that produced that now familiar, but still miraculous, photograph of the earth seen off beyond the threshold of the moon . . . "small and blue and beautiful in that eternal silence where it floats." This was one of the great revolutionary moments of the human consciousness, but the moment was not explicit in the photograph nor in the newspaper accounts of the voyage. Only the imagination could recognize it—make imaginative sense of it. Are we seriously to be told that the imagination has no role to play here because the event is in the newspapers? Or is it the publication in the newspapers of the imaginative labor which offends?

INTERVIEWER: The way the writer "takes the subject"—that depends a lot on what the writer knows about it, right? How far around and in he's been? Can I ask about the uses of public range, social reference, all that? Is there a way of getting beyond the cliché about "the value of the experience," saying something true about how general knowledge ought to sit in a writer?

MACLEISH: I don't know that anything as essential as experience can ever be a cliché, even when parroted in the way you mean. You have to live to write in more senses than one, and no one can ever live enough—there will always be cracks in the knowledge and they will always show. But we have been talking about this rather factitious distinction between the public world and the private world, and that does raise the question of knowledge of the public world. Well, there is one thing you can say about that, because poetry has said it over and over from the first beginnings. One of the dimensions of great poetry—one of the dimensions by which poetry becomes great —is precisely the public dimension: that vast landscape off beyond—the human background, total human background— what we call "the world." It is there in Shakespeare: even in *Hamlet,* the most inward of the great plays, Denmark is behind the scene—beyond the garden where the king is murdered. And so too, obviously, of Dante: Dante's Hell is under Italy— actual Italy, historic Italy. As Homer's Troy, Homer's Aegean, contains the poems. So Tu Fu's China. So the Thebes of *Oedipus. Oedipus Rex* is, I suppose, by common agreement one of the keys to the secret human heart, but what would the play be without Thebes?

The Greeks regarded what we call "public" experience as part of *human* experience. That's what a man was: he was a member of his city. And if he was a poet he was a *poet* who was a member of his city. This is what gives such ground and scope and humanity to Greek poetry at its greatest. The Greek poets knew what a city was *to them*—what a war was, a people. They *knew.* Compare them with Pound. I have great admiration for Pound: he is aware of the city, of the well-ordered state, of the long tradition—the enduring ethic. But he doesn't *know.* He hasn't been there. And it shows. Carl Sandburg was one of the few contemporary poets who was able to take the state in his stride. Perhaps he took it in too easy a stride: Edmund Wilson thought so—you remember his contemptuous dismissal. But Carl will have the last word there. This is perhaps one way of answering the question: that a man who excludes, who really—not perhaps willfully or explicitly but by subconscious habit, by conforming unthinkingly to the current fashion—*excludes* the public part of his experience is apt to end up finding himself excluded. We talk about the play within the play: there is also a play *without* the play—which contains everything.

INTERVIEWER: What about the question of work-life and

art-life—say in Stevens? Poetry here, business there. Aren't we
headed into a time when there's a demand that a writer get
himself wholly together—*mean* it across the board? He'll be
hung for fraud if he finds a condition of marginality acceptable
for poetry?

MACLEISH: Wallace Stevens "meant it": the fact that he had
a living to earn affected that no more than it affected Shakespeare. Stevens was the head, as I understood it, of the whole
trial operation of the Hartford Accident, with lawyers all over
the country trying cases for him. He tried very few cases himself, but he oversaw the trying of cases and was helpful and very
intelligent, a good lawyer and useful and a well-paid officer of
the Hartford Accident. I think very well paid. In other words,
his life, his professional life, what you called his work-life, was
successful. His poetry was something else. The trying of cases,
the defending of who ran over a child and so forth, never, *as
such,* enters his poetry. It might have if he had had a little
streak of Masters in him. It might have, but it didn't. His
metaphysical mind escaped—and escaped is the right word—
escaped out of Hartford Accident into those deeper and deeper
examinations of the metaphysical universe. So that the question with Stevens isn't really a question of public against private because his business life was private also. I don't think he
was ever interested in a political question in his life. I never
heard him mention one. But he is a perfect example—perhaps
the most successful and admirable example—of a man who
made a go of poetry *and* business. Your word is the right one.
Poetry and business in the modern world. I never made a go
of it. I tried everything from the law through journalism and
government service to teaching at Harvard, and for each one
I had to pay a price. Stevens made the art and the work go
together. He fitted them together. He had, as you say, carefully
planned work habits. Does this have anything to do with the
"marginality" of poetry in contemporary life? I don't think so.
I think it has to do with the "marginality" of poetry in *Ste-*

vens's life. In terms of the hours of his life, poetry was necessarily pushed to the margin. But in the margin it *was* his life. And it was superb poetry. Not in a relative sense: superb *as* poetry. Nothing else matters. Nothing matters with any man but the work. The rest is biography.

INTERVIEWER: Everyman his own margin maker, is that it? I mean, every poet . . .

MACLEISH: We look back at Mr. W. S. and we say to ourselves, well, we don't know much about him. We know he was an actor. Anyway, he supported himself somehow or other in the theater. Shall we say the theater makes poetry marginal except when Mr. W. S. practices it? Shall we make a distinction between a poet supported by patrons (or, in the contemporary world, by poetry audiences) and a poet who supports himself? Is the second "marginal" whereas the first isn't? Because the first is free to devote all his time to writing? But is he? He usually has to please his patron and that can be fairly time-consuming. The truth is that neither you nor I have ever known a poet who wasn't more or less in that situation—who wasn't with the left hand trying to store up enough birdseed so he could go on with the right hand and write some poetry.

INTERVIEWER: Marginal or not, the theater is a cooperative enterprise. It forces the writer into a public situation. How do you feel about losing control? Is that a special hell?

MACLEISH: It could be, I suppose. I have had two very different approaches to Broadway production. In the first I had no intention of a Broadway production whatever. I wrote *J. B.* because I had a theme that wouldn't leave me alone. I knew that it had to be a verse play and that was about all I knew to begin with. So I wrote it as a verse play and published the first part of it in the *Saturday Review* and the finished poem with my publishers, Houghton Mifflin. I thought that was the end of it. It never occurred to me that anybody would want to produce it. Then Curt Canfield, who was Dean of the Yale Drama School, said he wanted to produce it at Yale. I said,

"Fine, great." No changes of any kind except some cuts for length. Don Oenschlager designed the set—very handsome— and Curt directed with student actors and we opened. Brooks Atkinson came up to see it and reviewed it in the *Times*, and the next morning nine producers were on the telephone. Alfred deLiagre, with more courage, I thought, than sound sense, took it on and he interested Gadge Kazan, who was the great director of the generation. Gadge came up here during the summer and he and I spent weeks in this room going over and over the play. Still very little rewriting—almost none. Things for purposes of stage continuity. The real problems occurred during tryout in Washington. In other words, I was deep in a Broadway production before I rightly realized that I was headed for Broadway. It was in Washington we discovered that we had no "end"—that the end of the play had to be reconceived. But even then I did not "lose control" of the play. By this time Gadge and I were closer than brothers—communicated almost without words. We both knew the end was wrong, but what to do about it was my problem. So I rewrote the end of the play and rewrote it and rewrote it, and was very unhappy about it. And then we opened in New York. The publicity people were in a terrible situation. They had a verse play on a Biblical theme on their hands. And as if that wasn't enough, the newspapers were struck, so that everything was against us. Well, what happened was that we ran on Broadway for a year.

INTERVIEWER: And weren't ground up in a machine.

MACLEISH: Nor was I in the second Broadway play, *Scratch*, though *Scratch* was a Broadway project from the start. By which I mean that it began not with a play but with a producer. Stuart Ostrow wanted to make a musical out of Steve Benet's short story, "The Devil and Daniel Webster," with Bob Dylan and me as the concocters. I had little interest in that, and less and less the more I heard of it, but eventually I became excited about a straight play based on Steve's story, or what lay behind it, and Ostrow, when he read the first draft, gave up the idea of the musical. *Scratch,* in other words, was written not only *for* the Broadway stage, but practically *on* the Broadway stage. And yet, even so, I never felt I had lost control. It was a joint undertaking certainly—producer, director, actors, playwright —but the theme was mine from the start and the words were always mine—the play.

But if I were to generalize about this, I think I'd say *J. B.* was right and *Scratch* was wrong—wrong I mean *for me.* For a man who is primarily not a playwright, not a theater hand, to start out on Broadway is probably a mistake, Broadway being what it has become in the last ten years. If I were ever to write a play again—which I won't—I'd start with a play as I did in *J. B.,* get it produced, if I could, in one of the fine repertory theaters outside New York, and keep it outside until it was ready for the buzzards.

INTERVIEWER: That implies self-restraint. Where do you buy it in a culture that teaches writers they "personally" matter? Can you say anything about that?

MACLEISH: I don't know if there is anything I can say about it, but by God something ought to be said. Let me begin with two people whom I knew, one very well and one quite well: Ernest Hemingway and Scott Fitzgerald. The tragedy—and it is a tragedy—of Hemingway's fame is that his life and his dramatization of himself have been built up, not by him, or let me say, not altogether by him, to such a point that the myth of the man is more important than the achievement—the work. And the same thing is true of Scott, Scott having done less about dramatizing himself, but having had more done for him. In each case the *literary figure*—capital "L", capital "F" —has been so blown up, so exaggerated, that the work has been diminished. You would know better than I how permanently, but in any case damage has been done. And the same thing is true of Robert Frost. Robert was himself the villain there, because, as anybody who knew him knows, he worked very hard at his own reputation even when he had no need to—when his greatness was acknowledged. This was damaging only to him. But the real question is what you do about this sort of thing. I don't know that pontificating about it does any good. My own conviction is that the literary person as such just doesn't count —doesn't matter. Some are interesting and some are dull. The only thing that matters is the work. And the amplification of the amplifying device, which is the man himself, is not good for the art of writing, is not good for the writer, is not good. Ernest used to love to come up and go to the nightclubs in New York. Why? To be recognized? But, for God's sake, he had been recognized in better ways before. I am not throwing off on Ernest. He is still the great prose stylist of the century. But if ever there was a cult of personality . . . ! Well, the one thing a young writer ought to swear to on his sword never to do is never to dramatize himself, whatever he may want to do about his work.

INTERVIEWER: What are the other dangers a writer might be wise to look out for?

MACLEISH: Innumerable, of course, like all the ills humanity is heir to, but self-dramatization will stand for a lot of them. The essential is not to think of one's self as a writer and to do nothing which will put one's self in that popinjay attitude. You don't write as a writer, you write as a man—a man with a certain hard-earned skill in the use of words, a particular, and particularly naked, consciousness of human life, of the human tragedy and triumph—a man who is moved by human life, who cannot take it for granted. Donne was speaking of all this when he told his congregation not to ask for whom the bell tolls. His learned listeners thought he was speaking as a divine—as a stoic. He was speaking from his poet's heart: he meant that when *he* heard the bell *he* died. It's all in Keats's letters—that writer's bible which every young man or woman with this most dangerous of lives before him should be set to read. Keats is already a poet in these letters—he is certain, in spite of the reviewers, that he will be among the English poets at his death.

But they are not the letters of a poet. They are the letters of a boy, a young man, who will write great poems. Who never postures. Who laughs at himself and who, when he holds his dying brother in his arms, thinks of his dying brother, not the pathos of the scene. You can put it down, I think, as gospel that a self-advertising writer is always a self-extinguished writer. Why do anonymous writers speak to us most directly? Why are the old, old writers—the old Chinese and the vanished Greeks —most truly ours?

INTERVIEWER: What about the company a writer *does* keep. Does it matter?

MACLEISH: I don't suppose anything matters more. The subject of art is life. You learn life by living it. And you don't live it alone—even on Walden Pond—as *Walden* proves on every page. You live it with and by people—yourself in your relation with people, with and by living things, yourself in your relation to living things. The mistake is Scott Fitzgerald's mistake, for example—to lump all this as something called "experience" and to put yourself outside it looking in like a kind of glorified journalist of the ultimate reality. Scott dancing around the dance floor beside a couple of pederasts, asking them intimate questions, as though the answers would be answers. Ernest's urgent feeling that he had to know all sorts and kinds, as though he were still a reporter for the Kansas City *Star.* What you really have to know is one: yourself. And the only way you can know that one is in the mirror of the others. And the only way you can see into the mirror of the others is by love or its opposite—by profound emotion. Certainly not by curiosity— by dancing around asking, looking, making notes. You have to *live* relationships to *know*. Which is why a lifetime marriage with a woman you love is a great gift, and five marriages in a raddled row is a disaster to everyone, including the marrier. The great luck—the immeasurable luck—for a man trying to write the poem of his life is to have known good men and women and to have loved them well enough to learn the differences from himself. It won't guarantee the poem will get written but it is immeasurable luck. A Jim Agee. A B. Hand. A Mark Van Doren. Felix Frankfurter. Jack Bate. Mac Bundy. Carl Sandburg. Dean Acheson . . . my wife.

INTERVIEWER: What about writers as friends? Easy friends, I mean. Can the relation be other than competitive? I remember your story about traveling out to Montana when Hemingway had that car accident.

MACLEISH: You mean Hemingway's remark that I had come out to watch him die? You can't generalize from Hemingway. He knew I'd come at considerable cost and inconvenience (travel on Northwest Airlines in those days was anything but a pleasure), and it embarrassed him. Also, he had grown his first beard—the first I saw, anyway—and looked like anything but a dying man; Pauline had to fight the nurses out of the room. But to answer your question . . . my own observation had been that writers can be "easy friends" and often are—but not as writers. Mark Van Doren and I are the easiest of friends. Hemingway and I were friends—close friends, I won't lean on the "easy"—from '24 or '25 until along in the thirties. Dos was a close friend always. So was John Peale Bishop. But these were —are— human friendships, friendships between men, not literary friendships. Reading Scott Fitzgerald's letters to Ernest is illuminating in this connection: you see at once what was wrong with that friendship. Scott writes as a writer. And in friendship, in human relations, in life, there is no such thing as a writer: there is merely a *man* who sometimes writes. I can't imagine anything shallower than a friendship based on a common interest in the production of literature. *Look* at those letters of Scott's! They throw light on Scott's novels, sure, but on the relation of two remarkable men . . . ?

INTERVIEWER: What are the prices? What are the necessary disciplines of writing?

MACLEISH: The first discipline is the realization that there *is* a discipline—that all art begins and ends with discipline, that any art is first and foremost a craft. We have gone far enough on the road to self-indulgence now to know that. The man who announces to the world that he is going to "do his thing" is like the amateur on the high-diving platform who flings himself into the void shouting at the judges that he is going to do whatever comes naturally. He will land on his ass. Naturally. You'd think, to listen to the loudspeakers which surround us, that no man had ever tried to "do his thing" before. Every poet worth reading has, but those really worth reading have understood that to do your thing you have to learn first what your thing is and second how to go about doing it. The first is learned by the difficult labor of living, the second by the endless discipline of writing and rewriting and rerewriting. There are no shortcuts. Young writers a while back, misreading Bill Williams, decided to ignore the fact that poems are made of words as sounds as well as of words as signs— decided not to learn the art of words as sounds, not to be bothered with it. They were not interested in poems. They were interested in doing their thing. They did—and that was that.

INTERVIEWER: Who do you read now? Who counts?

MacLEISH: Read for pleasure or read from necessity? I suppose I read for pleasure as everyone else does—what comes along. What's "new," as Ezra used to say. (Not much *is* what it says it is but one always hopes.) But necessity is something else. You *have* to read in order to write, no matter what you pretend to yourself. Art is a seamless web, and we all latch into it where we find a loose end. But the problem is to find the connection. And hence the necessity. What astonishes me about myself is that my necessities haven't changed over fifty years. You would think they'd have to in a time like this, but they don't. Robert Frost is out of fashion—or so they tell me —but fashion is irrelevant: Robert is still what he always was, and still necessary to me. So, even more, is Yeats. So is Perse. So is Pound. Eliot. That particular, unique, and irreplaceable tone—timbre—of Carl Sandburg. And back of the men of my own time the necessity leads by the same curious—oh, it is curious enough—path: Hopkins, Rilke, Rimbaud, Emily, Emerson, Keats, Milton, Donne, and so to the great inland ocean of Shakespeare and back of that to Chaucer and Dante and the Greeks and off around the world to Li Po and Tu Fu. No pattern I or anyone else can see, but all of it somehow making a whole—all of it *necessary*. Necessary as bread. More than bread—water. Still. Fifty years later.

INTERVIEWER: Fifty years ago means the twenties. You have reason to remember the twenties; why does everyone else want to? Why all this nagging of that time?

MACLEISH: No idea. From any point of view, the decade of the twenties was a terrible decade: it was self-indulgent, it was fat, it was rich, it was full of the most loathsome kinds of open and flagrant money-making. All the worst aspects of the French came out as the franc dropped. And yet that decade in Paris was perfect. I suppose it was the right period for *us*. Because of the war, I was a lot older than I should have been to do what I was doing—trying to learn an art. But I was trying to do it alone, which is the best way to try to do it, and I was living in a city where you could *be* alone without ever being lonely, and I had Ada with me. She—I don't need to tell *you* —was a singer. A lovely singer with a beautiful, clear, high voice, and a superb musician. She was going great guns singing new songs for Stravinsky and Poulenc and Copland. So we were right in the middle of the most exciting period in almost a century of music. Also, the people who drifted along—Ernest, Dos, Scott, Gerald Murphy, above all, the Murphys—were people of extraordinary interest who were also—or became, most of them—close friends. I can see why this still interests *me*—I love to go back to it in my mind—but why anybody else forty, fifty, sixty years younger should be interested in it, I just don't understand.

INTERVIEWER: What was the special pull of the Murphys?

Why did they give up that mode of life? Did Gerald Murphy's friends try to persuade him to stick to the arts?

MACLEISH: Three questions. The last two are tragically easy to answer. Gerald gave up painting when his youngest child, Patrick, who had had tuberculosis and, he thought, recovered, became ill again. Gerald wasn't Irish for nothing. He bore the stigmata—including the deep Puritan wound which afflicts Irish Catholicism and distinguishes the Gaels of Eire from the Gaels of the Scottish islands in the Hebrides. Gerald took that second (and fatal) illness as a judgment on himself. He hadn't "earned" the right to art. When, after the agony was over, the Murphys settled in New York, Gerald threw everything out of his room but the bed and a chair—white plaster walls, a white bed and chair. Did his friends try to dissuade him? How could they? And yet I remember an ambiguous scene. A Paris concert hall. An "occasion" of some kind: the Murphys are in a box and Ada and I with them. Picasso appears in front of the box looking at Gerald—smiling at him. Gerald stares over his head. Picasso turns away. But I am not answering your questions. Why did they give up "that mode of life"? It was the other way around. Their older son, Baoth, who had always been well, happy, a golden child, died suddenly, brutally, at sixteen. Then Patrick—an extraordinary human being, "un monsieur," as Picasso said, "qui est par hazard un enfant"—died after years of dying, also at sixteen. Then there were the consequences of all that doctoring and hospitalization—years in Montana-Vermala, in the Adirondacks, Depression income. Their money was all but gone. They had never been "rich" by American standards, but they had always spent money as though they were, having a blithe contempt for money as such—a healthy conviction that money should be used for the purposes of life, the living of life, the defeat of illness and death. One has to pay for a faith like that, and Gerald and Sara paid without a whimper. He went back to Mark Cross, the business his father had founded. I never heard him complain of anything except the boredom. But he put up with that, supported his wife and daughter, saved his sister's holdings, and made Mark Cross, for a few, vivid years, a creative enterprise . . . not necessarily profitable, but real. "Merchant prince" he used to call himself in those days, mocking his life. But when he was dying (of cancer) René d'Harnoncourt, then the head of the Museum of Modern Art, told me I might tell him the museum had accepted his *Pear and Wasp* for its permanent collection. I feel sure he died thinking of himself as a painter. He should have. He was a painter. And a man. A man who loved life and learned how to live it. And how to die—something not all men learned even in that generation.

That or something like it would be the answer to your first question—the "special pull," I think you said. No one has even been able quite to define it. Scott tried in *Tender Is the Night.* Dos tried in more direct terms. Ernest tried by not trying. I wrote a "Sketch for a Portrait of Mme. G——M——," a longish poem. They escaped us all. There was a shine to life wherever they were: not a decorative *added* value, but a kind of revelation of inherent loveliness, as though custom and habit had been wiped away and the thing itself was, for an instant, *seen.* Don't ask me how.

INTERVIEWER: Did the Americans in Paris in the twenties know who they were? Was there any sense among them that what they were doing would have overwhelming impact before they were through?

MACLEISH: I can only answer for myself—what I saw and heard. Everyone was aware, I think, that work was being produced in Paris which was magnificent by any standard. This was true of all the arts—the arts generally—the arts as practiced by artists of many nationalities: French, Spanish, Russian, Irish, German, Greek, Austrian. We knew we belonged to a great, a greatly creative, generation—that we lived in a generative time. Everything seemed possible—*was* possible. To be young in a time like that was incredible luck—to be young and in Paris. That much is certain: the witnesses are innumerable. But when you narrow the circle to the American the answers are not so easy. American letters at the turn of the century had reached something which looked to my generation like rock bottom, and the achievements of Eliot and Pound during and after the First World War, though they had raised our hearts, had not wholly persuaded us that *we* belonged in this great resurgence of all the arts which was evident in Paris—this world resurgence of great art. So our excitement, real enough, was a little hesitant, a little tentative. Hemingway's *In Our Time* was the first solid American proof to appear on the Seine —proof that a master of English prose had established himself and that this master was indubitably American, American not only by blood but by eye and ear. But *In Our Time* was a collection of short stories. Would there be a great novel? A great *American* novel? We didn't know in Paris in the twenties. We only knew anything was possible.

INTERVIEWER: In that twenties community, how much exchange of ideas went on . . . reading of each other's manuscripts, advice sought and given . . . ?

MACLEISH: None. None so far as I was concerned. I met Hemingway a year or so after we got to Paris and Gerald Murphy about the same time . . . Dos, Estlin Cummings, Bishop, Scott . . . but there was no "community" in the sense in which you, I think, are using the word. No Americans-in-Paris community. That notion is a myth concocted after the event by critics with fish to fry. There was the literary-tourist world of the Dôme and the Rotonde but no work came out of that. The real "community" was, of course, Paris—the Paris of Valéry and Fargue and Larbaud—the world center of art which had drawn Picasso from abroad, and Juan Gris and Stravinsky and all the rest of that great international generation including, first and foremost, Joyce. The world center of poetry which held Alexis Léger down at the Quai d'Orsay in his anonymity as St.-J. Perse. That community—real community

—drew and sustained the young Americans who lived in Paris in those years, but they didn't belong to it nor did they communicate with it, except to watch and wonder like the rest of the world. I knew Fargue and Larbaud, and Jules Romains through Adrienne Monnier. Alexis Léger became a close friend many years afterward, when all this was gone and Paris was a Nazi slum. I knew Joyce and marveled at him. But I was not part of *that* Paris nor were any Americans I knew, with the possible exceptions of Tom Eliot and Ezra Pound, who sometimes appeared. In a touching letter toward the end of his life, Scott speaks of "the last American season" in Paris. If there ever was an "American season" in Paris in the twenties, Paris was not aware of it. Nor, I think, was anyone else.

INTERVIEWER: Can I try instant analysis about why we're so interested in that time, that romance? Part of what the period means, part of the reason people come back to it, is that the glamour is forgivable in a way that glamour isn't forgivable now. People could live as they lived without the sense that all around was an active enmity to their values, their standards, their way of perceiving. In a sense going back to the twenties —you called it that "self-indulgent" time—is trying to find a release from the pressure of justifiable hostility. Possible?

MACLEISH: I'm not sure I'd use the word "glamour"—not, certainly, of *our* life, Ada's and mine. But there was a certain relaxation. We were all of us out of that "worst of wars." Ernest had been shot up. Scott had not really been involved in it, but that was tragedy too. I had had a year of it in France. My brother had been killed. Almost everybody that we saw—certainly all the French, and all the English in Paris at that time —had lived through it. So the whole city gave off a sense that you had something coming to you—just what, you never asked . . . or learned.

INTERVIEWER: You were talking at lunch about people perceiving themselves as images of themselves rather than as genuine functions in the world and so on. Do you think that being a writer now is essentially a different kind of act from what it once was, a different kind of performance?

MACLEISH: Not "essentially"—essentially there is only one life a writer can live. But different—yes. Because the world is different. The economic "reality" is different. The Republic doesn't have the self-generated surge forward that it seemed to have a generation ago. We've come in out of the dream, and we have to think about the world we see around us, do something about it, at least be sensitive to it. Which means be sensitive to it *as* poets. And yet all the time and in spite of the changes in the world—the rapid and incoherent changes—the question at the center, the poet's question, remains the same. Who am I? The figures out on the lawn playing croquet have changed. They are not playing croquet anymore. They aren't dressed as they once were, and there's somebody with a gun back of the bush. But the question remains. So that the problem is to answer the old question in a new scene, a new setting, with other angles of light, refractions of sound, shadows moving—but still, somehow, to answer it.

INTERVIEWER: So writing now is different. But more difficult?

MACLEISH: Well, I have just had the experience, as I've said, of writing a play—*Scratch*—the whole purpose of which was to try to find out what has become of the Republic in this new world we've been talking about. I found the critic of the *Times*, who exercises the power of life and death in the New York theater, totally impenetrable by this idea, buttoned up, occluded. He was an Englishman at that period—an Englishman and an authority on the dance—and he simply didn't understand what was being said on the stage twenty feet in front of him. Which suggests to me that the problem of writing about the public world may have become more difficult than it was forty years ago. Or perhaps it is only the problem of getting through that particular infarct to the live audience behind him.

INTERVIEWER: I remember when you were teaching you were

strong for "alive" and "living" as "critical terms." What are the referents, anyway? What gives the edge?

MACLEISH: To start negatively, "alive" is what is not "literary." Or, in positive terms, what has a speaker—a voice. No writing is alive which is merely *written*. Donne, for example. Why is Donne so *present?* Why is Hopkins so much Hopkins? Or Cummings? Or Mark Van Doren? Or Agee? Cal Lowell? Wilbur? Not because they write well but because they *speak*. Each with his own voice. There's a man there, a woman— Emily. The lawyers have a useful word—"fungible." Wheat is fungible: substitute one bushel for another. Poets can't be substituted. Each has his own let's call it breath, except that it goes on and on with the words—doesn't end with the man. So that the words remain *his*. And alive.

INTERVIEWER: Breath?

MACLEISH: Well, the use of the language. The *way* a man *uses* it. You don't choose a word if you're a writer as a golf pro chooses a club with the *shot* in mind. You choose it with *yourself* in mind—*your* needs, *your* passions, feelings. It has to carry the green, yes, but it must also carry *you*. Not only your "meaning," but you yourself meaning it. You're quite right— this does seem to me the fundamental criterion in the use of language as material for art. You *create* your words in choosing them. You make them yours—spoken with your breath. Youngsters tend to think the trick is to break down the syntax —be careless—write the way they think they talk. Nothing could be farther from the truth. To make a word your own is a year's labor—maybe a life's.

INTERVIEWER: The MacLeish poems I like best give this sense that metaphors are racing and expending energy fiercely —the edge of a moment. "Cook County," "You, Andrew Marvell," "The Genius," for example. Did they come in a rush?

MACLEISH: Those are golden words; I shouldn't let myself think about them. Because even at my age a man shouldn't let himself believe what he most wants to believe. You delight me by saying some of my poems sound as though they had come in a rush, but none of them have with the exception of "You, Andrew Marvell," which was there at the end of a morning and finished by night. I am sure—I mean I am not sure at all but I believe—the master poets must come at their poems as a hawk on a pigeon in one dive. I can't. I chip away like a stonemason who has got it into his head that there is a pigeon in that block of marble. But there's a delight in the chipping. At least there's a delight in it when your hunch that the pigeon in there is stronger than you are carries you along. There is no straining then nor *are* you strained—all assurance and confidence. Oh, you can be fooled, of course—there may be nothing there but a stone. But until you are . . .

I said something a minute ago about a long breath that sustains itself. If you find anything like that in any poem, then the impulse which drove the poem at the start is still alive in the poem printed on the page. So that the length of that poem is not the length (endless) of the work but the length of the impulse: exhausted—and achieved—in a breath.

I used to run into students who thought impulse meant idea: you got an idea and somehow you made a poem of it. A poem made out of an idea could run on forever. No single breath there. Impulse as one finds it in this art—maybe in all art— is a glimpse. Of a relationship, a possible relationship—Baudelaire's *analogie universelle.* The impulse, the urge, the emotion, begins in that cloudy glimpse, and the whole labor of art is to create the form which will contain the relationship—turn glimpse into image. But in such a way that the poem—if you are lucky, if there *is* a poem at the end—will carry *not only* the image but the impulse which produced it, that single breath—its own.

INTERVIEWER: If I understand it, then really it's all in the end of "Reason for Music"—"meaning the movement of the sea." Can you say that in any other way? Can you translate?

MACLEISH:

>Why do we labor at the poem?
>Out of the turbulence of the sea,
>Flower by brittle flower, rises
>The coral reef that calms the water
>
>Generations of the dying
>Fix the sea's dissolving salts
>In stone, still trees, their branches immovable,
>Meaning,
>>the movement of the sea.

Translate? Well, I am not one of those who believe that poems can't be translated; it would be an impoverished world if they couldn't. But not, I think, *out* of their images. Suppose you say that poets, like those tiny coral insects—generations of the dying—fix the sea's dissolving salts in stone, still trees, their branches immovable, which means—what? The movement of the sea. What have you gained? It's obvious what you have lost: the rhythms which suspend the words in a relationship of their own without which the world of the poem—of any poem— collapses. (A fact of art which one of my admired contemporaries, Bill Williams, tried to forget, misleading a whole generation of the dying as a result.) But still what *have* you gained? Why do we labor at the poem? To hold the evanescent *still* in its evanescence. I think the poem says it better—but perhaps I should not attempt to judge.

INTERVIEWER: There's a struggle going on in the stillness, though. I'm thinking about "The Captivity of a Fly" . . . "My heart against the hard-rib bone beat like a fly." What is the theme exactly—"a prisoner of the open wall"? It comes back in Job, too, as though it were a "personal remark" in some way. "It had gone free, my heart, it might have gone free, but the shining world so shone."

MACLEISH: The image, of course, is the commonest of all

images—the fly against the windowpane that "flings itself in flightless flight." "So it loves light." And the refraction of the image is as obvious. We are all "prisoners of the open wall." What else is "the burden of the mystery" which so weighed on John Keats? Easy enough to turn away from the glass and go free—but not if you're a fly. Easy enough to put off the burden of the mystery—but not if you're human. You spoke of Job. Of course. Easy enough for Job to get down from his dung heap and walk off—if he could stop being Job, the man with a passion for justice and therefore the need to confront God. Job is the opposite of the existentialist as he is the opposite of the "good Catholic." His world *has* to mean, because God made it. It is because he loves God that he is certain there are meanings—not the other way around. What satisfies Sartre won't satisfy Job. Nor what satisfies Job's friends. He sees the light and so is prisoner of the glass.

INTERVIEWER: Are you ever completely satisfied with a finished work?

MACLEISH: Not at first. Not while the thing is still malleable. It's like the homicide experts in the movies who judge by the stiffening of the corpse: you can tell—God knows how—when a poem has settled into itself. After that you touch it at your peril: the whole thing may disintegrate if you change a word. It's for that reason I formed the habit long ago of putting new poems into a desk drawer and letting them lie there to ripen (or the opposite) like apples. I suppose everyone else does the same thing. I learned early and by sad experience never to publish a green poem. Who in hell wrote *that?* Instead, I pull them out after a few weeks or months and say, "Well . . . possibly . . ." and start all over. Or consign the whole thing to the wood fire and hope the seed, whatever it was, will sow itself again. I doubt if it does. It's sick of me by that time.

INTERVIEWER: Could we talk for a minute about "reputation"? Can a good writer make his way without cultivating his own reputation? Interviews, luncheons, appearance, back-scratching, all that crap. A lot of people still feel there is an Establishment to be cracked or supplanted before they can start to breathe.

MACLEISH: That word, "Establishment," has a lot to answer for. If it is intended to refer to anything more than the distinction between the old men *now* established and the young men who *want* to be—if, that is to say, it is intended to imply a kind of conspiracy by a few established characters to suppress *les autres*—it is a fraud, or worse, a kind of escape mechanism . . . an excuse. The real question is the one you put first: how to "arrive" in the world (if it is one) of the arts in our time, a world on which all those monsters you name—television and luncheons and appearances and the rest—batten and feed. Do you have to "arrive"? Not really, but it's convenient if you want to eat regularly. But suppose you do want to eat regularly, do you have to submit to all that nonsense? Because most of it, though there are some intelligent interviewers, *is* nonsense. I don't think so. The fact is that nothing matters ultimately in any art but the *work* of art—*the* poem, *the* fiction. *That* comes first and it is *that* which remains at the last. Cal Lowell began with a poem. So did Dick Wilbur. Frost began with a book of poems. To go at it the other way around is to invite disaster: straw without bricks. Believe in the work. Believe in your own work. No poem was ever suppressed—if it *was* a poem. Belayed, yes. Muffled. Ignored for a generation or a century. But not suppressed.

INTERVIEWER: You wrestled once with the problem of reputation in the arts—in "Poetical Remains." You talked about leaving behind an "anthological rubble," "mind mingled with mind," "odd and even coupled." What is the state of feeling behind the words?

MACLEISH: I suppose you start out (I can only suppose, because it must be a very private experience for each man) with that lust for fame to which Keats confessed and to which, I guess, we should all confess—all of us who practice an art, certainly. That lust for fame is a lust for personal fame. You want to be distinguished from the others who are remembered —if anybody indeed is going to be remembered. And then, as time goes by and you begin to get a little hindsight, you look back. What really does happen to poets? Most of them leave a few fragments which go into the rubble heap, where the next generation can feed on them. They don't intend to but they do. Well, eventually, thinking about all this, you get to the point where you realize that personal fame is not at all what you're concerned with really—that old Robert was right when he said he hoped to leave half a dozen poems which would be hard to get rid of. Wonderful way of saying it. You begin to see that what is really going to happen is not that half a dozen but two, three, four poems, or maybe lines of poems, or fragments—some things may get shelved, shored up, or left behind. But left behind not alone but in a conjunction. So that you begin to think of yourself in terms of the others who were with you in this place—your contemporaries. "Oh living men, Remember me, Receive me among you." And you realize that's how you are really going to end up. You're going to be part of that, of them. And finally you begin to think, that's the way it ought to be. You ought to make the world fruitful that way. Rot! Leaving those fragments—those few poems that will be hard to get rid of.

Obviously, these are very subjective emotions. But I think, even so, even if they are subjective, one can make some generalizations about them. How to go about it? Let me try this way. I think, as you move along . . . now, this may simply be a result of the blessed accident that befell me when I found myself, far too old, teaching at Harvard. I began to understand then, by teaching a course in which I tried to find out for myself what poetry is, what it *really* is. I began to understand that it is a part of a process which extends beyond poetry but which is most apparent *in* poetry, of trying to *see* human experience, trying to *see* "the world." "The world" being what a man feels *about* the world. Now if you realize this—what the purpose of your art is—you come to see that you are laboring at your art not only to make works of art but to make sense of your life —those dark and bewildering moments of experience. And to make sense of it not only for yourself. In other words, those poems are not works to be published for the glory of A. MacLeish—so that A. MacLeish may be spoken of. Not at all. They are steps in an attempt to stop time in terms of time so that it may be *seen.* To stop time, but to stop it on its own terms. Let men see it. Make it *visible* to men. Therefore, whatever you leave behind you exists in terms of those others who have read it, who were aware of it, who were moved by it. And the consequence is that you *do* have a totally different attitude toward fame. It isn't that you want to be admired any the less. Of course you want to be admired. Any poet wants to be admired—to be a great poet. But who is a great poet? Maybe a handful in the world's history. So that's irrelevant. What's really going to come out of your work is something else. If you have succeeded at all you have become part—however small a part—of the consciousness of your time. Which is enough. No?

BENJAMIN DeMOTT
Summer 1974

3. Pablo Neruda

Pablo Neruda was born Ricardo Eliecer Neftalí Reyes de Basoalto in Parral, Chile, on July 12, 1904. It was the land of his childhood, the spectacular forested area of southern Chile, that later kindled Neruda's imagination and recurred as vibrant images in his poetry. He took the name Neruda after the Czech short-story writer Jan Neruda and submitted his first poem to a magazine at age fifteen, already exploring the brooding themes of love, death, and the passage of time that were to dominate his poetry.

Over the next several years he produced many volumes of poetry, including *Veinte poemas de amor y una cancíon desesperada (Twenty Love Poems and a Song of Despair)*, which was published in 1924 and has sold almost two million copies to date, and *Residencia en la tierra (Residence on Earth)*, which appeared in 1933. In recognition of his achievements, the Chilean government appointed him to the consular service, and Neruda subsequently served as Chile's consul in several countries, including Spain, where in 1939 he used his office of consul to help the cause of the Spanish Loyalists.

An outspoken critic of U.S. influence in Latin America, Neruda won election as a Communist to the national Senate of Chile in 1945 but was forced into political exile in 1947.

He published his monumental *Canto general (General Song)*, often considered his masterpiece, in Mexico in 1950. The recipient of many prizes and honorary degrees, he was awarded the Nobel Prize in literature in 1971.

Following many years of exile Neruda returned to Chile in 1952. He was the Communist Party's candidate for president in 1970 until he withdrew his candidacy in order to support his friend Salvador Allende Gossens.

Married since 1951 to Matilde Urrutia, Neruda died on September 23, 1973, at the age of sixty-nine.

mi dirección hasta 20 de Junio

Hôtel du Quai Voltaire
19, Quai Voltaire
PARIS - 7ᵉ
—
TÉLÉPHONE
Hôtel : 548-42-91 (lignes groupées)
Bar : 222-28-11

30 marzo Abril

Querida Rita, Solo ayer
recibí la entrevista,
la corregiré este week-end
y te la mando el martes
y próximo (mayo) Perdo-
na, pero hubo toda
clase de aventuras con
tu <u>typescript</u>, pero
lo tendrás !

Te abrazamos,
Pablo

A page from Pablo Neruda's correspondence with interviewer Rita Guibert.

Pablo Neruda

"I have never thought of my life as divided between poetry and politics," Pablo Neruda said in his September 30, 1969, accept-*ance speech as the Chilean Communist Party candidate for the presidency. "I am a Chilean who for decades has known the misfortunes and difficulties of our national existence and who has taken part in each sorrow and joy of the people. I am not a stranger to them, I come from them, I am part of the people. I come from a working class family. . . . I have never been in with those in power and have always felt that my vocation and my duty was to serve the Chilean people in my actions and with my poetry. I have lived singing and defending them."*

Because of a divided Left, Neruda withdrew his candidacy after four months of hard campaigning and resigned in order to support a Popular Unity candidate. This interview was con-

ducted in his house at Isla Negra in January 1970 just before his resignation.

Isla Negra (Black Island) is neither black nor an island. It is an elegant beach resort forty kilometers south of Valparaiso and a two-hour drive from Santiago. No one knows where the name comes from; Neruda speculates about black rocks vaguely shaped like an island which he sees from his terrace. Thirty years ago, long before Isla Negra became fashionable, Neruda bought —with the royalties of his books—six thousand square meters of beachfront, which included a tiny stone house at the top of a steep slope. "Then the house started growing, like the people, like the trees."

Neruda has other houses—one on San Cristobal Hill in Santiago and another in Valparaiso. To decorate his houses he has scoured antique shops and junkyards for all kinds of objects. Each object reminds him of an anecdote. "Doesn't he look like Stalin?" he asks, pointing to a bust of the English adventurer Morgan in the dining room at Isla Negra. "The antique dealer in Paris didn't want to sell it to me, but when he heard I was Chilean, he asked me if I knew Pablo Neruda. That's how I persuaded him to sell it."

It is at Isla Negra where Pablo Neruda, the "terrestrial navigator," and his third wife, Matilde ("Patoja," as he affectionately calls her, the "muse" to whom he has written many love poems), have established their most permanent residence.

Tall, stocky, of olive complexion, his outstanding features are a prominent nose and large brown eyes with hooded eyelids. His movements are slow but firm. He speaks distinctly, without pomposity. When he goes for a walk—usually accompanied by his two chows—he wears a long poncho and carries a rustic cane.

At Isla Negra Neruda entertains a constant stream of visitors and there is always room at the table for last-minute guests. Neruda does most of his entertaining in the bar, which one enters through a small corridor from a terrace facing the beach.

On the corridor floor is a Victorian bidet and an old hand organ.
On the window shelves there is a collection of bottles. The bar
is decorated as a ship's salon, with furniture bolted to the floor
and nautical lamps and paintings. The room has glass-panel
walls facing the sea. On the ceiling and on each of the wooden
crossbeams a carpenter has carved, from Neruda's handwriting,
names of his dead friends.

Behind the bar, on the liquor shelf, is a sign that says NO SE
FIA *(no credit here). Neruda takes his role as bartender very*
seriously and likes to make elaborate drinks for his guests al-
though he drinks only Scotch and wine. On a wall are two
anti-Neruda posters, one of which he brought back from his last
trip to Caracas. It shows his profile with the legend "Neruda go
home." The other is a cover from an Argentine magazine with
his picture and the copy "Neruda, why doesn't he kill himself?"
A huge poster of Twiggy stretches from the ceiling to the floor.

Meals at Isla Negra are typically Chilean. Neruda has men-
tioned some of them in his poetry: conger-eel soup; fish with a
delicate sauce of tomatoes and baby shrimp; meat pie. The wine
is always Chilean. One of the porcelain wine pitchers, shaped
like a bird, sings when wine is poured. In the summer, lunch is
served on a porch facing a garden that has an antique railroad
engine. "So powerful, such a corn picker, such a procreator and
whistler and roarer and thunderer . . . I love it because it looks
like Walt Whitman."

Conversations for the interview were held in short sessions.
In the morning—after Neruda had his breakfast in his room—
we would meet in the library, which is a new wing of the house.
I would wait while he answered his mail, composed poems for
his new book, or corrected the galleys of a new Chilean edition
of Twenty Love Poems. *When composing poetry, he writes*
with green ink in an ordinary composition book. He can write
a fairly long poem in a very short time, after which he makes only
a few corrections. The poems are then typed by his secretary and
close friend of more than fifty years, Homero Arce.

*In the afternoon, after his daily nap, we would sit on a stone
bench on the terrace facing the sea. Neruda would talk holding
the microphone of the tape recorder, which picked up the sound
of the sea as background to his voice.*

INTERVIEWER: Why did you change your name, and why did
you choose "Pablo Neruda"?

NERUDA: I don't remember. I was only thirteen or fourteen
years old. I remember that it bothered my father very much
that I wanted to write. With the best of intentions, he thought
that writing would bring destruction to the family and myself
and, especially, that it would lead me to a life of complete
uselessness. He had domestic reasons for thinking so, reasons
which did not weigh heavily on me. It was one of the first
defensive measures that I adopted—changing my name.

INTERVIEWER: Did you choose "Neruda" because of the
Czech poet Jan Neruda?

NERUDA: I'd read a short story of his. I've never read his
poetry, but he has a book entitled *Stories from Malá Strana*
about the humble people of that neighborhood in Prague. It
is possible that my new name came from there. As I say, the
whole matter is so far back in my memory that I don't recall.
Nevertheless, the Czechs think of me as one of them, as part
of their nation, and I've had a very friendly connection with
them.

INTERVIEWER: In case you are elected president of Chile, will
you keep on writing?

NERUDA: For me writing is like breathing. I could not live
without breathing and I could not live without writing.

INTERVIEWER: Who are the poets who have aspired to high
political office and succeeded?

NERUDA: Our period is an era of governing poets: Mao Tse-
tung and Ho Chi Minh. Mao Tse-tung has other qualities: as
you know, he is a great swimmer, something which I am not.
There is also a great poet, Léopold Senghor, who is president

of Senegal; another, Aimé Césaire, a surrealist poet, is the mayor of Fort-de-France in Martinique. In my country, poets have always intervened in politics, though we have never had a poet who was president of the republic. On the other hand, there have been writers in Latin America who have been president: Rómulo Gallegos was president of Venezuela.

INTERVIEWER: How have you been running your presidential campaign?

NERUDA: A platform is set up. First there are always folk songs, and then someone in charge explains the strictly political scope of our campaign. After that, the note I strike in order to talk to the townspeople is a much freer one, much less organized; it is more poetic. I almost always finish by reading poetry. If I didn't read some poetry, the people would go away disillusioned. Of course, they also want to hear my political thoughts, but I don't overwork the political or economic aspects because people also need another kind of language.

INTERVIEWER: How do the people react when you read your poems?

NERUDA: They love me in a very emotional way. I can't enter or leave some places. I have a special escort which protects me from the crowds because the people press around me. That happens everywhere.

INTERVIEWER: If you had to choose between the presidency of Chile and the Nobel Prize, for which you have been mentioned so often, which would you choose?

NERUDA: There can be no question of a decision between such illusory things.

INTERVIEWER: But if they put the presidency and the Nobel Prize right here on a table?

NERUDA: If they put them on the table in front of me, I'd get up and sit at another table.

INTERVIEWER: Do you think awarding the Nobel Prize to Samuel Beckett was just?

NERUDA: Yes, I believe so. Beckett writes short but exquisite things. The Nobel Prize, wherever it falls, is always an honor to literature. I am not one of those always arguing whether the prize went to the right person or not. What is important about this prize—if it has any importance—is that it confers a title of respect on the office of writer. That is what is important.

INTERVIEWER: What are your strongest memories?

NERUDA: I don't know. The most intense memories, perhaps, are those of my life in Spain—in that great brotherhood of poets; I've never known such a fraternal group in our American world—so full of *alacraneos* (gossips), as they say in Buenos Aires. Then, afterwards, it was terrible to see that republic of friends destroyed by the civil war, which so demonstrated the horrible reality of fascist repression. My friends were scattered: some were exterminated right there—like García Lorca and Miguel Hernández; others died in exile; and still others live on in exile. That whole phase of my life was rich in events, in profound emotions, and decisively changed the evolution of my life.

INTERVIEWER: Would they allow you to enter Spain now?

NERUDA: I'm not officially forbidden to enter. On one occasion I was invited to give some readings there by the Chilean Embassy. It is very possible that they would let me enter. But I don't want to make a point of it, because it simply may have been convenient for the Spanish government to show some democratic feeling by permitting the entry of people who had fought so hard against it. I don't know. I have been prevented from entering so many countries and I have been turned out of so many others that, truly, this is a matter which no longer causes the irritation in me that it did at first.

INTERVIEWER: In a certain way, your ode to García Lorca, which you wrote before he died, predicted his tragic end.

NERUDA: Yes, that poem is strange. Strange because he was such a happy person, such a cheerful creature. I've known very few people like him. He was the incarnation . . . well, let's not say of success, but of the love of life. He enjoyed each minute of his existence—a great spendthrift of happiness. For that reason, the crime of his execution is one of the most unpardonable crimes of fascism.

INTERVIEWER: You often mention him in your poems, as well as Miguel Hernández.

NERUDA: Hernández was like a son. As a poet, he was something of my disciple, and he almost lived in my house. He went to prison and died there because he disproved the official version of García Lorca's death. If their explanation was correct, why did the fascist government keep Miguel Hernández in prison until his death? Why did they even refuse to move him to a hospital, as the Chilean Embassy proposed? The death of Miguel Hernández was an assassination too.

INTERVIEWER: What do you remember most from your years in India?

NERUDA: My stay there was an encounter I wasn't prepared for. The splendor of that unfamiliar continent overwhelmed me, and yet I felt desperate, because my life and my solitude there were so long. Sometimes I seemed locked into an unending Technicolor picture—a marvelous movie, but one I wasn't allowed to leave. I never experienced the mysticism which guided so many South Americans and other foreigners in India. People who go to India in search of a religious answer to their anxieties see things in a different way. As for me, I was profoundly moved by the sociological conditions—that immense unarmed nation, so defenseless, bound to its imperial yoke. Even the English culture, for which I had a great predilection, seemed hateful to me for being the instrument of the intellectual submission of so many Hindus at that time. I mixed with the rebellious young people of that continent; in spite of my consular post, I got to know all the revolutionaries—those in the great movement that eventually brought about independence.

INTERVIEWER: Was it in India that you wrote *Residence on Earth*?

NERUDA: Yes, though India had very little intellectual influence on my poetry.

INTERVIEWER: It was from India that you wrote those very moving letters to the Argentine, Hector Eandi?

NERUDA: Yes. Those letters were important in my life, because he, a writer I did not know personally, took it upon himself, as a good Samaritan, to send me news, to send me periodicals, to help me through my great solitude. I had become afraid of losing contact with my own language—for years I met no one to speak Spanish to. In one letter to Rafael Alberti I had to ask for a Spanish dictionary. I had been appointed to the post of consul, but it was a low-grade post and one that had no stipend. I lived in the greatest poverty and in even greater solitude. For weeks I didn't see another human being.

INTERVIEWER: While there you had a great romance with Josie Bliss, whom you mention in many poems.

NERUDA: Yes, Josie Bliss was a woman who left quite a profound imprint on my poetry. I have always remembered her, even in my most recent books.

INTERVIEWER: Your work, then, is closely linked to your personal life?

NERUDA: Naturally. The life of a poet must be reflected in his poetry. That is the law of the art and a law of life.

INTERVIEWER: Your work can be divided into stages, can't it?

NERUDA: I have quite confusing thoughts about that. I myself don't have stages; the critics discover them. If I can say anything, it is that my poetry has the quality of an organism—infantile when I was a boy, juvenile when I was young, desolate when I suffered, combative when I had to enter the social struggle. A mixture of these tendencies is present in my current poetry. I always wrote out of internal necessity, and I imagine that this is what happens with all writers, poets especially.

INTERVIEWER: I've seen you writing in the car.

NERUDA: I write where I can and when I can, but I'm always writing.

INTERVIEWER: Do you always write everything in longhand?

NERUDA: Ever since I had an accident in which I broke a finger and couldn't use the typewriter for a few months, I have followed the custom of my youth and gone back to writing by hand. I discovered when my finger was better and I could type again that my poetry when written by hand was more sensitive; its plastic forms could change more easily. In an interview, Robert Graves says that in order to think one should have as little as possible around that is not handmade. He could have added that poetry ought to be written by hand. The typewriter separated me from a deeper intimacy with poetry, and my hand brought me closer to that intimacy again.

INTERVIEWER: What are your working hours?

NERUDA: I don't have a schedule, but by preference I write in the morning. Which is to say that if you weren't here making me waste my time (and wasting your own), I would be writing. I don't read many things during the day. I would rather write all day, but frequently the fullness of a thought, of an expression, of something that comes out of myself in a tumultuous way—let's label it with an antiquated term, "inspiration"—leaves me satisfied, or exhausted, or calmed, or empty. That is, I can't go on. Apart from that, I like living too much to be seated all day at a desk. I like to put myself in the goings-on of life, of my house, of politics, and of nature. I am forever coming and going. But I write intensely whenever I can and wherever I am. It doesn't bother me that there may be a lot of people around.

INTERVIEWER: You cut yourself off totally from what surrounds you?

NERUDA: I cut myself off, and if everything is suddenly quiet, then that is disturbing to me.

INTERVIEWER: You have never given much consideration to prose.

NERUDA: Prose . . . I have felt the necessity of writing in verse all my life. Expression in prose doesn't interest me. I use prose to express a certain kind of fleeting emotion or event, really tending toward narrative. The truth is that I could give up writing in prose entirely. I only do it temporarily.

INTERVIEWER: If you had to save your works from a fire, what would you save?

NERUDA: Possibly none of them. What am I going to need them for? I would rather save a girl . . . or a good collection of detective stories . . . which would entertain me much more than my own works.

INTERVIEWER: Which of your critics has best understood your work?

NERUDA: Oh! My critics! My critics have almost shredded me to pieces, with all the love or hate in the world! In life, as in art, one can't please everybody, and that's a situation that's always with us. One is always receiving kisses and slaps, caresses and kicks, and that is the life of a poet. What bothers me is the distortion in the interpretation of poetry or the events of one's life. For example, during the P.E.N. club congress in New York, which brought together so many people from different places, I read my social poems, and even more of them in California—poems dedicated to Cuba in support of the Cuban Revolution. Yet the Cuban writers signed a letter and distributed millions of copies in which my opinions were doubted, and in which I was singled out as a creature protected by the North Americans; they even suggested that my entry into the United States was a kind of prize! That is perfectly stupid, if not slanderous, since many writers from socialist countries *did* come in; even the arrival of Cuban writers was expected. We did not lose our character as anti-imperialists by going to New York. Nevertheless, that was suggested, either through the hastiness or bad faith of the Cuban writers. The fact that at this present moment I am my party's candidate for president of the republic shows that I have a truly revolutionary history.

It would be difficult to find *any* writers who signed that letter who could compare in dedication to revolutionary work, who could equal even one-hundredth of what I have done and fought for.

INTERVIEWER: You have been criticized for the way you live, and for your economic position.

NERUDA: In general, that's all a myth. In a certain sense, we have received a rather bad legacy from Spain, which could never bear to have its people stand out or be distinguished in anything. They chained Christopher Columbus on his return to Spain. We get that from the envious *petite bourgeoisie,* who go around thinking about what others have and about what they *don't* have. In my own case, I have dedicated my life to reparations for the people, and what I have in my house—my books—is the product of my own work. I have exploited no one. It is odd. The sort of reproach *I* get is never made to writers who are rich by birthright! Instead, it is made to *me* —a writer who has fifty years of work behind him. They are always saying: "Look, look how he lives. He has a house facing the sea. He drinks good wine." What nonsense. To begin with, it's hard to drink bad wine in Chile because almost all the wine in Chile is good. It's a problem which, in a certain way, reflects the underdevelopment of our country—in sum, the mediocrity of our ways. You yourself have told me that Norman Mailer was paid some ninety thousand dollars for three articles in a North American magazine. Here, if a Latin American writer should receive such compensation for his work, it would arouse a wave of protest from the other writers—"What an outrage! How terrible! Where is it going to stop?"—instead of everyone's being pleased that a writer can demand such fees. Well, as I say, these are the misfortunes which go by the name of cultural underdevelopment.

INTERVIEWER: Isn't this accusation more intense because you belong to the Communist Party?

NERUDA: Precisely. He who has nothing—it has been said

many times—has nothing to lose but his chains. I risk, at every moment, my life, my person, all that I have—my books, my house. My house has been burned; I have been persecuted; I have been detained more than once; I have been exiled; they have declared me incommunicado; I have been sought by thousands of police. Very well then. I'm *not* comfortable with what I have. So what I have, I have put at the disposal of the people's fight, and this very house you're in has belonged for twenty years to the Communist Party, to whom I have given it by public writ. I am in this house simply through the generosity of my party. All right, let those who reproach me do the same and at least leave their shoes somewhere so that they can be passed on to somebody else!

INTERVIEWER: You have donated various libraries. Aren't you now involved in the project of the writers' colony at Isla Negra?

NERUDA: I have donated more than one entire library to my country's university. I live on the income from my books. I don't have any savings. I don't have anything to dispose of, except for what I am paid each month from my books. With that income, lately I've been acquiring a large piece of land on the coast so that writers in the future will be able to pass summers there and do their creative work in an atmosphere of extraordinary beauty. It will be the Cantalao Foundation— with directors from the Catholic University, the University of Chile, and the Society of Writers.

INTERVIEWER: *Twenty Love Poems and a Song of Despair*, one of your first books, has been and continues to be read by thousands of admirers.

NERUDA: I had said in the prologue to the edition which celebrated the publication of one million copies of that book —soon there will be two million copies—that I really don't understand what it's all about—why this book, a book of love-sadness, of love-pain, continues to be read by so many people, by so many young people. Truly, I do not understand it. Perhaps this book represents the youthful posing of many enigmas; perhaps it represents the answers to those enigmas. It is a mournful book, but its attractiveness has not worn off.

INTERVIEWER: You are one of the most widely translated poets—into about thirty languages. Into what languages are you best translated?

NERUDA: I would say into Italian, because of the similarity between the two languages. English and French, which are the two languages I know outside of Italian, are languages which do not correspond to Spanish—neither in vocalization, or in the placement, or the color, or the weight of the words. It is not a question of interpretative equivalence; no, the sense can be right, but this correctness of translation, of meaning, can be the destruction of a poem. In many of the translations into French—I don't say in all of them—my poetry escapes, nothing remains; one cannot protest because it says the same thing that one has written. But it is obvious that if I had been a French poet, I would not have said what I did in that poem, because the value of the words is so different. I would have written something else.

INTERVIEWER: And in English?

NERUDA: I find the English language so different from Spanish—so much more direct—that many times it expresses the meaning of my poetry, but does not convey the atmosphere of my poetry. It may be that the same thing happens when an English poet is translated into Spanish.

INTERVIEWER: You said that you are a great reader of detective stories. Who are your favorite authors?

NERUDA: A great literary work of this type of writing is Eric Ambler's *A Coffin for Dimitrios*. I've read practically all of Ambler's work since then, but none has the fundamental perfection, the extraordinary intrigue, and the mysterious atmosphere of *A Coffin for Dimitrios*. Simenon is also very important, but it's James Hadley Chase who surpasses in terror, in horror, and in the destructive spirit everything else that has been written. *No Orchids for Miss Blandish* is an old book, but it doesn't cease being a milestone of the detective story. There's a strange similarity between *No Orchids for Miss Blandish* and William Faulkner's *Sanctuary*—that very disagreeable but important book—but I've never been able to determine which was the *first* of the two. Of course, whenever the detective story is spoken of, I think of Dashiell Hammett. He is the one who changed the genre from a subliterary phantasm and gave it a strong backbone. He is the great creator, and after him there are hundreds of others, John MacDonald among the most brilliant. All of them are prolific writers and they work extraordinarily hard. And almost all of the North American novelists of this school—the detective novel—are perhaps the most severe critics of the crumbling North American capitalist society. There is no greater denunciation than that which turns up in those detective novels about the fatigue and corruption of the politicians and the police, the influence of money in the big cities, the corruption which pops up in all parts of the North American system, in "the American way of life." It is, possibly, the most dramatic testimony to an epoch, and yet it is considered the flimsiest accusation, since detective stories are not taken into account by literary critics.

INTERVIEWER: What other books do you read?

NERUDA: I am a reader of history, especially of the older chronicles of my country. Chile has an extraordinary history. Not because of monuments or ancient sculptures, which don't exist here, but rather because Chile was invented by a poet, Don Alonso de Ercilla y Zúñiga, page of Carlos V. He was a Basque aristocrat who arrived with the conquistadores—quite unusual, since most of the people sent to Chile came out of the dungeons. This was the hardest place to live. The war between the Araucanians and the Spanish went on here for centuries, the longest civil war in the history of humanity. The semisavage tribes of Araucania fought for their liberty against the Spanish invaders for three hundred years. Don Alonso de Ercilla y Zúñiga, the young humanist, came with the enslavers who wanted to dominate all America and *did* dominate it, with the exception of this bristly and savage territory we call Chile. Don Alonso wrote *La Araucana,* the longest epic in Castilian literature, in which he honored the unknown tribes of Araucania—anonymous heroes to whom he gave a name for the first time—more than his compatriots, the Castilian soldiers. *La Araucana,* published in the sixteenth century, was translated, and traveled in various versions through all of Europe. A great poem by a great poet. The history of Chile thus had this epic greatness and heroism at birth. We Chileans, quite unlike the other crossbred people of Spanish and Indian America, are not descended from the Spanish soldiers and their rapes or concubinages, but from either the voluntary or forced marriages of the Araucanians with Spanish women held captive during those long war years. We are a certain exception. Of course, then comes our bloody history of independence after 1810, a history full of tragedies, disagreements, and struggles in which the names of San Martín and Bolívar, José Miguel Carrera and O'Higgins carry on through interminable pages of successes and misfortunes. All this makes me a reader of books which I unearth and dust off and which entertain me enormously as I search for the significance of this country—so remote from everybody, so cold in its latitudes, so deserted . . . its saltpeter pampas in the north, its immense patagonias, so snowy in the Andes, so florid by the sea. And this is my country, Chile. I am one of those Chileans in perpetuity, one who, no matter how well they treat me elsewhere, must return to my country. I like the great cities of Europe: I adore the Arno Valley, and certain streets of Copenhagen and Stockholm, and naturally, Paris, Paris, Paris, and yet I still have to return to Chile.

INTERVIEWER: In an article entitled "My Contemporaries,"

Ernesto Montenegro criticizes the Uruguayan critic Rodríguez Monegal for expressing the vain wish that contemporary European and North American writers study their Latin American colleagues if they want to achieve the renovation of their prose. Montenegro jokes that it is like the ant saying to the elephant, "Climb on my shoulders." Then he cites Borges: "In contrast to the barbarous United States, this country (this continent) has not produced a writer of worldwide influence—an Emerson, a Whitman, a Poe . . . neither has it produced a great esoteric writer—a Henry James, or a Melville."

NERUDA: Why is it important if we do or don't have names like those of Whitman, Baudelaire, or Kafka on our continent? The history of literary creation is as large as humanity. We can't impose an etiquette. The United States, with an overwhelmingly literate population, and Europe, with an ancient tradition, can't be compared to our multitudes in Latin America without books or means of expressing themselves. But to pass time throwing stones at one another, to spend one's life hoping to surpass this or that continent seems a provincial sentiment to me. Besides, all this can be a matter of individual opinion.

INTERVIEWER: Would you like to comment on literary affairs in Latin America?

NERUDA: Whether a magazine is from Honduras or New York (in Spanish) or Montevideo or from Guayaquil, we discover that almost all present the same catalogue of fashionable literature influenced by Eliot or Kafka. It's an example of cultural colonialism. We are still involved in European etiquette. Here in Chile, for example, the mistress of the house will show you anything—china plates—and tell you with a satisfied smile: "It's imported." Most of the horrible porcelain exhibited in millions of Chilean homes is imported, and it's of the worst kind, produced in the factories of Germany and France. These pieces of nonsense are accepted as top quality because they have been imported.

INTERVIEWER: Is fear of nonconformity responsible?

NERUDA: Certainly in the old days everybody was scared of revolutionary ideas, particularly writers. In this decade, and especially after the Cuban Revolution, the current fashion is just the opposite. Writers live in terror that they will *not* be taken for extreme leftists, so each of them assumes a guerrilla-like position. There are many writers who only write texts which assert that they are in the front lines of the war against imperialism. Those of us who have continually fought that war see with joy that literature is placing itself on the side of the people; but we also believe that if it's only a matter of fashion and a writer's fear of not being taken for an active leftist, well, we are not going to get very far with that kind of revolutionary. In the end, all sorts of animals fit into the literary forest. Once, when I had been offended for many years by a few pertinacious persecutors who seemed to live only to attack my poetry and my life, I said: "Let's leave them alone, there is room for all in this jungle; if there's space for the elephants, who take up such a lot of room in the jungles of Africa and Ceylon, then surely there's space for all the poets."

INTERVIEWER: Some people accuse you of being antagonistic toward Jorge Luis Borges.

NERUDA: The antagonism towards Borges may exist in an intellectual or cultural form because of our different orientation. One can fight peacefully. But I have other enemies—not writers. For me the enemy is imperialism, and my enemies are the capitalists and those who drop napalm on Vietnam. But Borges is not my enemy.

INTERVIEWER: What do you think about Borges's writing?

NERUDA: He is a great writer, and people who speak Spanish are very proud that Borges exists—above all, the people of Latin America. Before Borges we had very few writers who could stand in comparison with the writers of Europe. We have had great writers, but a writer of the universal type, like Borges, is not found very often in our countries. I cannot say that he has been the *greatest*, and I hope he will be surpassed many times by others, but in every way he has opened the way and attracted attention, the intellectual curiosity of Europe, toward our countries. But for me to fight with Borges because everybody wants me to—I'll never do it. If he thinks like a dinosaur, well, that has nothing to do with my thinking. He understands nothing of what's going on in the contemporary world; he thinks that I understand nothing either. Therefore, we are in agreement.

INTERVIEWER: On Sunday we saw some young Argentines who were playing guitars and singing a *milonga* by Borges. That pleased you, didn't it?

NERUDA: Borges's *milonga* pleased me greatly, most of all because it is an example of how such a hermetic poet—let's use that term—such a sophisticated and intellectual poet can turn to a popular theme, doing it with such a true and certain touch. I liked Borges's *milonga* very much. Latin American poets ought to imitate his example.

INTERVIEWER: Have you written any Chilean folk music?

NERUDA: I've written some songs which are very well known in this country.

INTERVIEWER: Who are the Russian poets you like most?

NERUDA: The dominant figure in Russian poetry continues to be Mayakovsky. He is for the Russian Revolution what Walt Whitman was for the Industrial Revolution in North America. Mayakovsky impregnated poetry in such a way that almost all the poetry has continued being Mayakovskian.

INTERVIEWER: What do you think about the Russian writers who have left Russia?

NERUDA: People who want to leave a place ought to do so. This is really a rather individual problem. Some Soviet writers may feel themselves dissatisfied with their relationship to the literary organizations or with their own state. But I have never seen less disagreement between a state and the writers than in socialist countries. The majority of Soviet writers are proud of the socialist structure, of the great war of liberation against the Nazis, of the people's role in the revolution and in the Great War, and proud of the structures created by socialism. If there are exceptions, it is a personal question, and it is correspondingly necessary to examine each case individually.

INTERVIEWER: But the creative work cannot be free. It must always reflect the State's line of thought.

NERUDA: It's an exaggeration to say that. I have known many writers and painters who have absolutely no intention of eulogizing this or that in the State. There is a kind of conspiracy to suggest that this is the case. But it's not so. Of course, every revolution needs to mobilize its forces. A revolution cannot persist without development: the very commotion provoked by the change from capitalism to socialism cannot last unless the revolution demands, and with all its power, the support of all the strata of society—including the writers, intellectuals, and artists. Think about the American Revolution, or our own war of independence against imperial Spain. What would have happened if just subsequent to those events the writers dedicated themselves to subjects like the monarchy, or the restitution of English power over the United States, or the Spanish king's over former colonies. If any writer or artist had exalted colonialism, he would have been persecuted. It's with even greater justification that a revolution which wants to construct a society starting from zero (after all, the step from capitalism or private property to socialism and communism has never been tried before) must by its own force mobilize the aid of intellect. Such a procedure can bring about conflicts; it is only human and political that these occur. But I hope that with time and stability the socialist societies will have less need to have their writers constantly thinking about social problems, and that they will be able to create what they most intimately desire.

INTERVIEWER: What advice would you give to young poets?

NERUDA: Oh, there is no advice to give to young poets! They ought to make their own way; they will have to encounter the obstacles to their expression and they have to overcome them. What I would never advise them to do is to begin with political poetry. Political poetry is more profoundly emotional than any other—at least as much as love poetry—and cannot be forced because it then becomes vulgar and unacceptable. It is necessary first to pass through all other poetry in order to become a political poet. The political poet must also be prepared to accept the censure which is thrown at him—betraying poetry, or betraying literature. Then, too, political poetry has to arm itself with such content and substance and intellectual and emotional richness that it is able to scorn everything else. This is rarely achieved.

INTERVIEWER: You have often said that you don't believe in originality.

NERUDA: To look for originality at all costs is a modern condition. In our time, the writer wants to call attention to himself, and this superficial preoccupation takes on fetishistic characteristics. Each person tries to find a road whereby he will stand out, neither for profundity nor for discovery, but for the imposition of a special diversity. The most original artist will change phases in accord with the time, the epoch. The great example is Picasso, who begins by nourishing himself from the painting and sculpture of Africa or the primitive arts, and then goes on with such a power of transformation that his works, characterized by his splendid originality, seem to be stages in the cultural geology of the world.

INTERVIEWER: What were the literary influences on you?

NERUDA: Writers are always interchanging in some way, just as the air we breathe doesn't belong to one place. The writer is always moving from house to house: he ought to change his furniture. Some writers feel uncomfortable at this. I remember that Federico García Lorca was always asking me to read my lines, my poetry, and yet in the middle of my reading, he would say, "Stop, stop! Don't go on, lest you influence me!"

INTERVIEWER: About Norman Mailer. You were one of the first writers to speak of him.

NERUDA: Shortly after Mailer's *The Naked and the Dead* came out, I found it in a bookstore in Mexico. No one knew anything about it; the bookseller didn't even know what it was about. I bought it because I had to take a trip and I wanted a new American novel. I thought that the American novel had died after the giants who began with Dreiser and finished with Hemingway, Steinbeck, and Faulkner—but I discovered a writer with extraordinary verbal violence, matched with great subtlety and a marvelous power of description. I greatly admire the poetry of Pasternak, but *Dr. Zhivago* alongside *The Naked and the Dead* seems a boring novel, saved only in part by its description of nature, that is to say, by its poetry. I remember about that time I wrote the poem "Let the Rail Splitter Awake." This poem, invoking the figure of Lincoln, was dedicated to world peace. I spoke of Okinawa and of the war in Japan, and I mentioned Norman Mailer. My poem reached Europe and was translated. I remember that Aragon said to me, "It was a great deal of trouble to find out who Norman Mailer is." In reality, nobody knew him, and I had a certain feeling of pride in having been one of the first writers to allude to him.

INTERVIEWER: Could you comment on your intense affection for nature.

NERUDA: Ever since my childhood, I've maintained an affection for birds, shells, forests, and plants. I've gone many places in search of ocean shells, and I've come to have a great collection. I wrote a book called *Art of Birds*. I wrote *Bestiary, Seaquake,* and *The Rose of Herbolario,* devoted to flowers, branches, and vegetal growth. I could not live separated from nature. I like hotels for a couple of days; I like planes for an hour; but I'm happy in the woods, on the sand, or sailing, in direct contact with fire, earth, water, air.

INTERVIEWER: There are symbols in your poetry which recur, and they always take the form of the sea, of fish, of birds . . .

NERUDA: I don't believe in symbols. They are simply material things. The sea, fish, birds exist for me in a material way. I take them into account, as I have to take daylight into account. The fact that some themes stand out in my poetry—are always appearing—is a matter of material presence.

INTERVIEWER: What do the dove and guitar signify?

NERUDA: The dove signifies the dove and the guitar signifies a musical instrument called the guitar.

INTERVIEWER: You mean that those who have tried to analyze these things—

NERUDA: When I see a dove, I call it a dove. The dove, whether it is present or not, has a form for me, either subjectively or objectively—but it doesn't go beyond being a dove.

INTERVIEWER: You have said about the poems in *Residence on Earth* that "They don't help one to live. They help one to die."

NERUDA: My book *Residence on Earth* represents a dark and dangerous moment in my life. It is poetry without an exit. I almost had to be reborn in order to get out of it. I was saved from that desperation of which I still can't know the depths by the Spanish Civil War, and by events serious enough to make me meditate. At one time I said that if I ever had the necessary power, I would forbid the reading of that book and I would arrange never to have it printed again. It exaggerates the feeling of life as a painful burden, as a mortal oppression. But I also know that it is one of my best books, in the sense that it reflects my state of mind. Still, when one writes—and I don't know if this is true for other writers—one ought to think of where one's verses are going to land. Robert Frost says in one of his essays that poetry ought to have sorrow as its only orientation: "Leave sorrow alone with poetry." But I don't know what Robert Frost would have thought if a young man had committed suicide and left one of *his* books stained with blood. That happened to me—here, in this country. A boy, full of life, killed himself next to my book. I don't feel truly responsible for his death. But that page of poetry stained with blood is enough to make not only one poet think, but all poets. . . . Of course, my opponents took advantage—as they do of almost everything I say—political advantage of the censure I gave my own book. They attributed to me the desire to write exclusively happy and optimistic poetry. They didn't know about that episode. I have never renounced the expression of loneliness, of anguish, or of melancholia. But I like to change tones, to find all the sounds, to pursue all the colors, to look for the forces of life wherever they may be—in creation or destruction.

My poetry has passed through the same stages as my life; from a solitary childhood and an adolescence cornered in distant, isolated countries, I set out to make myself a part of the great human multitude. My life matured, and that is all. It was in the style of the last century for poets to be tormented melancholiacs. But there can be poets who know life, who know its problems, and who survive by crossing through the currents. And who pass through sadness to plenitude.

RITA GUIBERT
Winter 1971
Translated by Ronald Christ

4. Isaac Bashevis Singer

A rabbi's son, Isaac Bashevis Singer was born in Radzymin, Poland, on July 14, 1904. His family moved to Warsaw when he was a child, and it was there that he received a traditional Jewish education. Although Singer was fascinated by the Jewish folklore and legends that his parents told their four children in order to strengthen the youngsters' religious faith, he nonetheless followed the lead of his older brother, the novelist I. J. Singer, and chose to become a writer. Before joining his brother in New York City in 1935, Singer worked as a proofreader for a Yiddish journal and published stories, translations, and book reviews in a number of Polish periodicals.

Once in America he became a regular contributor to the *Jewish Daily Forward,* writing reviews and articles in addition to short stories and serialized novels. His first work to be translated into English, *The Family Moskat,* was published in 1950, and was an international success. It was followed in 1957 by a collection of short stories, *Gimpel the Fool and Other Stories,* some of which had appeared in translation by Saul Bellow in *Partisan Review.* Singer's other works of fiction include *The Magician of Lublin* (1960), *The Slave* (1962), *The Manor* (1967), *Enemies, A Love Story* (1972), and *Shosha* (1978). *In My Father's Court,* a memoir of his childhood in Poland, was published in 1966.

Singer has won nearly every major literary prize, including two National Book awards—one in children's literature for *A Day of Pleasure* in 1970 and a second in fiction for *A Crown of Feathers and Other Stories* in 1976. He is a member of the National Institute of Arts and Letters and the American Academy of Arts and Sciences. In 1978 he was awarded the Nobel Prize in literature.

Singer became an American citizen in 1943. Married since 1940 to Alma Haimann, he lives on New York's Upper West Side. His son by a previous marriage is a high-school teacher in Israel.

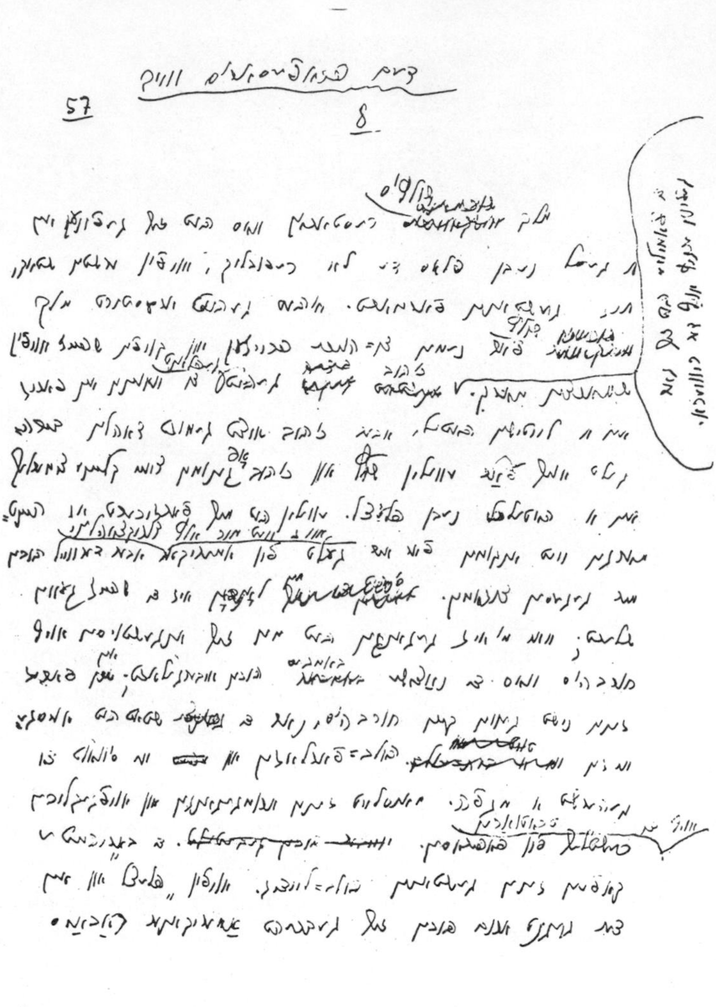

A manuscript page from "The Professor's Wife."

Isaac Bashevis Singer

Isaac Bashevis Singer lives with his second wife in a large, sunny five-room apartment in an Upper Broadway apartment house. In addition to hundreds of books and a large television set, it is furnished with the kind of pseudo-Victorian furniture typical of the comfortable homes of Brooklyn and the Bronx in the 1930s.

Singer works at a small, cluttered desk in the living room. He writes every day, but without special hours—in between interviews, visits, and phone calls. His name is still listed in the Manhattan telephone directory, and hardly a day goes by without his receiving several calls from strangers who have read something he has written and want to talk to him about it. Until recently, he would invite anyone who called for lunch, or at least coffee.

Singer writes his stories and novels in lined notebooks, in longhand, in Yiddish. Most of what he writes still appears first in the Jewish Daily Forward, *America's largest Yiddish-language daily, published in New York City. Getting translators to put his work into English has always been a major problem. He insists on working very closely with his translators, going over each word with them many times.*

Singer always wears dark suits, white shirts, and dark ties. His voice is high but pleasant, and never raised. He is of medium height, thin, and has an unnaturally pale complexion. For many years he has followed a strict vegetarian diet.

The first impression Singer gives is that he is a fragile, weak man who would find it an effort to walk a block. Actually, he walks fifty to sixty blocks a day, a trip that invariably includes a stop to feed pigeons from a brown paper bag. He loves birds and has two pet parakeets who fly about his apartment uncaged.

INTERVIEWER: Many writers when they start out have other writers they use as models.

SINGER: Well, my model was my brother, I. J. Singer, who wrote *The Brothers Askenazi.* I couldn't have had a better model than my brother. I saw him struggle with my parents and I saw how he began to write and how he slowly developed and began to publish. So naturally he was an influence. Not only this, but in the later years before I began to publish, my brother gave me a number of rules about writing which seem to me sacred. Not that these rules cannot be broken once in a while, but it's good to remember them. One of his rules was that while facts never become obsolete or stale, commentaries *always* do. When a writer tries to explain too much, to psychologize, he's already out of time when he begins. Imagine Homer explaining the deeds of his heroes according to the old Greek philosophy, or the psychology of his time. Why, nobody would read Homer! Fortunately, Homer just gave us the images and the facts, and because of this the *Iliad* and the *Odyssey* are fresh in our time. And I think this is true about all writing. Once a writer tries to explain what the hero's motives are from a psychological point of view, he has already lost. This doesn't mean that I am against the psychological novel. There are some masters who have done it well. But I don't think it is a good thing for a writer, especially a young writer, to imitate them. Dostoyevsky, for example. If you can call him a writer of the psychological school; I'm not sure I do. He had his digressions and he tried to explain things in his own way, but even with him his basic power is in giving the facts.

INTERVIEWER: What do you think of psychoanalysis and writing? Many writers have been psychoanalyzed and feel this has helped them to understand not only themselves but the characters they write about.

SINGER: If the writer is psychoanalyzed in a doctor's office, that is his business. But if he tries to put the psychoanalysis into the writing, it's just terrible. The best example is the one who wrote *Point Counter Point.* What was his name?

INTERVIEWER: Aldous Huxley.

SINGER: Aldous Huxley. He tried to write a novel according to Freudian psychoanalysis. And I think he failed in a bad way. This particular novel is now so old and so stale that even in school it cannot be read anymore. So, I think that when a writer sits down and he psychoanalyzes, he's ruining his work.

INTERVIEWER: You once told me that the first piece of fiction you ever read was the *Adventures of Sherlock Holmes.*

SINGER: Well, I read these things when I was a boy of ten or eleven, and to me they looked so sublime, so wonderful, that even today I don't dare to read Sherlock Holmes again because I am afraid that I may be disappointed.

INTERVIEWER: Do you think A. Conan Doyle influenced you in any way?

SINGER: Well, I don't think that the stories of Sherlock Holmes had any real influence on me. But I will say one thing —from my childhood I have always loved tension in a story. I liked that a story should be a story. That there should be a beginning and an end, and there should be some feeling of what will happen at the end. And to this rule I keep today. I think that storytelling has become in this age almost a forgotten art. But I try my best not to suffer from this kind of amnesia. To me a story is still a story where the reader listens and wants to know what happens. If the reader knows everything from the very beginning, even if the description is good, I think the story is not a story.

INTERVIEWER: What do you think about the Nobel Prize for literature going to S. Y. Agnon and Nelly Sachs?

SINGER: About Nelly Sachs, I know nothing, but I know Agnon. Since I began to read. And I think he's a good writer. I wouldn't call him a genius, but where do you get so many geniuses nowadays? He's a solid writer of the old school, a school which loses a lot in translation. But as far as Hebrew is concerned, his style is just wonderful. Every work of his is associated with the Talmud and the Bible and the Midrash. Everything he writes has many levels, especially to those who know Hebrew. In translation, all of these other levels disappear and there is only the pure writing, but then that is also good.

INTERVIEWER: The prize committee said that they were giving the Nobel Prize to two Jewish writers who reflected the voice of Israel. That leads me to wonder how you would define a Jewish writer as opposed to a writer who happens to be Jewish?

SINGER: To me there are only Yiddish writers, Hebrew writers, English writers, Spanish writers. The whole idea of a Jewish writer, or a Catholic writer, is kind of farfetched to me. But if you forced me to admit that there is such a thing as a Jewish writer, I would say that he would have to be a man really immersed in Jewishness, who knows Hebrew, Yiddish, the Talmud, the Midrash, the Hassidic literature, the Cabbala, and so forth. And then if in addition he writes about Jews and Jewish life, perhaps then we can call him a Jewish writer, whatever language he writes in. Of course, we can also call him just a writer.

INTERVIEWER: You write in Yiddish, which is a language very few people can read today. Your books have been translated into fifty-eight different languages, but you have said you are bothered by the fact that most of your readers, the vast majority of your readers, have to read you in translation, whether it's English or French. That very few writers can read you in Yiddish. Do you feel that a lot is lost in translation?

SINGER: The fact that I don't have as many readers in Yiddish as I would have liked to have bothers me. It's not good that a language is going downhill instead of up. I would like Yiddish to bloom and flower just as the Yiddishists say it *does* bloom and flower. But as far as translation is concerned, naturally every writer loses in translation, particularly poets and humorists. Also writers whose writing is tightly connected to folklore are heavy losers. In my own case, I think I am a heavy loser. But then lately I have assisted in the translating of my works, and knowing the problem, I take care that I don't lose too much. The problem is that it's very hard to find a perfect equivalent for an idiom in another language. But then it's also a fact that we all learned our literature through translation. Most people have studied the Bible only in translation, have read Homer in translation, and all the classics. Translation, although it does do damage to an author, it cannot kill him: if he's really good, he will come out even in translation. And I have seen it in my own case. Also, translation helps me in a way. Because I go through my writings again and again while I edit the translation and work with the translator, and while I am doing this I see all the defects of my writing. Translation has helped me avoid pitfalls which I might not have avoided if I had written the work in Yiddish and published it and not been forced because of the translation to read it again.

INTERVIEWER: Is it true that for five years you stopped writing entirely because you felt there was nobody to write for?

SINGER: It is true that when I came to this country I stopped writing for a number of years. I don't know exactly if it was because I thought there were no readers. There were many readers. Coming from one country to another, immigrating, is a kind of a crisis. I had a feeling that my language was so lost. My images were not anymore. Things—I saw thousands of objects for which I had no name in Yiddish in Poland. Take such a thing as the subway—we didn't have a subway in Poland. And we didn't have a name for it in Yiddish. Suddenly I had to do with a subway and with a shuttle train and a local, and my feeling was that I lost my language and also my feeling about the things which surrounded me. Then, of course, there was the trouble of making a living and adjusting myself to the new surroundings . . . all of this worked so that for a number of years I couldn't write.

INTERVIEWER: Do you think that Yiddish has any future at all, or do you think that very soon it will be a dead language completely?

SINGER: It won't be a dead language because Yiddish is connected with five or six hundred years of Jewish history . . . of important Jewish history. And whoever will want to study this history will have to study Yiddish. In a joke I say that I have a special comfort for Yiddish and this is that now we are having as a world population only about 3.5 billion people, but one hundred years from now we will have most probably 100 billion people, and every one of them will need a topic for a Ph.D. Imagine how useful Yiddish will be for all these students looking for a topic. They will bring out everything that was connected with Yiddish and analyze it and write things about it, articles and these things that you write for universities —theses. So, I don't think it will be forgotten. Take such a language as Aramaic. It's already two thousand years that the Jews didn't use Aramaic, and the language is still here. It has become now a part of Hebrew. Aramaic is used now in certificates and in divorce papers. Jews never forget really anything, especially a language which has created so much and has played such a part like Yiddish.

INTERVIEWER: When one thinks of contemporary writers writing in Yiddish, one thinks immediately of you. But then it is hard to come up with any other names. Are there any other writers writing in Yiddish whom you consider highly?

SINGER: There is one writer whom I consider highly. Really, he is a great writer. He's a poet. His name is Aaron Zeitlin. This man, he is my friend, but I don't praise him because he's my friend. He's really a great poet. I consider his writing of the same value as the poetry of Thomas Hardy, and I have a high opinion of Thomas Hardy. The others . . . there are a number of other Yiddish writers . . . some of them are well known, like Sholem Asch. There was David Bergelson. There was one very strong prose writer called A. M. Fuchs who is really a strong writer, but he wrote always on the same topic. He had only one story to tell with a million variations. But I would say that there is something about Yiddish writing which is very effective and yet very old-fashioned—because the modern Yiddish writer does not write about real Jewish things, though it happens he is the product of enlightenment. He was brought up with the idea that one should get out of Jewishness and become universal. And because he tried so hard to become universal, he became very provincial. This is the tragedy. Not with the whole of Yiddish writings but with a lot of it. And thank God when I began to write I avoided this misfortune. Even though I was discouraged all the time. They told me why do you write about devils and imps. Why don't you write about the situation of the Jews, about Zionism, about socialism, about the unions, and about how the tailors must get a raise, and so on and so on. But something in me refused to do this. They complained to me that I am obsolete. That I go back to the generations which have already vanished. That I'm almost a reactionary. But young writers are sometimes very stubborn. I refused to go their way and I was later glad that I had the character not to do what they wanted me to do. This type of writing has become so obsolete and so stale that it's not a question of getting translators in Yiddish, but really that we have very little to translate.

INTERVIEWER: When you say "this type of writing," you mean writing about unions and . . .

SINGER: About unions, about immigration, about progress, about anti-Semitism. This kind of journalistic writing in which one had the desire to create what they call a better world. To make the world better, to make the Jewish situation better. This kind of writing was very much in fashion in the twenties and I would say that the Yiddish writers never got out of it really.

INTERVIEWER: Don't you believe in a better world?

SINGER: I believe in a better world, but I don't think that a fiction writer who sits down to write a novel to make a better world can achieve anything. The better world will be done by many people, by the politicians, by the statesmen, by the sociologists. I don't know who is going to create it or if there will ever be a better world. One thing I am sure is that the novelists will not do it.

INTERVIEWER: The supernatural keeps cropping up in practically everything you write, particularly your short stories. Why this strong concern with the supernatural? Do you personally believe in the supernatural?

SINGER: Absolutely. The reason why it always comes up is because it is always on my mind. I don't know if I should call myself a mystic, but I feel always that we are surrounded by powers, by mysterious powers, which play a great part in everything we are doing. I would say that telepathy and clairvoyance play a part in every love story. Even in business. In everything human beings are doing. For thousands of years people used to wear woolen clothes and when they took them off at night they saw sparks. I wonder what these people thought thousands of years ago of these sparks they saw when they took off their woolen clothes? I am sure that they ignored them and the children asked them, "Mother what are these sparks?" And I am sure the mother said, "You imagine them!" People must have been afraid to talk about the sparks so they would not be suspected of being sorcerers and witches. Anyhow, they were ignored, and we know now that they were not hallucinations, that they were real, and that what was behind these sparks was the same power which today drives our industry. And I say that we too in each generation see such sparks which we ignore just because they don't fit into our picture of science or knowledge. And I think that it is the writer's duty, and also pleasure and function, to bring out these sparks. To me, clairvoyance and telepathy and . . . and devils and imps . . . all of these things . . .

INTERVIEWER: Ghosts?

SINGER: Ghosts and all these things which people call today superstition are the very sparks which we are ignoring in our day.

INTERVIEWER: Do you think they will be able to be explained scientifically, just as sparks can be explained today as electricity?

SINGER: I think the notion of science—what is scientific and what is not—will change in time. There are many facts which cannot be worked out in a laboratory, and still they are facts. You cannot show in a laboratory that there has ever been a Napoleon, you can't prove it as clearly as you can an electric current, but we know there *was* a Napoleon. What we call today ghosts and spirits and clairvoyance is also the sort of fact which you cannot just prepare and cannot make experiments with. But this doesn't mean that the fact is not true.

INTERVIEWER: How about the devil? In many of your writings the devil is the main character.

SINGER: Naturally, I use the devil and the imps as literary symbols. True, but the reason I use them as symbols is because I have a feeling for them. If I didn't have a feeling for these entities I would not use them. I still live with this idea that we are surrounded by all kinds of powers and I've been brought up with it and I still cling to it. Not that I try to, but they cling to me. If you extinguish the light at night and I am in a dark room, I am afraid. Just as I was when I was seven or eight years old. I have spoken to many rationalists who say how illogical that is, but when I ask them if they would consent to sleep a winter's night in a room with a corpse, they shiver. The fear of the supernatural is in everybody. And since we are all afraid of the supernatural, there is no reason why we shouldn't make use of it. Because if you are afraid of something, the very fact that you are afraid means that you have admitted that it exists. We aren't afraid of something which doesn't exist.

INTERVIEWER: You are the only Jewish writer who writes about the devil. Even Hebrew literature avoids the theme of the diabolical.

SINGER: It is true that Yiddish and Hebrew literature are both under the influence of the Enlightenment. They are both in a way modern kinds of literature. Writers were brought up with the idea that they had been sunk in the Middle Ages long enough, and that since modern literature should be rational and logical, they should deal with the real world. To them, when I began to write, I seemed a most reactionary writer, a writer who went back to the dark ages. But, as I was saying, young writers are sometimes very stubborn. What is to you *dark* is to me *real*. They all condemned me for it. But today, since this kind of writing has had a certain degree of success, they began somehow to make peace with it. Because you know how it is in this world: if something works it works. In fact, I didn't expect that anybody would be interested in my kind of writing. I was interested, and this was for me enough.

INTERVIEWER: Being as interested as you are in ritual and superstition, do you have any about yourself—in particular connected with your work and work habits?

SINGER: It is true that I believe in miracles, or, rather, grace from heaven. But I believe in miracles in every area of life *except* writing. Experience has shown me that there are no miracles in writing. The only thing that produces good writing is hard work. It's impossible to write a good story by carrying a rabbit's foot in your pocket.

INTERVIEWER: How do you come to write a story? Do you observe all the time, like a reporter? Do you take notes?

SINGER: I never go out to look for a story. I take notes, but never like a reporter. My stories are all based upon things that have come to me in life without my going out to look for them. The only notes I take are notes on an idea for a story. But it must be a story with a climax. I am not a slice-of-life writer. When such an idea comes to me, I put it down in a little notebook I always carry around. Finally the story demands to be written, and then I write it.

INTERVIEWER: In addition to writing stories and novels, you spent many years of your life in journalism. You still work as a journalist for the *Forward*.

SINGER: Yes. I am a journalist. Every week I write two or three journalistic articles. Journalism in Yiddish is quite different from journalism in other languages, especially in English. In America, a journalist is a man who either deals completely with facts, or he is a commentator of the political situation. In a Yiddish newspaper, even if it's a daily, it's actually a daily *magazine*. I can write articles in the *Forward* about life making sense or not, or that you shouldn't commit suicide, or a treatise on imps or devils being in everything. Our readers are accustomed to get the news mostly from the radio and television or from the English newspaper which comes out in the evening. When he buys the newspaper in the morning, he is not after the news; he wants to read articles. So if I am a journalist, I am not exactly the same kind of journalist who works for let's say *The New York Times*.

INTERVIEWER: Do you think working as a journalist for such a paper as the *Times* is a good background for somebody who wants to write novels and stories?

SINGER: I think that any information a human being gets,

especially a writer, is good for him. I don't think that being a journalist can do any damage to a writer.

INTERVIEWER: Do you know any other writers?

SINGER: Very few, because here in America I find there is no place to meet them. When I lived in Poland, I used to hang out at the writers' club. I'd be there every day. But there is nothing quite like that in America. I know practically no other writers. Once in a while I meet some writers at a cocktail party, and I like them; they are very fine people. But somehow it never goes beyond a superficial meeting. I am sorry about this. I would like to be friendly with more writers.

INTERVIEWER: Many contemporary writers are affiliated with the universities. What do you think of teaching as a way of making a living while writing?

SINGER: I think that journalism is a healthier occupation for a writer than teaching, especially if he teaches literature. By teaching literature, the writer gets accustomed to analyzing literature all the time. One man, a critic, said to me, "I could never write anything because the moment I write the first line I am already writing an essay about it. I am already criticizing my own writing."

It's not good when the writer is both a critic and a writer. It doesn't matter if he writes a review once in a while or even an essay about criticism. But if this kind of analyzing goes on all the time and it becomes his daily bread, it may one day become a part of his writing: it is very bad when the writer is half writer and half critic. He writes essays about his heroes instead of telling a story.

INTERVIEWER: Could you tell me something about the way you work. Do you work every day, seven days a week?

SINGER: Well, when I get up in the morning, I always have the desire to sit down to write. And most of the days I *do* write something. But then I get telephone calls, and sometimes I have to write an article for the *Forward.* And once in a while I have to write a review, and I am interviewed, and I am all the time interrupted. Somehow I manage to keep on writing. I don't have to run away. Some writers say that they can only write if they go to a far island. They would go to the moon to write not to be disturbed. I think that being disturbed is a part of human life and sometimes it's useful to be disturbed because you interrupt your writing and while you rest, while you are busy with something else, your perspective changes or the horizon widens. All I can say about myself is that I have never really written in peace, as some writers say that they have. But whatever I had to say I kept on saying no matter what the disturbances were.

INTERVIEWER: What do you consider the most difficult aspect of writing?

SINGER: Story construction. This is the most difficult part for me. How to construct the story so that it will be interesting. Easiest for me is the actual writing. Once I have the construction set, the writing itself—the description and dialogue—simply flows along.

INTERVIEWER: The hero of most Western writing is the Superman, the Prometheus character. The hero of Yiddish fiction, Jewish writing, seems to be the little man. He's a poor but proud man always struggling. And your own classic example of the little man would be Gimpel the Fool. How do you account for the fact that in so much of Yiddish fiction the hero is the little man?

SINGER: Well, the Yiddish writer was really not brought up with the idea of heroes. I mean there were very few heroes in the Jewish ghettos—very few knights and counts and people who fought duels and so on. In my own case, I don't think I write in the tradition of the Yiddish writers' "little man," because their little man is actually a *victim*—a man who is a victim of anti-Semitism, the economic situation, and so on. My characters, though they are not big men in the sense that they play a big part in the world, still they are not little, because in their own fashion they are men of character, men of thinking, men of great suffering. It is true that Gimpel the Fool is a little man, but he's not the same kind of little man as Sholom Aleichem's Tevye. Tevye is a little man with little desires, and with little prejudice. All he needed was to make a living. If Tevye could have made a living, he wouldn't have been driven out of his village. If he could have married off his daughters, he would have been a happy man. In my case, most of my heroes could not be satisfied with just a few rubles or with the permission to live in Russia or somewhere else. Their tragedies are different. Gimpel was not a little man. He was a fool, but he wasn't little. The tradition of the little man is something which I avoid in my writing.

INTERVIEWER: If most of your writing deals with a people without power, without land, without statehood, political organization, or even a choice of occupation, and who yet have a great moral response and an intensity of faith, are you in effect suggesting that the Jews were better off when they were restricted and discriminated against?

SINGER: I think there is no question that power is a great temptation and those who have power will sooner or later stumble into injustice. It was the good fortune of the Jewish people that for two thousand years they didn't have any power. The little bit of power that they did have they have certainly misused like anyone else who has power. But we were blessed for almost two thousand years with a complete lack of power, so because of this our sins were never as great as those who really had power over the life and death of other people. But I bring this up not to preach. I never really knew people who had a lot of power. Except when I describe Poles or when I describe once in a while a rich man whose power was in his money. But even so, these people were not really rich enough to wield much power.

INTERVIEWER: I can't help but get the feeling from your writing that you have grave doubts about the sufficiency of knowledge or even wisdom.

SINGER: Well, in a way it is true. Yiddish writing was all built on the ideas of the Enlightenment. Enlightenment, no matter how far it will go, will not bring the redemption. I have never believed that socialism or any other *ism* is going to redeem humanity and create what they call the "new man." I have had many discussions with writers about this. When I was young, when I began to write, people really believed that once the means of production belonged to the government, the "new man" would result. I was clever enough or maybe foolish enough and skeptical enough to know that was a lot of nonsense; no matter who owns the railroads or the factories, men will remain the same.

INTERVIEWER: Is there anything that you think will save humanity?

SINGER: Nothing will save us. We will make a lot of progress, but we will keep on suffering, and there will never be an end to it. We will always invent new sources of pain. The idea that man is going to be saved is a completely religious idea, and even the religious leaders never suggest that we will be saved on this earth. They believe that the soul is going to be saved in another world, that if we behave here well, there is a hope that our soul will go to paradise. The idea of creating a paradise here on this earth is not Jewish and certainly not Christian, but a completely Greek or pagan idea. As the Jews say, from a pig's tail you cannot make a silk purse. You cannot take life and suddenly turn it into one great delight, one ocean of pleasure. I never believed in it, and whenever people speak about a better world, while I admit that conditions can be made better and I hope that we can do away with wars, still there will be enough sickness and enough tragedy so that humanity will keep on suffering more or less in the same way as it always has. Being a pessimist to me means to be a realist.

I feel that in spite of all our sufferings, in spite of the fact that life will never bring the paradise we want it to bring, there is something to live for. The greatest gift which humanity has received is free choice. It is true that we are limited in our use of free choice. But the little free choice we have is such a great gift and is potentially worth so much that for this itself life is worthwhile living. While I am in one way a fatalist, I also know that what we have reached up until now is largely because of free will, not because conditions have changed, as the Marxists believe.

INTERVIEWER: Many readers look upon you as a master storyteller. Others feel that you have a far more significant purpose in your writing than merely to tell stories.

SINGER: Well, I think that to write a story *well* is the duty of a storyteller. To try with all his might that a story should come out right. What I call right is that the construction should be right, the description right, that there should be equilibrium between form and content, and so on. But this is not everything. In each story, I try to say something, and what I try to say is more or less connected with my ideas that this world and this kind of life is not everything, that there is a soul and there is a God and there may be life after death. I always come back to these religious truths although I am not religious in the sense of dogma. I don't keep to all the rules of organized religion. But the basic truths of religion are near to me and I always contemplate them. I would consider myself more of a Jewish writer than most of the Yiddish writers because I am more a believer in the Jewish truths than they. Most of them believe in progress. Progress has become their idol. They believe that people will progress to such a degree that the Jews will be treated well, they will be able to assimilate, mix with the Gentiles, get good jobs, and perhaps be president one day. To me all these hopes are very little and very obsolete and very petty. I feel that our real great hope lies in the soul and not in the body. In this way I consider myself a religious writer.

INTERVIEWER: Sometimes reading you I think of certain Far Eastern philosophers, such as the Indian philosopher Krishnamurti. Were you at all influenced by Buddhist or Hindu writings?

SINGER: I read these writers too late to have been really influenced by them. But when I read them in my later years, a short time ago, I said to myself I have thought these same thoughts without having read them. When I read the Bhaga-vad-Gita, it looked to me so very near, and I almost wondered if I had read this in a former life. This is true also about the sayings of Buddha and other Far Eastern writings. The so-called eternal truths are really eternal. They are in our blood and in our very essence.

INTERVIEWER: Some commentators on the current scene, notably Marshall McLuhan, feel that literature as we have known it for hundreds of years is an anachronism, that it's on the way out. The reading of stories and novels, they feel, is soon to be a thing of the past, because of electronic entertainments, radio, television, film, stereophonic records, magnetic tapes, and other mechanical means of communication yet to be in-vented. Do you believe this to be true?

SINGER: It will be true if our writers will not be good writers. But if we have people with the power to tell a story, there will always be readers. I don't think that human nature is going to change to such a degree that people will stop being interested in a work of imagination. Certainly, the true facts, the real facts, are always interesting. Today nonfiction plays a very big part . . . to hear stories about what happened. If people get to the moon, journalists will tell us, or films will tell us, what happened there, and these will be more interesting stories than anything a fiction writer can produce. But still there will be a place for the good fiction writer. There is no machine and no kind of reporting and no kind of film that can do what a Tolstoy or a Dostoyevsky or Gogol did. It is true that poetry has suffered a great blow in our times. But not because of television or because of other things, but because poetry itself became bad. If we are going to have numbers of bad novels, and bad novelists imitate each other, what they write will neither be interesting nor understood. Naturally, this may kill the novel, at least for a time. But I don't think that literature, good literature, has anything to fear from technology. The very opposite. The more technology, the more people will be interested in what the human mind can produce *without* the help of electronics.

INTERVIEWER: So you would encourage young people today to think of serious writing as a way of life?

SINGER: When it comes to business, to the finances of writing, I really don't know. It may be that a time will come when the novelist will get such small royalties that he will not be able to make a living. I just cannot tell you about this. But if a young man would come to me and I can see that he has talent and he asks me if he should write, I would say go on and write and don't be afraid of any inventions and of any kind of progress. Progress can never kill literature, any more than it can kill religion.

INTERVIEWER: It's hard to keep from noticing that among the most widely read and respected authors in the United States today there is a large percentage of Jewish authors—yourself, Saul Bellow, Philip Roth, Henry Roth, Bernard Malamud. Even non-Jewish writers are writing on Jewish themes and producing best-sellers, as, for example, James Michener with his novel *The Source.* How do you account for the post–World War II popularity of Jewish writers and Jewish themes?

SINGER: I think that for many centuries the Jew was completely ignored in literature. They wrote about the Jew always in the way of a cliché. Either the Jew was a usurer, a bad man, a Shylock, or he was a poor man, a victim of anti-Semitism. In other words, they either scolded him or they pitied him. And because of this the Jew's way of life, his way of love, was a secret to humanity. It's only a short time ago that Jewish writers began to write about Jews the same way as Americans write about Americans and English writers about Englishmen. They tell everything about them, the good and the evil. They don't try to apologize for them. They don't try to scold them. And I would say that since there was a lot of curiosity about Jewish life, I am not astonished that Jewish literature is now in vogue. This doesn't mean that it is always going to be so. I believe that sooner or later things will even out. How many Jews are good writers or bad writers I don't know. I don't think that we are producing as many good writers as people think. We have a lot of able, gifted writers, and able people, but I see as few great writers among us as there are few great writers among other people! There are a very few great writers anywhere.

HAROLD FLENDER
Fall 1968

5. Henry Green

Henry Green is the pseudonym of Henry Vincent Yorke, who was born in 1905 in Tewkesbury, England. The third son of wealthy parents, he spent most of his childhood after the age of six away from his West Country home, attending a series of boarding schools, including Eton. He completed his formal education at Oxford, where he decided to become a writer, and while still a student, he published his first novel, *Blindness* (1926), at the age of twenty-one. In 1929 *Living* appeared, but it was ten more years before his next novel, *Party Going*, was completed. It was followed by *Pack My Bag* (1940), which Green described as an interim autobiography.

During the Second World War Green joined the Auxiliary Fire Service, which provided the basis for his novel *Caught*, written between 1940 and 1942. After the war he returned to his family's engineering firm in the Midlands, where he worked for most of his life while continuing to write in his free time.

His writing style, combining the spare use of words with a poet's sense of symbolism and imagery, earned him accolades from critics and colleagues alike. Included among the latter was Rebecca West, who once called Green "the best writer of his time."

His postwar novels included *Loving* (1945), *Back* (1946), *Concluding* (1948), *Nothing* (1950), and *Doting* (1952). From 1953 until his death in 1973 Green published nothing further.

From a draft of Henry Green's novel *Loving*. The conversation at the top of the page is between Raunce, the hero of the book, and his female employer, who is addressing him here as Arthur not because that is his name but because her footmen have always been called Arthur.

Gian Berto Vanni

Henry Green

Henry Green is a tall, gracious, and imposingly handsome man, with a warm, strong voice and very quick eyes. In speech he displays on occasion that hallmark of the English public school: the slight tilt of the head and closing of the eyes when pronouncing the first few words of some sentences—a manner most often in contrast to what he is saying, for his expressions tend toward parable and his wit may move from cozy to scorpion-dry in less than a twinkle. Many have remarked that his celebrated deafness will roar or falter according to his spirit and situation; at any rate he will not use a hearing aid, for reasons of his own, which are no doubt discernable to some.

Mr. Green writes at night and in many longhand drafts.

In his autobiographical novel, Pack My Bag, *he has described prose in this way:*

Prose is not to be read aloud but to oneself at night, and it is not quick as poetry, but rather a gathering web of insinuations which go further than names however shared can ever go. Prose should be a long intimacy between strangers with no direct appeal to what both may have known. It should slowly appeal to feelings unexpressed, it should in the end draw tears out of the stone.

An ancient trade compliment, to an author whose technique is highly developed, has been to call him a "writer's writer"; Henry Green has been referred to as a "writer's writer's writer," though practitioners of the craft have had only to talk with him momentarily on the subject to know that his methods were not likely to be revealed to them, either then or at any other time. It is for this reason—attempting to delve past his steely reticence —that some of the questions in the interview may seem unduly long or presumptuous.

Mr. Green, who has one son, lives in London, in a house in Knightsbridge, with his beautiful and charming wife, Dig. The following conversation was recorded there one winter night in the author's firelit study.

INTERVIEWER: Now, you have a body of work, ten novels, which many critics consider the most elusive and enigmatic in contemporary literature—and yourself, professionally or as a personality, none the less so. I'm wondering if these two mysteries are merely coincidental?

GREEN: What's that? I'm a trifle hard of hearing.

INTERVIEWER: Well, I'm referring to such things as your use of a pseudonym, your refusal to be photographed, and so on. May I ask the reason for it?

GREEN: I didn't want my business associates to know I wrote novels. Most of them do now, though . . . *know* I mean, not write, thank goodness.

INTERVIEWER: And has this affected your relationships with them?

GREEN: Yes, yes, oh yes—why, some years ago a group at our Birmingham works put in a penny each and bought a copy of a book of mine, *Living*. And as I was going round the iron foundry one day, a loam moulder said to me, "I read your book, Henry." "And did you like it?" I asked, rightly apprehensive. He replied, "I didn't think much of it, Henry." Too awful.

Then, you know, with a customer, at the end of a settlement which has deteriorated into a compromise painful to both sides, he may say, "I suppose you are going to put this in a novel." Very awkward.

INTERVIEWER: I see.

GREEN: Yes, it's best they shouldn't know about one. And one should never be known by sight.

INTERVIEWER: You have, however, been photographed from the rear.

GREEN: And a wag said: "I'd know that back anywhere."

INTERVIEWER: I've heard it remarked that your work is "too sophisticated" for American readers, in that it offers no scenes of violence—and "too subtle," in that its message is somewhat veiled. What do you say?

GREEN: Unlike the wilds of Texas, there is very little violence over here. A bit of child killing, of course, but no straight shootin'. After fifty, one ceases to digest; as someone once said: "I just ferment my food now." Most of us walk crabwise to meals and everything else. The oblique approach in middle age is the safest thing. The unusual at this period is to get anywhere at all—God damn!

INTERVIEWER: And how about "subtle"?

GREEN: I don't follow. *Suttee*, as I understand it, is the suicide—now forbidden—of a Hindu wife on her husband's flaming bier. I don't want my wife to do that when my time comes—and with great respect, as I know her, she won't . . .

INTERVIEWER: I'm sorry, you misheard me; I said, "subtle" —that the message was too subtle.

GREEN: Oh, *subtle.* How dull!

INTERVIEWER: . . . yes, well now I believe that two of your novels, *Blindness* and *Pack My Bag,* are said to be "autobiographical," isn't that so?

GREEN: Yes, those two are mostly autobiographical. But where they are about myself, they are not necessarily accurate as a portrait; they aren't photographs. After all, no one knows what he is like, he just tries to give some sort of picture of his time. Not like a cat to fight its image in the mirror.

INTERVIEWER: The critic Alan Pryce-Jones has compared you to Jouhandeau and called you an "odd, haunted, ambiguous writer." Did you know that?

GREEN: I was in the same house with him at Eton. He was younger than me, so he saw through me perhaps.

INTERVIEWER: Do you find critical opinion expressed about your work useful or interesting?

GREEN: Invariably useless and uninteresting—when it is from daily papers or weeklies, which give so little space nowadays. But there is a man called Edward Stokes who has written a book about me and who knows all too much. I believe the Hogarth Press is going to publish it. And then the French translator of *Loving,* he wrote two articles in some French monthly. Both of these are valuable to me.

INTERVIEWER: I'd like to ask you some questions now about the work itself. You've described your novels as "nonrepresentational." I wonder if you'd mind defining that term?

GREEN: "Nonrepresentational" was meant to represent a picture which was not a photograph, nor a painting on a photograph, nor, in dialogue, a tape recording. For instance, the very deaf, as I am, hear the most astounding things all round them which have not in fact been said. This enlivens my replies until, through mishearing, a new level of communication is reached. My characters misunderstand each other more than people do in real life, yet they do so less than I. Thus, when writing, I "represent" very closely what I see (and I'm not seeing so well now) and what I hear (which is little) but I say it is "nonrepresentational" because it is not necessarily what others see and hear.

INTERVIEWER: And yet, as I understand this theory, its success does not depend upon any actual sensory differences between people talking, but rather upon psychological or emotional differences between them as readers, isn't that so? I'm referring to the serious use of this theory in communicative writing.

GREEN: People strike sparks off each other; that is what I try to note down. But mark well, they only do this when they are talking together. After all, we don't write letters now, we telephone. And one of these days we are going to have TV sets which lonely people can talk to and get answers back. Then no one will read anymore.

INTERVIEWER: And that is your crabwise approach.

GREEN: To your question, yes. And to stop one's asking why I don't write *plays,* my answer is I'd rather have these sparks in black and white than liable to interpretation by actors and the producer of a piece.

INTERVIEWER: Do you consider that all your novels have been done as "nonrepresentational"?

GREEN: Yes, they all of course represent a *selection* of material. The Chinese classical painters used to leave out the middle distance. Until *Nothing* and *Doting* I tried to establish the mood of any scene by a few but highly pointed descriptions. Since then I've tried to keep everything down to bare dialogue and found it very difficult. You see, to get back to what you asked a moment ago, when you referred to the emotional differences between readers—what one writes has to be all things to all men. If one isn't enough to enough readers, they stop reading, and the publishers won't publish anymore. To disprove my own rule I've done a very funny three-act play and no one will put it on.

INTERVIEWER: I'm sorry to hear that, but now what about the role of *humor* in the novel?

GREEN: Just the old nursery rhyme—"Something and spice makes all things nice," is it? Surely the artist must entertain. And one's in a very bad way indeed if one can't laugh. Laughter relaxes the characters in a novel. And if you *can* make the reader laugh, he is apt to get careless and go on reading. So you as the writer get a chance to get something into him.

INTERVIEWER: I see, and what might that something be?

GREEN: Here we approach the crux of the matter which, like all hilarious things, is almost indescribable. To me the purpose of art is to produce something alive, in my case, in print, but with a separate, and of course one hopes, with an everlasting life of its own.

INTERVIEWER: And the qualities then of a work of art . . .

GREEN: To be alive. To have a real life of its own. The miracle is that it should live in the person who reads it. And if it *is* real and true, it does, for five hundred years, for generation after generation. It's like having a baby, but in print. If it's really good, you can't stop its living. Indeed, once the thing is printed, you simply cannot strangle it, as you could a child, by putting your hands round its little wet neck.

INTERVIEWER: What would you say goes into creating this life, into making this thing real and true?

GREEN: Getting oneself straight. To get what one produces to have a real life of its own.

INTERVIEWER: Now, this page of manuscript you were good enough to show me—what stage of the finished work does this represent?

GREEN: Probably a very early draft.

INTERVIEWER: In this draft I see that the dialogue has been left untouched, whereas every line in the scene otherwise has been completely rewritten.

GREEN: I think if you checked with other fragments of this

draft, you would find as many the other way around, the dialogue corrected and the rest left untouched.

INTERVIEWER: Here the rewriting has been done in entire sentences, rather than in words or phrases—is that generally the way you work?

GREEN: Yes, because I copy everything out afresh. I make alterations in the manuscript and then copy them out. And in copying out, I make further alterations.

INTERVIEWER: How much do you usually write before you begin rewriting?

GREEN: The first twenty pages over and over again—because in my idea you have to get everything into them. So as I go along and the book develops, I have to go back to that beginning again and again. Otherwise, I rewrite only when I read where I've got to in the book and I find something so bad I can't go on till I've put it right.

INTERVIEWER: When you begin to write something, do you begin with a certain *character* in mind, or rather with a certain *situation* in mind?

GREEN: Situation every time.

INTERVIEWER: Is that necessarily the *opening* situation—or perhaps you could give me an example; what was the basic situation, as it occurred to you, for *Loving*?

GREEN: I got the idea of *Loving* from a manservant in the Fire Service during the war. He was serving with me in the ranks, and he told me he had once asked the elderly butler who was over him what the old boy most liked in the world. The reply was: "Lying in bed on a summer morning, with the window open, listening to the church bells, eating buttered toast with cunty fingers." I saw the book in a flash.

INTERVIEWER: Well, now after getting your initial situation in mind, then what thought do you give to the plot beyond it?

GREEN: It's all a question of length; that is, of proportion. How much you allow to this or that is what makes a book now.

It was not so in the days of the old three-decker novel. As to plotting or thinking ahead, I don't in a novel. I let it come page by page, one a day, and carry it in my head. When I say carry I mean the *proportions*—that is, the length. This is the exhaustion of creating. Towards the end of the book your head is literally bursting. But try and write out a scheme or plan and you will only depart from it. My way you have a chance to set something living.

INTERVIEWER: No one, it seems, has been able to satisfactorily relate your work to any source of influence. I recall that Mr. Pritchett has tried to place it in the tradition of Sterne, Carroll, Firbank, and Virginia Woolf—whereas Mr. Toynbee wished to relate it to Joyce, Thomas Wolfe, and Henry Miller. Now, *are* there styles or works that you feel have influenced yours?

GREEN: I really don't know. As far as I'm consciously aware, I forget everything I read at once, including my own stuff. But I have a tremendous admiration for Céline.

INTERVIEWER: I feel there are certain aspects of your work the mechanics of which aren't easily drawn into question because I don't find terms to cover them. I would like to try to state one, however, and see if you feel it is correct or can be clarified. It's something Mr. Pritchett seems to hint at when he describes you as "a psychologist poet making people out of blots," and it has to do with the degree to which you've developed the "nonexistence of author" principle. The reader does not simply forget that there is an author behind the words, but because of some annoyance over a seeming "discrepancy" in the story must, in fact, *remind* himself that there is one. This reminding is accompanied by an irritation with the author because of these apparent oversights on his part, and his "failings" to see the particular *significance* of certain happenings. The irritation gives way then to a feeling of pleasure and superiority in that he, the reader, sees *more* in the situation than the author does—so that all of this now belongs to *him*.

And the author is dismissed, even perhaps with a slight contempt—and only the *work* remains, alone now with this reader who has had to take over. Thus, in the spell of his own imagination the characters and story *come alive* in an almost incredible way, quite beyond anything achieved by conventional methods of writing. Now, this is a principle that occurs in Kafka's work, in an undeveloped way, but is obscured because the situations are so strongly fantasy. It occurs in a very pure form, however, in Kafka's *Journals*—if one assumes that they were, despite all said to the contrary, *written to be read,* then it is quite apparent, and, of course, very funny and engaging indeed. I'm wondering if that is the source of this principle for you, or if, in fact, you agree with what I say about it?

GREEN: I don't agree about Kafka's *Journals,* which I have by my bed and still don't or can't follow.

But if you are trying to write something which has a life of its own, which is alive, of course the author must keep completely out of the picture. I hate the portraits of donors in medieval triptyches. And if the novel *is* alive, of course the reader will be irritated by discrepancies—life, after all, is one discrepancy after another.

INTERVIEWER: Do you believe that a writer should work toward the development of a particular *style?*

GREEN: He can't do anything else. His style is himself, and we are all of us changing every day—developing, we hope! We leave our marks behind us, like a snail.

INTERVIEWER: So the writer's style develops with him.

GREEN: Surely. But he must take care not to let it go too far —like the later Henry James or James Joyce. Because it then becomes a private communication with himself, like a man making cat's cradles with spider's webs, a sort of Melanesian gambit.

INTERVIEWER: Concerning your own style and the changes it has undergone, I'd like to read a sample paragraph—from *Living,* written in 1928—and ask you something about it. This paragraph occurs, you may perhaps recall, as the description of a girl's dream—a working-class girl who wants more than anything else a home, and above all, a child . . .

"Then clocks in that town all over town struck 3 and bells in churches there ringing started rushing sound of bells like wings tearing under roof of sky, so these bells rang. But women stood, reached up children drooping to sky, sharp boned, these women wailed and their noise rose and ate the noise of bells ringing."

I'd like to ask about the style here, about the absence of common articles—"a," "an," and "the"—there being but one in the whole paragraph, which is fairly representative of the book. Was this omission of articles throughout *Living* based on any particular theory?

GREEN: I wanted to make that book as taut and spare as possible, to fit the proletarian life I was then leading. So I hit on leaving out the articles. I still think it effective, but would not do it again. It may now seem, I'm afraid, affected.

INTERVIEWER: Do you think that an elliptical method like that has a function other than, as you say, suggesting the tautness and spareness of a particular situation?

GREEN: I don't know, I suppose the more you leave out, the more you highlight what you leave in—not true of taking the filling out of a sandwich, of course—but if one kept a diary, one wouldn't want a minute-to-minute catalogue of one's dreadful day.

INTERVIEWER: Well, that was written in 1928—were you influenced toward that style by *Ulysses?*

GREEN: No. There's no "stream of consciousness" in any of my books that I can remember—I did not read *Ulysses* until *Living* was finished.

INTERVIEWER: That was your second novel, and that novel seems quite apart stylistically from the first and from those that followed—almost all of which, while "inimitably your own," so to speak, are of striking diversity in tone and style. Of them, though, I think *Back* and *Pack My Bag* have a certain similarity, as have *Loving* and *Concluding*. Then again, *Nothing* and *Doting* might be said to be similiar in that, for one thing at least, they're both composed of . . . what would you say, ninety-five percent? . . . ninety-five percent dialogue.

GREEN: *Nothing* and *Doting* are about the upper classes— and so is *Pack My Bag*, but it is nostalgia in this one, and too, in *Back*, which is about the middle class. Nostalgia has to have its own style. *Nothing* and *Doting* are hard and sharp; *Back* and *Pack My Bag*, soft.

INTERVIEWER: You speak of "classes" now, and I recall that *Living* has been described as the "best proletarian novel ever written." Is there to your mind, then, a social-awareness responsibility for the writer or artist?

GREEN: No, no. The writer must be disengaged or else he is writing politics. Look at the Soviet writers.

I just wrote what I heard and saw, and, as I've told you, the workers in my factory thought it rotten. It was my very good friend Christopher Isherwood used that phrase you've just quoted, and I don't know that he ever worked in a factory.

INTERVIEWER: Concerning the future of the novel, what do you think is the outlook for the Joycean-type introspective style and, on the other hand, for the Kafka school?

GREEN: I think Joyce and Kafka have said the last word on each of the two forms they developed. There's no one to follow them. They're like cats which have licked the plate clean. You've got to dream up another dish if you're to be a writer.

INTERVIEWER: Do you believe that films and television will radically alter the format of the novel?

GREEN: It might be better to ask if novels will continue to be written. It's impossible for a novelist not to look out for other media nowadays. It isn't that everything has been done in fiction—truly nothing has been done as yet, save Fielding, and he only started it all. It is simply that the novelist is a communicator and must therefore be interested in any form of communication. You don't dictate to a girl now, you use a recording apparatus; no one faints anymore, they have blackouts; in Geneva you don't kill someone by cutting his throat, you blow a poisoned dart through a tube and *zing,* you've got him. Media change. We don't have to paint chapels like Cocteau, but at the same time we must all be ever on the lookout for the new ways.

INTERVIEWER: What do you say about the use of symbolism?

GREEN: You can't escape it, can you? What, after all, is one to do with oneself in print? Does the reader feel a dread of anything? Do they all feel a dread for different things? Do they all love differently? Surely the only way to cover all these readers is to use what is called symbolism.

INTERVIEWER: It seems that you've used the principle of "nonexistent author" in conjunction with another—that since identified with Camus, and called the absurd. For a situation to be, in this literary sense, genuinely absurd, it must be convincingly arrived at, and should not be noticed by readers as being at all out of the ordinary. Thus it would seem normal for a young man, upon the death of his father, to go down and take over the family's iron foundry, as in *Living;* or to join the service in wartime, as in *Caught;* or to return from the war, as in *Back*—and yet, in abrupt transitions like these, the situations and relationships which result are almost sure to be, despite any dramatic or beautiful moments, fundamentally *absurd.* In your work I believe this reached such a high point of refinement in *Loving* as to be indiscernable—for, with all the critical analyses that book received, no one called attention to the absurdity of one of the basic situations: that of *English* servants in an *Irish* household. Now, isn't that fundamental situation, and the absence of any reference to it throughout the book, intended to be purely absurd?

GREEN: The British servants in Eire while England is at war is Raunce's conflict, and one meant to be satirically funny. It is a crack at the absurd southern Irish and at the same time a swipe at the British servants, who yet remain human beings. But it is meant to torpedo that woman and her daughter-in-law, the employers.

As to the rest, the whole of life now is of course absurd—hilarious sometimes, as I told you earlier, but basically absurd.

INTERVIEWER: And have you ever heard of an actual case of an Irish household being staffed with English servants?

GREEN: Not that comes quickly to mind, no.

INTERVIEWER: Well, now what is it that you're writing on at present?

GREEN: I've been asked to do a book about London during the blitz, and I'm into that now.

INTERVIEWER: I believe you're considered an authority on that—and, having read *Caught,* I can understand that you would be. What's this book to be called?

GREEN: *London and Fire, 1940.*

INTERVIEWER: And it is not fiction?

GREEN: No, it's an historical account of that period.

INTERVIEWER: Then this will be your first full-length work of nonfiction?

GREEN: Yes, quite.

INTERVIEWER: I see. *London and Fire, 1940*—a commissioned historical work. Well, well; I daresay you'll have to give up the crabwise approach for this one. What's the first sentence?

GREEN: "My 'London of 1940' . . . opens in Cork, 1938."

INTERVIEWER: . . . I see.

TERRY SOUTHERN
Summer 1958

6. John Cheever

John Cheever was born on May 27, 1912, in Quincy, Massachusetts. A writer since the age of ten, Cheever attended Thayer Academy in South Braintree, Massachusetts, but was expelled before graduation. He perversely benefited from this experience when he sold his first short story, "Expelled," to *New Republic* editor Malcolm Cowley.

During the 1930s Cheever's short fiction appeared in a number of magazines, but he quickly became identified as a leading contributor to *The New Yorker*. His first collection of short stories, *The Way Some People Live*, was published in 1943 while he was in the army. After the war he taught advanced composition at Barnard College and wrote scripts for the television series *Life with Father*. But in 1951 a Guggenheim Fellowship permitted him to turn his full attention to his writing, and his second collection of short fiction, *The Enormous Radio and Other Stories*, came out in 1953. A 1956 National Institute of Arts and Letters Award made a trip to Italy possible, and provided Cheever with a new setting for a number of his stories. Cheever's first novel, *The Wapshot Chronicle* (1957), earned him the National Book Award, and its sequel, *The Wapshot Scandal* (1964), was awarded the Howell's Medal for fiction.

A steady succession of novels and short fiction have followed, many of them focusing on the isolation and discontent of contemporary American life. These works include *Bullet Park* (1969), *The World of Apples* (1973), *Falconer* (1977), and, most recently, *The Stories of John Cheever*, winner of the Pulitzer Prize and the National Book Critics Circle Award in 1979.

A member of the National Institute of Arts and Letters and the American Academy of Arts and Sciences, Cheever has been married to the former Mary Winternitz for nearly forty years. They have three grown children, one of whom is the novelist Susan Cheever.

The main entrance to Falconer--the only entrance for
convicts,their visitors and the staff--was crowned by an
esuctheon representing Liberty,Justice and,between the two,
the power of legislation. Liberty wore a mob-cap and carried a
pike. Legislation was the federal eagle,armed with hunting arrows.
Justice was conventional;blinded,vaguely erotic in her clinging
robes and armed with a headsman's sword. The bas-relief was
bronze but black these days--as black as unpolished anthracite or
onyex. How many hundreds had passed under this--this last
souvenir they would see of man's struggle for cohreence. Hundreds,
one guessed,thousands,millions was close. Above the escutchen was
a declension of the place-names:Falconer Jail 1871,Falconer
Reformatory,Falconer Federal Penitionary,Falconer State Prison,
Falconer Correctional Facility and the last,which had never
caught on:Daybreak House. Now cons were inmates,the assholes
were officers and the warden was a superindendent. Fame is
chancey,God knows but Falconer--with it's limited accomodations
for two thousand miscreants was as famous as Old Bailey. Gone
was the water-torture,the striped suits,the lock-stepthe balls
and chains and there was a soft-ball field where the gallows had
stood but at the time of which I'm writing leg-irons were still
used in Auburn. You could tell the men from Auburn by the noise
they made.

A page from the manuscript of *Falconer*.

John Cheever

The first meeting with John Cheever took place in the spring of 1969, just after his novel Bullet Park *was published. Normally, Cheever leaves the country when a new book is released, but this time he had not, and as a result many interviewers on the East Coast were making their way to Ossining, New York, where the master storyteller offered them the pleasures of a day in the country—but very little conversation about his book or the art of writing.*

Cheever has a reputation for being a difficult interviewee. He does not pay attention to reviews, never rereads his books or stories once published, and is often vague about their details. He dislikes talking about his work (especially into "one of those machines") because he prefers not to look where he has been, but where he's going.

For the interview Cheever was wearing a faded blue shirt and khakis. Everything about him was casual and easy, as though we were already old friends. The Cheevers live in a house built in 1799, so a tour of buildings and grounds was obligatory. Soon we were settled in a sunny second-floor study where we discussed his dislike of window curtains, a highway construction near Ossining that he was trying to stop, traveling in Italy, a story he was drafting about a man who lost his car keys at a nude theater performance, Hollywood, gardeners and cooks, cocktail parties, Greenwich Village in the thirties, television reception, and a number of other writers named John (especially John Updike, who is a friend).

Although Cheever talked freely about himself, he changed the subject when the conversation turned to his work. Aren't you bored with all this talk? Would you like a drink? Perhaps lunch is ready, I'll just go downstairs and check. A walk in the woods, and maybe a swim afterwards? Or would you rather drive to town and see my office? Do you play backgammon? Do you watch much television?

During the course of several visits we did in fact mostly eat, drink, walk, swim, play backgammon, or watch television. Cheever did not invite me to cut any wood with his chain saw, an activity to which he is rumored to be addicted. On the day of the last taping, we spent an afternoon watching the New York Mets win the World Series from the Baltimore Orioles, at the end of which the fans at Shea Stadium tore up plots of turf for souvenirs. "Isn't that amazing," he said repeatedly, referring both to the Mets and their fans.

Afterward we walked in the woods, and as we circled back to the house, Cheever said, "Go ahead and pack your gear, I'll be along in a minute to drive you to the station" . . . upon which he stepped out of his clothes and jumped with a loud splash into a pond, doubtless cleansing himself with his skinny-dip from one more interview.

INTERVIEWER: I was reading the confessions of a novelist on writing novels: "If you want to be true to reality, start lying about it." What do you think?

CHEEVER: Rubbish. For one thing the words "truth" and "reality" have no meaning at all unless they are fixed in a comprehensible frame of reference. There are no stubborn truths. As for lying, it seems to me that falsehood is a critical element in fiction. Part of the thrill of being told a story is the chance of being hoodwinked or taken. Nabokov is a master at this. The telling of lies is a sort of sleight of hand that displays our deepest feelings about life.

INTERVIEWER: Can you give an example of a preposterous lie that tells a great deal about life?

CHEEVER: Indeed. The vows of holy matrimony.

INTERVIEWER: What about verisimilitude and reality?

CHEEVER: Verisimilitude is, by my lights, a technique one exploits in order to assure the reader of the truthfulness of what he's being told. If he truly believes he is standing on a rug, you can pull it out from under him. Of course, verisimilitude is also a lie. What I've always wanted of verisimilitude is probability, which is very much the way I live. This table seems real, the fruit basket belonged to my grandmother, but a madwoman could come in the door any moment.

INTERVIEWER: How do you feel about parting with books when you finish them?

CHEEVER: I usually have a sense of clinical fatigue after finishing a book. When my first novel, *The Wapshot Chronicle*, was finished, I was very happy about it. We left for Europe and remained there, so I didn't see the reviews and wouldn't know of Maxwell Geismar's disapproval for nearly ten years. *The Wapshot Scandal* was very different. I never much liked the book, and when it was done I was in a bad way. I wanted to burn the book. I'd wake up in the night and I would hear Hemingway's voice—I've never actually heard

Hemingway's voice, but it was conspicuously his—saying, "This is the small agony. The great agony comes later." I'd get up and sit on the edge of the bathtub and chain-smoke until three or four in the morning. I once swore to the dark powers outside the window that I would never, *never* again try to be better than Irving Wallace. It wasn't so bad after *Bullet Park,* where I'd done precisely what I wanted: a cast of three characters, a simple and resonant prose style, and a scene where a man saves his beloved son from death by fire. The manuscript was received enthusiastically everywhere, but when Benjamin DeMott dumped on it in the *Times,* everybody picked up their marbles and ran home. I ruined my left leg in a skiing accident and ended up so broke that I took out working papers for my youngest son. It was simply a question of journalistic bad luck and an overestimation of my powers. However, when you finish a book, whatever its reception, there is some dislodgement of the imagination. I wouldn't say derangement. But finishing a novel, assuming it's something you want to do and that you take very seriously, is invariably something of a psychological shock.

INTERVIEWER: How long does it take the psychological shock to wear off? Is there any treatment?

CHEEVER: I don't quite know what you mean by treatment. To diminish shock I throw high dice, get sauced, go to Egypt, scythe a field, screw. Dive into a cold pool.

INTERVIEWER: Do characters take on identities of their own? Do they ever become so unmanageable that you have to drop them from the work?

CHEEVER: The legend that characters run away from their authors—taking up drugs, having sex operations, and becoming president—implies that the writer is a fool with no knowledge or mastery of his craft. This is absurd. Of course, any estimable exercise of the imagination draws upon such a complex richness of memory that it truly enjoys the expansiveness —the surprising turns, the response to light and darkness—of any living thing. But the idea of authors running around helplessly behind their cretinous inventions is contemptible.

INTERVIEWER: Must the novelist remain the critic as well?

CHEEVER: I don't have any critical vocabulary and very little critical acumen, and this is, I think, one of the reasons I'm always evasive with interviewers. My critical grasp of literature is largely at a practical level. I use what I love, and this can be anything. Cavalcanti, Dante, Frost, anybody. My library is terribly disordered and disorganized; I tear out what I want. I don't think that a writer has any responsibility to view literature as a continuous process. I believe that very little of literature is immortal. I've known books in my lifetime to serve beautifully, and then to lose their usefulness, perhaps briefly.

INTERVIEWER: How do you "use" these books . . . and what is it that makes them lose their "usefulness"?

CHEEVER: My sense of "using" a book is the excitement of finding myself at the receiving end of our most intimate and acute means of communication. These infatuations are sometimes passing.

INTERVIEWER: Assuming a lack of critical vocabulary, how, then, without a long formal education, do you explain your considerable learning?

CHEEVER: I am not erudite. I do not regret this lack of discipline, but I do admire erudition in my colleagues. Of course, I am not uninformed. That can be accounted for by the fact that I was raised in the tag end of cultural New England. Everybody in the family was painting and writing and singing and especially reading, which was a fairly common and accepted means of communication in New England at the turn of the decade. My mother claimed to have read *Middlemarch* thirteen times; I daresay she didn't. It would take a lifetime.

INTERVIEWER: Isn't there someone in *The Wapshot Chronicle* who has done it?

CHEEVER: Yes, Honora . . . or I don't remember who it is . . . claims to have read it thirteen times. My mother used to leave *Middlemarch* out in the garden and it got rained on. Most of it is in the novel; it's true.

INTERVIEWER: One almost has a feeling of eavesdropping on your family in that book.

CHEEVER: The *Chronicle* was not published (and this was a consideration) until after my mother's death. An aunt (who does not appear in the book) said, "I would never speak to him again if I didn't know him to be a split personality."

INTERVIEWER: Do friends or family often think they appear in your books?

CHEEVER: Only (and I think everyone feels this way) in a discreditable sense. If you put anyone in with a hearing aid, then they assume that you have described them . . . although the character may be from another country and in an altogether different role. If you put people in as infirm or clumsy or in some way imperfect, then they readily associate. But if you put them in as beauties, they never associate. People are always ready to accuse rather than to celebrate themselves, especially people who read fiction. I don't know what the association is. I've had instances when a woman will cross a large social floor and say, "Why did you write that story about me?" And I try to figure out what story I've written. Well, ten stories back apparently I mentioned someone with red eyes; she noticed that she had bloodshot eyes that day and so she assumed that I'd nailed her.

INTERVIEWER: They feel indignant, that you have no right to their lives?

CHEEVER: It would be nicer if they thought of the creative aspect of writing. I don't like to see people who feel that they've been maligned when this was not anyone's intention. Of course, some young writers try to be libelous. And some old writers, too. Libel is, of course, a vast source of energy. But these are not the pure energies of fiction, but simply the libelousness of a child. The sort of thing one gets in freshman themes. Libel is not one of my energies.

INTERVIEWER: Do you think narcissism is a necessary quality of fiction?

CHEEVER: That's an interesting question. By narcissism we mean, of course, clinical self-love, an embittered girl, the wrath of Nemesis, and the rest of eternity as a leggy plant. Who wants that? We do love ourselves from time to time; no more, I think, than most men.

INTERVIEWER: What about megalomania?

CHEEVER: I think writers are inclined to be intensely egocentric. Good writers are often excellent at a hundred other things, but writing promises a greater latitude for the ego. My dear friend Yevtushenko has, I claim, an ego that can crack crystal at a distance of twenty feet; but I know a crooked investment banker who can do better.

INTERVIEWER: Do you think that your inner screen of imagination, the way you project characters, is in any way influenced by film?

CHEEVER: Writers of my generation and those who were raised with films have become sophisticated about these vastly different mediums and know what is best for the camera and best for the writer. One learns to skip the crowd scene, the portentous door, the banal irony of zooming into the beauty's crow's-feet. The difference in these crafts is, I think, clearly understood, and as a result no good film comes from an adaptation of a good novel. I would love to write an original screenplay if I found a sympathetic director. Years ago René Clair was going to film some of my stories, but as soon as the front office heard about this, they took away all the money.

INTERVIEWER: What do you think of working in Hollywood?

CHEEVER: Southern California always smells very much like a summer night . . . which to me means the end of sailing, the end of games, but it isn't that at all. It simply doesn't correspond to my experience. I'm very much concerned with trees . . . with the nativity of trees, and when you find yourself in a place where all the trees are transplanted and have no history, I find it disconcerting.

I went to Hollywood to make money. It's very simple. The people are friendly and the food is good, but I've never been happy there, perhaps because I only went there to pick up a check. I do have the deepest respect for a dozen or so directors whose affairs are centered there and who, in spite of the overwhelming problems of financing films, continue to turn out brilliant and original films. But my principal feeling about Hollywood is suicide. If I could get out of bed and into the shower, I was all right. Since I never paid the bills, I'd reach for the phone and order the most elaborate breakfast I could think of, and then I'd try to make it to the shower before I hanged myself. This is no reflection on Hollywood, but it's just that I seemed to have a suicide complex there. I don't like the freeways, for one thing. Also, the pools are too hot . . . 85 degrees, and when I was last there, in late January, in the stores they were selling yarmulkes for dogs—my God! I went to a dinner and across the room a woman lost her balance and fell down. Her husband shouted over to her, "When I told you to bring your crutches, you wouldn't listen to me." That line couldn't be better!

INTERVIEWER: What about another community—the academic? It provides so much of the critical work . . . with such an excessive necessity to categorize and label.

CHEEVER: The vast academic world exists like everything else, on what it can produce that will secure an income. So we have papers on fiction, but they come out of what is largely an industry. In no way does it help those who write fiction or those who love to read fiction. The whole business is a subsidiary undertaking, like extracting useful chemicals from smoke. Did I tell you about the review of *Bullet Park* in *Ramparts*? It said I missed greatness by having left St. Boltophs. Had I stayed, as Faulkner did in Oxford, I would have probably been as great as Faulkner. But I made the mistake of leaving this place, which, of course, never existed at all. It was so odd to be told to go back to a place that was a complete fiction.

INTERVIEWER: I suppose they meant Quincy.

CHEEVER: Yes, which it wasn't. But I was very sad when I read it. I understood what they were trying to say. It's like being told to go back to a tree that one spent fourteen years living in.

INTERVIEWER: Who are the people that you imagine or hope read your books?

CHEEVER: All sorts of pleasant and intelligent people read the books and write thoughtful letters about them. I don't know who they are, but they are marvelous and seem to live quite independently of the prejudices of advertising, journalism, and the cranky academic world. Think of the books that have enjoyed independent lives. *Let Us Now Praise Famous Men. Under the Volcano. Henderson the Rain King.* A splendid book like *Humboldt's Gift* was received with confusion and dismay, but hundreds of thousands of people went out and bought hardcover copies. The room where I work has a window looking into a wood, and I like to think that these earnest, lovable, and mysterious readers are in there.

INTERVIEWER: Do you think contemporary writing is becoming more specialized, more autobiographical?

CHEEVER: It may be. Autobiography and letters may be more interesting than fiction, but still, I'll stick with the novel. The novel is an acute means of communication from which all kinds of people get responses that you don't get from letters or journals.

INTERVIEWER: Did you start writing as a child?

CHEEVER: I used to tell stories. I went to a permissive school called Thayerland. I loved to tell stories, and if everybody did their arithmetic—it was a very small school, probably not more than eighteen or nineteen students—then the teacher would promise that I would tell a story. I told serials. This was very shrewd of me, because I knew that if I didn't finish the story by the end of the period, which was an hour, then everyone would ask to hear the end during the next period.

INTERVIEWER: How old were you?

CHEEVER: Well, I'm inclined to lie about my age, but I suppose it was when I was eight or nine.

INTERVIEWER: You could think of a story to spin out for an hour at that age?

CHEEVER: Oh, yes. I could then. And I still do.

INTERVIEWER: What comes first, the plot?

CHEEVER: I don't work with plots. I work with intuition, apprehension, dreams, concepts. Characters and events come simultaneously to me. Plot implies narrative and a lot of crap. It is a calculated attempt to hold the reader's interest at the sacrifice of moral conviction. Of course, one doesn't want to be boring . . . one needs an element of suspense. But a good narrative is a rudimentary structure, rather like a kidney.

INTERVIEWER: Have you always been a writer, or have you had other jobs?

CHEEVER: I drove a newspaper truck once. I liked it very much, especially during the World Series, when the Quincy paper would carry the box scores and full accounts. No one had radios, or television—which is not to say that the town was lit with candles, but they used to wait for the news; it made me feel good to be the one delivering the good news. Also, I spent four years in the Army. I was seventeen when I sold my first story, "Expelled," to *The New Republic*. *The New Yorker* started taking my stuff when I was twenty-two. I was supported by *The New Yorker* for years and years. It has been a very pleasant association. I sent in twelve or fourteen stories a year. At the start I lived in a squalid slum room on Hudson Street with a broken windowpane. I had a job at MGM with Paul Goodman, doing synopses. Jim Farrell, too. We had to boil down just about every book published into either a three-, five-, or twelve-page précis for which you got something like five dollars. You did your own typing. And, oh, carbons.

INTERVIEWER: What was it like writing stories for *The New Yorker* in those days? Who was the fiction editor?

CHEEVER: Wolcott Gibbs was the fiction editor very briefly, and then Gus Lobrano. I knew him very well; he was a fishing companion. And, of course, Harold Ross, who was difficult but I loved him. He asked preposterous queries on a manuscript—everyone's written about that—something like thirty-six queries on a story. The author always thought it outrageous, a violation of taste, but Ross really didn't care. He liked to show his hand, to shake the writer up. Occasionally he was brilliant. In "The Enormous Radio" he made two changes. A diamond is found on the bathroom floor after a party. The man says, "Sell it, we can use a few dollars." Ross had changed "dollars" to "bucks," which was absolutely perfect. Brilliant. Then I had "the radio came softly" and Ross penciled in another "softly." "The radio came softly, softly." He was absolutely right. But then there were twenty-nine other suggestions like, "This story has gone on for twenty-four hours and no one has eaten anything. There's no mention of a meal." A typical example of this sort of thing was Shirley Jackson's "The Lottery," about the stoning ritual. He hated the story; he started turning vicious. He said there was no town in Vermont where there were rocks of that sort. He nagged and nagged and nagged. It was not surprising. Ross used to scare the hell out of me. I would go in for lunch. I never knew Ross was coming, until he'd bring in an egg cup. I'd sit with my back pressed against my chair. I was really afraid. He was a scratcher and a nose picker, and the sort of man who could get his underwear up so there was a strip of it showing between his trousers and his shirt. He used to hop at me, sort of jump about in his chair. It was a creative, destructive relationship from which I learned a great deal, and I miss him.

INTERVIEWER: You met a lot of writers during that time, didn't you?

CHEEVER: It was all terribly important to me, since I had

been brought up in a small town. I was in doubt that I could make something of myself as a writer until I met two people who were very important to me: one was Gaston Lachaise and the other was E. E. Cummings. Cummings I loved, and I love his memory. He did a wonderful imitation of a woodburning locomotive going from Tiflis to Minsk. He could hear a pin falling in soft dirt at the distance of three miles. Do you remember the story of Cummings's death? It was September, hot, and Cummings was cutting kindling in the back of his house in New Hampshire. He was sixty-six or -seven or something like that. Marion, his wife, leaned out the window and asked, "Cummings, isn't it frightfully hot to be chopping wood?" He said, "I'm going to stop now, but I'm going to sharpen the ax before I put it up, dear." Those were the last words he spoke. At his funeral Marianne Moore gave the eulogy. Marion Cummings had enormous eyes. You could make a place in a book with them. She smoked cigarettes as though they were heavy, and she wore a dark dress with a cigarette hole in it.

INTERVIEWER: And Lachaise?

CHEEVER: I'm not sure what to say about him. I thought him an outstanding artist and I found him a contented man. He used to go to the Metropolitan—where he was not represented—and embrace the statues he loved.

INTERVIEWER: Did Cummings have any advice for you as a writer?

CHEEVER: Cummings was never paternal. But the cant of his head, his wind-in-the-chimney voice, his courtesy to boobs, and the vastness of his love for Marion were all advisory.

INTERVIEWER: Have you ever written poetry?

CHEEVER: No. It seems to me that the discipline is very different . . . another language, another continent from that of fiction. In some cases short stories are more highly disciplined than a lot of the poetry that we have. Yet the disciplines are as different as shooting a twelve-gauge shotgun and swimming.

INTERVIEWER: Have magazines asked you to write journalism for them?

CHEEVER: I was asked to do an interview with Sophia Loren by the *Saturday Evening Post.* I did. I got to kiss her. I've had other offers but nothing as good.

INTERVIEWER: Do you think there's a trend for novelists to write journalism, as Norman Mailer does?

CHEEVER: I don't like your question. Fiction must compete with first-rate reporting. If you cannot write a story that is equal to a factual account of battle in the streets or demonstrations, then you can't write a story. You might as well give up. In many cases, fiction hasn't competed successfully. These days the field of fiction is littered with tales about the sensibilities of a child coming of age on a chicken farm, or a whore who strips her profession of its glamour. The *Times* has never been so full of rubbish in its recent book ads. Still, the use of the word "death" or "invalidism" about fiction diminishes as it does with anything else.

INTERVIEWER: Do you feel drawn to experiment in fiction, to move toward bizarre things?

CHEEVER: Fiction *is* experimentation; when it ceases to be that, it ceases to be fiction. One never puts down a sentence without the feeling that it has never been put down before in such a way, and that perhaps even the substance of the sentence has never been felt. Every sentence is an innovation.

INTERVIEWER: Do you feel that you belong to any particular tradition in American letters?

CHEEVER: No. As a matter of fact, I can't think of any American writers who could be classified as part of a tradition. You certainly can't put Updike, Mailer, Ellison, or Styron in a tradition. The individuality of the writer has never been as intense as it is in the United States.

INTERVIEWER: Well, would you think of yourself as a realistic writer?

CHEEVER: We have to agree on what we mean before we can

talk about such definitions. Documentary novels, such as those of Dreiser, Zola, Dos Passos—even though I don't like them —can, I think, be classified as realistic. Jim Farrell was another documentary novelist; in a way, Scott Fitzgerald was, though to think of him that way diminishes what he could do best . . . which was to try to give a sense of what a very particular world was like.

INTERVIEWER: Do you think Fitzgerald was conscious of documenting?

CHEEVER: I've written something on Fitzgerald, and I've read all the biographies and critical works, and wept freely at the end of each one—cried like a baby—it is such a sad story. All the estimates of him bring in his descriptions of the '29 crash, the excessive prosperity, the clothes, the music, and by doing so, his work is described as being heavily dated . . . sort of period pieces. This all greatly diminishes Fitzgerald at his best. One always knows reading Fitzgerald what time it is, precisely where you are, the kind of country. No writer has ever been so true in placing the scene. But I feel that this isn't pseudohistory, but his sense of being alive. All great men are scrupulously true to their times.

INTERVIEWER: Do you think your works will be similarly dated?

CHEEVER: Oh, I don't anticipate that my work will be read. That isn't the sort of thing that concerns me. I might be forgotten tomorrow; it wouldn't disconcert me in the least.

INTERVIEWER: But a great number of your stories defy dating; they could take place anytime and almost anyplace.

CHEEVER: That, of course, has been my intention. The ones that you can pinpoint in an era are apt to be the worst. The bomb-shelter story ("The Brigadier and the Golf Widow") is about a level of basic anxiety, and the bomb shelter, which places the story at a very particular time, is just a metaphor . . . that's what I intended anyhow.

INTERVIEWER: It was a sad story.

CHEEVER: Everyone keeps saying that about my stories, "Oh, they're so sad." My agent, Candida Donadio, called me about a new story and said, "Oh, what a beautiful story, it's so sad." I said, "All right, so I'm a sad man." The sad thing about "The Brigadier and the Golf Widow" is the woman standing looking at the bomb shelter in the end of the story and then being sent away by a maid. Did you know that *The New Yorker* tried to take that out? They thought the story was much more effective without my ending. When I went in to look at page proofs, I thought there was a page missing. I asked where the end of the story was. Some girl said, "Mr. Shawn thinks it's better this way." I went into a very deep slow burn, took the train home, drank a lot of gin, and got one of the editors on the telephone. I was by then loud, abusive, and obscene. He was entertaining Elizabeth Bowen and Eudora Welty. He kept asking if he couldn't take this call in another place. Anyhow, I returned to New York in the morning. They had reset the whole magazine —poems, newsbreaks, cartoons—and replaced the scene.

INTERVIEWER: It's the classic story about what *The New Yorker* is rumored to do—"remove the last paragraph and you've got a typical *New Yorker* ending." What is your definition of a good editor?

CHEEVER: My definition of a good editor is a man I think charming, who sends me large checks, praises my work, my physical beauty, and my sexual prowess, and who has a stranglehold on the publisher and the bank.

INTERVIEWER: What about the beginning of stories? Yours start off very quickly. It's striking.

CHEEVER: Well, if you're trying as a storyteller to establish some rapport with your reader, you don't open by telling him that you have a headache and indigestion and that you picked up a gravelly rash at Jones Beach. One of the reasons is that advertising in magazines is much more common today than it was twenty to thirty years ago. In publishing in a magazine you are competing against girdle advertisements, travel advertise-

ments, nakedness, cartoons, even poetry. The competition almost makes it hopeless. There's a stock beginning that I've
always had in mind. Someone is coming back from a year in
Italy on a Fulbright Scholarship. His trunk is opened in cus-
toms, and instead of his clothing and souvenirs, they find the
mutilated body of an Italian seaman, everything there but the
head. Another opening sentence I often think of is, "The first
day I robbed Tiffany's it was raining." Of course, you can open
a short story that way, but that's not how one should function
with fiction. One is tempted because there has been a genuine
loss of serenity, not only in the reading public, but in all our
lives. Patience, perhaps, or even the ability to concentrate. At
one point when television first came in no one was publishing
an article that couldn't be read during a commercial. But
fiction is durable enough to survive all of this. I don't like
the short story that starts out "I'm about to shoot myself" or
"I'm about to shoot you." Or the Pirandello thing of "I'm
going to shoot you or you are going to shoot me, or we are
going to shoot someone, maybe each other." Or the erotic
thing, either: "He started to undo his pants, but the zipper
stuck . . . he got the can of three-in-one oil . . ." and on
and on we go.

INTERVIEWER: Certainly your stories have a fast pace, they
move along.

CHEEVER: The first principle of aesthetics is either interest
or suspense. You can't expect to communicate with anyone if
you're a bore.

INTERVIEWER: William Golding wrote that there are two
kinds of novelists. One lets meaning develop with the characters or situations, and the other has an idea and looks for a myth
to embody it. He's an example of the second kind. He thinks
of Dickens as belonging to the first. Do you think you fit into
either category?

CHEEVER: I don't know what Golding is talking about. Cocteau said that writing is a force of memory that is not under-

stood. I agree with this. Raymond Chandler described it as a direct line to the subconscious. The books that you really love give the sense, when you first open them, of having been there. It is a creation, almost like a chamber in the memory. Places that one has never been to, things that one has never seen or heard, but their fitness is so sound that you've been there somehow.

INTERVIEWER: But certainly you use a lot of resonances from myths . . . for example, references to the Bible and Greek mythology.

CHEEVER: It's explained by the fact that I was brought up in southern Massachusetts, where it was thought that mythology was a subject that we should all grasp. It was very much a part of my education. The easiest way to parse the world is through mythology. There have been thousands of papers written along those lines—Leander is Poseidon and somebody is Ceres, and so forth. It seems to be a superficial parsing. But it makes a passable paper.

INTERVIEWER: Still, you want the resonance.

CHEEVER: The resonance, of course.

INTERVIEWER: How do you work? Do you put ideas down immediately, or do you walk around with them for a while, letting them incubate?

CHEEVER: I do both. What I love is when totally disparate facts come together. For example, I was sitting in a café reading a letter from home with the news that a neighboring housewife had taken the lead in a nude show. As I read I could hear an Englishwoman scolding her children. "If you don't do thus and so before Mummy counts to three" was her line. A leaf fell through the air, reminding me of winter and of the fact that my wife had left me and was in Rome. There was my story. I had an equivalently great time with the close of "Goodbye My Brother" and "The Country Husband." Hemingway and Nabokov liked these. I had everything in there: a cat wearing a hat, some naked women coming out of the sea, a dog with a shoe in his mouth, and a king in golden mail riding an elephant over some mountains.

INTERVIEWER: Or Ping-Pong in the rain?

CHEEVER: I don't remember what story that was.

INTERVIEWER: Sometimes you played Ping-Pong in the rain.

CHEEVER: I probably did.

INTERVIEWER: Do you save up such things?

CHEEVER: It isn't a question of saving up. It's a question of some sort of galvanic energy. It's also, of course, a question of making sense of one's experiences.

INTERVIEWER: Do you think that fiction should give lessons?

CHEEVER: No. Fiction is meant to illuminate, to explode, to refresh. I don't think there's any consecutive moral philosophy in fiction beyond excellence. Acuteness of feeling and velocity have always seemed to me terribly important. People look for morals in fiction because there has always been a confusion between fiction and philosophy.

INTERVIEWER: How do you know when a story is right? Does it hit you right the first time, or are you critical as you go along?

CHEEVER: I think there is a certain heft in fiction. For example, my latest story isn't right. I have to do the ending over again. It's a question, I guess, of trying to get it to correspond to a vision. There is a shape, a proportion, and one knows when something that happens is wrong.

INTERVIEWER: By instinct?

CHEEVER: I suppose that anyone who has written for as long as I have, it's probably what you'd call instinct. When a line falls wrong, it simply isn't right.

INTERVIEWER: You told me once you were interested in thinking up names for characters.

CHEEVER: That seems to me very important. I've written a story about men with a lot of names, all abstract, names with the fewest possible allusions: Pell, Weed, Hammer, and Nailles, of course, which was thought to be arch, but it wasn't meant to be at all. . . .

INTERVIEWER: Hammer's house appears in "The Swimmer."

CHEEVER: That's true, it's quite a good story. It was a terribly difficult story to write.

INTERVIEWER: Why?

CHEEVER: Because I couldn't ever show my hand. Night was falling, the year was dying. It wasn't a question of technical problems, but one of imponderables. When he finds it's dark and cold, it has to have happened. And, by God, it did happen. I felt dark and cold for some time after I finished that story. As a matter of fact, it's one of the last stories I wrote for a long time, because then I started on *Bullet Park*. Sometimes the easiest-seeming stories to a reader are the hardest kind to write.

INTERVIEWER: How long does it take you to write such a story?

CHEEVER: Three days, three weeks, three months. I seldom read my own work. It seems to be a particularly offensive form of narcissism. It's like playing back tapes of your own conversation. It's like looking over your shoulder to see where you've run. That's why I've often used the image of the swimmer, the runner, the jumper. The point is to finish and go on to the next thing. I also feel, not as strongly as I used to, that if I looked over my shoulder I would die. I think frequently of Satchel Paige and his warning that you might see something gaining on you.

INTERVIEWER: Are there stories that you feel particularly good about when you are finished?

CHEEVER: Yes, there were about fifteen of them that were absolutely BANG! I loved them, I loved everybody—the buildings, the houses, wherever I was. It was a great sensation. Most of these were stories written in the space of three days and which run to about thirty-five pages. I love them, but I can't read them; in many cases, I wouldn't love them any longer if I did.

INTERVIEWER: Recently you have talked bluntly about having a writer's block, which had never happened to you before. How do you feel about it now?

CHEEVER: Any memory of pain is deeply buried, and there is nothing more painful for a writer than an inability to work.

INTERVIEWER: Four years is a rather long haul on a novel, isn't it?

CHEEVER: It's about what it usually takes. There's a certain monotony in this way of life, which I can very easily change.

INTERVIEWER: Why?

CHEEVER: Because it doesn't seem to me the proper function of writing. If possible, it is to enlarge people. To give them their risk, if possible to give them their divinity, not to cut them down.

INTERVIEWER: Do you feel that you had diminished them too far in *Bullet Park*?

CHEEVER: No, I didn't feel that. But I believe that it was understood in those terms. I believe that Hammer and Nailles were thought to be social casualties, which isn't what I intended at all. And I thought I made my intentions quite clear. But if you don't communicate, it's not anybody else's fault. Neither Hammer nor Nailles were meant to be either psychiatric or social metaphors; they were meant to be two men with their own risks. I think the book was misunderstood on those terms. But then I don't read reviews, so I don't really know what goes on.

INTERVIEWER: How do you know when the literary work is finished to your satisfaction?

CHEEVER: I have never completed anything in my life to my absolute and lasting satisfaction.

INTERVIEWER: Do you feel that you're putting a lot of yourself on the line when you are writing?

CHEEVER: Oh yes, oh yes! When I speak as a writer I speak with my own voice—quite as unique as my fingerprints—and I take the maximum risk at seeming profound or foolish.

INTERVIEWER: Does one get the feeling while sitting at the

typewriter that one is godlike, or creating the whole show at once?

CHEEVER: No, I've never felt godlike. No, the sense is of one's total usefulness. We all have a power of control, it's part of our lives: we have it in love, in work that we love doing. It's a sense of ecstasy, as simple as that. The sense is that "this is my usefulness, and I can do it all the way through." It always leaves you feeling great. In short, you've made sense of your life.

INTERVIEWER: Do you feel that way during or after the event? Isn't work, well, work?

CHEEVER: I've had very little drudgery in my life. When I write a story that I really like, it's . . . why, wonderful. That is what I can do, and I love it while I'm doing it. I can feel that it's good. I'll say to Mary and the children, "All right, I'm off, leave me alone. I'll be through in three days."

ANNETTE GRANT
Fall 1976

7. Irwin Shaw

Irwin Shaw was born in Brooklyn, New York, on February 27, 1913. Although he entered Brooklyn College, he was forced to withdraw when he failed freshman calculus, and for a time held several miscellaneous jobs, including driving a truck, before being readmitted. At school Shaw played varsity football and wrote one-act plays for the college dramatic society; after graduation he began writing radio scripts while completing plays and short fiction in his spare time. At age twenty-three his antiwar play, *Bury the Dead* (1936), was successfully produced on Broadway. It was followed by *Siege* (1937), *The Gentle People* (1939), *Quiet City* (1939), *Retreat to Pleasure* (1940), and other plays.

Drafted into the army in 1942, Shaw served in North Africa and Europe. He remained in Paris after the war, joining the community of expatriate American writers. After his considerable success as a playwright, Shaw turned to novels; his first, *The Young Lions,* was inspired by his war experiences and was published in 1948. He has since published many other works of fiction as well as such screenplays, as *Act of Love* (1954) and *Desire under the Elms* (1958). His best-selling novels include *The Troubled Air* (1950), *Lucy Crown* (1956), *Voices of a Summer Day* (1965), *Rich Man, Poor Man* (1970), *Evening in Byzantium* (1973), *Nightwork* (1975), *Beggarman, Thief* (1977), and most recently, *The Top of the Hill* (1979).

Shaw is the father of a son, Adam, who is also a writer, and divides his time between Klosters, Switzerland, and Southampton, New York.

and the President is giving a ball and the Garde Republicain
is out ~~marching marching~~ with their breastplates and
horsehair ~~plumes~~ *tails* and the North Africans are rioting for autonomy
~~xxx~~ at the Place de la Republique and all the policemen
have dents in their ~~bxx xxxxi~~ shiny steel helmets. Mass
is being ~~sung~~ *celebrated* at St Sulpice and they are burying an actor
in Pere LaChaise.~~xxx~~ There are long lines outside the
mail windows at the American Express, ~~and~~ the young lieutenants
are leaving for ~~Indo-china.~~ There is a fair on the Champs de
Mars and the phrenologists are doing well next to the
shooting galleries. They are selling perfume on the Rue de
la Paix and the merchants are worried about this year's
Burgundy in the wine market and ~~they the great~~ *a thousand deep* baskets
of watercress are being stacked at Les Halles. The buses
are coming ~~into~~ *in from the Orly airfield to* the Gare des Invalides with the passengers
from New York and South Africa and Warsaw and the trains
going south have whole cars filled with bicycles for *the*
~~xxx xxxxxxxxx people going out vacation~~ *vacationers en route* to the Côte
d'Azur. It is August and half the shops are closed, with
their iron shutters down, and it is ~~winter~~ *February* and the porters
wait/at the Gare de l'est *with wheelchairs* for the skiers with broken legs.
On the gray island in the river, they are turning out
the ~~tiny succeeding~~ *450 long-lived,* four-horsepower Renaults *a day* and the
Communists are painting Americans Go Home *iron* on the/bridges.
They are selling canaries near the Hotel de Ville and
putting out newspapers on the Rue Réamur and the headlines

A page from the manuscript of *Paris! Paris!* by Irwin Shaw.

Irwin Shaw

Editor's Note: *Two interviews with Irwin Shaw appear below. The first took place when* The Paris Review *was in its infancy, over twenty-five years ago. Shaw has remained a friend to the editors of the magazine, and so it seemed appropriate to ask him for an update.*

INTERVIEWERS: You know, I've been reading that story you spoke about, the last one in your collection of short stories *Mixed Company*, the one called "The Green Nude." It's pretty funny.

SHAW: What do you mean by that? Pretty funny?

INTERVIEWERS: As a matter of fact, it's very funny. A very funny story.

SHAW: Damn right it's funny. Didn't I tell you it was?

INTERVIEWERS: No, I really mean it's a funny story. A damn good one. I didn't mean . . .

SHAW: I *told* you it was funny.

INTERVIEWERS: Yes, I remember you did, and you were quite right too . . .

SHAW: Well, that's good. Let's get this thing started right. I don't want to have to start by throwing you out of here.

INTERVIEWERS: Yes, we don't want this to read "exit one interviewer," at least not so early in the piece. . . .

SHAW: Here, let me fix you a drink.

Irwin Shaw is not always as sensitive when discussing his own work. But he is a writer intensely proud of his creative efforts: two best-selling novels, The Young Lions *and* The Troubled Air; *a number of plays; and short stories considered among the finest in contemporary literature. His sensitivity is somewhat belied by his physique, for at first sight there is little in Irwin Shaw of what is popularly imagined as the sensitive artist. He has the heavy shoulders and short legs of the backfield star, the muscled forearms of the pelota champion (which, ironically, is one of the few sports he doesn't play), and the large, close-cropped head typical of another of his pleasures—boxing. Ernest Hemingway once told the author Peter Viertel that there is only one way to handle Irwin Shaw in a boxing match: "Rip off your glove and sink your fingers deep into the bulge of his forearm, severing a few of the muscles there and rendering the arm more or less useless." Hemingway demonstrated on Viertel, who has the scars left to prove it, along with the rueful admission that there isn't a man around, much less Irwin Shaw, who can stand up to* that *sort of punishment.*

Irwin Shaw has had to fight for success from the start. Born in Brooklyn, he is one of the few inhabitants of that community who recognized its limitations and from the age of twelve made a concerted effort to get himself enough money to cross the East River into Manhattan. He has come a long way from Brooklyn.

He reached New York, then Hollywood, and in the past years has lived in Europe: in Paris, in Rome, and now, the summer of 1953, in a villa perched on one of the foothills of the Pyrenees, with a view over the pink roofs of Saint-Jean-de-Luz to the lighthouse of Ciboure and the sea. In such pleasant surroundings, happy with his lovely wife and young son, Irwin Shaw continues to write with the concentration and driving energy that has brought him here: writing for him is an intense and private occupation that allows no spectators from the outside world. He refuses to discuss work on which he is currently engaged. In the mornings he won't be disturbed; his wife answers the phone for him. In the afternoons he abandons his typewriter for other activities, all performed with enormous vigor. He plays a ferocious brand of tennis on the courts of the Chantaco Club in Ascain down the road, or travels at great speed in his Hillman-Minx across the Spanish border to the bullfights. In the evening, more often than not, Irwin Shaw plays chemin de fer in the casino in Biarritz, again with an intensity that is said to discourage those who consider calling "Banco" when he holds the deal. Even when relaxed at home, turning a large martini glass in his hand, Irwin Shaw dominates a room that includes a brown grand piano; an impressive panoramic view of the Pyrenees; a tapestry-sized portrait of an iron-faced woman on a green horse, one Maria-Léonie Mortier de Trevisé, Princesse de Fancigny-Cystria (the landlady, Irwin Shaw calls her); and four ceiling-height sepia-brown plaques depicting the four seasons. All these Irwin Shaw overpowers, his laugh one of zestful enjoyment of life, and his humor the sharp, quick natural wit peculiar to one whose formative years were spent in Brooklyn.

When the interviewers called on Irwin Shaw, they found him with a huge bandage encasing his left hand. It turned out that it covered a wound inflicted by the convertible mechanism of his Hillman-Minx clipping down hard at the end of his fingers, an accident jarringly out of character. The interviewers were sympa-

*thetic, but pleased somehow; if only for a moment Mr. Shaw
appeared in a more natural perspective, his tragedy the small
polite domestic nuisance that occurs to the completely average
citizen in his completely average home.*

SHAW: Well, shall we get off "The Green Nude"?

INTERVIEWERS: Mr. Shaw, did you begin by writing short
stories, or plays?

SHAW: If you really want to know, my first job was writing
Dick Tracy.

INTERVIEWERS: You mean you wrote the words in the bal-
loons of the comic strip?

SHAW: No, no, no. It was a radio show. I pushed Dick Tracy
into situations and rescued him five times a week. It made me
a living and gave me time to do my own writing.

INTERVIEWERS: And you grew up in Brooklyn?

SHAW: I never left Brooklyn until I had made enough money
to get out. I spent all my childhood and I did all my growing
up there.

INTERVIEWERS: There's considerable Brooklyn background
in your earliest stories.

SHAW: Naturally. It was the freshest in my mind then, when
I started to write. But don't forget that almost every writer will
tell you that events that happened to him before he starts
writing are the most valuable to him. Once he starts writing
he seems to observe the world through a filter. I believe that's
true about writers: that the unconscious observation of things,
a kind of absorbing of life that goes on before he becomes a
writer, that is what is most useful to him. When he starts
observing things professionally and taking notes and trying to
remember, he may collect a lot more but he loses the spontaneous quality and the flow. He becomes too systematic. It's his
job to be, but he never gets anything as valuable as what he
got unconsciously. He has become the observer rather than
the actor. The best portrayal of the type that I know is the

character of Tregorin in Chekov's *The Seagull,* and then there's Philip Quarles in Huxley's *Point Counter Point* who wrote notes on his own reactions while his son was dying of meningitis.

INTERVIEWERS: Does the professional writer remain the observer rather than the actor throughout his career?

SHAW: He's apt to. Once trained, he stays the observer. Occasionally, he may find himself in a situation of pressure strong enough to change him—like war—and even then he must be deeply involved in it to lose his observer's outlook.

INTERVIEWERS: Can you tell us something about the novel that came out of your war years?

SHAW: Yes, *The Young Lions.* Well, I started off with a very grandiose idea indeed, one that eventually proved not to be feasible and I had to give it up. I had three main stories, all based on character: Christian Diestl, the German sergeant; Noah Ackerman, a young American Jew; and Michael Whiteacre, a product of the theater and radio world of Broadway and Hollywood. To link these three I introduced a fourth character, a bullet—the bullet fired by Whiteacre in the Black Forest which kills Diestl. I wanted to show it as lead in the ground, the miners that got it out, the engineers, the smelters, the sorters, the packagers, then the long chain of supply in the army that put the bullet finally in Whiteacre's cartridge belt. My idea was to show how we are all linked in this world— soldiers, civilians, the most sophisticated, the most primitive— the link being, in our time, death. There are other links, of course, but the strongest and most fundamental one in our century is killing. But I gave up the idea, even though it was the thing that gave me the impetus for the entire book. Aside from being grandiose, I think it was finally unnecessary. I found by concentrating on just three characters, I could say the things I had to say better than by trying to flesh out a rigid and theoretical skeleton.

INTERVIEWERS: And how about the characters in *The Young*

Lions? Where do they come from? Are they based on real life or imagination?

SHAW: The major characters are inventions for the most part. Some of the minor characters I know.

INTERVIEWERS: Two minor characters in *The Young Lions* seem to be too overdrawn to be from real life.

SHAW: What? What was that?

INTERVIEWERS: Two minor characters . . .

SHAW: Who? Who?

INTERVIEWERS: Well, one of them was a Frenchman who ate martini glasses.

SHAW: Oh, that one. I knew *him.* He was a wild man, a good friend of mine. Used to beat up cops and eat martini glasses. I don't believe he's still at it, but he used to be a wild one, that Frenchman. Now who's the other?

INTERVIEWERS: The other was an army general, a division commander. He did something that doesn't seem consistent with the average general's behavior. He stood on a little hill under enemy fire and urged a *platoon* to come up with him and advance towards the German lines.

SHAW: I never knew his name, but there was a legend that came out of the Normandy fighting about such a general—the sort of leadership you heard tell of General Roosevelt in Sicily. The fiction writer is constantly stumbling over the outrageousness of fact. Anyway, this particular fact isn't so outrageous. Plenty of generals got killed in the war. They didn't get killed eating Red Cross doughnuts.

INTERVIEWERS: Your main characters, though, are inventions?

SHAW: For the most part, yes. Some of the things that happened to Noah in *The Young Lions* happened to a man I knew, but he was an invention, regardless. I formed the character myself, for my own purposes and the purposes of the book, and put him through a series of events, some of which had actually happened and which I thought were fitting for the character. I didn't know Christian Diestl at all, although I talked to as many German prisoners of war as I could during the war, and to whomever I could in Germany and Austria right after the war. He wasn't an absolute invention—his dialogue and appearance in the first chapter were more or less suggested by something somebody once told me as having happened to her. But after that, it was all invented—taking into account the fact that here and there I used a story I'd heard or a scene I'd been a witness to, and which was useful for the character. Diestl, himself, I wanted to use as a symbol and an explanation, as well as an individual human being. I wanted to show how a man can start out decent, intelligent, well meaning, as so many people in Germany must have been, even in the greatest days of Nazism—and wind up bestialized, almost bereft of humanity, almost dead to the instincts of survival even, as the Germans finally were, by believing in one false thing, which spreads and spreads and finally corrupts them entirely. The false thing I had Diestl believing in was the conviction that at that one time and in that one place (Austria) the end justified the means. The belief, in the course of the book, corrupts him to a point of fanaticism at which no horror any longer has the power to move or disgust him.

INTERVIEWERS: Christian Diestl, then, symbolizes one of the more important morals of *The Young Lions*, that . . .

SHAW: What? What do you mean?

INTERVIEWERS: Well, critics of *The Young Lions* and your other novel, *The Troubled Air*, specify you as one of the few remaining novelists that try to put a message, or a moral, into their work. That perhaps you had an ax to grind.

SHAW: Who said that?

INTERVIEWERS: I don't know, but it seems to us to have been said.

SHAW: I don't believe I grind axes in my novels.

INTERVIEWERS: Well, perhaps some people have felt there was a tendency to stress points, to moralize.

SHAW: To propagandize?

INTERVIEWERS: Something like that, yes.

SHAW: That's the sort of thing critics say. You have to understand that a critic, in order to be a critic, always has to have his own pet theory about a writer. He has to put you in some definite category, stuff you in a pigeonhole, and it doesn't make much difference to him if a great deal of your work, or even most of it, belongs in another category entirely. When this happens, when what you've written doesn't fall into the critic's chosen terrain, he ignores it. Those critics who call me a propagandist ignore my stories about young men and women, like "The Girls in Their Summer Dresses." I don't think critics should categorize the writer; they should allow him scope. Don't be too disappointed if I say that what I was trying to do in *The Young Lions* was to show the world at a certain point in its history, its good and evil, and as many people as I could crowd into the book struggling through that world, trying to find some reason for trying to stay alive in it.

INTERVIEWERS: And in *The Troubled Air*?

SHAW: I wanted to show the decent and average American faced with social pressures of which he doesn't approve—in this case Red-baiting in the radio world. I picked a man who was decent, with a kind of modest, half-exhausted desire to do good, a man trying to coast through life without being a son of a bitch. I couldn't pick a more positive person, a mean man, or a saint (I've never found a saint in the radio business anyhow). He had to be the decent, average American faced with a quite un-American problem—a problem to which there was no successful solution—and facing it with his only weapon, that of resignation—of the self-destroying and profitless, at least for the moment, gesture. But he doesn't resign immediately; he hedges and tries to qualify his position, a compromise that is his tragedy and his defeat.

INTERVIEWERS: You can't say, then, that *The Troubled Air* doesn't express attitudes.

SHAW: Sure, it expressed attitudes, and I admit some of them were attitudes which I myself hold very strongly. But I don't think the novel was built around them. There were a lot of other ideas there with which I disagree violently, and the novel wasn't built around them either. Personally, I don't see how I could have been grinding any ax, but then that's just my opinion and I'm not a critic. *The Troubled Air* was attacked by the Communists as being reactionary and the editor of a minor book club got my publisher to swear I wasn't a Communist before he'd consider the book. That's what happens when you try to put down more than one point of view.

INTERVIEWERS: I wish you'd say something more about critics. There's something in the tone of your voice . . .

SHAW: What do you mean?

INTERVIEWERS: I mean when you get going on critics . . .

SHAW: I don't "get going." You just asked me what I thought and I was trying to tell you. For instance, I don't think most American critics want to accept the defeat of a decent man. If a hero is defeated it's got to be because of something wrong in him. In *The Troubled Air* the hero, for reality's sake, was not presented as a winner of the [Congressional] Medal of Honor for heroism; but even so, for all that, he behaved with a thousand times more guts than any of the people in the radio business are actually behaving at this minute. He was finally hedged in and defeated by extremists on both sides, the Left and Right. Now, there's something most American critics don't want to swallow. How such a man can be licked by something like the emotional climate of his country. It's too pessimistic and unheroic. The critics never . . .

INTERVIEWERS: Would you like to make a definitive statement about critics here and now?

SHAW: Listen, I did that long ago. I put down my final thoughts on the critics in the preface to a play called *The Assassins.* I was furious then. It's all in there and you can read it anytime.

INTERVIEWERS: But that was only about drama critics.

SHAW: Mostly, but I got in something about the other ones too.

INTERVIEWERS: But weren't you a critic once yourself?

SHAW: Yes. I reviewed the drama for a season for *The New Republic*.

INTERVIEWERS: Did you like being a critic?

SHAW: Not much. It wore out the pleasure of going to the theater. There's an almost unavoidable feeling of smugness, of self-satisfaction, of teacher's pettishness, that sinks into a critic's bones, and I was afraid of it. You see it in all our newspapers and reviews. They've even gone so far as to dub this the Age of Criticism, and every time one of them comes out with a book proving that Melville had a wart on his right nostril instead of on his left, as had been generally supposed up to then, all the other critics start shivering in ecstasy and murmuring "Sainte-Beuve come again." They're so damned polite to each other they swallow the worst kind of piddling nonsense from each other as though it was sugar candy.

INTERVIEWERS: One more question about criticism, if we may. Are you your own severest critic? Do you . . . ?

SHAW: I am forced to say that I have many fiercer critics than myself.

INTERVIEWERS: Do you *really* enjoy writing, Mr. Shaw?

SHAW: I used to enjoy it more. It's tougher now, as one's power dwindles. Also, the variety of choice increases. There used to be only one sentence to write. You wrote it and it was good and you let it stay. As you grow older and more experienced you find that where you had one sentence before, you have thirty possibilities now and you have to stew to find the best.

INTERVIEWERS: As a successful writer, do you think that failure is a detriment? Particularly to the young writer who is the most easily discouraged?

SHAW: Sure, it's a detriment, but I don't see how you're

going to avoid it. And perhaps it isn't a bad idea for a young writer to taste failure before success, because he's going to know a lot more of failure before he's done.

INTERVIEWERS: That sounds pretty pessimistic.

SHAW: Why pessimistic? It stands to reason. Look, failure is inevitable for the writer. Any writer. I don't care who he is, or how great he is, or what he's written. Sooner or later he's going to flop and everybody who admired him will try to write him off as a bum. He can't help it. He's bound to write something bad. Shakespeare wrote a few bad plays. Tolstoy was turning out some pretty dreadful stuff at the end of his life. Name me one great writer who hasn't had some failure.

INTERVIEWERS: Yes, but aren't you judging failure on a pretty relative basis? Failure for Shakespeare or Tolstoy merely means something that doesn't measure up to the standard of his work. It's not the same thing as failure for a young writer starting on a career.

SHAW: Why isn't it? Failure was just as bitter for Tolstoy and Shakespeare during their lifetimes. Do you think they could comfort themselves with posterity? Or about measuring up to standards and that kind of business?

INTERVIEWERS: Well, what about success? Certainly that's beneficial to a writer?

SHAW: To a certain extent it is. But everybody forgets that a writer who has had success—even one who's made a lot of money on one book—may have waited fifteen years for that one book, and before he can produce another one, it may be another fifteen years, if ever. And I'm not only talking about commercial or critical failure. There's the kind of running failure that dogs a writer all his life—ideas that only get half-written, false beginnings, first drafts that suddenly go dead and have to be thrown away, even crucial paragraphs that stiffen under your hand and refuse to be revived. And then, whole books—even if they've been well received—that nag you long after they've been published, because you see where you could have done something better with them. And then, American writers, more than any others, are haunted by the fear of failure, because it's such a common pattern in America. The ghost of Fitzgerald, dying in Hollywood, with his comeback book unfinished, and his best book, *Tender Is the Night,* scorned—his ghost hangs over every American typewriter. An absolutely necessary part of a writer's equipment, almost as necessary as talent, is the ability to stand up under punishment, both the punishment the world hands out and the punishment he inflicts upon himself. If he doesn't have the faith in himself, the energy, the ambition, to shake it off or absorb it and plow ahead, he'll wind up a one-book man or a two-book man, and hitting the bottle instead of the typewriter. Failure is more consistent—for everybody—than success. It's like living in a rainy belt—there are some sunny days, but most of the time it's wet outside and you'd better carry your umbrella. Anyway, failure is apt to produce self-pity, and it's been my experience that self-pity can be very productive.

INTERVIEWERS: Do you approve of rich wives for the struggling artist?

SHAW: I certainly do; largely because of the income-tax situation. I can say this because I can swear that my wife is not now, nor has ever been, rich.

INTERVIEWERS: And how about writing for the movies?

SHAW: It's not as good as a rich wife, but I think it only harms those writers who were bound to be harmed by something anyway. And you get an interesting technical exercise there—writing in handcuffs—which might one day be of considerable use in your own things.

INTERVIEWERS: Do you think you have been embittered or disappointed by your experiences in Hollywood?

SHAW: On the contrary. When I first went out there at the age of twenty-three, I had no illusions at all. I was almost as cynical about Hollywood as you seem to be. Now after seeing all the good movies that have been made since then, against all obstacles, I have some hope for the movies, which is more than I started out with.

INTERVIEWERS: To get back to your early writing. There is considerable preoccupation with the rise of Hitler, with anti-Semitism in Europe, and with oncoming war generally. And yet, as a play, *Bury the Dead* was violently antiwar.

SHAW: That's right. I think the course of my writing during the thirties pretty well reflects what most of my generation was preoccupied with then. We began in the Depression, very dedicated and oppressed and doom-conscious. In the early thirties we were against a new war at any cost. We believed that simply by protesting against war we could avoid it. We kept saying to ourselves "we won't fight again *ever* about anything." My play was produced in 1936 and the play that won the Pulitzer Prize for that year was Robert Sherwood's *Idiot's Delight,* and that was a fierce attack on munitions makers. Congress had just passed the neutrality bill and there was the Oxford Movement in England. So you can see . . .

INTERVIEWERS: Then what was it that began to change you? It didn't happen overnight, did it?

SHAW: It took a little while, I guess. We believed that people believed the same thing the world over, but what we didn't know or wouldn't believe was that in Germany and Italy and Russia people who thought as we did were being lined up against walls and machine-gunned. Then there was the civil war in Spain, which had its great effect on us; that, plus the growth of Hitlerism and the persecution of the Jews, all of that business. At first it was too much for us to believe, but bit by bit we began believing it. I think I was recording in my short stories what we, our age, felt then. In almost everything I wrote, even these simple stories, little sketches really, of the young men and girls in New York, this thing was hanging like a backdrop. Even a simple story called "Search Through the Streets of the City," which was about a man who runs into a girl he once had an affair with and finds she's married the wrong man, has an atmosphere of draft boards and headlines and impending disaster.

INTERVIEWERS: Do you think your writing since the war has the same preoccupation?

SHAW: Pretty much the same. We've lived in a sick world since 1914. It's no accident that Kafka has become so popular. He's enjoying the popularity of the prophet whose prophecies have come true. He prophesied the final emergence of the Victim as the archetype of the modern man—the Victim who is slowly teased and tortured and destroyed by forces that are implacable and pitiless and that cannot be understood. And since we have to live in this atmosphere of perpetual doom, it's natural that it should permeate one's writing. War has now been taken out of all human contact. We can hardly conceive or bear to think of the faculties now achieved for mass destruction. This isn't even the kind of killing with regret, with compassion, that I tried to write about in *The Young Lions.*

INTERVIEWERS: There was a sermon in *The Young Lions,* given by an old pastor in the ruined church at Dover. That was important, then?

SHAW: Yes, that was very important. I tried to have that old man say what my only belief is about war—not to be proud of the thousands of bombers you send against the enemy and their cities, of the blind, indiscriminate, million-quality of your killing, no matter how necessary you may think it is. And when a soldier kills another soldier, he must kill with a sense of sin and tragedy. The sin is as much the soldier's as it is of the enemy he kills by his hand, and that is the way a soldier loves his enemy, moved by a curious sense of sin that belongs to them both. That's probably the fundamental thing I tried to say in the novel.

INTERVIEWERS: Would you say it was kind of an obsession with you, this compassion? It seems to be in many of your later stories, particularly those about the war—in a story like "Act of Faith," for instance?

SHAW: It's something I believe in strongly.

INTERVIEWERS: But not an obsession?

SHAW: I don't know. I don't think I believe in obsessions. I don't agree with Graham Greene, if that's what you mean. I read what he said in your last issue about the writer's need to be obsessed. I admire Greene, but there I disagree with him. Or disagree with him to the extent of the value he places on a *single* obsession. Writers, especially if they live long enough, can be gripped by different obsessions, or at the same time by several obsessions. For example—T. S. Eliot, if he was obsessed by anything in his great early work, was obsessed by a sense of revulsion and disgust with the modern world. Now he's obsessed with the idea of redemption through faith, and his work, as far as I'm concerned, has suffered because of it. I didn't like *The Cocktail Party* one bit. I thought it unworthy of him. I realize this isn't a fashionable theory, at least not among the critics.

INTERVIEWERS: Back to the critics again?

SHAW: Well, it's what I've been telling you. They have to have a theory to peg you with and anything that doesn't fit that theory they tend to ignore. This business of obsession is another of their theories. Hemingway is supposed to be obsessed with violence. But it seems to me that Hemingway has done a lot of writing that couldn't be more tranquil. You remember the fishing scenes in *The Sun Also Rises* that were done about the Pyrenees, right out the window there *(he waved his bandage-encased hand, the size of a bear paw, at the mountains).* They're remarkable for the feeling they give of peace and nature and communion and friendship between two men who have gone fishing. But I've never heard it said that Hemingway was obsessed by friendship. What was Stendhal's obsession? To write sentences as clear as those in the Code Napoléon? Does that explain why *The Charterhouse of Parma* is a great novel? Every novelist has a different purpose—and often several purposes which might even be contradictory. For example, I find myself wanting to expose how bitter the world is and at the same time how glorious it is to live in it. You can't talk abstractly about the purpose of the novel. The novelist is a free agent, he can't be pinned down.

INTERVIEWERS: You were saying a while back about *The Troubled Air* that the best recourse of the honorable man who can think and is in such a situation is to resign. This applies particularly to the intellectual in America?

SHAW: Remember, I was writing about a particular man, a particular problem, and a particular atmosphere, which I hope is not going to remain unchanged. Still, for a long time, the intellectual in America has had, at least socially and psychologically, a difficult time. In the thirties the Communists were making their first big dent, and it was they who began to belittle the intellectuals in places like New York. They were joined by the violent right-wing newspapers who hated Roosevelt and expressed their contempt of the intellectuals by inventing such phrases as the "brain trust."

INTERVIEWERS: You'd say that the intellectual, and particularly the writer, is much better respected in Europe than in the States?

SHAW: Not in Europe, generally. Remember what happened to the intellectuals in Germany and in Russia. But in Western Europe, yes. Look at François Mauriac, a Nobel Prize winner and one of the best living French novelists, writing a column on anything he pleases, on politics or a play he's seen the night before, or a point of religious doctrine, twice a week, which is published on the front page of *Figaro,* the biggest conservative paper in France. Can you imagine either one of our two living Nobel Prize winners—Pearl Buck or William Faulkner—writing a column like that for *The New York Times?*

INTERVIEWERS: What is thought of the writer in America, then?

SHAW: He's a freak. People feel uncomfortable when he's around. He has odd, inconsistent ways of making his living, and nine times out of ten he can't earn his living by writing. He's distrusted and maybe he's subversive. An American writer is always a potential witness for an investigating committee. Right now, the situation has worsened: at least in the thirties an occasional writer was asked to the White House. Now, attacking writers as among the most eggheaded of intellectuals is considered a good way of guaranteeing an election. I might mistrust intellectuals, but I'd mistrust nonintellectuals even more.

INTERVIEWERS: Can you tell us something about the theater. Do you find it an easier medium than the novel?

SHAW: It's the hardest of them all. Young novelists come a dime a dozen, but the playwright must be older, more experienced, and in more complete control of his craft. The scope of the novel is such that mistakes can be made, even serious mistakes, without impairing the value of the work. But the theater audience is hypercritical and the form of the play is extremely exacting, and one mistake and you're through. I've had a hard time with the theater. I've always been anxious to write plays. I read all kinds of plays and books on the theater and books about how to write plays, but all I learned was that playwriting is something nobody can teach you.

INTERVIEWERS: But your first success, *Bury the Dead,* came when you were twenty-three years old. You learned pretty fast.

SHAW: Look, I wrote five plays before *Bury the Dead.* They were all bad, and I didn't show them to anybody. I had to write them to practice, and that's the way I learned. Since *Bury the Dead,* I've written seven plays, all but *The Gentle People* flops. I like the theater as a form, but I'm not so sure about its being the right one for me. You never can tell what's going to happen. My play *The Gentle People* was translated into French and produced in Paris last winter, fifteen years after it was done at home. It was perhaps the greatest theatrical success I've had. They called it *Phillipe et Jonas* and the French appreciated it as I meant it to be: a combination fairy tale and joke. In New

York it was accepted by critics and audiences alike as a head-on melodrama.

INTERVIEWERS: You don't seem to have much regard for the New York theater audience.

SHAW: Oh, but I do. I have a fine play in mind I'll write for them someday. The curtain slides up on a stage bare except for a machine gun facing the audience. Then after a pause in which the audience is given time to rustle their paper bags and their programs, wheeze and cough and settle in their seats, the actor enters. He's a tall man dressed in evening clothes. He comes downstage to the footlights and, after a little bow, smiles charmingly at the audience, giving them more time to mumble and rustle and cough and whisper and settle in their seats. Then he walks upstage, adjusts the machine gun, and blasts them.

INTERVIEWERS: Oh, yes . . . Perhaps we ought to move on to the short story. What about the technique of the short story?

SHAW: Well, that's something I've been thinking about for twenty-five years and I'm not sure. The form of the short story is so free as to escape restriction to any theory. Theories just don't seem to hold up. I had a theory when I began and I know I haven't been able to follow it out.

INTERVIEWERS: What was that?

SHAW: I wanted to write stories in each one of which the style and shape would be dictated, as far as possible, not by me but by the material itself. That is, I wanted to make the attempt to cut the umbilical cord between the creator and the character. The Promethean writer would be the one who sounded like a Russian artillery officer when he was writing "The Cossacks," a Dublin lush when he was writing "Counterparts," and a German professor when he was writing "Disorder and Early Sorrow." I know it's impossible, but some damned interesting writing might come out of the attempt.

INTERVIEWERS: Where do you get your ideas for your short stories?

SHAW: All over. Watching, listening, remembering. A lot of them from my friends or people I meet. Sometimes from a general feeling or belief which is strong enough to make me invent characters and situations to state it. For example, my story "The Eighty-Yard Run," which was about an exfootball player, a minor hero, who turns into a complete failure by the age of thirty-five, came as a result of my seeing around me so many men, all of whose best moments had come in their youth. I wanted to express that and show the subtle disappointments and inadequacies which bring so many promising young men to failure so early. Americans are at their best in their youth, and for me, at least, nothing is more characteristic of that best side and best moment of Americans than the race down the football field under a kickoff, in which are mingled gaiety, grace, recklessness, good-humored ferocity, skill at high speed, all taking place in a particular atmosphere of health and holiday that is duplicated nowhere else in the world. It was a productive symbol both for me and for the reader, and I built my story around the feelings of past joy and present regret that remembering it gave me.

INTERVIEWERS: Do you write your stories immediately after you hear them or think of them?

SHAW: No. I have to wait to get the story in proper perspective. I've been working now on a story I've been carrying around in my head since August 1944.

INTERVIEWERS: Do you keep a notebook?

SHAW: Yes, I do. I take a great many notes. If I have an idea for a short story, I jot it down. Now look, haven't you fellows got enough? I don't see what good these damn interviews are anyway. All this has been said before. Conceivably, writing can still be original, but talking or writing *about* writing can't. Holy man, I want to play some tennis.

INTERVIEWERS: You going to play tennis with that hand?

SHAW: Damn right. Funny thing about this hand of mine. I usually work on a typewriter. Can't, of course, with this hand,

and the funny thing is that I've been reading Proust for two weeks and I find this pen I'm using writes the longest Proustian sentences you ever saw. I can't seem to do anything about it.

INTERVIEWERS: One more thing. Would you happen to have a photograph of yourself lying about? We'll have an artist do a line sketch off it to preface the interview.

SHAW: I suppose there's one. I take terrible pictures. I wish I was vain enough not to have any more taken and call in all those that are still out. You know, a woman was speaking to me the other day about a photograph she'd seen of me. You know what she said to me? She said to me, "My, now that I've seen you, that photograph must have been taken when you were much older, Mr. Shaw, much older."

JOHN PHILLIPS
GEORGE PLIMPTON
Winter 1953

❖❖❖

INTERVIEWERS: The first interview is especially acid about critics. Have your views changed over the years?

SHAW: My views naturally have mellowed. Most of the critics have been more or less kind to me, and the public has been most kind, and I reach my readers regardless of what the critics have written. So that when I get a bad review now, it doesn't bother me as much as it once did.

INTERVIEWERS: Do you read the reviews of your books?

SHAW: Not much anymore, no. Not often. I sometimes glance at them, but I know that all writers are the same way. They forget a thousand good reviews and remember one bad one. Therefore, an excessive amount of spleen is vented on the one critic. You have to expect the raps when you have achieved popularity as a writer, which in high literary circles is regarded as proof of venality and deliberate debasement of artistic standards. The popularity that I've enjoyed in the last few years has tended to soften the effect of critical blows. There was one critic I was very angry with, who came up to the party for Jim Jones's *Whistle*—after Jim had died—and I was in the receiving line. I put out my hand. He said, "You really want to shake my hand?" I said, "Sure. Forget it." But there are a couple of critics I won't forget, from the so-called New York literary establishment, who have their own pets and standards, which I don't understand, and who have a tendency to either snub me or downgrade me. Naturally, I have some sharp things to say about them in the privacy of my own home. But I'd rather not say anything about them here, because the real juicy throat-cutting stories I'm saving for my memoirs.

INTERVIEWERS: You have recently spoken of a Jewish cabal which is at the forefront of this country's critical evaluation. . . .

SHAW: Well, it's not really a Jewish cabal. . . . It's something that started in the old *Partisan Review,* and it just so happened that quite a few people were Jews, but it had nothing particularly to do with Jews. They were Trotskyites. Anyone who was at all political and not a Trotskyite they considered a Stalinist. Unfortunately, they all wrote well and were maliciously entertaining. Then they became violent patriots during the war, though not one of them ever served in the armed services as far as I know. They didn't fight in the war. They didn't ever play football. They live in a dusty atmosphere of books and intrigue, and they don't like people like me who have entered more than they have into the mainstream of American life. And they've kept their lofty attitudes ever since. They and their disciples have gone out and worked for *Time* magazine, and *Newsweek* and *The New York Review of Books* and even now in the Sunday *Times* book-review section. They have a very haughty attitude towards people like me, mostly because —at least I think—because of the fact that my books sell a lot and people in general like them. They disregard all the great writers who were enormously popular, like Dickens, Balzac, Dostoyevsky, Tolstoy, and for that matter Fitzgerald and Mark Twain and Hemingway. Anyway, I don't let them bother me much. As I wrote somewhere when writing about James Jones, "Posterity makes the judgments, not *The Saturday Review of Literature,* or *The New York Review of Books,* or even the Sunday *Times* book-review section. There are going to be a lot of surprises in store for everybody."

INTERVIEWERS: Do you think writers have it easier today than when you started out?

SHAW: In some ways they do, and then again they don't. When I started out, in the early 1930s, there were a great many magazines that published short stories. And writers of fiction, when they begin, are more likely to try the short form. At that time there was a great market for it, greater interest in the short story, and the young writer had a chance to practice his craft, to get criticism and meet with editors. Since that time, unfortunately, the short-story market has dwindled to almost nothing, and that form of expression has become almost obsolete for all writers in America except those who are willing to publish in small magazines or those writers who have enough of a reputation that they can use the limited space in two or three magazines throughout the country. However, from the point of view of finances, getting started as a writer has become more feasible. Although the number of newspapers has dwindled—and that used to be a field where a lot of beginning writers could serve their apprenticeship—there are many other forms that are lucrative. The chief one is television, which devours huge amounts of the written word, as does advertising and industry. The demand for quality in the writing in magazines like *Time, Newsweek,* etcetera, is attractive to bright young people of talent, and the proliferation of special-interests magazines offers a multitude of opportunities for financial security. However, those are dangerous places for writers to start in with, because the money is good and the writing quickly falls into a routine and people who had started out as serious are very likely to find themselves in a financial as well as an artistic bind, since working in those mediums is an all-day, all-week job. And they are liable to find themselves artistically exhausted when they want to work on something of their own. On the other hand, in my experience I've found that if you're young enough, *any* kind of writing you do for a short period of time —up to two years, perhaps—is a marvelous apprenticeship. I told my son, who wanted to be a writer, that his newspaper experience—he was lucky enough to get four years of newspaper experience under demanding editors on the U.P.I. and *The Washington Post*—could only help him. But you must avoid giving hostages to fortune, like getting an expensive wife, an expensive house, and a style of living that never lets you afford the time to take the chance to write what you wish. So that, while writers in general can make a living much more easily than when I first started in the 1930s, the serious writer who doesn't want to compromise at all finds it much more difficult. Still, we're fortunate enough. The other day I got a contract from a magazine in Budapest. To reprint a short story of mine they agreed to pay me fifty dollars, out of which there would be deducted a thirty percent tax, a ten percent agent's fee, and furthermore I was required to send at my own expense two books to some bureaucratic organization of the Hungarian government. You can imagine how well writers are doing in Budapest.

INTERVIEWERS: How have you changed as writer since the interview in *The Paris Review* with you twenty-five years ago? Habits, energies, attitudes?

SHAW: My habits have remained more or less the same ever since I stopped writing for the theater. Writing for the theater, when you live among actors, you find yourself leading a nocturnal life. You're staying up until four or five o'clock in the morning, and you work at night more than you do in the day.

Now that I'm away from the theater, I find I get up very early in the morning and, for the most part, work four or five hours, then go out. I used to ski or play tennis, then come back about four or five o'clock and go over what I'd done. My attitudes have been changed, I imagine, but somebody would have to read all my books to find out how they have, I imagine, that my characters have become much more complicated than when I first began, which would be normal. I've become more gentle in my irony. I'm liable to do more with failure and death. My attitude toward women is much less romantic than it was, which is also normal. I'm not as hopeful as I was when I was young. And I can see through trickery and cheating a lot better than I did back then, since I've been exposed to quite a bit of it and some lessons have seeped in. I've also become —naturally, since I have had a family now for a long time— much more involved in the relations between members of a family. In fact, the book I'm doing now is just about that.

INTERVIEWERS: Have your views changed since that first interview about the writer in America?

SHAW: Yes, they have, because times have changed. First of all, when I gave that interview it was at the height of the McCarthy period when writers *were* being hounded. After that, remember, we had Kennedy, and Kennedy was a man who liked writers and even *I* got invited to the White House. Also, Ernest Hemingway did a great deal toward making the writer an acceptable public figure; obviously, he was no sissy. He was a he-man. He made money by his trade, his art. He knew everybody. He moved in very aristocratic and socially acceptable circles. So that helped a great deal. Also, today there are so many more writers. Everybody knows somebody who is writing for television or for the movies. They get much more publicity. People write about them as human beings much more than they used to, and so that has changed. Of course, it hasn't changed completely. A couple of years ago in Switzerland, a gentleman in the insurance business, an American, came to me and he said, "You live here?" I said, "Yes." He said, "Well, what do you *do*?" I said, "I'm a writer." He said, "Yes, I know. But what do you do for a *living*?" But that attitude has changed somewhat. I don't think that the writer anymore is regarded as a freak by Americans. What I said then was accurate, but now no longer is.

INTERVIEWERS: If a writer's powers do diminish over a period of time, in what areas does this seem to occur?

SHAW: Since, by all rights, my powers should be in full flood of diminishment, that's a hard question for me to answer honestly. I think that for myself I write with the same enthusiasm—if not with the same speed. I find myself redoing things much more than I did then. But, remember, that is a particularly American question, because in Europe a writer is supposed to improve up until he's about seventy-five. Europeans seem to have a career curve that's much more regular than that of Americans . . . there are very few flash-in-the-pans in Europe, especially among writers. In America we have the feeling of the doomed young artist. Fitzgerald was the great example of that, who started losing his power at the age of twenty-nine, according to the critics. The fact that he didn't was only found out posthumously. But unless a man becomes an alcoholic or is tormented by life in a terrible way, he shouldn't lose his powers as he grows older. For example, Isaac Singer is seventy-five years old, and although he was born in Poland and doesn't write in English, still he's an American, and he's going as strong as ever. He should be a model for us all. People who light up like Roman candles come down in the dark very quickly. Curiously, the United States is just full of writers who have one big work in their life and that's all. Tom Heggen killed himself after *Mister Roberts*. So did Ross Lockridge after *Raintree County*.

INTERVIEWERS: Could it be that some writers really only have one book in them . . . and writer's block is simply an excuse?

SHAW: I don't think so. The great writers—Dostoyevsky,

Tolstoy, Dickens, Meredith, Thackeray—just kept bringing them out. They didn't care if they repeated themselves. It didn't bother them that they wrote echoes. We seem to go by a different timing mechanism than these writers. The only man who wrote a great deal in our time was John O'Hara, because he went on the wagon and had nothing else to do. I've gone on the wagon, but my body doesn't believe it. It's waiting for that whiskey to get in there . . . to get me going. I never drink while I'm working, but after a few glasses, I get ideas that would never have occurred to me dead sober. And some of the ideas turn out to be valuable the next day. Some not.

INTERVIEWERS: How important to a writer are the adjutants to the profession—editor, publisher, agent?

SHAW: That depends very largely upon the writer. I know writers, very good ones, who lean upon their editors very heavily. There's no onus attached to that, but they want constant reassurance. They are doubtful about their own directions, and they often go to their editors while writing a book for help. I, on the other hand, never show anything to anybody until I've finished it. The only exception I've made to that is my son, because he represents a whole new generation; when I write about young people I want to see whether I'm getting it straight or not. Editors can be very useful. I had a great editor, Saxe Cummins at Random House, who helped me cut more than a hundred thousand words out of *The Young Lions.* If I had kept them in it might have been a terrible flop. The editors I had at *The New Yorker* quietly helped me in peculiar, small ways. One thing they taught me was the value of cutting out the last paragraph of stories, something I pass down as a tip to all writers. The last paragraph in which you tell what the story is about is almost always best left out. The editors I have now are valuable in other ways, occasionally pointing out something they think is a weakness and in getting things straight. In the novel it's hard to keep track of everybody. They also help keep a hold on reality. They say, "That street didn't run that way."

For example, in "The Sailor Off the Bremen" I described a walk down into Greenwich Village in which a beating took place near the YWCA. My poor editor at *The New Yorker* took the time to walk down and time it and come back and tell me I had done it correctly. Also, I wrote a story about North Africa during the war—this was *before* I got to North Africa—and I described it as hot, with everybody suffering from the heat. The editors found out just before publication that in the early days of the invasion it had been cold and blustery and everybody was freezing. An editor for prose isn't as important as an editor, say, for film, where the whole thing can be changed by an editor. But the most brilliant example of that in our time, I think, was Ezra Pound's editing of *The Wasteland*, which made the poem infinitely better. Well, there are very few people like Pound around and very few people like T. S. Eliot who'll listen. So I don't hope for that.

The writer works in a lonely way, and these people who work around him are supportive and useful in a general way. Publishers. Agents. I had a very nice agent, a long time ago, who approved of my stuff and sold my short stories. But once she said, "I don't think this short story you sent in to me is right. I think you should do this and that to it." So I said, "My dear young lady, you have one job, which is selling my stories, and I have another job, which is writing them. Let's you stick to your job, and I'll stick to mine." My present agent, Irving B. Lazar, does a very good job of selling my work, but I get no criticism from him, which is a happy combination for both of us. Irving is famous, you know, not only as an agent but for his fear of germs. He'll ask the hotel concierge for twenty towels to put between his bed and his bathroom so that after a shower he can walk back into the bedroom on a path of towels. At the Hotel Chantaco, in Saint-Jean-de-Luz, he used up so many towels that the concierge called him on the phone and asked him to leave, which got Swifty so angry he took all the towels and threw them over the balcony. Once, he and Howard

Hughes, who was also nuts about germs, found themselves in the men's room of a casino in Las Vegas, and it became a question of which one was going to risk opening the door for the other; in normal circumstances either would push the door with his *shoulder* rather than risk contamination by using his hands. Both tried to outwait the other. They'd be in there to this day if someone had not pushed the door to come in, and both men were able to slip out without touching anything at all.

INTERVIEWERS: Could we ask: What are the writer's responsibilities to his talent compared with his responsibilities to his state of well-being, his family?

SHAW: Well, a writer is a human being. He has to live with a sense of honor. If when I got out of college I had abandoned my family to starvation, which is just about where we were, I think I'd have been a much worse writer. I know that the romantic idea is that everybody around a writer must suffer for his talent. But I think that a writer is a citizen (which is one of the reasons I went into the war), that he's a part of humanity, part of his nation, part of his family. He may have to make some compromises.

INTERVIEWERS: Why did you eventually stop writing for *The New Yorker*?

SHAW: Because my friends on it, my editors, died, and I didn't like the policy of the new people who came in. It's a very good magazine, but I felt that I had either outgrown it or fallen behind it. I think there would be differences of opinion there. They've tried to get me to write for them again, since 1952, when I quit, but I just didn't feel that I belonged there anymore, although I like many of their short stories. My favorite short-story writer is John Cheever, who writes for them all the time. But it's not within my field anymore. I found that I could publish the stories I wanted to write other places. *The New Yorker* has been very hospitable to me. I had great editors there, starting with Wolcott Gibbs, William Maxwell, Gus Lobrano, and above all—Harold Ross.

INTERVIEWERS: What constitutes a good editor?

SHAW: A good editor is a man who understands what you're talking and writing about and doesn't meddle too much. A good editor can put his finger on a weakness or on a *longueur* or on a failure in development without trying to tell you how to repair it. That was the one thing *The New Yorker* never tried to do with me. They never tried to rewrite me. There were times when they said, "Well, we don't like the story this way, but if you change it in a certain way we'll take it." Occasionally their ideas were acceptable, and at other times I'd say, "Nothing doing," and I'd publish the story someplace else. For example, "The Eighty-Yard Run" was first submitted to *The New Yorker,* and they turned it down. Another story that became quite famous, "Night Birth and Opinion," which got the best reviews in the book of short stories in which it was included, was turned down. Editors are not infallible. Also, sometimes the prejudices of the group of editors might militate against a certain kind of story. *The New Yorker* editors are the least athletic group of people I've ever seen, and also they were against violence, although they did publish "The Sailor Off the Bremen," which is the first long story they ever published and the first politically serious story they'd ever accepted.

INTERVIEWERS: Didn't that particular story have something to do with a change in their policy toward short stories?

SHAW: It did indeed. That was the first really serious story they published, and the first time they published a story that long. Now they publish stories twenty thousand words long. I was very grateful to them for doing "Sailor Off the Bremen," especially since I'd already sent it off to *Esquire,* and had told *The New Yorker* the story wasn't for them. But the editors wormed it out of me, and both *Esquire* and *The New Yorker* chose it the same day, which put me in an ethical predicament, since to submit a manuscript to more than one publisher at a time in those days was considered immoral on the part of the writer. But I preferred at that moment to have it in *The New Yorker,* and that's what I did.

INTERVIEWERS: It's true, isn't it, that you wrote "Sailor Off the Bremen" and "The Girls in Their Summer Dresses," perhaps your most famous short stories, in one week? You were twenty-five. You wrote "The Girls in Their Summer Dresses" in one afternoon, I think you told me.

SHAW: Morning.

INTERVIEWERS: Morning. You left it on the kitchen table, and your wife, Marian, tossed it out the window.

SHAW: Well, that's not quite how it happened. We had one room up on the twenty-eighth floor of this hotel on Eighth Avenue, both busted. We were waiting for the rehearsals of *The Gentle People* to start. I wrote "The Girls in Their Summer Dresses" one morning while Marian was lying in bed and reading. And I knew I had something good there, but I didn't want her to read it, knowing that the reaction would be violent, to say the least, because it's about a man who tells his wife that he's going to be unfaithful to her. So I turned it facedown, and I said, "Don't read this yet. It's not ready." It was the only copy I had. Then I went out and took a walk, had a drink, and came back. She was raging around the room. She said, "It's a lucky thing you came back just now, because I was going to open the window and throw it out." Since then she's become reconciled to it, and I think she reads it with pleasure, too.

INTERVIEWERS: Could you tell us something about Harold Ross of *The New Yorker?*

SHAW: Ross pretended that he was a ruffian and an ignoramus, and he would send back my copy with all sorts of queries saying, "What does this mean? I can't find this word in the dictionary." But he only did it in the interest of clarity—he liked lucid prose—and I'd go in with Lobrano, the editor, mostly, and we'd fight it out. Sometimes Ross would say,

"Well, I don't understand this story at all, but if you guys like it so much, it's gonna be in."

He was a wonderful fellow and a very good friend and marvelous to be with, and I missed him enormously when he died. He could learn to change, which is why *The New Yorker* is still going strong after its dilettantish beginnings. When you think its first cover was the fop with the monocle looking at a butterfly, and they wound up publishing *In Cold Blood* by Truman Capote and *Hiroshima* by John Hersey, you can see the ability to grow that made Ross and made the magazine.

INTERVIEWERS: Do you see any change or progression in your own approach to fiction these days? What does one learn regarding technique, say, as one becomes older and more experienced? Does one stick to a formula that apparently works?

SHAW: Well, as you can see from the variety of things I've written, I haven't stuck to any formula. In a previous interview I said that when I was young, I tried to write each story, each play, each novel in the style suitable to the material and not in a style that could be recognized just as mine. However, that's a very hard purpose to fulfill. Most great writing in America and elsewhere, writers stick to the same style, like William Faulkner and Ernest Hemingway. But I wanted to be more various. That may have come about because of my training in the theater, where characters have to cut the umbilical cord from the writer and talk in their own voices. Of course, the master of that was James Joyce. He could sound like anybody, and did. But we're not all Joyces.

INTERVIEWERS: Do you have any general opinion about young writers starting off?

SHAW: So many young writers I've met are uneducated. They don't read. They don't read what started things . . . produced the trends. They don't know the classics. If they become enthusiastic, it's about someone like Kurt Vonnegut, who is uncopyable. If they try to copy him, they're in for disaster.

INTERVIEWERS: What words of advice would you offer them?

SHAW: Keep going. Writing is finally play, and there's no reason why you should get paid for playing. If you're a real writer, you write no matter what. No writer need feel sorry for himself if he writes and enjoys the writing, even if he doesn't get paid for it.

INTERVIEWERS: Why do writers protest so much that writing is no fun at all; why do they complain about the agonies of creation?

SHAW: I don't believe them. What do they do it for, then? Writing is like a contact sport, like football. Why do kids play football? They can get hurt on any play, can't they? Yet they can't wait until Saturday comes around so they can play on the high-school team, or the college team, and get smashed around. Writing is like that. You can get hurt, but you enjoy it.

WILLIE MORRIS
LUCAS MATTHIESSEN
Spring 1976

8. Kingsley Amis

Kingsley Amis was born in London on April 16, 1922. He studied at the City of London School, and at St. John's College, Oxford, from which he was graduated in 1949.

Although he never consciously decided to become a writer ("It just seemed to happen"), the publication of his first novel, *Lucky Jim* (1954), brought him both critical and popular recognition as one of postwar Britain's most promising young writers, as well as the Somerset Maugham Award. Another novel, *That Uncertain Feeling*, followed in 1955, and a poetry collection, *A Case of Samples*, appeared in 1956. An article in the *Spectator* in 1954 first identified him as a leading exponent—along with the poets Philip Larkin and John Wain—of a new literary style that stressed an anti-Romantic viewpoint and austerity of tone, and whose practitioners were sometimes collectively referred to as the Movement by English critics, even though no such formal group existed.

Amis's critics have noted that his subsequent works have slowly moved away from humor toward increasingly serious themes. He has written several critical and biographical studies, a book of short stories, and many novels, including *Take a Girl Like You* (1960), *One Fat Englishman* (1963), *The Anti-Death League* (1966), *Girl, 20* (1971), *Ending Up* (1974), and *Jake's Thing* (1979). Amis has also published an assortment of genre fiction: *Colonel Sun* (1968), a spy thriller; *The Green Man* (1969), a ghost story; and *The Riverside Villas Murder* (1973), a classic mystery story. His second book of poetry, *A Look Round the Estate*, was published in 1967, and his *Collected Poems 1944–1979* appeared in 1979.

Amis is currently an Honorary Fellow at St. John's College, Oxford University. Married to the novelist Elizabeth Jane Howard, he has two sons and a daughter from his first marriage. The Amises live in London.

11th April 1975 *Bell tolls a end* *3rd Edmund* *Where is John III buried, and when?* 1

Prologue
I
Hubert Anvil's voice rose above the sound of the choir and ~~the winding multitude of~~ full orchestra, reaching
the vertex
~~strings~~ of the loftiest dome in the Old World and the western doors of the longest

nave in Christendom. For this was the Cathedral Basilica of St George at Coverley, the

mother church of all England and of the English Empire overseas. That bright May morn-

ing it was as full as it had ever been in the three centuries since its consecration,

and it could scarcely have held a more distinguished assembly at any time: the young
Portugal
King William V himself; the kings of ~~Catalonia~~, of Naples, of Sweden, of Lithuania and

a dozen other realms; the Dauphin and the Crown Prince of Muscovy; the viceroys of

Brazil, India and New Spain, here after weeks of travelling; the brother of the Emper-
~~Prince High~~ *Emperor* *Beirut* ~~clergy who ranged~~
or of Almaigne; the Christian Delegate of the Sultan-Caliph of Turkey; the incumbent
the Vicar of the Pontiff of Constantinople, twelve and ~~from~~
Gilyanshi -Archbishop, Primate of United England, ~~and~~ no fewer than ~~eleven~~ cardinals, ~~in~~, less ~~six~~
pre-eminent ~~more~~ *besides*
~~mixed~~ clergy from all over the Catholic world—these and hundreds ~~of others~~ had con-
solemn
gregated for the ~~official~~ obsequies of His Most Devout Majesty, King John III of Eng-

land and her Empire.
He had been a good
~~The reigning and rightful~~-king, worthy of his title in matters of faith and observances,
mutually-respectful held in tender affection ~~dearly~~
enjoying ~~excellent~~ relations with both Convocation and the Papal Curie, ~~much loved~~ by
A large number
the people. ~~Many~~ of those attending his Requiem Mass would have been moved as much by

a sense of personal loss as by simple duty or the desire to assist at a great occas-
and
ion. Just as many, perhaps, were put in awe by the sizes ~~majesty and~~ richness of the
renowned
setting. Apart from Wren's magnificent dome, the most ~~celebrated~~ of the sights to be
in commemorating of
seen was the vast Turner ceiling ~~commemorating~~ the Holy Victory, the fruit of four and
there was nothing like it anywhere.
a half years' ~~of~~ virtually uninterrupted work. The western window by Gainsborough, be-
, mother of Constantine the Great,
ginning to blaze now as the sun caught it, showed the birth of St Helena at Colchest-
still-brilliant
er. Along the south wall ran Blake's frescoes depicting ~~the progress of~~ St Augustine's
progress ~~of light~~
/ through England. Holman Hunt's oil painting of the martyrdom of St George was less
tale
celebrated for its merits than for the ~~story~~ of the artist's journey to Palestine ~~with~~ in
hope
the ~~intention~~ of securing authenticity for his setting; and one of the latest addition

s, the Ecce Homo mosaic by David Hockney, had attracted downright adverse criticism
only
for its excessively traditionalist, almost archaising style. But ~~nothing but~~ admira-
,
tion had ever attended--to take a diverse selection--the William Morris spandrels on

A Kingsley Amis manuscript page.

Kingsley Amis

Kingsley Amis, the former Angry Young Man, lives in a large, early-nineteenth-century house beside a wooded common. To reach it, one makes a journey similar to that described by the narrator of Girl, 20 *when he visits Sir Roy Vandervane: first by tube to the end of the Northern Line at Barnet; then, following a phone call from the station to say where one is, on foot up a stiff slope; and finally down a suburban road. But instead of being picked up en route by Sir Roy's black chum, Gilbert, I was intercepted by Amis's tall and imposing blond wife, the novelist Elizabeth Jane Howard.*

Amis's study was a picture of bohemian disorder. Scattered across the floor were several teetering piles of poetry books and a mass of old 78 r.p.m. jazz records, while the big Adler typewriter on his desk was almost hidden behind a screen of empty bottles of sparkling wine which he'd recently sampled in his capacity as drink correspondent of Penthouse. *A more sober note was struck by some shelves containing a complete* Encyclopaedia Britannica, *a thirteen-volume* O.E.D., *and various other authoritative tomes, but this was quickly dispelled by the sight of a small sherry cask in one corner, full, I was told, of whisky.*

For someone whose only regular exercise is strolling to and from the local pub, Amis at fifty-three is well preserved, with just a modest paunch hinted at beneath the light blue pullover and brown slacks he was wearing when we met. Early photos show him with thick, wavy hair; it's gray now, but there's still plenty of it, conventionally styled, and only a little longer at the back and sides than it was twenty years ago. He has a mobile face that lends itself to the impersonations for which he is famous (and of which I caught a tantalizingly brief glimpse), and an educated but far from affected voice that reminds one at times of the actor Kenneth More. The interview did not take place in his study, but in a pleasant, book-lined sitting room with a prospect of the back lawn through lofty French windows. We talked for about two hours, from eleven-fifteen until one-fifteen, Amis perched on the edge of a sofa rather than sitting back in it so as not to aggravate a troublesome disk. He chose his words carefully, sometimes pausing to think things out, but rarely needing to rephrase an answer. At about midday he had a Scotch, which was replenished shortly before the interview closed.

INTERVIEWER: You've said that "until the age of twenty-four, I was in all departments of writing *abnormally unpromising.*" This suggests that you *were* trying to write before this.

AMIS: Oh, indeed yes. I've been trying to write for as long as I can remember. But those first fifteen years didn't produce much of great interest. I mean, it embarrasses me very much to look back on my early poems—very few lines of any merit at all and lots of affectation. But there were quite a lot of them. That's a point in one's favor, I think, to work these poisons out of one's system on paper: bad influences, like Dylan Thomas and Yeats—I'm not saying they're bad poets, but I do think they're bad influences, especially on a young writer. As regards prose, that was even worse. My first novel, which will never see the light of day, was really affectation from beginning to end —well, it did have a few jokes which I lifted for later stuff, and some bits of background from the town I was living in at the time, Berkhamsted, that were usable in *Take A Girl Like You*, many years later.

INTERVIEWER: Have you always had the capacity for making people laugh?

AMIS: I was the, or a, school wit at twelve years old. Well, not wit exactly—someone who could imitate the masters. I've always been a fair mimic; one of my party pieces is FDR as heard by the British over shortwave radio in 1940. This perhaps has something to do with writing fiction; a novelist is a sort of mimic by definition.

INTERVIEWER: Did the fact that you were an only child have any bearing on your development as a writer? Either the amount of reading you did, or the fact that you had to use your imagination more?

AMIS: I think it's . . . well, writing for me is to a large extent self-entertainment, and the only child is driven to do that. For example, I'm an expert whistler—I won't give you a sample— but that takes hours of practice, the sort of thing one hasn't got time for if one's part of a large family, I imagine. And as for reading, well, of course I got a lot done. Again, totally heterogeneous material, what we would now call very bad literature: the boys' comics of those days—which were, of course, compared with today's comics, positively Flaubertian in their style and Dickensian in their character portrayal—all the way up through hardbound books of adventure stories and such, and taking in real writers like Dickens himself, Shakespeare, and so on, in much the same sort of spirit. I think it's very important to read widely and in a wide spectrum of merit and ambition on the part of the writer. And ever since, I've always been interested in these less respectable forms of writing—the adventure story, the thriller, science fiction, and so on—and this is why I've produced one or two examples myself. I read somewhere recently somebody saying, "When I want to read a book, I write one." I think that's very good. It puts its finger on it, because there are never enough books of the kind one likes: one adds to the stock for one's own entertainment.

INTERVIEWER: Did you draw on your childhood memories for *The Riverside Villas Murder?*

AMIS: To some extent. None of the events: I wasn't lucky enough to be seduced by the pretty next-door neighbor, nor did I find a corpse in the sitting room. But the feeling and the adolescent attitudes were as close as I could remember to my own. The attitude to sex, to girls, to parents and school—that was all out of my emotional experience.

INTERVIEWER: You served in the Royal Signals in the war. Did *My Enemy's Enemy* owe anything to this?

AMIS: Well, as you know, there were three stories of army life. And the shortest one, "Court of Enquiry," was based on an experience of my own. I was the unfortunate Lieutenant Archer who was given a bad time by his company commander. But the other two stories were total fiction.

INTERVIEWER: Archer describes his vision of an acceptable postwar England as "as full of girls and drink and jazz and books and decent houses and decent jobs and being your own boss." Was this your England, too?

AMIS: Oh, yes, that's very much how I felt. And when I voted Labor by proxy in 1945, this is what I had in mind. I didn't expect the Government to bring me girls, but I did share in the general feeling of optimism and liberty abroad at that time.

INTERVIEWER: Did you publish anything before *Lucky Jim?*

AMIS: Right at the end of my Oxford stay I coedited *Oxford Poems 1949* with James Michie, and naturally got some of my own poems into that. But apart from poems and a review or two, I don't think there was anything.

INTERVIEWER: There still seem to be misconceptions about the origins of *Lucky Jim.* Am I right in saying that it wasn't based on Swansea University, where you were lecturing at the time?

AMIS: Yes. It was conceived, if that's the right word, way back in 1946, when I happened to visit Philip Larkin, who was on the library staff at Leicester University. The young man surrounded by bores whom for various reasons he doesn't dare to offend—that was all there. The contribution of Swansea, so to speak, was just to give me information about how things were run: what the faculty is, who the registrar is and what he does, what classes are like, what exam responsibilities are like, etcetera. But there's no character in the book, however minor, who was actually there at Swansea.

INTERVIEWER: Why was *Lucky Jim* such a long time coming?

AMIS: Well, being busy and being lazy, which so often go together, my first year at Oxford after the war was spent celebrating not being in the army. Then I had to work hard for my final exams. At Swansea it took me some time to get to grips with the heavy work load, and meanwhile there were also domestic responsibilities in the form of a wife and two young children who turned up very fast, one after the other. And another point was lack of a possible place to write in. The only requirement, I think, is a room to oneself, however small. Fortunately my wife received a small legacy and we got a house in Swansea which had such a room in it and *instantly* I began *Lucky Jim.* But that was a slow process: I had to redraft the whole thing. The first draft was very feeble, so I showed it to friends, particularly Philip Larkin again, who made very constructive suggestions. And then I started again from scratch, a thing I haven't done since. So it was not only delayed by external circumstances, but also, I think, by inexperience.

INTERVIEWER: I think it's difficult for anyone under thirty today to see Jim as a true rebel, despite what he may have appeared then.

AMIS: Yes, well, rebellion escalates, doesn't it? My father thought that he, my father, was a rebel. Though of course by the time I was taking any notice of his views, he was as stolidly conservative, not to say reactionary, as anybody I've ever met. And it's true that Jim's rebelliousness is by any standards mild, certainly by today's standards. But then I think the degree to which he was intended to be seen by the author as a rebel has been exaggerated. He didn't want to change the System. He certainly didn't want to *destroy* the System.

INTERVIEWER: He wanted to be his own man?

AMIS: Yes. He didn't like the bits of the System that were immediately in his neighborhood, that was all. If he had happened to be in the music department, the professor of which is sympathetically portrayed, I think he'd have had a very different time.

INTERVIEWER: What was your reaction to being called an Angry Young Man?

AMIS: Mixed. I mean, no writer, especially a young and unknown writer, resents publicity of any kind—whatever he may say. I'm sure I didn't. But the other side of that was being lumped together with some very strange people. Again, not that I'm denigrating them. But all of us in that nonexistent Movement—which is really only a string of names—felt that, I think. But this is what literary journalists have to do, don't they? Discern trends and groups even when there isn't much of a trend, and nothing in the way of a group.

INTERVIEWER: Do you think it's ironic that many of the so-called Angries like William Cooper, John Wain, John Braine, and yourself were writing in a traditional style?

AMIS: Yes, there was certainly no rebelliousness at all of treatment or presentation. And we were, in that sense, reactionaries rather than rebels. We were trying to get back, let's say, to the pre-Joyce tradition, really—but not very consciously. It's always dangerous to suppose that what looks in retrospect like something planned, something willed, was actually planned at the time. This is all a matter of instinct, of feeling. But there was a general resemblance to that degree.

INTERVIEWER: What are your own feelings about experimental prose?

AMIS: I can't bear it. I dislike, as I think most readers dislike, being in the slightest doubt about what is taking place, what is meant. I don't want full and literal descriptions of everything, and I'm prepared to take a hint from the author as well as the next man, but I dislike mystification. Part two about experiment, I'd say, is that it's usually thought of as entirely to do with style and intelligibility. But there are other forms. I mean after all, can't one have experiments in mixing farce and horror, comedy and seriousness . . . ?

INTERVIEWER: As you've tried to do?

AMIS: Yes, though I wouldn't call myself an experimental writer, because it has this other connotation. But *The Green Man,* for example, in its modest way, was a kind of experiment. I mean, "Can a ghost story be combined with a reasonably serious study of human relations, in this case the problem of selfishness?" The alcoholism is part of that, but the central figure there, Allington, finds himself becoming more and more insecure because he doesn't really take any notice of other people. And the result is that by undergoing these harrowing experiences he at last notices his young daughter, and talks to her in a way that he hasn't done before. So at the price of losing his wife and making an utter fool of himself, he's at last made contact with another person, so one feels in that sense hopeful about his future.

INTERVIEWER: Why are you so unhappy with your third novel, *I Like It Here?*

AMIS: Well, it was written partly out of bad motives. Seeing that *That Uncertain Feeling* had come out in 1955, and it was now 1957 and there was no novel on the way, I really cobbled it together out of straightforwardly autobiographical experiences in Portugal, with a kind of mystery story rather perfunctorily imposed on that. The critics didn't like it, and I don't blame them really. I had a look at it the other day and parts of it are not too bad. But it's really a very slipshod, lopsided piece of work.

INTERVIEWER: There's one passage in the book that I'd like to use as a cue: the reference to Fielding as "the only non-contemporary novelist who could be read with unaffected and wholehearted interest." Why do you dismiss the vast majority of the classics like this?

AMIS: Well, this is a hard one. I mean, I know that I should read them more, and I know enough about the classics to know what I'm missing. But . . . it's a question of what one is reading for. And if I read the classics that I haven't read, it would be out of a sense of duty. It's not that I don't admire many of the classics, but it's a distant and rather too respectful admiration.

INTERVIEWER: Did having to teach English literature exacerbate this?

AMIS: No, in a way it had the opposite effect. Being forced by the syllabus to read all those unread people was good—I got a lot of entertainment out of it, and I found out a lot. Again, one can't say this had any direct effect on what I wrote.

INTERVIEWER: What is it about Fielding that you like?

AMIS: Well, I describe it to some extent in the passage you mention. Apart from his wit, and, I think, attractive though sometimes heavy irony, he seems to be very concerned not to bore the reader, to keep the narrative going along. And he was great enough to transcend the conventional love story current at his time—well, not transcend exactly, but to write very well and understandably and very deeply within that set of conventions, and I can't think of any other writer who could do that.

INTERVIEWER: Which twentieth-century writers have influenced you?

AMIS: Well, there's the early Joyce, P. G. Wodehouse, Evelyn Waugh, Anthony Powell, Elizabeth Taylor, and early Angus Wilson among novelists. And poets . . . oh, Hardy I admire, but don't feel very warm to—A. E. Housman, Philip Larkin, John Betjeman, the early R. S. Thomas, parts of Robert Frost, parts of Robert Graves, some poems by Yeats. It's not a complete list—in fact I was once worried by this, that I couldn't name more than a dozen admired contemporaries. But I mentioned it to Robert Graves, and he said, "Nonsense. You ought to be concerned if you admire *more* than that number. It shows you have no discrimination." Which is a good point!

INTERVIEWER: Waugh was quoted in *The Paris Review* as saying that writing for him was an exercise in the use of language rather than an attempt to explore character. How do you react to this?

AMIS: I've come to see it in that way more and more. I certainly feel that this is what I'm trying to do. But I think this is connected—and trying not to sound too somber here—with growing older. Because the world that seemed so various and new, well, it does contract. One's burning desire to investigate human behavior, and to make, or imply, statements about it, does fall off. And so one does find that early works are full of energy and also full of vulgarity, crudity, and incompetence, and later works are more carefully finished, and in that sense better literary products. But . . . there's often a freshness that is missing in later works—for every gain there's a loss. I think it evens out in that way.

INTERVIEWER: You've described the creation of characters as "a mysterious process." Can you enlarge on that?

AMIS: Yes, well, the whole thing *is* mysterious, and it's interesting that writers with very different approaches all say this as soon as you ask them. They say: "The thoughts that I have are not mine. My works are not my own." And so on. . . . The development of character is a sort of by-product of the development of the central idea. I always start with a situation which may occur to one. Or you may see an example of it in what's around you, and things grow out of that. With *Lucky Jim,* for instance, the situation was this young man surrounded by all these hostile powers, and there was a ready-made setting which seemed to fit this situation. And as soon as one has got this far, a lot of options become closed. With a woman who is a sort of sexual bore, who covers about a third of Jim's life, we're on the road to the kind of person that the character Margaret has got to be. And since the story would be finished if, in the second chapter, Jim said, "Look, leave me alone. Go away," we *can't* have him say that, he must have reasons for not saying that. And so that develops the cowardly, or if you like, decent side of his character. And this happens all the way along in my experience. When you think you're inventing, what you're really doing is following up the implications of your original idea.

INTERVIEWER: I think Waugh said he used suddenly to find his characters taking to drink, or surprising him in other ways.

AMIS: Yes, well, this would fall into place later. Graham Greene said he would find an episode or a character turning up after the first ten thousand words which he had no idea how to use. But then thirty thousand words later it would come up. And experience had taught him never to destroy what he had written, because it would always be fitted into the design later.

INTERVIEWER: Do you keep a notebook?

AMIS: Yes, but it's not a very fat notebook. It contains things like scraps of dialogue that one overhears or thinks of . . . very short descriptions of characters . . . comic incidents seen, or conceivably invented. But I don't write synopses. I used to at one time. I mean, I kept a very thick and detailed notebook for *Take A Girl Like You*—about a hundred pages. But I think that was partly nervousness, because I knew that its theme, and using a female protagonist, was going to put a severe strain on my resources. And I was limbering up, as it were, to write that.

INTERVIEWER: I came across an echo of Graham's speech to Jenny on the barrier between the attractive and the unattractive in a recent article about Joe Ackerley.* Apparently, E. M. Forster once made the same complaint to Ackerley, who was very handsome as a young man.

AMIS: Really? Yes, well, that idea—the division into two nations of the attractive and the unattractive—had been in my mind, as it were independently, for many years. And then the time came, quite suddenly, without realizing it: here was the moment to put these ideas into a character's mouth.

INTERVIEWER: Roger Micheldene, the hero of *One Fat Englishman*, describes America as "a semi-permanent encampment of a nation of parvenus." Was that your own reaction?

AMIS *(laughs)*: No, not at all. I think the pro- and anti-American stuff hasn't, if I may say so, been properly understood. What I was doing was knocking *British* anti-Americanism, and I thought, Put all the usual tired old arguments into the mouth of a very unsympathetic character. I thought this was quite a good way of showing up all those British attitudes. But I must have muffed it somewhere along the line because American reviewers fell into two classes: one lot said, "Mr. Amis makes some shrewd hits on the deficiencies in our culture." And they were meant to be very unshrewd hits. Others said, half rightly, "Mr. Amis's objections to American life are very old hat. If they were ever accurate, they no longer are so. It's all been done better by American writers." Well, that's true, except that they got the name wrong. Roger Micheldene's objections were all of those things.

INTERVIEWER: Roger really is a shit of the first water—in the same league as Bertrand Welch and Bernard Bastable. Do you enjoy creating such characters?

AMIS: Yes. Well, it's very hard to dislike them. I think it was Christopher Ricks, reviewing *One Fat Englishman*, who said,

*J. R. Ackerley was literary editor of the *Listener* from 1935 to 1959.

after listing Roger's appalling deficiencies, "Nevertheless, one can't help feeling that the author liked the character. I did too." Of course I like him. After all, life tells us all the time that it's possible to like the people that you violently disapprove of—not only from a moral pinnacle—but would hate to find yourself involved with. But nevertheless, I can't help feeling that I'd quite enjoy a couple of drinks with Roger.

INTERVIEWER: Irving Macher, the young novelist, is a pretty nasty piece of work, too.

AMIS: Yes.

INTERVIEWER: I'd like to use him as a cue for a digression on American novelists. You've said, "Not one of them has succeeded in establishing an oeuvre." Isn't that rather a sweeping statement?

AMIS *(aggressively):* Yeah? . . . Well, I'd like to hear *your* candidates for that position.

INTERVIEWER: Well *(pause)* how about Gore Vidal?

AMIS: Yes, well, it may be laziness, but on the rare occasions when I do pick up Vidal, whose early books I enjoyed before he was as celebrated as he is now, he seems to me to suffer from American cleverness: the fear of being thought stupid, or dull, or behind the times. I think that's a very bad attitude for the novelist to adopt. He must not mind being thought boring and pompous from time to time—let's hope he avoids it, but if he runs too far in the opposite direction, he's heading for disaster.

INTERVIEWER: Perhaps we should concentrate on the phrase "establish an oeuvre," which does at least allow that there might have been some very good American novels written.

AMIS: Oh yes, indeed. Individual books, and two or three books or more by many American novelists. But the enemies are smartness, and in many cases, the desire to be American. And being American is, I think, a very difficult thing in art, because all the elements are European, and to give them a distinctive American stamp is something you can't *try* to do— it can only be hoped that in the end this will emerge. The lure of the Great American Novel—it's no longer, perhaps, the *Great* American Novel, because that sounds like the dull, or traditional, American novel—but the Important, the Significant, the New, the most American American Novel . . . I think that marsh light is still burning hard.

INTERVIEWER: By the time *One Fat Englishman* came out, you'd shifted from Swansea to Cambridge. Was it Dr. Leavis who said that Peterhouse had given a fellowship to a pornographer?

AMIS: So I was told, yes.

INTERVIEWER: But wasn't that all wrong? Because in fact you're not at all explicit about sex.

AMIS: I wouldn't have thought so. I mean, I have to follow my own rule of always letting readers know what's taking place. But with regard to sexual matters, not in detail. The reader should know whether it took place or not, whether it was a success or not, and what they felt about it. But anybody who can get sexual titillation out of my sex scenes must be very easily stimulated. I shy away from explicit sex mainly because it's socially embarrassing. The comparison I usually draw is with being told these things by an acquaintance—and after all, the novelist is only an acquaintance, isn't he, as far as the reader's concerned?—and to be told in detail what he's been up to for over half an hour—the equivalent of a chapter, say —would be embarrassing, wouldn't it? *I* would find it embarrassing.

INTERVIEWER: Your next novel, *The Anti-Death League*, was something of a watershed. I think you announced that you were no longer content just to do straightforward social comedy. Was this because, as somebody suggested, you weren't being taken seriously because you were funny?

AMIS: Who knows? When starting to think about any novel, part of the motive is: I'm going to show them, this time. Without that, a lot of what passes under the name of creative energy would be lost. It's an egotistical self-assertion, if you like

—the mere act of writing a book is that. And it may well be that my feeling when thinking of *The Anti-Death League* was, to some extent, I'm going to show them that I can be overtly serious. And this did mystify some of the critics. One rang up in some agitation and said, "Can I come see you? I've just read your new book, and I'm not happy about it." I thought, Oh, dear. So I said, "Come along by all means." I wondered what he wanted—and he had to do this by a series of hints, clearing his throat a great deal—and what it turned out to be was: Was I serious? Or was it all an elaborate farce or irony, couched in the form of some supposedly serious story? So I reassured him: I said, "It's all right. Don't worry. The serious parts in that *are* serious." "Right," he said, and gave the thing a favorable notice. The idea that what's funny can't be serious dies hard, but I think it's dying because of *Catch-22*, Evelyn Waugh, and so on.

INTERVIEWER: I wondered whether *The Anti-Death League* might have owed something to the changes in your own life at that time.

AMIS: I think that alterations in your own life *may* have an immediate effect on a book. But I think much more usually these things are delayed. What happens in *The Anti-Death League* had been brewing inside me for a long time, the result of realizing that one isn't going to be young forever, and noticing more and more that there is pain and sorrow in the world. And again, ceasing to be young, that there are certain fundamental questions to be answered. I mean, the answer to them all may be *"No. Nothing."* But they've got to be answered, and the novelist naturally answers them for himself in fiction.

INTERVIEWER: Doesn't *The Anti-Death League* contain some of your favorite characters: James Churchill? Brian Leonard?

AMIS: Yes. Max Hunter, Ayscue, and Moti Naidu—

INTERVIEWER: Oh, him too?

AMIS: Yes, in fact he's the favorite of all of them. The

novelist always has favorites, and often he's a minor character, as in this case. And Naidu is the one I admire most. He's the one who has the right attitudes. I'm no mystic. I'm certainly no Buddhist or Hindu thinker, because being a Westerner I don't understand any of that. But when Naidu makes his plea to Churchill, saying that Churchill's withdrawal is a selfish escape, and he's *not* thinking of his girl friend but of himself; and that his enemy is, as he puts it, "bad feelings of all descriptions" which he must try to put away; and that everybody must try to become a man, he is as near to being the author's voice as anybody usually is in one of my novels.

INTERVIEWER: You also kill off L. S. Caton.

AMIS: Well, I was running out of things to do with L. S. Caton, and this was a good place to get rid of him because he clearly had no place in that novel at all. So I brought him in and had him shot. I mean, I thought it was a good idea to have somebody shot, and what better candidate than he?

INTERVIEWER: *Colonel Sun* seemed to underline your preference for genre fiction over the mainstream novel. Is this because you believe that, say, writers like Eric Ambler, Gavin Lyall, and Geoffrey Household are achieving more within their spheres than many straightforward novelists?

AMIS: Well, I start from the same place as the genre writers start from: they cannot afford to bore me, and I cannot stand being bored, so we begin at the same place. And they have all sorts of things forced on them: some sort of pace, a feeling of conflict, climaxes, anticlimaxes, suspense, and so on. They have to do that. And having done that, they can then erect other matters.

INTERVIEWER: Do you think it's easier to strip away the facades of characters when they're in situations of suspense?

AMIS: Oh, yes. That's the old, well-tried, and valuable lever that such writers have always used: put people into conditions of extremity of some sort, and you won't find out *all* about them, but you'll get to the inside of them quicker than you would in the "drawing room, gin, and Jaguar" type of novel.

INTERVIEWER: Do you keep an ideal reader in mind when you write?

AMIS: Not really, except as regards clarity. Occasionally I say to my wife, "This is what I mean, does what I've written convey it?"

INTERVIEWER: Can writing—humor particularly—be directed by any sort of formula?

AMIS: No, none. I was going to say, "Be unexpected." But then noncomic writing must do that too. And "Be expected" is an important rule too. It's a letdown if the comedian doesn't finally actually really sit on his hat.

INTERVIEWER: You've mentioned science fiction. What is it about it that attracts you?

AMIS: To start with, as always, something rather simple and perhaps even childish. Because I was attracted to it as a lad on sensational grounds: grounds of excitement, wonder—as they always say—and a liking for the strange, the possibly horrific. That's the beginning. And then of course as science fiction came out of the pure monster and robot phase and started to do other things, it became a very efficient vehicle for both social satire, and for investigation of the human character in a different way from the straightforward novel: humanity's character considered as a single thing, rather than the characters of individual beings reacting on one another. Of course many science-fiction writers aren't equipped to tackle these rather grand themes, but I think it might well happen. So in one way science fiction is more ambitious than the novel we're used to, because these great abstractions can be discussed: immortality, how we feel about the future, what the future means to us, and how much even we're at the mercy of what's happened in the past. All these things it can do.

INTERVIEWER: Is it fair to see *I Want It Now* as an attack on the rich?

AMIS *(laughs):* Well, some rich. That's so to speak the vehicle of what the novel is trying to say. It's about power, to some extent, and responsibility. And certain kinds of rich people are notorious for the way they wield power without responsibility. But if you were to ask, "How did you think up *I Want It Now?*" I'd say it began like this: after spending the evening with some very unpleasant rich people in Tennessee, my wife said, "Just think what it would be like to be Mabel's daughter" —Mabel hadn't got a daughter—and I thought, *Yes.* And so I tried to imagine what it would be like. And then clearly there would have to be a character who was going to come and take her away from this situation, and since he was going to do a kind of Sleeping Beauty operation on her, he must not be at all attractive—at least superficially. So where do we find energetic people who are not at all attractive to all appearances, though with a surface charm and so on? *Television!* And that is what I meant earlier by one's options being closed by the nature of the central situation. "What would it be like to be Mabel's daughter?" Well, that fixes Mabel. That fixes her daughter. It fixes the hero/liberator character. It fixes his environment, and it also fixes his relations with the people alongside him in television. And then the satellites of the rich woman also fall into place. So an awful lot seems suddenly to have been done for you—I mean, you've done it all yourself, but it feels as if it's suddenly emerged.

INTERVIEWER: This book also contains another of your favorite characters, doesn't it?

AMIS: Oh yes, George Parrott—again a minor character— who switches from being the hero's sworn enemy, to being his unwilling and highly critical ally, rather than his friend. I enjoyed making George up a lot, and had to exercise "artistic restraint" to avoid letting him run away with me. But he began merely as a plot device. Somebody had to give a little bit of help at a critical juncture, and somebody earlier had to appear as a kind of bogeyman and the kind of rich suitor that the heroine was used to receiving. Well, to save on the cost, as it were, those have got to be the same chap. Oh, and he also had to give the hero some information, and it was really that, I suppose, which made him develop. Because if a character is to impart essential information, and to have to spend two or three pages doing so, then clearly to avoid boring the reader if possible, the author's got to take a lot of trouble with that character's conversational style and try to make it internally amusing, as well as merely a vehicle for conveying the essential information. So Parrott's style of expression had to be eccentric, which again gives the character more depth, I suppose.

INTERVIEWER: As you said earlier, Maurice Allington, the hero of *The Green Man,* is an alcoholic. Can we talk about drink—

AMIS: Sure, anytime—

INTERVIEWER: Specifically, the part it plays in your novels, and, if relevant, the part it plays in your creative life?

AMIS: Yes. Well, as far as my books are concerned, it's a device that corresponds to the thriller writer's lever of being able to strip a character rather bare quite quickly and fairly plausibly. I don't say that the drunk man is the real man, and the sober man merely a shell. But you find out something different about people when they're drunk. Of course, you sometimes find that they're not different at all—that you merely get more of the same, perhaps said rather more loudly and incoherently, but basically the same. Other people change. Allington's alcoholism—or near-alcoholism, because he's still able to run his life and the inn—was a plot detail that occurred to me very early. I don't think it had been done before: ghosts that are seen only by an alcoholic, and so can be dismissed as delirium, or fancies, or even as lies. So it had that function, as well.

INTERVIEWER: I think you've also said that pubs have a special role in your books.

AMIS: This is very much a thing in my own life as well. The pub is the great piece of neutral territory, for which there are rules, as there are in other parts of social life, but they're rather different rules. And of course some kinds of people dislike pubs. Others expand in the most extraordinary way when they find themselves in one. The obligations are different, and the relations between the people are changed. There's one small revelation in *I Want It Now* when there's a pub scene right at the end. It concerns Lord Baldock, whom we've thought of as a very stuffy person and one of the rich up to now. In the pub, it's noted, he seems to be able to find his way to the bar with no trouble at all. Again, a very small, mini-revelation about him, but perhaps the reader feels, well, we would have liked to have known a bit more about him, as seen in a pub setting.

INTERVIEWER: Does drink play any part in your creative life?

AMIS: Well, it may play an adverse part. . . .

INTERVIEWER: Presumably you can't write when you've drunk too much?

AMIS: No, there comes a fairly early point when the stimulating effect turns into an effect that produces disorder and incoherence. But I find writing very nervous work. I'm always in a dither when starting a novel—that's the worst time. It's like going to the dentist, because you do make a kind of appointment with yourself. And this is one of the things I've learnt to recognize more and more with experience: that you realize it's got to be . . . next week. Not today—but if you don't sit down by the end of next week, it'll go off the boil slightly. Well, it can't be next Wednesday, because somebody from *The Paris Review* is coming to interview you, so it had better be Thursday. And then, quaking, you sit down at the typewriter. And that's when a glass of Scotch can be very useful as a sort of artistic icebreaker . . . artificial infusion of a little bit of confidence which is necessary in order to begin at all. And then each day's sitting down is still rather tense, though the tension goes away as the novel progresses, and when the end is even distantly in sight, the strain becomes small, though it's always there. So alcohol in moderate amounts and at a fairly leisurely speed is valuable to me—at least I think so. It could be that I could have written better without it . . . but it could also be true that I'd have written far less without it.

INTERVIEWER: Do you have a daily routine?

AMIS: Yes. I don't get up very early. I linger over breakfast reading the papers, telling myself hypocritically that I've got to keep up with what's going on, but really staving off the dreadful time when I have to go to the typewriter. That's probably about ten-thirty, still in pyjamas and dressing gown. And the agreement I have with myself is that I can stop whenever I like and go and shave and shower and so on. In practice, it's not till about one or one-fifteen that I do that—I usually try and time it with some music on the radio. Then I emerge, and nicotine and alcohol are produced. I work on until about two or two-fifteen, have lunch, then if there's urgency about, I have to write in the afternoon, which I really hate doing—I really dislike afternoons, whatever's happening. But then the agreement is that it doesn't matter how little gets done in the afternoon. And later on, with luck, a cup of tea turns up, and then it's only a question of drinking more cups of tea until the bar opens at six o'clock and one can get into second gear. I go on until about eight-thirty and I always hate stopping. It's not a question of being carried away by one's creative afflatus, but saying, "Oh dear, next time I do this I shall be feeling tense again."

INTERVIEWER: What are the pitfalls in writing humor?

AMIS: There's one obvious one: you must never make one character laugh at what another says or does. Dornford Yates's "Berry" novels, which are quite good fun in a sedate sort of way, are ruined by everybody collapsing with merriment whenever Berry shows up. The other pitfall is: you must never offer the reader anything simply *as* funny and nothing more. Make it acceptable as information, comment, narrative, etcetera, so that if the joke flops the reader has still got *something*. Wodehouse understood this perfectly, even better than Shakespeare did.

INTERVIEWER: Do you revise as you go?

AMIS: Yes. A page takes me quite a long time. Two pages a day is good. Three pages is splendid.

INTERVIEWER: Is that foolscap?

AMIS: No, it's quarto more. So it's about a thousand words, probably.

INTERVIEWER: Do you compare notes with your wife?

AMIS: Oh yes, we consult each other all the time. And if neither of us is up against some hideous deadline, we read work in progress to each other at the end of the day. We both find this very valuable. You know: "How should I convey this difficult information? Is it plausible that he should say that?" You can get reassurance, or you can get criticism or other suggestions. But I'm sure reading aloud's awfully important, anyway. I think both of us get quite as much from ourselves from these readings as we get from the other person. And I was interested to see that Kipling, whom I've been working on recently, used to read his work aloud to himself, too. And I would guess—he doesn't say so—with much the same objective in mind: to find stylistic weaknesses.

INTERVIEWER: Presumably your wife is an exception to your rule about modern women novelists being generally unreadable?

AMIS: Yes indeed she is. I would have put her on my list of modern novelists I read. If she weren't an exception, I could never have married her—a lot of people fail to see that.

INTERVIEWER: What is it you dislike most about women novelists?

AMIS: Well, I think it's a little unfair to them and to me to say "women novelists" like that.

INTERVIEWER: *Some* women novelists, then. I think you've disparaged the NW1 syndrome.

AMIS: Yes, the NW1 novel*—I suppose it's a handy term. Well, it's dressed-up autobiography, autobiography in fiction that is what I basically object to, because it's very rare for life to present one with a story, merely a repetitious account of a situation: things getting a little worse—generally a little worse —and sometimes a little better, and conflict seems to be omitted, and there's no sense of purpose on the part of the characters or the part of the author. I like to feel when beginning a novel that some problem is being presented, some choice is necessary, something's got to be worked to. . . .

INTERVIEWER: The funny way Roy talks in *Girl, 20* underlined for me the lengths you go to make dialogue sound authentic. All those "sort of's" and "you know's."

AMIS: Well, dialogue's a very powerful weapon, isn't it? Again, traditionally the novelist has to characterize people quite quickly by the way they talk: their various idioms, whether they talk plainly, or in a flowery style. But I do find dialogue quicker to write than narrative—narrative I always find rather painful. Dialogue is more fun . . . but I always try over the phrases, fooling the reader into believing that this is how people actually talk. In fact, inevitably, it's far more coherent than any actual talk. I don't say I succeed all that often, but when in doubt I will repeat a phrase to myself seven or eight times, trying to put myself in the place of an actor speaking the part. And all these "I mean's" and "sort of's" and "you know's" are important because there are characters who find it difficult to lay their tongues on what they mean the first time, and I think this should be indicated.

INTERVIEWER: I couldn't help liking Roy in spite of everything.

AMIS: Oh, I'm very fond of Roy. Again, one can't write a

---

*Amis's description of the environs of an NW1 novel is as follows: "A postal area of (North-west) London inhabited partly by intellectuals, trendies, weedies, fashionable journalists, and media men."

whole book about someone one doesn't like. It overlaps a great deal with boredom: the novelist can't write about somebody that bores him. And the fact that he won't bore you, I hope, with what he says, makes him, to some extent, sympathetic immediately. One would hate to fall within the circle of Roy's responsibilities—irresponsibility is what the book's really about —but one couldn't think of a better chap to have a boozy lunch with.

INTERVIEWER: There's a lot about music in the book. I believe it's very important to you.

AMIS: Yes, I would put music slightly ahead of literature. I think a world without music would be worse than a world without books—I don't know whether a world without literature, exactly. But I've always responded to it in an uneducated sort of way—I've done some half-hearted attempts at semi-self-education. And I find it a necessity. I find it—what can one say?—refreshing and uplifting.

INTERVIEWER: Would you have liked to have been a musician?

AMIS: Yes. Of course one always has these fantasies about how if things had been different, what other paths one might have pursued. But music would be the first one I would choose if suddenly set down at the age of twelve. One reason is a sort of personal social one that musicians cannot function on their own—even if they're concert pianists playing a piano recital.

INTERVIEWER: Is this why you like writing for television? The need to work with others?

AMIS: Yes, I think it's probably the main motive. Another motive, of course, is trying to do something you haven't done before. Seeing if you can broaden your talent, which is a thing I've always thought necessary.

INTERVIEWER: Flexing new muscles?

AMIS: Yes. And the other thing, as you say, is working with others. Of course, if it doesn't go well, it's disastrous, and you say, "Why did I ever leave the typewriter to get involved with these people and have my sovereign wishes frustrated?" But when it goes well, it's very exciting.

INTERVIEWER: What do you like about journalism?

AMIS: Well, I like a task. I like being forced to read a book occasionally. And there's still some very, very minor literary critic inside my head, and there's still something of a teacher, too. It's a habit that's hard to get out of. And again, it's a change.

INTERVIEWER: All part of the business of entertaining yourself, as well?

AMIS: Yes. And there are also opportunities for stating some critical point you don't think has been emphasized enough.

INTERVIEWER: I thought your last novel, *Ending Up*, was very bleak.

AMIS: Yes, well, no book is the author's last word on any subject or expresses what he feels all the time. So if I were to walk under a bus this afternoon, then *Ending Up* would be my last novel, and people might say, "Well, he ended in a fit of pessimism and gloom." This wouldn't really be so. Each novel can only represent a single mood, a single way of looking at the world, and one feels bleak from time to time, and takes a fairly pessimistic view of one's own future and chances. But there are other times when one doesn't, and out of that other books would emerge.

INTERVIEWER: I think you've said it was partly inspired by the communal setup you have here, with relatives and friends living in?

AMIS: Yes. The starting point is so often: What would happen if . . . ? In this case, What would it be like if we were all old and all, or some of us, handicapped to some degree? It was a kind of purposeful exaggeration of what is only slightly present or potentially present in existing circumstances.

INTERVIEWER: Did you know that Mencken had had nominal aphasia when you wrote the book?

AMIS: No. That happened because a friend of mine suffered

from this mildly. It's cleared up now, and he's a close enough friend for me to ask him, "Do you mind if I exaggerate this?" "Not at all," he said, "if you think you can get a laugh out of it." I'm surprised that nobody's done it before.

INTERVIEWER: What are you doing at the moment? Is there any work in progress?

AMIS: Well, you find me at a time when that dreaded Thursday week, or something of the sort, is on the horizon. I've got quite a lot of a book in my head, yes, and this will be a sort of science fiction of the sort where the author proposes some change back in history, and deals with the results of that change. In this case, if the Reformation had never taken place. Then make the date 1976, say, when the book will probably come out, and show a different England and a different world.

INTERVIEWER: I gather you're also compiling the *Oxford Book of Light Verse?*

AMIS: Yes, I've done a bit of work on that already. It means that I shall virtually have to read the whole of English poetry in a decreasingly ample length of time, but I'll enjoy that because it's something to do in the afternoon.

INTERVIEWER: Could we just close with a summary of what really motivates you as a novelist?

AMIS: Well, as I've said before, self-entertainment is one thing. Another is feeling—I'm sorry, I can't help sounding pretentious here—feeling that this is what I've been designed to do . . . that I'd be failing in my duty to who knows what if I didn't go on producing writing of certain sorts. I don't feel any particular duty to the public. But a different matter, really, is duty to the reader, which determines not whether you shall write, but *how* you write. I don't think I've ever written anything that is designed purely as a sop to the reader: I don't put in bits of sex to increase sales. But I always bear him in mind, and try to visualize him and watch for any signs of boredom or impatience to flit across the face of this rather shadowy being, the Reader.

(I was busy packing up my gear when Amis said he would like to add an important postscript to his final answer.)

AMIS: And then of course there's always vanity. You remember that Orwell said, when he was answering his own question, why I write, that his leading motive was the desire to be thought clever, to be talked about by people he had never met. I don't think he was being arrogant, I think he was being very honest.

MICHAEL BARBER
Winter 1975

9. James Dickey

James Dickey, the son of a suburban Atlanta attorney, was born on February 2, 1923. He joined the air force after his freshman year at Clemson University, flying over one hundred combat missions during the Second World War, and he later described this experience as a kind of seasoning: "I look on existence from the standpoint of a survivor." He has also attributed his initial interest in writing to the war and the long hours between missions.

After the war Dickey returned to school and subsequently received an M.A. in English from Vanderbilt University. While teaching English at Rice University, Dickey began publishing his poetry in the *Sewanee Review,* the *Atlantic, Partisan Review,* and *Harper's.* Another tour of duty during the Korean War, a year-long European sabbatical, additional teaching posts, and six years in the advertising business preceded the publication of his first poetry collection, *Into the Stone and Other Poems* (1960), which gave his literary career its decisive push forward. In 1965 his volume of poetry *Buckdancer's Choice* won both the Melville Cane Award and the National Book Award. The following year he was appointed to succeed Stephen Spender as consultant in poetry to the Library of Congress. Dickey's other books of poetry include *Drowning With Others* (1962), *Helmets* (1964), the prose poem *Jericho* (1974), *The Zodiac* (1976), *God's Images* (1977), and *The Strength of Fields* (1979), the title poem of which he delivered at the inauguration of President Jimmy Carter in 1976. He is also the author of a volume of poetry criticism, *Babel to Byzantium* (1968), as well as of the novel *Deliverance,* which he later adapted for the popular motion picture.

Poet-in-Residence and professor of English at the University of South Carolina, Columbia, since 1969, Dickey lives with his second wife, Deborah Dobson. He has two sons and a grandson.

Falling

Transcontinental   low moon   the states are dark   each successively
as dark as the last. There is some leak of air somewhere in the cabin
And someone is disturbed. In her blue uniform, there near the galley
With racks of trays, she gets a blanket, and begins to pin it up
over the faint ear-whistle of air coming in from the darkness.
Then she is in total dark and cold. The door blew out   and she found
Herself with her arms and legs in the killing dark and her cry   one
Long way turning to wind. Can this be me   here in this place turning
in myself   feeling around me the flutter   of garments   in this
Cold of God   and yet I am spaced some way or other   on air   I can
Flare my hands and feet in it   death is still three or four miles
Down   it is not so cold as it was   but cold. I have try to look
At everything in the dark. There are lights   a highway   towns
And there the glitter of water   the moon racing slowly through
The curves of a river   a lake opens its eye   the darks change
Throughout the enormous air. I can spread my legs   and my skirt
Catches on the air   I can circle until there is little there is no
Sense of falling   but flight   (delicately) maintained   the air whistles
faintly but I am suspended between earth and heaven   the plane I was
on is probably landing in Chicago   I have been falling for hours
It is warmer   I can see the shape of the continent   lose its
Shape   If I fell into water I might live   so let me begin
To plane across the air in my jacket and skirt   moving like an owl
Across the space of midnight   toward the glitter of water   It is
a journey through the uncreated   through chaos   where nothing
Holds   Here is a usual young woman flying upon the dark like a goddess
Heading for the slowly opening eye   of water   cross-country
Cross-country through the country of the air   possessing for an
Instant the continent as a diess would possess it   travelling above the
Heads of sleepers on farms   the hawmows sharpening as I pass over
Them   the boys' penises rising   the farm girls feeling the goddess
In them brooding on the four boats of the beds   dreaming of fire
Of comets and javelin fireworks   a great woman scrawled in stars
Overhead in the calm night   and will wake to see a woman   struggling
the stars struggling to become a woman. Water is nearer and now I am
Over but cannot fall into it   I am streaking like a jet in my jet
Stewardess's uniform And the ground is closer   the dark
Cufielda a total dark and I have just time to fling off my one
Shoe   to pull off my stockings   It is abnormally easy to undress
Tumbling   I can assume any position the air has to offer   take off
The sad wings of my jacket   the bat's guiding leather of my skirt
The intimate flying-garment   The inner flying garment of my slip
The long airstreams of my stockings   my brassiere letting my breasts
warm on the air   and my girdle   and all of us float down almost
Together   but myself gradually leaving them   finally fighting away
From my head my shoe, the last thing   and will descend now in this
state into the warm fields   trying as I can to land   on my back.
whoever finds me will find me as I am   and will not understand
why but will, more deeply. It will all be broken this kind of thing
Is what one does when there is nothing to be done   makes a gesture
understood by nothing or by no one   in the dark   and will lie

In the fields   life broken out   but with one breath   believing   I could
Have made it back to water I overpassed   when in the goddess state
have flown too close to
the goddess state to

James Dickey

In 1960, when he was thirty-eight—an age at which most men have abandoned pretenses at having creative gifts—James Dickey published his first book of poetry, Into the Stone, *a Scribner's Poets of Today volume that he shared with two other unknown poets, Paris Leary and Jon Swan. In the years since, Dickey has become one of the most powerful voices in American poetry.*

But, ironically, it was fiction, not poetry, that made Dickey's name a household word. After toying with Deliverance *for nearly ten years, he finished it in a great thrust of energy in 1969. Those who knew Dickey closely, however, were aware that* Deliverance, *while a publishing phenomenon, was not the center of his creative objective. He once remarked to a student, "*The Eye-Beaters *is worth a hundred* Deliverances."

This interview took place in Dickey's Lake Katherine home

*in Columbia, South Carolina. It was recorded in three sessions
(two in May 1972 and one in May 1974) in his huge den with
an inch-thick gray carpet and an appropriate wall of books.
Dickey, a large, bearish man, has a voice to match. Throughout
the tapings he poised on his chair's edge, sucking air through
his teeth in anger at incompetent poets, and often shaking with
laughter at good one-liners. On the first day he wore a pink shirt
with French cuffs; the next sessions found him garbed in jackets
and pants of leather or suede. After each day's taping, Dickey
played the guitar, took his interviewer canoeing, or demonstrated his skill with the bow and arrow. He is adroit with all
three, perhaps excelling on the six-string. He has contributed
numerous guitar tapes to the Library of Congress in addition to
providing some of the music for* Deliverance.

This fall, his long poem, The Zodiac, *will be published,
followed soon after by his second novel,* Alnilam.

INTERVIEWER: You have said you got where you are today,
an established poet and novelist, "the hardest way possible,
unsolicited manuscripts." Can you tell us about it?

DICKEY: It was very difficult to do; I didn't have any precedent; I didn't know any writers, editors, publishers, or agents.
They might have been in the outer part of the solar system as
far as I was concerned. I just knew that I liked to write and I
had some ideas that I thought might work out as poems. So I
wrote them, then sent them around. As they say, I could have
papered my bedroom wall with the rejections.

I began to send stuff out when I was at Vanderbilt, and the
only way that I knew where to send anything was to go into
the stacks of the library and get a magazine out that I admired,
like the *Sewanee Review,* and get the address off the masthead
and send the poem to the guy who was the editor at that
address. I sent poems in and I kept getting back these form
rejections. In 1948 or 1949 I remember with what wonder I

saw a true human handwriting on the rejection slip. It said, "Not bad."

INTERVIEWER: What made you decide to commit yourself to writing?

DICKEY: Like most American writers I kind of backed into it. I liked poetry; I liked to read it. I'm the kind of person who can't be interested in a thing without wanting to see if I can't get out there and do a little of it myself. If I see somebody shooting arrows, I want to get a bow and see if I can shoot some myself.

INTERVIEWER: Did the legendary Vanderbilt crowd have much effect on you?

DICKEY: There is no sense in which it could be said that I was a latter-day Fugitive or Agrarian. But Donald Davidson was my teacher, and he's the single best teacher that I've ever had with the possible exception of Monroe Spears. He made poetry and intellectual life important; all you had to do was walk into his classroom and you knew you were in the presence of some important spirit. I got interested in anthropology, astronomy, the kind of thing that Donald Davidson stood for. But the whole Vanderbilt ethos and Agrarianism and cultural pluralism were just academic subjects to me. I'm much more interested in them now than when I was in the milieu that produced them.

INTERVIEWER: What did you do when you graduated?

DICKEY: I took an M.A. in 1950 and became an instructor in technical English and report writing at what was then called Rice Institute in Houston, Texas, but almost immediately after my appointment I went off to the Korean War.

INTERVIEWER: When did you get into the advertising business?

DICKEY: A few years after the war—1956, and I stayed in it until 1962. I worked with three different agencies—first I was with McCann-Erickson, on the Coca-Cola account, where I was known not as Jungle Jim, but as Jingle Jim. I then moved to Atlanta and worked with an agency called Liller Neal and Battle, where I worked on fertilizer accounts, mainly. Also banks and Pimento products. I then took a position as creative director and vice-president of an Atlanta agency called Burke Dowling Adams, where I engineered the advertising campaign dealing with the awarding of the transcontinental run by Delta to the West Coast. Now, in connection with my film work, I fly that airline all the time.

INTERVIEWER: How important was your work to you? Do you regret leaving it?

DICKEY: No. I'm glad I left it. But if I had four or five different lives, or the proverbial nine lives, I would like to spend one of them in business. It's a fascinating and exciting way to live. It's very frustrating; it's got its hang-ups; it's a man-killing pace; and it's tremendously difficult. But I love business people and I met some really terrific people whom otherwise I wouldn't have known. I wouldn't have had any relationship to them unless *that* were the relationship: making deals, working with them on their problems, and selling their products. I enjoyed it. There's something about the nine-to-five existence and the five-thirty cocktails after work on Friday afternoons and talking over the problems of the week with your buddies who are working on the same problems that's really kind of nice. I remember it with affection and with a certain amount of gratitude. Nevertheless, I don't have that many lives. I have only one, so when it was time for me to leave, I left.

INTERVIEWER: What were you writing during your business period?

DICKEY: I wrote my whole first book, *Into the Stone*, on company time. I had a typewriter and I had a bunch of ads stacked up in those famous brown envelopes with work orders on them. When I had a minute or two, I'd throw a poem into the typewriter and try to work out a line or get a transition from one stanza to the next. But the business world gives you almost no time to do anything but business. You are selling your soul to the devil all day and trying to buy it back at night. This can work out fine for a while, but after that the tensions and the difficulties begin to mount up and you see that you are going to have to make a choice. This took place with me after about five and a half or six years.

INTERVIEWER: What made you decide to make your final commitment to writing, to say, "This is it, I am leaving"?

DICKEY: Age. I knew I couldn't have it both ways much longer, and as they say in the pro football games or basketball games on Sunday afternoons, "The clock is running." I didn't have that much time. I needed a lot more time to do my work and not *their* work. And there is also the feeling of spending your substance, your vital substance, on something that is really not that important—of giving the best of yourself, every day, to selling soda pop. You just don't want to let yourself go that easily. You can't. Or I couldn't, anyway.

INTERVIEWER: Do you think in some ways it is a commitment to a kind of artificial moral order?

DICKEY: Well, if you work for the Coca-Cola Company, the first thing you're told is how many people's jobs and lives depend on the drink and how old and venerable and honorable the company is, that the pension plans are good, the medical plans are good, and so on. But after all, it's only soda pop, and you're quite sure in the end that you don't want to spend your vital substance on something that's not any more important than a soft drink. If you go with the Coca-Cola Company, Pepsi-Cola, R.C., or any of them, you enlist yourself in a war that was going on before you were born, and will go on after you die. It's a little bit—I hate to drag this in—like Vietnam. You fight limited engagements in limited areas and nobody ever wins.

INTERVIEWER: After *Into the Stone* came out, did you think that you were going to succeed as a poet?

DICKEY: I didn't know then, and I still don't know. The

Guggenheim people wrote to me and asked me if I would like to stand for a fellowship and to send in whatever I had to offer. I was in one of those Scribner three-decker, large economy-size packages of young poets with Paris Leary and Jon Swan, and I sent them that, and presto, lo and behold, they gave me some money—several thousand dollars. I said to Maxine, "This is our escape hatch. Let's sell the house and go and live in Italy. Why the hell not? When are we ever going to get another chance?" I swore I was going to go back to Europe before I was forty. I made it at the age of thirty-nine.

INTERVIEWER: What sort of effect did Europe have on you and your writing?

DICKEY: Italy was especially good. First of all, there was what Davidson used to talk about all the time, cultural pluralism: different wines, different dishes, different paintings, different life-styles, all kinds of different things which give such richness and variety to life. What we'll end up with if the world gets increasingly Americanized is life in a gigantic Rexall's. Of course, you can go into Rexall's and get a lot of things you need. You can also get a lot of things you don't need, but might be interested in having. There are a lot of diversified products in Rexall's. But Rexall's is Rexall's. It's not the same as going to a bullfight or going to a folk dance in Sicily or going into the Uffizi Museum in Florence.

When an American goes to Europe, he doesn't go there to get just another version of America. He wants *difference.* You see fields of tulips in Holland. You never saw anything like that in your life. You see cliffs down on the Amalfi Drive, you see people in an Italian village. The guys having a drink together: why, by God, they fall into each other's arms—and they just *saw* each other last night; they were probably drunk together last night. You don't see Americans do that. Americans are pushing each other away all the time, even the men and women.

INTERVIEWER: Would you advise a young writer to go abroad for a while?

DICKEY: Yes. I believe that a broad scan of experience can be nothing but beneficial to a young writer. It may be confusing at the beginning, but the increment of his personal memory bank can be only for the best. To cite but one example, look at Hemingway's experience of Paris. Take others: Henry James's experience of London, J. B. Priestley's sojourn in Arizona, and Stephen Crane's in Cuba. You name it.

INTERVIEWER: What other advice would you give?

DICKEY: I don't know. The talent game is a tough game. Luck plays an enormous part in it. It's not like business, though luck has a very strong place in business too. You can write one good poem by luck or hazard that's going to make people want your work. Whether or not you can produce anything good later on is not the important thing. It's that you struck it right then. It's the same with a novel—I wrote *Deliverance.* The movies bought it; it was serialized, written into a dozen languages; it's the best novel I can write, but there's also an enormous element of luck in it. I wrote the right book at the right time. People were caught up in a savage fable of decent men fighting for their lives and killing and getting away with it. My next novel could be a failure.

INTERVIEWER: How can a young poet know if his work is really worthwhile?

DICKEY: You never know that. I don't know it; Robert Lowell doesn't know it; John Berryman didn't know it; and Shakespeare probably didn't know it. There's never any final certainty about what you do. Your opinion of your own work fluctuates wildly. Under the right circumstances you can pick up something that you've written and approve of it; you'll think it's good and that nobody could have done exactly the same thing. Under different circumstances, you'll look at exactly the same poem and say, "My Lord, isn't that *boring.*" The most important thing is to be excited about what you are doing and to be working on something that you think will be the greatest thing that ever was. One of the difficulties in writing poetry is to maintain your sense of excitement and discovery about what you write. American literature is full of people who started off excited about poetry and their own contribution to it and their own relationship to poetry and have had, say, a modicum of success and have just gone on writing poetry as a kind of tic, a sort of reflex, when they've lost all their original excitement and enthusiasm for what they do. They do it because they have learned to do it, and that's what they *do*. You have to find private stratagems to keep up your original enthusiasm, no matter what it takes. As you get older, that's tougher and tougher to do. You want to try to avoid, if you possibly can, the feeling of doing it simply because you *can* do it.

INTERVIEWER: What are some of these private stratagems?

DICKEY: A very great deal of exercise, to keep the body moving, because when the body moves the mind is inclined to move with it. At times, a certain amount of alcohol helps. The point is to get to a certain *level* at which the creative flow can best take place. Any means to effect this end is to the good.

INTERVIEWER: How do ideas for poems come to you?

DICKEY: Well, I can give you one example, of course there are many. But, I remember when I was in Okinawa and the war was over and we went out to one of the invasion beaches near Buckner Bay, me and my cofliers, and we went swimming and there was an old amtrack there in ten feet of water that the Japanese had stove in—big holes in the sides of it—and I swam down and sat in the driver's seat. That image stayed with me and years later, twenty or twenty-five years later, I wrote "The Driver."

INTERVIEWER: You also write about things that an ordinary person would pass by, like the jump of a fish, or the movement of trees, or light.

DICKEY: That could almost be cited as the definition of a

poet: someone who notices and is enormously taken by things that somebody else would walk by. The major thing for a writer to do is develop some means of selecting the *best* of his memories and ideas and images and to build on them and reluctantly let the others go.

INTERVIEWER: Can you describe the genesis and working out of a poem based on an image that most people would pass by? "Dust," for example?

DICKEY: "Dust" was a collusion between or among two or three different kinds of elements. I wanted to try to utilize a stanza form with a short first line, evolving into longer lines, and at the end coming back to a short line. This is purely a technical problem. The second element was literary: I wanted to work with the Biblical statement, "But dust thou art, to dust returneth." The third element that was important was the sense of lying about half drunk in a California afternoon and looking up through the sunlight shining through the window and really noticing—as one will do when one is about half drunk—these strange little things in the air. They are always spiral shaped and it seemed to me that this might have something to do with venereal disease, with the spirochete and so on. So that was the fourth element. I tried to get all of them together in one poem.

INTERVIEWER: You speak of technical elements. How do you feel about free verse?

DICKEY: I go back and forth. Sometimes I like to write in very strictly measured forms. I think there are tremendous advantages accruing to that. But then I also want to try to open out the poem and make what I have recently been calling the "balanced poem," and make gaps within the lines and write in bursts of words. You shouldn't restrict yourself . . . what Ivor Winters did, and say that it's got to be this way or it's no good at all. You should experiment. You should wander around a bit; you should risk being wrong. Actually, free verse is not a term that I myself care much for. I would call it unrhymed, irregular verse, because I remember what Mr. Eliot said, "No verse is free for the poet that wants to do a good job," and it really *isn't* free. What you are talking about is that you are not writing a rhyming or a regular verse, but more of an open, organic form.

INTERVIEWER: Does form ever control your subject matter?

DICKEY: I used to be much interested in inventing forms; for example, the form in "The Hill Below the Lighthouse" dictated the subject matter. What I did was to work out a refrain scheme—I call it a returning rhyme—so that each stanza had an end line which was italicized. And the end stanza of the poem—the sixth or seventh, I forget which—was made up of the refrained lines themselves.

INTERVIEWER: Do you show your poems in a working stage to anyone else?

DICKEY: It depends. There are some things that I show to certain selected people if I think the words have reached the stage where their future development might prove good. But generally I keep the successive drafts of a poem to myself, because I conceive the poetic process as quite a private matter between the poet, his hand, and the blazing white island of paper which he is trying to populate or eliminate.

INTERVIEWER: How many drafts do you usually do?

DICKEY: It depends on the poem. With a longer one like "The Firebombing," I'd say certainly one hundred and fifty to one hundred and seventy-five, because you are searching all the time for some kind of order—some constitution to order whatever it is you are trying to say. Then, you are also trying to render it unforgettable. We poets are shameless people. We try to give whoever reads our poems something that they simply cannot shake. And if you try to do this in a long poem, you have to have some kind of executive order that makes the parts contribute to the whole, so that the audience will remember both the whole and the parts that contributed to it.

INTERVIEWER: What about a shorter poem like "Remnant Water"?

DICKEY: Oh, there are over thirty drafts of that. It's a kind of Vermeer, a still-life piece; this is relatively unusual for me. Most of my things depend on violence and length. But "Remnant Water" is a short piece, and so the whole revolves around the placement of each single word and not the presentation of an action, as it does in "The Firebombing." I worked on that an awful long time. It might point a new direction, I don't know. But it is necessary that one experiment; that a poet should work out different kinds of direction.

INTERVIEWER: Do you ever have the temptation to change a poem after it's published?

DICKEY: I have a paranoid thing about making absolutely sure before I let anything go out under my name that it is as good as I can do at that particular time. I might have second thoughts about it later, but I'm willing to stand on it when I turn it loose; therefore, it gets very hard for me to turn one loose.

INTERVIEWER: When you think about *Poems: 1957–1967*, what poem are you least enchanted with yourself?

DICKEY: Well, I don't know. The title poem "Drowning with Others" is one that I would like to make into a much longer poem—much, much longer. It's anthologized all over the damn place—but I can see possibilities in it now that I didn't see then.

INTERVIEWER: It's always ironic that the more successful a person gets, the more under attack he comes. I've noticed that there is an increasing amount of bitterness by a great number of people toward your work. Do you have any sort of response to their criticism?

DICKEY: Most of the time I don't even know what it is. It seems to me that a lot of it is politically oriented. For some reason or other I've had the right-wing monkey put on my back. But I'm not right wing; I'm not left wing; I'm not any wing.

INTERVIEWER: After all, you did work for Eugene McCarthy at one time as a speech writer.

DICKEY: Yes, I did. He was my closest friend in Washington. That doesn't concern people. The fact that William Buckley is also a very close friend *does* concern people because that gives them an automatic put-down. I just don't worry about it. I've got too much work to do. It seems to be an invariable rule that people who don't have a strong creative drive, but find themselves in the creative competitive market, are eventually and inevitably going to put other writers down by means of politics.

INTERVIEWER: Some of your detractors have mentioned the fact that they felt that you should use your influence, your place in the world, for the "betterment of man."

DICKEY: If I knew what it was, I might do that. But I don't know. There's this tendency in American life to assume that because someone is good or maybe just notorious or publicized in one realm that he's a universal authority on everything. So, Frank Sinatra or John Wayne can tell you how to vote. What competence do *they* have in politics? Or that a poet can tell you about ecology or something of that sort. A poet is only a professional sensibility. His opinion in politics is no better than anyone else's ninety-nine percent of the time. But they're always being interviewed and always being asked their political opinion: what should we do with the military, what should we do with the economy, with government spending, etcetera. Poets don't know anything about that. If they did, they wouldn't be poets. This is not to say that they are precluded from knowing anything about it at *all;* it is to say, however, that just because they are poets their opinions should not be paid any more attention to than anybody else's. It does not give them any privilege or any insight or any clairvoyance as to the political and economic and military future of America.

INTERVIEWER: You don't feel, then, that since a poet has a highly developed sensitivity about our universe and about our place in the world and our society, he should make public pronouncements about the direction our society is taking?

DICKEY: I think in that way lies madness. No; all he's got is his own sensibility and his own opinions as a private citizen. But he has no privilege. Insight, yes. Maybe a poet could come along who could solve all our problems, but I haven't seen him yet. The history of poets pronouncing on public issues is notoriously dismal.

INTERVIEWER: I remember you quoted Auden talking about poetry: "for poetry makes nothing happen." Do you believe that?

DICKEY: I think that if it does make anything happen, it's deep in the individual's sensibilities; it's not in the public arena. As John Peale Bishop says, when the poet, or the critic, mounts the soapbox, the garbage remains in the streets.

INTERVIEWER: Did your job as poetry consultant to the Library of Congress involve you in the political world? One thinks of Archibald MacLeish trying to get Pound out of prison.

DICKEY: Well, Archie was the *librarian* of Congress, and his name is engraved in gold just inside the entrance way of the Library. The consultancy is quite a different thing. I did try to get several of the incarcerated Russian poets out of prison without success. My position was not such as that which Archie occupied. My name is not engraved in gold letters, and I would not have had the capacity to occupy the position which Archie had, nor would I have accepted it if offered. My position was that of being the only equivalent that the United States has of poet laureate. Frost was in the chair, Robert Lowell was in the chair, and Robert Penn Warren was in the chair. The job is as the incumbent conceives it: he can do as much or as little with it as he likes. He can lecture, he can initiate programs that the Library will implement, he can arrange for lectures in the

Coolidge auditorium, he can travel for the State Department, or he can do nothing at all except accept the position as a sinecure. I chose to be a working consultant. I set up an arrangement with the local ETV station to film the readings that I proposed, so that the Library would have the nucleus of a filmed archive of writers, novelists, and poets that would eventually be the equivalent of the spoken archives that the Library is famous for. Videotape made this possible. Universities and students may now go to the Library of Congress to see and hear, for example, John Updike reading from his works. Also John Cheever, William Stafford, Josephine Miles, and many another.

It is also part of the tradition of the consultancy that the consultant take at least one extended trip. Frost, for example, went to Russia. I went to New Zealand, Australia, Japan, and Alaska. I made the job hard, and now that it is over, I am glad that I did.

INTERVIEWER: You got into what you call your *one* political foray when Yevtushenko was here, in this country. Why?

DICKEY: Well, he's a close friend. I like him very much, but I profoundly disapprove of the kind of thing he does. He uses poetry as a pretext for making bohemian speeches. He's a great deal better poet than Allen Ginsberg, but he does the same *sort* of thing. I don't think poetry is well served by that. Poetry *can* speak on topical things eloquently. Look at Yeats on the riots of 1916, for example. But we should not be led into the corner of assuming that poetry is no good which does not speak on news items. If a man wants to write about the circle that's made in the water when a fish jumps, he should be able to write about that and should not be charged off as irrelevant because he's not writing about the Vietnam riots. You should have the whole gamut: political action, the jump of the fish, or the space program. You should have anything you want.

INTERVIEWER: It seems Allen Ginsberg is the diametrical opposite of you.

DICKEY: I certainly hope so. I think Ginsberg has done more harm to the craft that I honor and live by than anybody else by reducing it to a kind of mean that enables the most dubious practitioners to claim they are poets because they think, If the kind of thing Ginsberg does is poetry, I can do *that*. They damn themselves to a life of inconsequentiality when they could have been doing something more useful. They could have been garbage collectors, or grocery store managers. Poetry is, as Yeats has said, "a high and lonely profession." It is very easy, too easy, to pick up on the latest thing in the newspapers and write a poem. That's all Ginsberg does. He just doesn't have any talent. I'll do a Ginsbergian poem or a Robert Bly poem for you right now.

INTERVIEWER: Do you consider them in the same school?

DICKEY: Well, not exactly the same, but they take off from the same . . . launching pad. Their poem goes:

> *It is the hour when the Americans in Vietnam are*
> *examining their hands.*
> *The dead are lying below the tangles of jungle brush.*
> *All over Minnesota snow is beginning to fall over the*
> *missile silos.*

INTERVIEWER: A southern writer said, "James Dickey first came to my attention as a reviewer and I thought he was one of the roughest around." You've been pretty rough on some of your contemporaries. For what reason?

DICKEY: Well, I'm not all that rough. I have a very naïve feeling as a reviewer. I don't believe that a reviewer or a critic can really criticize well unless he can praise well. I always liked that about Randall Jarrell. He praised well. James Agee praises well. You've got to be able to like the right things to be enabled to dislike the wrong things. People misconstrue John Simon. He *does* praise well. He doesn't find much to praise, but he praises well. John Simon hates so much so vehemently because he likes so little so strongly.

INTERVIEWER: Let's talk about someone that you do like strongly. What attracts you so much to William Stafford?

DICKEY: It's because he has the ability to say amazing things without seeming to raise his voice. He's kind of *murmuring*. I've never encountered a poet like that. He's not doing a lot of vast, tearing, rhetorical stuff like Lowell does, or a lot of kinky, tricky self-derogation like John Berryman. He's talking like an American midwestern farmer who just has this capacity to say startling, quiet stuff.

INTERVIEWER: Do you feel that Stafford is making a more significant contribution to American letters than Lowell is?

DICKEY: Yes, I do. I think Stafford will mean more to people over a longer period. Maybe not to the makers of textbooks or anthologies, but he's a people's poet of the finest kind; he's instantly understandable, and he gives you an enormous amount to think about without hollering at you, or without beating you down. Roethke was like that. Stafford, in a completely different way, has that same quality. He doesn't have the crazy, apocalyptic kind of a feel that Roethke has, but he's got an easy going, quiet, authoritative, human, imaginative voice.

INTERVIEWER: Did you know Roethke?

DICKEY: Yes, I did indeed. I knew him quite well during the last two years of his life. He was a strange, terrifying, and terrified man. He seemed to have no confidence in himself. He was constantly afraid of being fired from the University of Washington because of his drunkenness and his periodic insanity. He feared becoming destitute, though he had a fine house on John Street overlooking the sea, a devoted wife, and friends who would have gone to the gallows for him. None of this seemed to do him any good. He read, it seemed, every scrap of paper on his work that appeared in print, and conceived endless literary enmities toward this, that, and the other literary critic or rival poet. Despite the fact that he was a little hard to live with, he was on the whole a lovable man, and it is still difficult for me to believe that he is gone from us.

INTERVIEWER: You had an article in the *Atlantic,* "The Greatest American Poet: Theodore Roethke." Why is he the greatest?

DICKEY: I don't see anyone else that has the kind of deep, gut vitality that Roethke's got. Whitman was a great poet, but he's no competition for Roethke. Lowell is a fine poet. He's a narrow, tragic, personal, confessional kind of writer. He's very good. But you can be interested in his hang-ups, his family, for just so long. In order to read Lowell and to like Lowell or Anne Sexton or any of the people that follow after Lowell, what is presupposed is that their life and their situation is going to be eternally fascinating to you. And it isn't. I *am* interested in Roethke's relationship to the ocean, because that gets me *into* it. I can participate. I can't enter Lowell's family. Of course, Lowell is an enormously powerful writer. The measure of his ability is that he can *make* you interested in his family; whereas Sylvia Plath, writing poems like "Daddy," is ridiculously bad; it's embarrassing. Lowell is a big writer, and he *compels* you to be interested. People like Sylvia Plath or Anne Sexton just embarrass you.

INTERVIEWER: How do you respond to the emergence of Sylvia Plath as a celebrated figure?

DICKEY: She's not very good. She's just someone who killed herself out of literary desperation—out of desperation to be literarily notable. Someone ought to write an article called "The Suicide Certification," which assumes that if you're a poet and you kill yourself, then you have *got* to be good. No way.

INTERVIEWER: One time you called it "suicide chic."

DICKEY: Well, of course, if you're taking your own life, that's a horrible situation. Al Alvarez seems to think, in his recent book on suicide, that she was just doing it as a gesture and she hoped it wouldn't come off. So she killed herself by mistake. She's the Judy Garland of American poetry. If you want to kill yourself, you don't make an *attempt;* you do it. You make sure that the thing comes off. Suicide *attempts,* and then writing *poems* about your suicide attempts, is just pure bullshit! Sylvia Plath is of a certain talent, a very modest talent. Anne Sexton is better than she is, and I don't care much for her, either.

INTERVIEWER: What is your opinion of the famous southern women writers—Eudora Welty, Carson McCullers, Katherine Anne Porter, and Flannery O'Connor?

DICKEY: The women of the South have brought into American literature a unique mixture of domesticity and grotesquery. There have been two routes open to the southern woman writer. She could research a historic subject—such as Elizabeth Madox Roberts did in *The Great Meadow,* which deals with the opening up of Kentucky—couple this with domestic images from her own life, and write her fiction out of these two considerations; or she could deal with eccentric village types, such as Carson McCullers and Eudora Welty frequently do and Flannery O'Connor does to an extreme. The southern women writers of the two generations which produced our great ones were singularly immobile, but then so was Emily Brontë. They had little breadth of experience, but much penetration into a specific and still milieu. They are remarkable writers. But their scope is limited to the local and domestic with, in some cases, an admixture of the grotesque. I like it all. This is the way my women see things, and it is an interesting way that sheds light.

INTERVIEWER: Is there something about the South that is peculiarly advantageous for the writing of poetry and fiction?

DICKEY: Yes, I think there is. Due to their past, their history, their rural background, Southerners are lonely people. They very seldom have anyone to talk to. The result of this has been that when a Southerner encounters another human being he talks his head off. Add to this the very strong folklore and the legendary quality of local stories, anecdotes, and jokes, and you have the basis for southern poetry and also for southern fiction.

Out of this situation, plus a certain superficial literariness (as in the case of Faulkner), came a great literature. But there are certain obvious defects. One of these is the eternal sameness of southern fiction, which almost always deals with a family either in a single generation or covering several generations. One cannot reasonably assume that a wide reading public is going to be interested in yet another novel dealing with the Lutrell family in Ellijay, Georgia, with its criminally inclined son and its seduceable daughter. With poetry it is quite different. A mystical element enters. It enters into the landscape, the rivers, and the animals. Our greatest poetry has been written out of southern landscape, and not out of southern people. This is to the good, I think.

INTERVIEWER: Has the poetry of Robert Frost, particularly the country poems, been of interest or impact?

DICKEY: I don't care much for Robert Frost, and have never been able to understand his reputation. He says a good thing now and then, but with a strange way of averting his eyes while saying it which may be profound and may be poppycock. If it were thought that anything I wrote was influenced by Robert Frost, I would take that particular work of mine, shred it, and flush it down the toilet, hoping not to clog the pipes.

INTERVIEWER: Did you know him?

DICKEY: Yes, I knew him slightly, and spent a couple of afternoons with him when I was teaching at the University of Florida in 1955, and a more sententious, holding-forth old bore who expected every hero-worshiping adenoidal little twerp of a student-poet to hang on his every word I never saw.

INTERVIEWER: One of the things I think that you do enjoy is an audience. Can that be the death of a poet, if he enjoys performing?

DICKEY: It sure killed off poor Dylan Thomas. He didn't write even *one* poem in the last six years of his life. Everybody adored him, paid him a lot of money; why should he write another book of *poems,* and maybe give the critics a shot at him that would lower his reading fee? Everybody *loved* him; he was screwing all the coeds in America, drinking all the whiskey, and he'd get up there and read his poems, and then he'd go on and read them somewhere else. He got a lot of dough for it. I mean, what incentive for him to write *was* there? To survive, a poet has to find some way of maintaining his original enthusiasm for *poetry,* not for the by-products of poetry, not for the fringe benefits of poetry, but for *it.*

INTERVIEWER: One time you were answering some irate poet and you said, "It's ironic to me that so many poets go about defending themselves in the wrong way; the real test lies in the poem."

DICKEY: Listen, a poet's pages are filled up with what he's done, that he can live on and trade on; but he has *got* to find some way to love that white empty page, those words he hasn't said yet.

INTERVIEWER: I think some people thought that you came out with *Deliverance* as a kind of afterthought, but I know from talking to you earlier that you had thought about *Deliverance* a long time. Why did you decide to finally go ahead and do it?

DICKEY: Well, I did think about it a long time. I started it about ten years ago and finished it about two years ago. It is misleading to leave it at that, because it would cause people to believe that I did nothing but work on *Deliverance* all that time —year after year. I wrote seven or eight other books during that time. *Deliverance* was really not high on the priority list at all. As Thomas Lovell Beddoes said of his own involvement with his lifelong work, never finished, called *Death's Jest Book,* "I just gave it another kick whenever I got around to it." But, by damn, when it began to look like *Deliverance* was really capable of being finished, then I started leaning on it and pushing, and working on it until it finally *did* get finished. Nobody was more surprised than I was, because this novel was just something lying around in a drawer. I liked the story, and I got to where I was interested in the characters, and so on. I didn't know anything about writing novels—I still don't know much about it.

INTERVIEWER: What sort of process did you go through in writing the novel—shifting from poems to a fictional work?

DICKEY: The main problem for me, as I recall, was finding out ways to do without the poetic line, because I had really relied heavily on the line, and the way the human eye moves across the page, what happens when you read a line of verse and the way it goes into the next line. I had to learn a whole new set of conventions, to work with the sentence and the paragraph, which I didn't know very much about.

Deliverance was originally written in a very heavily charged prose, somewhat reminiscent of James Agee. But it was too juicy. It detracted from the narrative thrust, which is the main thing that the story has going for it. So I spent two or three drafts taking that quality out. I wanted a kind of unobtrusively remarkable observation that wouldn't call attention to itself. That's why I made the narrator an art director. He's a guy who *would* see things like this; a writer would perform all kinds of cakewalks to be brilliant stylistically, which would have interfered with the narrative drive of the story.

INTERVIEWER: You have so many interesting set pieces in there. One that struck me was that section beginning "there is always something wrong with people in the country" which you ended "and I saw that the only way out was by water from the country of the nine-fingered people." Did you ever feel like putting something like that into a poem?

DICKEY: No, it was the other way around, because some of the same events which are depicted in *Deliverance* have been in poems—such as the boat going by the effluent pipe where the chicken heads and the feathers are. I wrote it into poetry first. Then I pulled it out of the poem and used it in the novel.

INTERVIEWER: Did you feel as if you were reducing it, changing it to prose?

DICKEY: It really wasn't a question of changing it over from one thing to the other. It was a question of reconceiving it in terms of another medium. The poems that I wrote were as a kind of three-part sequence, as I remember, called "On the Coosawattee." The same events and circumstances and physical situation over twenty years ago in north Georgia were what I was trying to reconceive in terms of the novel.

INTERVIEWER: What do you feel *Deliverance* is going to say later on?

DICKEY: I don't know. It has been variously reviewed. I don't really read very many reviews of anything I write. If somebody comes up to me and says, "Jim, there's a fabulous review in the *Atlantic* and you must read it; he's crazy about the book," then I'll read it. If the guy says it's a horrible review and that I'm the anti-Christ himself, then I don't read it, because I don't want to go around filled with resentment against some stranger. That bleeds off your energies; you take them out in useless hatred. I need the energy for other things. I've known writers who are absolutely destroyed by adverse opinion, and I think this is a lot of shit. You shouldn't allow that to happen to yourself, and if you do, then it's *your* fault. My course is set; I know what I'm going to do. As Stephen Dedalus says, in *A Portrait of the Artist as a Young Man*, "I'm ready to make a lifelong mistake." I believe in making a lifelong mistake, but I don't believe in being guided by people who write about me. Why, there's not anything that could ever be said about a person either good or bad that hasn't been said about me. But it doesn't matter. I'm going to write my way, and if that doesn't agree with people's sensibilities or even their digestions, it doesn't make any difference to me. If it's a lifelong mistake, it won't be the first one that's been made.

INTERVIEWER: What sort of contribution do you, yourself, feel that *Deliverance* will make?

DICKEY: I'll tell you what I really tried to do in *Deliverance*. My story is simple: there are bad people, there are monsters among us. *Deliverance* is really a novel about how decent men kill, and the fact that they get away with it raises a lot of questions about staying within the law—whether decent people have the right to go outside the law when they're encountering human monsters. I wrote *Deliverance* as a story where under the conditions of extreme violence people find out things about themselves that they would have no other means of knowing. The late John Berryman, who was a dear friend of mine, said that it bothered him more than anything else that a man could live in this culture all his life without knowing whether he's a coward or not. I think it's necessary to know.

INTERVIEWER: You don't feel, then, as some critics have said, that this particular work can be viewed as an exercise in violence?

DICKEY: No. At least not in the sense that Peckinpah's *Straw Dogs* is an exercise in violence. What I don't like about Sam's work is that it has that obvious element of contrivance in it. *Deliverance* is something that could happen. You run up against bad men who would just as soon shoot you as look at you. In fact, some of them would rather. So what do you do? This is a story about what you *do*.

INTERVIEWER: Do you feel that it is in the tradition of the grand male fraternity that dominates Hemingway's fiction?

DICKEY: Hemingway's people are bullfighters and boxers. Their *business* is violence. My men are decent guys. Lewis is a survival freak who is a nut on special disciplines, such as archery, canoeing, and so on. Suburban people, especially these fellows, are supposed to get out there and look at nature a little bit . . . have fun before it all disappears. Lewis might be a little obsessive about it. But the other guys— Ed Gentry, the narrator, for example, is just a decent guy with the job of providing for his family who happens to be fascinated with Lewis. Ed Gentry is not a bullfighter, a boxer, a tournament archer, or a racing canoeist. He's a guy who has a tangential relationship with these things that his obsessed buddy insists on talking about and doing. Drew is another decent guy, and is untroubled. He's America's own man. He's what the culture develops and the culture hopes for . . . a decent family man, he tends to his business, he does his job, and he has a couple of mild hobbies, like playing the guitar. Bobby, the other fellow, is a fat, lecherous, country-club guy who never should have been up in the woods to begin with. We get those men together and we have them beset by the blind fury of two disgusting human beings; and we see what the decent guys do.

INTERVIEWER: Is this kind of a warning to us?

DICKEY: I don't know whether it is or not.

INTERVIEWER: Some people felt like it might have been a kind of social commentary, thinly disguised.

DICKEY: I don't know. My interest was in just simply writing the story, and letting the symbolism fall where it may. Hemingway was right about that. You don't try to build in, self-consciously, a bunch of preconceived symbols. If we make a real river, and real canoes, and real men, and real monsters, and real arrows, and real shotguns, and real woods, and real rapids and white water, then all the other stuff will take care of itself.

INTERVIEWER: What of your writing now? What's it like being a post-*Deliverance* writer?

DICKEY: It's not so bad. My preoccupation is with poetry, and everything else is a spin-off from that—novels, literary criticism, screenplays, whatever. If I lose poetry, which is the center of my creative wheel, I lose everything. I don't propose to let that happen. I want to write another book of poems, and then maybe have a big collection in a few years. Then I want to turn away from everything I've ever done in poetry and strike out in a completely new direction, if I can find what it is.

INTERVIEWER: Do you have any ideas?

DICKEY: The main thing in poetry is the discovery of an idiom and the exploitation of it over an area of thought for a long period of time. It is discovering an idiom such as Christopher Marlowe did—he really discovered blank verse—that's important. He didn't do it all himself. He found it too early. But Shakespeare *did* do it. I want to get at a kind of new way of using the English language which would not be mannered in such a way as, say, John Berryman is mannered, and would not be so lax as, say, Randall Jarrell is lax. I don't mean to make them into two possible poles, but we could use them as a starting place. There are some possibilities of the English language which have never even been hinted at. I don't know whether I can get at them or not. It may be a little like the blind man in the blacked-out room looking for the black cat that ain't there. That's very much the feeling I have, and yet I believe I can touch him every now and then. One of these days, I'm going to grab him.

INTERVIEWER: Who do you go back to and want to read again?

DICKEY: My writing really couldn't be assessed by what my tastes are, because I love to read and I'll read anything. I love to read good-bad poets, like Roy Campbell and Vachel Lindsay. If I want to turn my critical apparatus on and write an article, then I can turn my critical apparatus on and write an article. Nothing is easier. But I also like the thrill of a wide reading net, and a lot of the bad poets appeal to me just as much as the good ones do. This may be unfortunate.

INTERVIEWER: If you had to have a frank conversation with Berryman or Vachel Lindsay, what would you say to them?

DICKEY: I'll tell you what I would talk about with Berryman, if I could get him back. Of course, his body lies shattered on the ice of the midwinter Mississippi River. But Berryman was a man of intense friendships. His friendships meant more to him than his love affairs—more than anything else. His experience was very narrow. Sitting around drinking with Delmore Schwartz, or with Randall, or Lowell, was about as intense as John ever got. There was a poem of his in his posthumous book that was based on a phone call that I made to him when I was drunk and he was drunk, and it was a very moving thing for me to open up Berryman's posthumous book and to come upon a poem titled "Damn You, Jim D., You Woke Me Up." His friendships were all-important to him, and *that's* what I would talk to John Berryman about.

INTERVIEWER: How about Lindsay?

DICKEY: It would have to do with the relation of the poet to the public by means of the public reading, communicating with hundreds of strangers. Lindsay was the first great proponent and probably the greatest practitioner of this form of human communication. The next great one was Dylan Thomas, who could read, in his rich South Welsh voice, the telephone book and make it sound like Scripture. People are very deeply moved by the sound of the human voice that says —that seems to say—deep rhythmical things. In my own time a whole generation of poets has been sustained by public appearances and by the deep need of people to be moved by true, imaginative words.

INTERVIEWER: You've known a great many poets personally. Do you find some common characteristic—in their madness, their vision, their discipline?

DICKEY: I would have to put the answer in the form of a paradox. Most of them are what the world would call weak men and women. They are wayward, licentious, heavy drinkers, irresponsible, unable to maintain a household properly, and subject to unpredictable vagaries of conduct. But, turning the coin to its other side, the best of them are incredibly strong people who will drive headfirst through a steel wall to get their work done. This is the type of person I admire most. I admire the type as I do, I suspect, because I am one of them.

INTERVIEWER: Do you keep in touch with fellow poets?

DICKEY: I am almost completely out of touch with them. They often write to me, but because of my heavy schedule I almost never have the time to answer. My correspondence deals with current and future projects which I am embarked upon. I would like nothing better than to engage in lengthy literary correspondence about time, life and its meaning, love, death, sex, and art with poets such as Robert Lowell or James Wright, but I do not have the time. I suspect that they don't either, but I like to think that they would welcome such a correspondence, could it be done. But it can't. My letters should never be collected, for most of them concern business, which is a very dull subject, for me no less than for anyone else who might be so underprivileged as to read them.

INTERVIEWER: We've talked a good deal about American poets, but English poets are always on the scene; some critics contend that the best contemporary English poet is Philip Larkin.

DICKEY: Oh, my Lord. Philip Larkin is a small kind of *vers de société* writer. He's one of these Englishmen of the welfare state who write self-effacing poems about how much he hates his record collection. That's not what we need. We need something that will affirm the basic possibility. This self-effacing stuff is so goddamned easy, it's tiresome.

INTERVIEWER: Is this the same poetic attitude you were discussing when, in reviewing James Merrill, you said, "his characters are always coming across each other in museums"?

DICKEY: That's right. But I don't have anything against Philip Larkin, or Ted Hughes—who's different. He's a guy who has a kind of ersatz violence that's equally easy to do. Hughes writes the kind of stuff I throw away. Larkin's all right; he's pleasant and kind of low-key—but that's all. No, no, the only really good guy over there and the only one who has any originality or interest for me is W. S. Graham, the Scottish poet. He's the real stuff.

INTERVIEWER: Why do you like Graham?

DICKEY: He has an original language. He can say amazing things. Larkin can't say anything amazing. Ted Hughes gives you the effect of a weight lifter who can't get the weight up.

INTERVIEWER: If there is a direction now in America, what do you think it is?

DICKEY: It could be toward some new and strange simplicity. Stafford has made a run at it.

INTERVIEWER: Is the country more a part of it than the city?

DICKEY: You have to keep to your sources as a writer. There are good writers who have the urban consciousness. John Hollander is one of them. He's a very fine writer. Auden is another one. He's always a little bit embarrassed by landscapes, or mountains or rivers, or any of the big natural forms.

INTERVIEWER: Except Iceland.

DICKEY: Yes, except Iceland. I don't know what he *did* in Iceland, or what he saw up there, but he was always a little bit embarrassed by nature, and he'd rather write about the city and the glass and chromium kind of culture we have. He didn't like it, but he was *used* to it and he knew it. I think the really good poets of now, and the ones who are going to be good, are going to be poets of dying nature. They're going to be like Lewis in *Deliverance*: people who are paranoid about getting out and seeing a little bit of this world before it disappears. I think the great poet, who is going to come, is going to be the poet who can see in a single grass blade—a single surviving grass blade —heaven and earth, or the lost paradise. There are not going to be that many more grass blades. The animals are going, the trees are going, the flowers are going, everything is going. So the poet who is going to be the great poet of the future is going to be that poet who can tell us what that last grass blade, popping up through the cement, means—*really*.

INTERVIEWER: In *This Is My Best*, in which you are collected, you said that you considered "The May Day Sermon" to be your best poem. Do you still?

DICKEY: Yes I do. Certainly. It's the best I can do—my big effort.

INTERVIEWER: Why does it work for you?

DICKEY: I think because it's got that kind of poetical wildness that I seek for. "Falling" has some of it also.

INTERVIEWER: What do you mean by "wildness"?

DICKEY: Something that no one could imagine if he hadn't felt it. It's really a kind of madness I feel when I'm writing. It's not an induced madness from alcohol or other things of that nature. I don't know what it is, but it lets me achieve the kind of thing I did in "Falling," and especially in "The May Day Sermon."

INTERVIEWER: You've talked about age being the great enemy, and here you are fifty years old.

DICKEY: Well, for me it can go two ways. One of them is that I'm at the end, right now, and I've already said my thing and there's no more for me to do. The other side of the coin is that I'm at the beginning, that I have finally arrived at the beginning and it's all to do yet, and what I've done up to this time is nothing at all compared to what might be possible. I think it's necessary for a writer to have this sense of possibility and also to have the sense of being finished, because you don't know which it is.

INTERVIEWER: What are you working on now?

DICKEY: A poem called "The Zodiac." It's about twenty-five pages long, and it's far better than "The May Day Sermon" . . . if I can just last. It is the best I can do. . . . But boy, I'll tell you, the thing that is exciting to me is that I have spent fifty years crawling up the hill of Parnassus on my hands and knees, and now I want to see if I can fly.

FRANKLIN ASHLEY
Spring 1976

10. Joseph Heller

Joseph Heller was born in the Coney Island section of Brooklyn, New York, on May 1, 1923. He graduated from Lincoln High School in 1941 and enlisted in the air force a year later. After completing cadet training in 1944, he was assigned to a combat unit and flew a total of sixty missions prior to being discharged in 1945 at the end of the Second World War. Heller's experiences as a bomber pilot eventually became the catalyst for his war novel, *Catch-22*, considered by many to be a masterwork of twentieth-century American fiction.

After the war Heller resumed his education under the G.I. bill of rights, obtaining from New York University—where he was elected to Phi Beta Kappa—a B.A. degree in 1948 and an M.A. degree in English literature from Columbia University in 1949. Later that year he studied at Oxford University on a Fulbright Scholarship and, after returning to the United States, taught freshman composition at Pennsylvania State University from 1950 to 1952—preceding John Barth as an English instructor there by one year. Heller worked in the advertising departments of *Time, Look,* and *McCall's* magazines for the next ten years while beginning to write the short fiction that he would later sell to *Esquire* and the *Atlantic.* In his spare time he also began *Catch-22,* which was written over an eight-year period. Published in 1961, it quickly developed a cult following and ultimately became a fixture on the hardcover and paperback best-seller lists. By 1980 *Catch-22* had sold over eight million copies.

His other work includes a play, *We Bombed in New Haven* (1968), and two highly successful novels, *Something Happened* (1974) and *Good as Gold* (1979). Heller was awarded a National Institute of Arts and Letters grant in 1963, and has since taught fiction and dramatic writing at Yale University and other schools.

Married to the former Shirley Held of Brooklyn since 1945, he is the father of two and lives on Manhattan's Upper West Side.

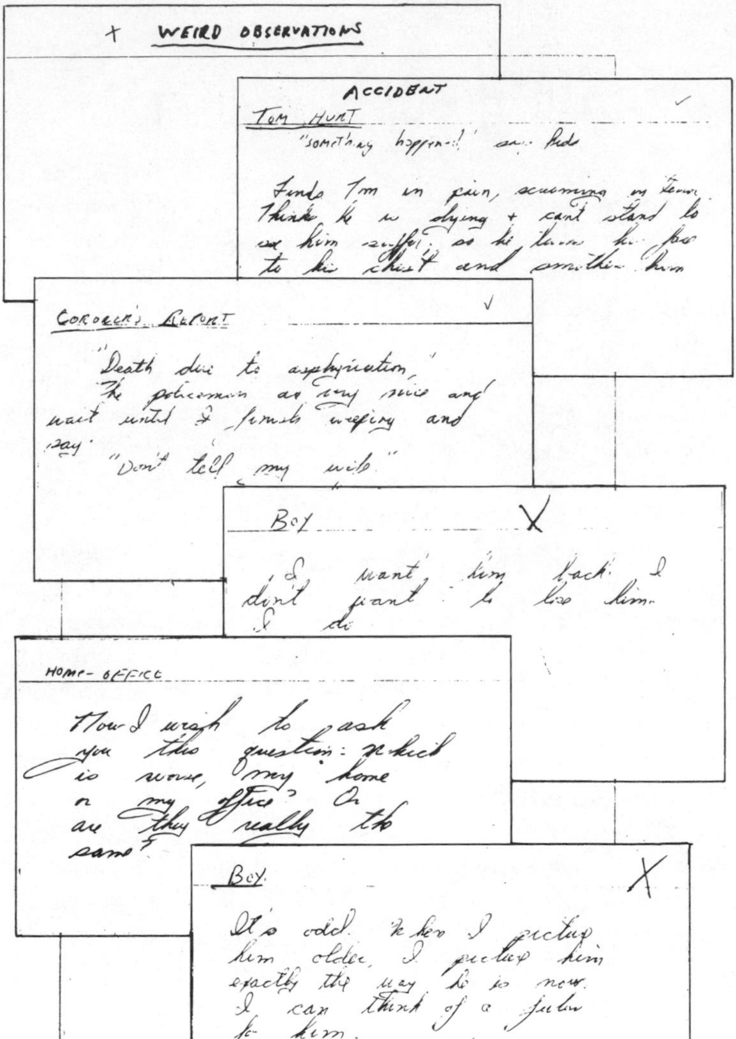

Three-by-five notecards for *Something Happened.*

Joseph Heller

*This interview with Joe Heller took place during the week of the
publication of* Something Happened—*a literary event of considerable significance, since the novel is only the second of the
author's career. The first, of course, was* Catch-22. *The fact that
it has taken more than a decade to produce a second work of
fiction seems of small concern to Heller, since he has evolved
a definite and unique pattern of work that is not at all determined by deadlines and other arbitrary demands. He says he
always wanted to be a writer. His earliest story was pecked out
on a neighborhood boy's typewriter and ultimately rejected by
the* Daily News *short-short story editor. His career moved at its
own pace. He did no writing during his war years in Italy. His
first accepted story appeared in The* Atlantic *(along with a
companion piece of fiction by James Jones) in 1948.* Catch-22
wasn't published until ten years later. Heller has no illusions

about the difficulty of making a living as a novelist. He tells his creative-writing class at the start of every academic year that even if every word a writer writes is published, he will almost surely have to supplement his income, usually by teaching (as Heller does), or perhaps by marrying money. The exigencies of such a career do not seem to have marked Heller himself. He sits very much at ease—an impressive figure (his considerable crop of hair seems to surround his face like a lion's ruff), trim (he keeps himself in firm shape by jogging and sticking to a strict diet), and with the detachment of someone talking about a third person he begins describing in a voice strong with the inflections of his native Brooklyn the unique process through which his novels have come to him. . . .

HELLER: In 1962 I was sitting on the deck of a house on Fire Island. I was frightened. I was worried because I had lost interest in my job then—which was writing advertising and promotion copy. *Catch-22* was not making much money. It was selling steadily (eight hundred to two thousand copies a week)—mostly by word of mouth—but it had never come close to the *New York Times* best-seller list. I had a wife and two children. I had no idea for another book. I was waiting for something to happen(!), wishing I had a book to start. My novels begin in a strange way. I don't begin with a theme, or even a character. I begin with a first sentence that is independent of any conscious preparation. Most often nothing comes out of it: a sentence will come to mind that doesn't lead to a second sentence. Sometimes it will lead to thirty sentences which then come to a dead end. I was alone on the deck. As I sat there worrying and wondering what to do, one of those first lines suddenly came to mind: "In the office in which I work, there are four people of whom I am afraid. Each of these four people is afraid of five people." Immediately, the lines presented a whole explosion of possibilities and choices—characters (working in a corporation), a tone, a mood of anxiety, or insecurity. In that first hour (before someone came along and asked me to go to the beach), I knew the beginning, the ending, most of the middle, the whole scene of that particular "something" that was going to happen; I knew about the brain-damaged child and, especially, of course, about Bob Slocum, my protagonist, and what frightened him, that he wanted to be liked, that his immediate hope was to be allowed to make a three-minute speech at the company convention. Many of the actual lines throughout the book came to me—the entire "something happened" scene with those solar plexus lines (beginning with the doctor's statement and ending with "Don't tell my wife" and the rest of them) all coming to me in that first hour on that Fire Island deck. Eventually I found a different opening chapter with a different first line ("I get the willies when I see closed doors") but I kept the original, which had spurred everything, to start off the second section.

INTERVIEWER: Was it the same process of "receiving" a first line with *Catch-22?*

HELLER: Just about. I was lying in bed in my four-room apartment on the West Side when suddenly this line came to me: "It was love at first sight. The first time he saw the chaplain, Someone fell madly in love with him." I didn't have the name Yossarian. The chaplain wasn't necessarily an army chaplain—he could have been a *prison* chaplain. But as soon as the opening sentence was available, the book began to evolve clearly in my mind—even most of the particulars . . . the tone, the form, many of the characters, including some I eventually couldn't use. All of this took place within an hour and a half. It got me so excited that I did what the cliché says you're supposed to do: I jumped out of bed and paced the floor. That morning I went to my job at the advertising agency and wrote out the first chapter in longhand. Before the end of the week I had typed it out and sent it to Candida Donadio, my agent. One year later, after much planning, I began chapter two.

INTERVIEWER: Is there any accounting for this unique procedure?

HELLER: I don't understand the process of imagination—though I know that I am very much at its mercy. I feel that these ideas are floating around in the air and they pick me to settle upon. The ideas come to me; I don't produce them at will. They come to me in the course of a sort of controlled daydream, a directed reverie. It may have something to do with the disciplines of writing advertising copy (which I did for a number of years), where the limitations involved provide a considerable spur to the imagination. There's an essay of T. S. Eliot's in which he praises the disciplines of writing, claiming that if one is forced to write within a certain framework, the imagination is taxed to its utmost and will produce its richest ideas. Given total freedom, however, the chances are good that the work will sprawl.

INTERVIEWER: Can you remember some other opening lines . . . ?

HELLER: Well, people have always asked what happened to Dunbar, a character who disappeared in *Catch-22*. So I was thinking of writing a novel about him. The opening line I came up with was obviously cultivated by an advertising slogan for Bigelow rugs that was widespread at the time: "A name on the door deserves a Bigelow on the floor." My variation of it was, "Dunbar woke up with his name on the door, and a Bigelow on the floor, and wondered how he had got there. . . ." So it was a novel about amnesia, Dunbar finding himself in a plush office, not knowing the secretary's name, or how many people were working for him, or what his position was—and gradually finding out. It did not work. I couldn't take my mind past a certain point.

INTERVIEWER: Do you have last lines that come along with those first lines?

HELLER: I had a closing line for *Something Happened* before I began writing the book. It was "I am a cow." For six years

I thought that was good. I had it on one of my three-by-five notecards. Then I wasn't all that happy with it, and finally I discarded it. But it seemed good at the time, and besides, I can't start writing until I have a closing line.

INTERVIEWER: Once you have an opening (and closing) line in mind, what dictates whether you will continue?

HELLER: I think writers move unconsciously toward what they think they can do. The two novels I have written, *Catch-22* and *Something Happened,* I chose to write and write in the way I did because of an instinctive feeling that I could handle the subject matter and the method of dealing with each of them. I have certain gifts. I can be funny—for one-half a page at a time, sometimes even more, though I wouldn't want to push my luck and try to be funny for ten. I can be humorous in several ways—with irony, with dialogue, with farcical situations, and occasionally with a lucky epigram or an aphorism. My inclination, though, is to be serious. But on the other hand, I cannot write an effective straightforward, separate narrative. I can't write description. I've told my editor that I couldn't write a good descriptive metaphor if my life depended on it. In *Catch-22* there is really very little physical description. There is very little in *Something Happened.* Bob Slocum tends to consider people in terms of one dimension; his tendency is to think of people—even those very close to him, his wife, daughter, and son and those he works for—as having a single aspect, a single use. When they present more than that dimension, he has difficulty in coping with them. Slocum is not interested in how people look, or how rooms are decorated, or what flowers are around.

INTERVIEWER: Do you find it restricting to tell the novel through the limited persona of Bob Slocum?

HELLER: It's true that I myself could have been much funnier, much more intelligent, much cleverer with words than Slocum is. But I must limit him, because if he had all my attributes he wouldn't be working for that company; he'd be

writing *Catch-22*. Still, even though I can't have him talk like
Nietzsche or Marcuse, I have unlimited possibilities with him
as long as I can establish the personality of someone who is only
sure that he is sure of nothing. He is utterly unset, undefined,
ambivalent. Thus, I can put him into any frame of mind, have
him react from just about any emotional perspective. The
opportunities were not too few but too many.

INTERVIEWER: Yes, but . . .

HELLER: Besides, your question suggests that Slocum's function is to inform. I don't think, even as an author, that I have
knowledge to give to readers. Philosophers might and scientists
can. It's possible for me to express something that you can
agree or disagree with, but certainly you will have heard it
before. So I don't think the "what" distinguishes a good novel
from a bad one but rather the "how"—the aesthetic quality of
the sensibility of the writer, his craft, his ability to create and
communicate.

I don't have a philosophy of life, or a need to organize its
progression. My books are not constructed to "say anything."
When I was at college, in every literary discussion there was
always such an emphasis on "What does he say? What's the
message?" Even then I felt that very few authors had anything
to say. What was important to me was "What does it do?"
This refutes, of course, the idea that the message is the objective of a novel. In fact, any "message" becomes part of the
texture, stirred so much that it's as negligible as a teaspoon of
salt in a large stew. Think of the number of artists who have
done still lifes—a view of a river, or a vase of flowers . . . there
is nothing about the choice of subject that is going to startle
anybody. What will distinguish one still life from another is
what the artist brings to it. To a certain extent that is true of
the novelist.

INTERVIEWER: What is your own feeling about Slocum?

HELLER: I told several people while I was writing the book
that Slocum was possibly the most contemptible character in

literature. Before I was finished, I began feeling sorry for him. That has happened to me before. That's why there are two generals in *Catch-22*. General Dreedle certainly had bad qualities, but then there were certain characteristics I liked (he was straightforward, honest, not a conniver), and I found I didn't want to attribute certain unsympathetic qualities to him. So I invented General Peckem as a sort of substitute scapegoat. Very hard to like *him*. But as for Slocum, many of my friends to whom I showed the book found not only compassion for him but strong identification. That surprised me, but I suppose it shouldn't have. He *is* very human.

INTERVIEWER: Does the reaction to your work often surprise you?

HELLER: Constantly. And I rely on it. I really don't know what I'm doing until people read what I've written and give me their reactions. I didn't know what *Catch-22* was all about until three months after it came out, when people, often total strangers who had no interest in saying the right (or wrong) things to me, began coming up and talking about the book. It meant different things to them. I thought the chaplain was the second most impressive character in the book (after Yossarian). But it turned out to be Milo. Then, it surprised me that things in *Catch-22* turned out to be very funny. I thought I was being humorous, but I didn't know I would make people laugh. In my apartment one day I heard this friend of mine in another room laughing out loud, and that was when I realized I could be comic. I began using that ability consciously—not to turn *Catch-22* into a comic work, but for contrast, for ironic effect. I really don't think authors know too much about the effect of what they're doing.

INTERVIEWER: Doesn't that bother you . . . that the author (you) has such a tentative grip . . . ?

HELLER: No. It's one of the things that makes it interesting. I would only be nervous if I were told that what I'd done was no good and no one would want to read it. I protect myself from that by submitting the first chapter to my agent, and to my editor, and, after about a third of the book is done, to other friends. They can be tough on me.

INTERVIEWER: Do you have an audience you keep in mind when you write?

HELLER: Since writing is really performing for people, unconsciously I must have an audience I'm writing for—someone who is really me, I suppose, with my degree of sensibility, my level of education, my interest in literature. . . .

INTERVIEWER: What sort of a discussion do you have with your friends about your work when it's in progress?

HELLER: It's never a discussion. They simply tell me what they think is good or bad. I do not always believe them. I try not to talk about it to anyone for years. I think of writing as private enterprise . . . since so much comes from rumination. Nothing is more personal than one's thoughts; I think I'd prefer to keep it that way.

INTERVIEWER: What are the best circumstances for this sort of ruminating?

HELLER: I have to be alone. A bus is good. Or walking the dog. Brushing my teeth is marvelous—it was especially so for *Catch-22*. Often when I am very tired, just before going to bed, while washing my face and brushing my teeth, my mind gets very clear . . . and produces a line for the next day's work, or some idea way ahead. I don't get my best ideas while actually writing . . . which is the agony of putting down what I think are good ideas and finding the words for them and the paragraph forms for them . . . a laborious process. I don't think of myself as a naturally gifted writer when it comes to using language. I distrust myself. Consequently, I try every which way with a sentence, then a paragraph, and finally a page, choosing words, selecting pace (I'm obsessed with that, even the pace of a sentence). I say to myself what I hope to put down on paper, but I hope not aloud. I think sometimes I move my lips, not only when I'm writing, but when I'm thinking of what I'm going to be having for dinner.

INTERVIEWER: How long can you keep at it?

HELLER: I ordinarily write three or four handwritten pages and then rework them for two hours. I can work for four hours, or forty-five minutes. It's not a matter of time. I set a realistic objective: How can I inch along to the next paragraph? Inching is what it is. It's not: How can I handle the next chapter? How can I get to the next stage in a way that I like? I think about that as I walk the dog or walk the twenty minutes from my apartment to the studio where I work.

INTERVIEWER: Do you put these ideas down as they occur to you?

HELLER: I keep a small sheath of three-by-five cards in my billfold. If I think of a good sentence, I'll write it down. It won't be an idea ("have him visit a brothel in New Orleans"). What I put down is an actual line of intended text ("In the brothel in New Orleans was like the time in San Francisco"). Of course, when I come back to it, the line may change considerably. Occasionally there's one that sings so perfectly the first time that it stays, like "My boy has stopped speaking to me and I don't think I can bear it." I wrote that down on a three-by-five card, perhaps on a bus, or after walking the dog. I store them in filing cabinets. The file on *Something Happened* is about four inches deep, the one on *Catch-22* about the length of a shoe box.

INTERVIEWER: Are there card files for unfinished work—like the Dunbar book you mentioned . . . ?

HELLER: No. I don't unfinish anything I start, and I don't start—as I've said—until I see the whole thing in my head.

INTERVIEWER: What are some of the other sources for material?

HELLER: I pick up a lot from friends. Mel Brooks. George Mandel. Especially Mandel. He talked about his experiences in the war. Once, he told me about talking to an army psychiatrist who asked him about his dreams, and George made one up about holding a fish in his hand. That's a bit in *Catch-22*. I've picked up a lot from him. He had the oddest medical ailment at one time—a stone in his salivary gland. It's very rare. And we can conclude that it was a very *small* stone. Well, it turns up in the hospital scene about the mixed-up records in *Catch-22*. Just a year ago Mandel suddenly became aware that Schrafft's no longer existed in New York, and that the *World-Telegram* wasn't being published anymore—somehow he hadn't noticed—and he said, "My God, soon there'll be nothing left." That went down on one of those three-by-five cards and was used in one of Bob Slocum's digressions in *Something Happened*. He's been very helpful.

INTERVIEWER: What about the influences from your reading?

HELLER: Every once in a while I can identify an influence. There's a page and a half in *Something Happened* which I wrote during my Jamesian period . . . the use of the word "ah?" When Slocum tells the psychiatrist he doesn't have auditory hallucinations but thinks he smells excrement, the psychiatrist says "Ah?" a number of times. It's out of *The Ambassadors*. The influence is not especially pronounced.

INTERVIEWER: What about personal contact with contemporary writers? Is that of use?

HELLER: I don't think writers are comfortable in each other's presence. We can talk, of course, for five minutes or so, but I don't think we want to socialize. There's always an acute status consciousness relating to how high or low a writer exists in the opinion of the person he's talking to. I've noticed that the opening gambit in conversation between two writers—and I'm always very uncomfortable hearing it—is "I like your work." I've heard it so often. It's so condescending. What if the person had not done any work? He would not be spoken to at all. This sort of relationship is peculiar to writers—after all, our status is never challenged by anyone else, one's jeweler, or a dress manufacturer. No, I don't think two novelists who have enjoyed a high measure of success can exist into their middle years living close to each other if both continue writing—I don't believe human nature can accept such a situation. The fact is there are few people with whom I would want to spend even a full weekend . . . to be in the same house or on a fishing trip with, unless I knew them well enough to go off by myself if I wanted to. I don't want to have to entertain them. In a novel you can't spend sixty pages writing about that sort of relationship.

INTERVIEWER: You wouldn't go on a fishing trip with Bob Slocum?

HELLER: No.

INTERVIEWER: How close is *Something Happened* to your own experience?

HELLER: Neither of my books was intended to be autobiographical. Both were based to a certain extent on experience —*Something Happened* is about someone who works in a company (which I have done) and who has a family (which I have), but it's also based to a great extent on my experience as an observer of other people and a reader of other writers. It's an imaginative work, after all—the most important ingredient in writing fiction is that *choice* is always available: *Who* will? *What* will? I told my wife and children years ago when they knew what *Something Happened* was about that they might think it was an exposé of their family life, and I told them— truthfully—that it was not about them. I did not feel (I said this half-facetiously to my wife) that she was interesting enough, or for that matter, that I myself was, to write a novel about.

I have had no experience with a brain-damaged child. But it turns out that the insecurity Bob Slocum feels not knowing how to deal with it is typical of parents who *do* have that experience . . . what's called "denial"—the refusal to accept the condition. Every time Slocum starts talking about the child, he starts digressing—and it's an accurate reaction.

INTERVIEWER: How do you compare the two novels?

HELLER: I think one difference between the two books is that *Catch-22* is concerned with physical survival against exterior forces or institutions that want to destroy life or moral self. *Something Happened* is concerned very much with interior, psychological survival in which the areas of combat are things like the wishes a person has, whether they are fulfilled or not, the close, intimate situations we have with our children when they're small and as they grow older, the memories we have of our relationship with parents as *they* grow older—these are some of the areas of disturbance in *Something Happened.* Of course, these areas are much more difficult to deal with than those in *Catch-22.* Given an Adolf Hitler, or inefficient or corrupt people, or people without sensibilities, we know what the dangers are, and we know what we must try to do. There's a line in *Something Happened:* "It was after the war that the struggle began."

INTERVIEWER: How long did it take you to write the climactic passage about the "something" which happens at the end of *Something Happened?*

HELLER: Two minutes. It had all been done years before sitting on that deck in Fire Island.

INTERVIEWER: Do titles come to you easily?

HELLER: There have only been a few. "Something Happened" turned up in the fall of '63 when I was walking with George Mandel past Korvettes or Brentano's and a kid came running past and yelled over his shoulder to another, "Hey come on, *something's happened*"—some sort of traffic accident I guess it must have been.

INTERVIEWER: You've spoken about music being important while you are working?

HELLER: It overcomes those noises that might distract me— a leaking faucet, my daughter's rock music in the other part of the apartment, or someone else's radio across the courtyard. I have tapes. I mostly listen to Bach, his choral music. Beethoven is OK; he's great, but Bach, for me, is the best.

INTERVIEWER: What about the necessary disciplines of writing?

HELLER: Well, I don't have social luncheons with people. By not having lunch with people it means that I do not have two martinis, which usually means the afternoon is not shot, since all I can do after two martinis is read the newspaper.

INTERVIEWER: Still, a considerable amount of time . . .

HELLER: I am a mysteriously slow writer. I say "mysteriously" because there is no accounting for it. I didn't start working on *Something Happened* until two years after that day on the Fire Island deck. In the meantime I started a musical comedy, wrote the final screenplay for *Sex and the Single Girl,* and then a television thing that turned out to be a sort of pilot of *McHale's Navy*—none of this especially serious stuff. Then the play *We Bombed in New Haven* took me away—not the writing of it (that only took six weeks) but the time spent working on the two productions. All this delay turned out to be for the better. When I went back to the two hundred and fifty pages I'd managed to get down on paper over those two years, I was able to write the book the way I wanted. I had learned more, and read more. The original forty pages became a hundred and twenty pages; the thirty pages of the second section became eighty; the seventy pages on the wife became a hundred—all of it much different in texture and mood from what I originally had in mind. It has happened with each novel. Originally, I didn't think *Catch-22* could be long enough to be more than a novelette. The addition became not padding but substance with a meaning and quality of its own. I missed my deadline for *Catch-22* by four or five years. I felt that it was the only book I was going to write, so I wanted to do it as well as I could. Actually, I wasn't ever sure I was going to be a writer. When I started *Catch-22,* I thought writing novels might be a useful way to kill time. I remember thinking that when I had the book one-third done and my agent was showing it to editors, that if they all had said, "No," I would not have finished the book. I don't have that narcissistic drive, the megalomania involved in spending years working on a book that no one is really interested in publishing. As it happened, there was no difficulty in finding a publisher. *Catch-22*, by the way, was the first novel I'd ever started.

INTERVIEWER: Has success changed your attitude about living or writing?

HELLER: I don't think so. And one reason is that it came to me so late. I don't think it's good to achieve too much at too early an age. What else can the future give you if you've already got all that your imagination has dreamt up for you? A writer is only discovered once in a lifetime, and if it happens very early the impossibility of matching that moment again can have a somewhat corrosive effect on his personality and indeed on the work itself.

INTERVIEWER: It seems to be a peculiarly American dilemma.

HELLER: It stems from a fundamental insecurity that afflicts successful Americans, particularly those who are self-made and have succeeded in a field in which there is a high element of risk. They never feel that they deserve their success, or that it is permanent; in fact, they seem to fear that their next book is going to cost them everything that they've gained . . . sort of like doubling up at roulette . . . betting on the black five times in a row. Actors suffer the same way. They can't believe it when they are successful. They're positive that an angel looking like Claude Rains is going to appear and say that a mistake has been made and "We're taking it all away from you." I'm not immune to it myself. It bothers me tremendously. But I like to think I'm over the hurdle. If I had finished my two books by the age of twenty-eight, well, I'd have a lot to worry about. That's not enough. But two books at age fifty-one means that the next one won't be due until I'm nearly seventy. I can coast for quite a while.

INTERVIEWER: Could you imagine not starting up again?

HELLER: If I thought I might never get an idea for another novel—one of those lines dropping in that provides a whole book—I don't think it would distress me. I've got two books under my belt now. I would be content to consider that a lifetime's work, and I could just putter around and find other things to do. I've been very lucky. I've written two books that were unusual and unusually successful.

INTERVIEWER: When did you begin writing?

HELLER: I wanted to be a writer when I was in the sixth grade —of course I wanted to be one without working at it. I wanted to be published in the New York *Daily News,* which published one short story a day in those days, or in *The New Yorker.* I remember writing a story about the Russian invasion of Finland and sending it to the *Daily News,* which, of course, rejected it. I was eleven years old. All my writing was imitative of what I was reading: the magazines that my older brother or sister would bring home; what the circulating libraries carried out in Coney Island, where we lived—why, I think I can remember Jerome Weidman's work in the 1930s better than he does. In 1948, when my first story came out in the *Atlantic* and nearly won the "Atlantic First," I thought I was pretty hot stuff. About that same time, Norman Mailer's *The Naked and the Dead* was published, and he was on the cover of *Saturday Review.* We were about the same age—twenty-six or twenty-seven—and it put me in my place.

INTERVIEWER: What about other fields of writing? Have you considered nonfiction?

HELLER: I don't do nonfiction well, and since I work so hard at writing, I might as well concentrate on what I know I can do. I'm too conscious of myself as a writer to be a journalist. I'm a show-off. When I write, I want people to notice me and that I'm doing something different from other people. A journalist—at least the ones I admire—is a writer who can make me forget his involvement so that I can concentrate on the subject of the piece, not the personality of the author. The journalist and the novelist have completely different intelligences. Journalists almost always compose on typewriters. They rarely do more than one draft. Somehow they think in terms of openings, development, conclusion—all in almost automatic sequences. I envy that gift. But if I had it, I'd be a journalist. You can't have it both ways.

INTERVIEWER: Have you had any of those first lines come to mind since finishing *Something Happened?*

HELLER: Dozens! I think when a book is finished and the editor likes it, and it's been handed in, an author goes through a period of nervous craziness. Some writers invest in Canadian uranium stocks; others change agents or wives or commit suicide. Some writers hear voices. It's not a good time in which to trust one's own judgment. The author has been too busy and intent. I remember one first line that came to me during this time was, "The kid, they say, was born in a manger, but frankly I have my doubts." It's not a bad line, but I wouldn't think a book would come out of it. . . . I did go further for a while, and I liked the idea, but it led me ultimately to remember Eliot's opening line about the Magi coming to the manger in, I think, *Ash-Wednesday*—"a cold coming we had of it"—and I gave it up after that. So I guess I'll have to wait around for another line to drop in. . . .

GEORGE PLIMPTON
Winter 1974

11. William Gass

William Gass was born in Fargo, North Dakota, on July 30, 1924, and grew up in Warren, Ohio. He was graduated magna cum laude from Kenyon College, where he majored in philosophy, and in 1954 earned a Ph.D. in philosophy from Cornell University. One impulse behind his fiction has been a fascination with literary theory and experimental construction. "I try to make things out of words," he has said, "the way a sculptor might make a statue out of stone."

Although Gass's first stories had been published in *Accent,* it was his first novel, *Omensetter's Luck,* twelve years in the writing, that brought him recognition as an important literary presence upon its publication in 1966. A collection of stories, *In the Heart of the Heart of the Country,* as well as an experimental novella, *Willie Masters' Lonesome Wife,* appeared in 1968. He has published two collections of essays, *Fiction and the Figures of Life* (1970) and *The World Within the Word* (1978), in addition to *On Being Blue,* a single long essay that came out in 1976. His criticism and short fiction have been extensively reprinted in anthologies such as *The Best American Short Stories,* and various chapters of his work-in-progress, *The Tunnel,* have been published in the *American Review, TriQuarterly,* and other magazines during the past decade. His most recently published book is *House VI,* an essay on architecture, with photographs and drawings by Peter Eisenman.

William Gass has been both a Guggenheim and Rockefeller Foundation Fellow, as well as the recipient of two awards from the National Academy of Arts and Letters (in 1975 and 1979), and twice a judge for the National Book Awards.

The father of three children by his first marriage, Gass is now married to Mary Alice Henderson. They have twin daughters and live in St. Louis, where he is the David May Distinguished Professor in the Humanities at Washington University.

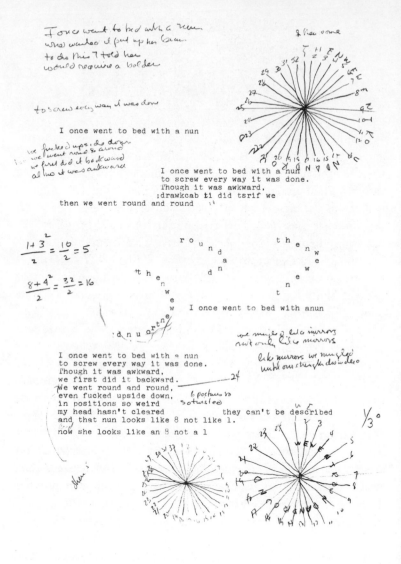

I once went to bed with a nun
who wanted I put up her ...
to do this I told her
would require a bolder

I knew some

to screw every way I was done

I once went to bed with a nun

we fucked upside down
we went round & around
we first did it backward
al tho it was awkward

I once went to bed with a nun
to screw every way it was done.
Though it was awkward,
;drawkcab ti did tsrif we
then we went round and round

$$\frac{1+3^2}{2} = \frac{16}{2} = 5$$

$$\frac{8+4^2}{2} = \frac{32}{2} = 16$$

r o u n d a n d

t h e n w e

t h e n w e

I once went to bed with anun

we mingle like mirrors
not only like mirrors

like mirrors we mingled
until our strength dwindled

I once went to bed with a nun
to screw every way it was done.
Though it was awkward,
we first did it backward.
we went round and round,
even fucked upside down,
in positions so weird
my head hasn't cleared
and that nun looks like 8 not like 1.
now she looks like an 8 not a 1

6 postures so
so twisted

they can't be described

$\frac{1}{3}$ o

A William Gass manuscript page.

William Gass

In the book-bound alcove off the bare room where he writes when at home, William Gass gave this interview in July of 1976. Sitting in cutoffs and T-shirt, sipping on a bottle of Ballantine ale, Gass, at age 53, resembles a boyish headmaster at his Sunday ease. When he talks, the small shifts of his compact body, the voice's inflections, and the mind's dartings reveal a writer harsh on himself and his work, though generous in his responses.

INTERVIEWER: Do you feel you are writing full throat now?

GASS: I hope so, but if I am a hound, at what am I baying? I am basically a closet romantic, a tame wild man. When I was in college, I closed the closet door behind me. Then, for all sorts of reasons, some artistic if you like, but at bottom personal as bottoms are, I became a formalist: I became detached; I emphasized technique; I practiced removal. I was a van. I took away things. And I became a toughie, a hard-liner. When I was in high school, I chanted Thomas Wolfe and burned as I thought Pater demanded and threatened the world as a good Nietzschean should. Then, at college, in a single day I decided to change my handwriting . . . which meant, I realized later, a change in the making of the words which even then were all of me I cared to have admired. It was a really odd decision. Funny. Strange. I sat down with the greatest deliberation and thought how I would make each letter of the alphabet from that moment on. A strange thing to do. Really strange. And for years I carefully wrote in this new hand; I wrote everything —marginal notes, reminders, messages—in a hand that was very Germanic and stiff. It had a certain artificial elegance, and from time to time I was asked to address wedding invitations, but when I look at that hand now I am dismayed, if not a little frightened, it is so much like strands of barbed wire. Well, that change of script was a response to my family situation and in particular to my parents. I fled an emotional problem and hid myself behind a wall of arbitrary formality. Nevertheless, I think that if I eventually write anything which has any enduring merit, it will be in part because of that odd alteration. I submitted myself to a comparatively formal, rather rigorous, kind of philosophical training. I stuffed another tongue in my mouth. It changed my tastes. It wasn't Shelley any longer, it was Pope. It wasn't even Melville, it was James. Most of these changes were for the better because, being a little older, I saw more in my new choices than I had in my old ones. But now, after maybe twenty years of not going near Nietzsche—of even being embarrassed by my youthful enthusiasms—I find him exciting again. My handwriting has slowly relaxed and is now the sloppy kindergarten scrawl I had as a child. I suspect the same kind of thing is happening in my work. I am ready to go in any direction. But I hope I've learned that the forms are inherent, that the formal discipline is inherent, so that when

I want to start improvising I won't have forgotten how to dance. It wasn't until I was ready to come out of my formal phase that I began to read Rilke. Once I took my thumb out of my mouth—well—soon there was no dike. So now I try to manage two horses: there is one called Valéry and another called Rilke. I remember I once compared writing to the image of the charioteer in the Phaedrus. Intellectually, Valéry is still the person I admire most among artists I admire most; but when it comes to the fashioning of my own work now, I am aiming at a Rilkean kind of celebrational object, thing, *Ding*.

INTERVIEWER: How much did this change have to do with your family?

GASS: I think a lot of it was deeply personal. Every powerful reason is a cause, accounts for a condition. When you decide to change your handwriting, and when you sit down and spend a day or more making new characters, you've got to be in an outraged and outrageous state of mind. I simply rejected my background entirely. I decided, as one of my characters says, to pick another cunt to come from. Did I come out of that hole in the wallpaper, Rilke has his hero Malte wonder. I just had to make myself anew—or rather, *seem* to. So I simply started to do it. And I think it very obvious now, though it wasn't obvious to me then, that I should pick the way I formed words to be the point where I should try to transform everything. The alphabet, for Christ's sake—I would have changed that, if I'd been able. So all along one principal motivation behind my writing has been to be other than the person I am. To cancel the consequences of the past. I am not the person who grew up in some particular place, though people try to label me as a local midwestern writer. But I never had roots: all my sources (as a writer) were chosen. I chose to be influenced by this or that book or chose to be defined as the author of this or that. I think that for a long time I was simply emotionally unable to handle my parents' illnesses. My mother was an alcoholic and my father was crippled by arthritis and his own character.

I just fled. It was a cowardly thing to do, but I simply would not have survived. I still hate scenes unless I make them. My situation certainly wasn't more severe than most people endure at some time in their lives, but I was not equipped to handle it. What is perhaps psychologically hopeful is that in *The Tunnel* I am turning back to inspect directly that situation, and that means I haven't entirely rejected it. On the other hand, I am taking a damn long time to write the book. But I don't know. What is psychologically best for a writer is what produces his best work. I suspect that in order for me to produce my best work I have to be angry. At least I find that easy. I am angry all the time.

INTERVIEWER: Have you spent a good part of your writing life getting even?

GASS: Yes . . . yes. Getting even is one great reason for writing. The precise statement of the motive is tricky, but the clearest expression of my unwholesome nature and my mean motives (apart from trying to write well) appears in a line I like in "In the Heart of the Heart of the Country." The character says, "I want to rise so high that when I shit I won't miss anybody." But maybe I say it's a motive because I like the line. Anyway, my work proceeds almost always from a sense of aggression. And usually I am in my best working mood when I am, on the page, very combative, very hostile. That's true even when I write to praise, as is often the case. If I write about Colette, as I am now, my appreciation will be shaped by the sap-tongued idiots who don't perceive her excellence. I also take considerable pleasure in giving obnoxious ideas the best expression I can. But getting even isn't necessarily vicious. There are two ways of getting even: one is destructive and the other is restorative. It depends on how the scales are weighted. Justice, I think, is the word I want.

INTERVIEWER: Isn't there a line in *Willie Masters' Lonesome Wife* about the pencil moving against the page with anger?

GASS: Something like that, sure. I am developing a theory

about that in an essay I'm writing on creativity. One doesn't want to generalize from what might be just a private psychology, but it seems to me the emotion is central. There is another sentence from *Willie* that should be mentioned here, though: "how close in the end is a cunt to a concept; we enter both with joy." That's the other line of mine I remember with pleasure. And both express something very close to me. If someone asks me, "Why do you write?" I can reply by pointing out that it is a very dumb question. Nevertheless, there is an answer. I write because I hate. A lot. Hard. And if someone asks me the inevitable next dumb question, "Why do you write the way you do?" I must answer that I wish to make my hatred acceptable because my hatred is much of me, if not the best part. Writing is a way of making the writer acceptable to the world—every cheap, dumb, nasty thought, every despicable desire, every noble sentiment, every expensive taste. There isn't very much satisfaction in getting the world to accept and praise you for things that the world is prepared to praise. The world is prepared to praise only shit. One wants to make sure that the complete self, with all its qualities, is not just accepted but approved . . . not just approved—whoopeed.

INTERVIEWER: Did your years at Kenyon College have much influence on your later aesthetic positions?

GASS: Not directly. I was already very fascinated by Ransom's stuff when I was in high school. I wrote an article on Ransom and sent it to him at the *Kenyon Review*. It was god-awful, but he was very sweet and returned it with a nice letter. I'd never met him, but I was so in love with the man's "manner" I scrawled his initials in the books of his I owned and pretended to others that he'd signed them. When I got to Kenyon he did remember my essay, or was polite enough to pretend to. And that "manner" was real. When I was going to school there, the faculty were very much under the influence of Ransom and the New Criticism, but I think that influence was so widespread you'd have found it most places. I did audit a few courses that

Ransom taught, but I didn't take any courses in English while I was at Kenyon. I was busy taking philosophy and other things of that sort. And I found that I fought English classes. I was such a smart ass I thought I knew much more than the instructor. No, my pretentions got ground beneath another heel. I couldn't get published in the literary magazine—not a colorful fart, not a thumbprint. The students were very good writers; some of them were publishing in the *Review* already. And I held a small, limp pen; I was terrified and crushed; I couldn't get anywhere; I was unbelievably bad; I was lousy. I knew the formalist ideas were in the air, of course, but I didn't really come face to face with them in any extensive way until I went to grad school, so I think that the influence of Kenyon was predominantly philosophical.

INTERVIEWER: What was your orientation when you were working on your Ph.D. in philosophy at Cornell?

GASS: I wanted to work in aesthetics, but they didn't have anybody who was interested in the area, and I didn't take any courses in the subject. They had a nice elderly man the students called "Bedsprings" because he rocked from his toes to his heels all the time and stared at the girls. Most of my courses were in language analysis, philosophy of science, logic, and the theory of meaning. The faculty finally settled on allowing me one wild paper a year which they would be agreeable about and not grade. What I eventually ended up doing was working with the philosophy of language and the theory of metaphor with Max Black. I had to learn to write analytical stuff for all these people, and it is not my natural manner. I hated it in lots of ways because I was working against the grain all the time. But it was very good for me. It was a superb faculty.

INTERVIEWER: Do you still retain that rigor?

GASS: I can still use it, though it isn't easy. I still admire it. I hope I can recognize its many fakes. Now I don't have to be what one would call rigorous very often anymore except in some classroom situations, because when I'm writing I find it very difficult to harmonize a desire for a certain kind of style with the rigor and precision appropriate to a certain kind of subject. The only compromise I can manage is expressed by the hope that I've done a reasonably thorough job on any philosophical issue before I start to write, so that beneath that fluffy, flamboyant style and all that sweet, sugary rhetoric there is some real cake—some sense at least of the complications of the problem. But I don't pretend to be treating issues in any philosophical sense. I am happy to be aware of how complicated, and how far from handling certain things properly I am, when I am swinging so wildly around.

INTERVIEWER: It seems that the style no matter how flamboyant is always very precise.

GASS: Well, I hope so, and you are a kind person to suggest it. Rigor is achieved by pushing things very hard and trying to uncover every possible ramification, nuance, and aspect, and then ordering those things very, very carefully. I think that's always valuable. Still, the kind of ordering you get in philosophy is quite different from the kind you try for in literature, although there is a similarity—an analogy. That's one of the reasons why I admire mathematicians, I guess. You found beauty listening to Austin give a lecture—he presented a beautiful landscape of the mind. Everything was so crisp and beautifully drawn. It was like watching a good draftsman. It wasn't as profound or original as Wittgenstein, for instance, but it was really a pleasure to hear such a careful disposal of ideas: a trash bag anybody'd be happy to plug on TV.

INTERVIEWER: Is Austin's and Searle's notion of speech acts of any use to you as a writer?

GASS: If you start talking about speech acts, what you are doing is connecting the notion of writing with a concept of performance. I think contemporary fiction is divided between those who are still writing performatively and those who are not. Writing for voice, in which you imagine a performance in the auditory sense going on, is traditional and old-fashioned

and dying. The new mode is not performative and not auditory. It's destined for the printed page, and you are really
supposed to read it the way they teach you to read in speed-
reading. You are supposed to crisscross the page with your eye,
getting references and gists; you are supposed to see it flowing
on the page, and not sound it in the head. If you do sound it,
it is so bad you can hardly proceed. It can't all have been
written by Dreiser, but it sounds like it. *Gravity's Rainbow* was
written for print, *J.R.* was written by the mouth for the ear.
By the mouth for the ear: that's the way I'd like to write. I can
still admire the other—the way I admire surgeons, bronc bust-
ers, and tight ends. As writing, it is that foreign to me.

INTERVIEWER: But in *Willie Masters' Lonesome Wife* . . .

GASS: Oh, sure, there I'm playing around with it. . . . Yes,
I was trying out some things. Didn't work. Most of them didn't
work. I was trying to find a spatial coordinate to go with the
music, but my ability to manipulate the spatial and visual side
of the medium was so hopelessly amateurish (I was skating on
one galosh), and the work also had to go through so many
hands, that the visual business was only occasionally successful,
and most of that was due to the excellent design work of Larry
Levy, not me. Too many of my ideas turned out to be only ideas
—situations where the reader says, "Oh yeah, I get the idea,"
but that's all there is to get, the idea. I don't give a shit for ideas
—which in fiction represent inadequately embodied projects—
I care only for affective effects. I'm still fooling around with
visual business, but I am thinking of a way to make them
sound. One problem, for instance, is trying to get the sense (in
print) of different lines of language being sounded at the same
time, or alternately, or at different speeds or pitch, as in music.

INTERVIEWER: You've said that the love of the word as a
resonance or shape is the least understood of all aesthetic
phenomena.

GASS: One of the things which children do early on is discover the ability they have to surround themselves with their

own sensory world. Shit, piss, and bellow, kick and wiggle: that's it! I think that what often makes writers is a continued sense of the marvelous palpable quality of making words and sounding them. My God, how Beckett has it. I have a very strong feeling about that love of making sounds. I think it must have been very enjoyable—in the old days—to form letters with your quill or pen and hand. I, for example, still have an old typewriter. An electric takes away from the expressiveness of the key. It was very important for Rilke to send a copy of the finished poem in his beautiful hand to somebody, because *that was* the poem, not the printed imitation. Writing by hand, mouthing by mouth: in each case you get a very strong physical sense of the emergence of language—squeezed out like a well-formed stool—what satisfaction! what bliss! That's another reason why I like the metaphor, in *Willie Masters,* of cunt and concept. As an artist you are dealing with a very abstract thing when you are dealing with language (and if you don't realize that, you miss everything), yet suddenly it is there in your mouth with great particularity—drawl, lisp, spit. When the word passes out into the world, that particularity is ignored; print obliterates it; type has no drawl. But if you can write for that caressing, slurring, foulmouthed singing drunken voice . . . that's a miracle. Gertrude Stein said poetry was caressing nouns, and I think she was right, only I wouldn't leave out verbs or prepositions, articles or adverbs, anything. . . .

As a writer you are, of course, aware of the arbitrary relationship of symbol-sounds to their meanings; but no real writer wants it that way. In doing *On Being Blue,* I was struck by the way in which meanings are historically attached to words: it is so accidental, so remote, so twisted. A word is like a schoolgirl's room—a complete mess—so the great thing is to make out a way of seeing it all as ordered, as right, as inferred and following. Now, when you take language out of the realm in which it is produced and put it in poetry and fiction, you transform it completely. Maybe *that* is the least understood aesthetic phenomenon. That process of transformation is perhaps the essence of creative activity. And if you take really bowel-turning material from the point of view of its pragmatic importance in the world, and surround it like kitty litter with stuff that is there purely for play, then you can get an electric line between the two poles clothes would turn white simply hanging on. The electricity of Elizabethan drama is total. They are talking always of life and death matters, but they are standing there playing with their mouths.

INTERVIEWER: Do you sound words over and over to yourself at the typewriter?

GASS: Yes. One time, two times, three times, times, times, times. . . . That's the final test. When that goes well, all's well —well, nearly all's well. And it stands. A bad line or a missed start will get scratched down so deeply in my head like a schoolkid's desk he's trying to carve "fuck," "cunt," and his name on, that it becomes extremely hard for me to start over and go at the sentence in a different way. I am almost never able to do that. If I've a botch at the beginning, I have to keep fiddling around until I have somehow fiddled it into a squeak, the squeak into the score. This damn imprinting is one of the hardest things I have to overcome. But I also appreciate Valéry's account of how a poem came to him because and while he was walking the meter. When work is going well for me— which is rarely—I have a clear metrical sense of sound and pace. This whole problem is vital. When one section is singing, it sings the rest. I've heard many of the speeches in Elkin that way. The song began and sang itself. Prose gives you flexibility, and you want to use it to shift the whole mode or manner of voice within a paragraph or within a single sentence. So you must have a notion, some clues, which will do the job. Joyce fiddled around with a lot of things trying to get that done, but I didn't get those clues of his until I heard him on records. Then I realized how he should be sung and that he had in mind a notation which isn't present in the book.

One problem is that the reader isn't conditioned, hasn't the time, intelligence, patience, to perform the work. When you think of being a good reader, you tend to think of yourself or somebody as having a sharp eye, quick intelligence, who pays attention, follows this resonance of meaning or that, and has a good memory for what happened before, and all that admirable true crap. But who thinks of the reader as an oral interpreter? When I read a traditional novel, I never remember anything except language, the rhythms in the language patterns, and I do have a good memory for that. I think I forgot the basic plot of *Middlemarch* hours after I read it, and it was of course a terrific book. But the impression, the quality of its style, that I think I shall remember forever. One used to read Henry James aloud. It's the only way to read him. But it takes time; you've got to figure out how to do it, and all this alters the temporal reach of the work entirely. Beckett is our best example. You look at the text and you see all those pauses. You say to yourself, yes, there are pauses, but you don't pause. You don't perform it. If you don't perform it, you ain't got it. In music, you can't *think* the rests, pretend the silences. There happen to be some splendid Beckett manuscripts at Washington University, and they taught me a great deal. I went over a little story called "Ping" one day with the idea of reading it aloud. It's about six or seven pages, but it is a half an hour or more in the reciting. If you do it properly, well spaced, larded with silence, then it's overpowering. You gotta wait, you know, and wait, and wait, and wait, and we just don't do that sort of thing—the world turns—who has time to wait between two syllables for just a little literary revelation? A lot of modern writers, I remember saying, are writing for the fast mind that speeds over the text like those noisy bastards in motorboats. The connections are all spatial and all at various, complicated, intellectual levels. They stand to literature as fast-food to food.

INTERVIEWER: Have you considered giving the reader some

kind of extratextual directions on how to read, as Barth does in *Lost in the Funhouse?*

GASS: "The Pedersen Kid" has some. *Willie* is full of them. I keep fussing around, trying to find ways to symbolize what I want. But notation . . . notation . . . what a difficulty! The myth is that Joyce tried to indicate that the speed passages in *Finnegans Wake* should be taken by variously spacing the words. In the novel I'm working on now, I want, for instance, a certain word to sound like a bell the whole time the reader is reading certain lines. I want this bong going bong all the bonging time. I'm trying to figure out what device will work —on the page—not only to give the proper instruction to the reader, but make him begin to hear it—dead dead dead dead —the way it's supposed to go. But as soon as you try to note it, the page goes crazy, and you get a dozen other things you want no part of.

INTERVIEWER: Is the reader an adversary for you?

GASS: No. I don't think much about the reader. Ways of reading are adversaries—those theoretical ways. As far as writing something is concerned, the reader really doesn't exist. The writer's business is somehow to create in the work something which will stand on its own and make its own demands; and if the writer is good, he discovers what those demands are, and he meets them, and creates this thing which readers can then do what they like with. Gertrude Stein said, "I write for myself and strangers," and then eventually she said that she wrote only for herself. I think she should have taken one further step. You don't write *for* anybody. People who send you bills do that. People who want to sell you things so they can send you bills do that. People who want to tell you things so they can sell you things so they can send you bills do that. You are advancing an art—the art. That is what you are trying to do.

INTERVIEWER: How important is it to you to establish some verisimilitude of character to release language?

GASS: Not terribly important. But what you are suggesting is. What I want to do is establish the legitimacy of the verbal source, which is sometimes a character, but it is sometimes a situation or some other kind of excuse. It must seem the right source. You mustn't turn on your tub tap and get crankcase oil. But this has little relationship to how people actually might talk or how oil might actually flow. People tell me that my characters are going crazy, and perhaps they believe that because I don't pay enough attention to verisimilitude. I don't think they are crazy, but the heightened language, the rapid shifts of feeling, the kinds of construction I am fond of—these do make readers think that the mind they are experiencing is not an ordinary one, that the consciousness they've been made conscious of is unusual, and that therefore it must be unhinged, extreme. I have a problem with dialogue because it is difficult for me to envision the total context in which the heightened language I sometimes want to use for conversation is justifiable.

INTERVIEWER: It seems to me that a number of the voices in your fiction are obsessional.

GASS: That's an impression which may come from my methods of construction. A particular piece is likely to be the exploration of a symbol or a certain set of symbols, and this constrains the text. No meaning can go away without returning. If you're writing an ordinary, naturalistic novel, you would be normally interested in the range and extent of experiences and responses and other people. I'm not. You'd want to give the impression of a large world, as if the land was larger than the feet of your fiction. Like Lowry, I want closure, suffocation, the sense that there is nowhere else to go. Also, I think the voices tend to reinforce the impression because I often locate the work in a single consciousness. Solipsism is one of the risks of the letter "I." If we were really listening in on any person's subconscious talk, it would sound pretty obsessional. One is consumed by one's self.

INTERVIEWER: Is "Icicles" a kind of sport for you? It does create a voice—the real estate salesman—we might hear on TV.

GASS: The central images I wanted to develop led to that—basically the idea of the icicles as a kind of property, then as part of real estate. And pretty soon I was into the real estate business. I couldn't give this language to the main character, but I did want to carry a certain notion of property forward as far as possible. I sort of backed into that, starting—as I usually do—with a concrete symbol that I wanted to explore: what can I do with the image of the icicle. I ended up deep in philosophical materialism.

INTERVIEWER: That is the way a lot of your stories start?

GASS: Almost invariably now. The only story that didn't start that way was my first one, "The Pedersen Kid," which had its story line first. All the others have begun with a very concrete everyday image—insects, icicles—or in the case of the novel subordinate suns circling the larger theme of luck—skipping stones, and so on. That's where the unity, if you can find it in my work, comes from. I am exposing a symbolic center. When I think the exposure is complete, I am finished with the story. It's more than peeling a peach.

I used to collect names as possibilities. Certain characters in a sense emerged from their names. I never conceive a character and then seek to christen it. I always have to have the words. I can't even get a story going until I have the title. The title, though, is a direct statement of the central image. If I try to think out in outline some linear structure, then I start pushing my material in that direction like a baby in a pram. When you arrive at your destination, all you still have is a baby in a pram. I want the work to write itself, every passage to emerge from the ones which have come before, so I have to keep looking at what I've done to see what will come out. Usually nothing does and I have to rewrite my beginning until something does suggest itself.

INTERVIEWER: Do some of these images become emblematic for you? Spiders, for example.

GASS: Yes, they become a certain kind of emblem. I am very fond of spiders. I am as fond of them as my family allows me to be. I used to have a house out in the country and it sheltered many spiders. Once, quite a large, handsome spider spun his web in the john, where I could conveniently watch him. And of course the family wanted that ughyukky spider removed. I regarded it as a convenient symbol of the imagination: spinning, lying in wait, sucking dry. Maybe my family wanted the imagination removed. But partly I used the spider because, in general, I like insects. I like to watch them operate. I think animals have the same fascination, but except for a few household pets, you have to go out to the zoo to see them. You can watch a spider the way you can sometimes watch people on the New York subway. You can inspect them. Raccoons move too much, and are hard to get close to. That's one reason I spend a lot of time examining objects. They hold still. They aren't threatened or embarrassed by your stare. I don't *regard* as much as I once did, but I realized that I was looking for sources of language, and now my source of language is almost always other language instead of things in the world. Words are the supreme objects. They are *minded* things.

INTERVIEWER: You described the most important intellectual experience of your life, seeing Wittgenstein, as almost wholly with content. How important is the notion of activity to you?

GASS: That was Wittgenstein's famous definition of philosophy: it was an activity, a certain way of doing which was without end. That notion is very similar to the one Valéry had about poetry. He was interested in the activity of writing, the consciousness in the act of composing, creating, and less so (he said) in the final result—which wasn't for him final, only the sign of an absolute weariness. Well, I'm very interested in the process, of course. I can become my subject. But I am interested in the process because of what I want it to lead to—the story, the poem. Perfection. But the process is a great lure, and you can postpone failure by dallying along the way like Ulysses. I can hardly get from one sentence to the next.

INTERVIEWER: Is that why you write so slowly?

GASS: I write slowly because I write badly. I have to rewrite everything many, many times just to achieve mediocrity. Time can give you a good critical perspective, and I often have to go slow so that I can look back on what sort of botch of things I made three months ago. Much of the stuff which I will finally publish, with all its flaws, as if it had been dashed off with a felt pen, will have begun eight or more years earlier, and worried and slowly chewed on and left for dead many times in the interim.

INTERVIEWER: You've said that when you first started writing you wrote only sentences. Was this the result of your philosophical skepticism about language or a program of exercises?

GASS: Experiments. I have no skepticism about language. I know it can bamboozle, but I am a believer. No. My experiments were stimulated by my reading of Gertrude Stein. I didn't really get to know her work until I was in graduate school. Talk about having your head tipped. I suddenly realized that I don't know anything about the basic forms that I was supposed to be managing. Nothing. So I studied her very carefully. I am still studying her, and I have always learned a lot. She made me understand how little I knew about what could be done with the basic units of all writing. And she raised philosophical questions about what the basic unit really was, or whether there was one, and about the functions of grammar. In philosophy we were interested in some of the same things then, but we weren't then raising important aesthetic issues. Now every issue is aesthetic. I don't know which is worse. But one of the wonderful things about Gertrude is that her repetitions rearrange the aesthetic grammar of the sentence and impose this new or special grammar upon the ordinary syntax of English. When I started to examine what she was up to, I realized that I had to begin to get a feel, the way a painter would, of what happens when you try a sentence this way or try it that. To write sentences out of context is a fool's business, but I set about doing the fool's business. You can't really talk very sensibly about the content of a sentence out of the context of its use, but you can talk a lot about the form of the sentence and how the forms are interlaced and how they interact within a sentence. I practiced a long time, I mean a long time, writing sentences and connecting sentences and generally fiddling around. I think I learned something. But not enough. I'm still doing it.

INTERVIEWER: How do you define the aesthetic difference?

GASS: Much of it is musical, most of it is defined by the gut, and theoretically—well, it gets "defined" by negation. Most sentences are *formed* for the sake of communication. For efficiency, clarity; but rhetorical forms are there for the sake of effect, for persuasion. There are poetic forms too. Of course, you end up simply feeling that things are going right or, alas, that they are not.

INTERVIEWER: Does it have to go against the grain to be right for you?

GASS: I don't think so, but it's true that I'm unlikely to trust anything that isn't against the grain. I am unlikely to trust a sentence that comes easily. I should love to be able to write with ease, but I can't, and when I do push ahead or rush on, the result is invariably poor. I have a bad attitude toward things which come easy—wine, women, work, or song—an attitude quite false to the facts, of course.

INTERVIEWER: Two words recur throughout your criticism—"model" and "metaphor." What is their importance to you?

GASS: I love metaphor the way some people love junk food. I think metaphorically, feel metaphorically, see metaphorically. And if anything in writing comes easily, comes unbidden, often unwanted, it is metaphor. "Like" follows "as" as night the day.

Now, most of these metaphors are bad and have to be thrown away. Who saves used Kleenex? I never have to say: "What shall I compare this to?" A summer's day? No. I have to beat the comparisons back into the holes they pour from. Some salt is savory. I live in a sea. But that's why I am so lost in the Elizabethans, because they seem to have sunk in the same ocean. What is not metaphorical, is not.

Leave nothing well enough alone is my motto, and I have been studying the phenomenon of language called metaphor since graduate school. Metaphor has been thought to be a pet of language, a peculiar relation between subject and predicate mainly: unhealthy, odd. But you can make metaphors by juxtaposing objects, and in lots of other ways. Suppose the relation between literary language and the world were itself metaphorical? Suppose the relation between language and life is like the relation between the subject and the predicate in a metaphor? If the analogy held, then one might find in it a way to express the relationship between literature and the world which wouldn't be quite so severe as the formalist position I once took required, and yet avoid the imbecility which makes it into some "meaningful" commentary. I've been principally interested in establishing the relationship between fiction and the world. If we can see that relation as a metaphorical one, then we are already several steps in the direction of models. Theory, in science, is frequently conceived as that which flows from a model. Indeed, making the model and constructing the theory are not always two different activities. The kinds of misinterpretation which arouse my wrath—not to say contempt—are paralleled, one finds, by misinterpretations of scientific facts/theories/laws which lead to paradoxes and confusions of every kind.

INTERVIEWER: If fiction is a metaphor, what is a good metaphor for fiction?

GASS: I have thrown out a number of them, and I wouldn't regard any of them as much good. A fiction is certainly not a mirror dawdling down a road. If I could think of a good one, I would put it in a novel. It's not an emotional model of the world—that's too narrow. It's more like a phenomenological model.

INTERVIEWER: A character in *The Tunnel* is writing a limerical history of the world. Why don't you write poetry other than your limericks?

GASS: I can't. I would love to. When I was young I tried, but it was awful. Not just bad, but monumentally so. I tend to use the word "poetry" as a generic term for everything I approve of, but I am unable to manage those narrower forms for any length of time or with any success. I can explore prose sentences and prose-paragraph structures. Those can be pretty tight sometimes, and certainly as formal as a poem. But when it comes to the damn poetry itself—well, I don't really know why I am so bad. Maybe I'm just a big dog and need a lot of room to turn around in. I can get away with a limerick because it is a very short form. I can turn out couplets, too, but not enough of them to make a whole poem. I have to be constantly discovering my form while I am working. In poetry, when you write the first two lines you have to have flung out the form fourteen or twenty-five lines ahead of you, but it takes me more than twenty-five lines to find the form I should have flung out ahead of me in the first place.

INTERVIEWER: You mentioned "playing around with form" before. How does that work in, say, "In the Heart of the Heart of the Country"?

GASS: Suppose somebody says, "Why don't you write a piece of journalism about how it is to live in the Midwest?" It is not an interesting suggestion, and I don't think I am going to do it, but I nevertheless get curious. I take a few notes. I take a lot of notes. The notes are of themselves a kind of form. Here are a lot of little headings: under this, such and such, under that, so and so. Then you begin to see that you've got these little blocks of information, and you start thinking, Maybe I

could harden these up and move them around. So you start
thinking what kind of pattern of presentation would achieve
the best effect. It is like establishing a kind of very large sentence. You ask yourself what kind of existing form your notes
are closest to. Notes! of course! you cry out. You can hear me,
I imagine. And so word resemblance leads you on, not form.
So you've really got a musical problem, certain paragraphs you
are arranging, and you imagine you are orchestrating the flow
of feelings from one thing to another. You want each note to
have a certain integrity, but of course you are already thinking
of how notes fit together. And you've got this private metaphor
of note card and note in music. Once you get your key signa-
ture, the theme inherent in the notes begins to emerge: the
relationship between art and life and all that. And the town
you've started to describe is called Brookston, but you don't
want to call it that, and in a moment the B you've reduced it
to is reminding you of Byzantium, which goes with the theme,
so you decide to explore Byzantium poems, though with an
ironic twist. You start out with "So I have sailed the seas and
come . . . to B." Have I really come to be? No. Certain themes
are developed that parallel themes in Yeats. The story moves
through a series of suggestions, of formal relationships. And
eventually what you want to do is take account of the kind of
formal relationship that begins to emerge simply from a set of
notes—simply from an accumulation of data—from the flow
of commentary and the appreciation of a set of poems. For
me any piece is a play of various forms against one another.
When I am playing with forms, it is often simply to find a
form for something odd like the garbage. I love lists. They
begin with no form at all . . . often, anyway. A list of
names is very challenging. There is one right order, and the
problem is to find it.

INTERVIEWER: You are doing this damn thing on the floor
of your study, shuffling and threading these cards—or forms.

The reader is reading the story once, ten times, twenty times. He will never catch up with you.

GASS: He doesn't need to. If you convey, in the kind of story I've been going on about, if you convey a certain note-taking quality, a little crude sociology, that's all that's necessary. All these other devices are primarily for the psychological side of the creative process, not for the reader. The reader has to feel a certain set of moves. He doesn't have to know the calculations. Still, if you took the trouble to label the sections of "In the Heart . . ." as you would describe a rhyme scheme, you'd find a pattern. I played with lots of different patterns before I found one that suited me. But what suits ultimately is not the fact that something fits an abstract pattern. You have to feel a resolution and a movement in the fit, otherwise it's no good. Most of these formal tics are private.

INTERVIEWER: Is much of the activity of your writing simply to amuse you or interest you as an exploration, with no hope that the reader will catch any of this? Is it necessary for you in order to keep writing?

GASS: Amuse may be the wrong word because it hurts so much, but in essence what you are suggesting is correct. Psychologically these games are necessary. Every writer plays them, though what they are varies a good deal. It is also a protective device which can be dangerous. You may feel that certain things which you have put down on the page are justified because you know how they satisfy your blessed apparatus. That, of course, won't do. I think for most writers there are little private projects which each work undertakes, and that these are best studied by people who are interested in the psychology of the writer. The Homeric parallels in *Ulysses* are of marginal importance to the reading of the work but fundamental to the writing of it. Proust had to be suckered by Bergson. And so on. These beliefs and these forms have to do with the security and insecurity of going forward into the void.

Writers have certain compulsions, certain ordering habits, which are a part of the book only in the sense that they make its writing possible. This is a widespread phenomenon. Certain rituals have to be gone through—in cooking, for example—which don't affect the final product at all.

INTERVIEWER: Sometimes a writer—Nabokov, for example—will engross the reader in his little games. What then?

GASS: I'm in favor of fun. Nabokov surfaces a lot of his game, however, and forces the reader, or the assiduous commentator, into paper chases. I don't think much of that, though I guess the assiduous commentator gets no quarter. Nabokov wants people to follow his private games with the same kind of interest he takes in them himself. Sometimes the intricacies and the little secrets and the codes really work for the reader; things open up and then it is really quite wonderful. Powerful private symbols are related to this. Lowry, for example, was obsessed with certain things. All great writers are. Lowry put down those obsessions on the page, and because they are there, he believes they will have an effect. It is the kind of error the beginning writer makes too—all this stuff that is so important to him never really gets to the page at all.

INTERVIEWER: What is a working day like for you?

GASS: Well, we usually get breakfast and the kids off to school by nine o'clock, and I start to work soon after. It's essential that I be in the midst of something, so I try to quit work with new material that now needs revision in the typewriter. In the morning I can start right off working on those revisions and hope that by the end of the day the process of revising will have sent me forward into some new material. If I get interrupted while I am, in a sense, at the end of something—a sentence, a paragraph, a scene—then I'm liable to have trouble getting back into things. At Yaddo I worked all morning, all afternoon, a great part of the evening, every day. At home I usually work in the morning and for a couple of hours in the afternoon. Lately I have been getting some work done in the evening, but that's because I have not been teaching at all. I haven't been talking about grading papers, preparing lectures, that sort of thing. The real writing process is simply sitting there and typing the same old lines over and over and over and over and sheet after sheet after sheet gets filled with the same shit. And then I discard or abandon material for weeks, months, during which time I start something new. Usually I have a great many projects going at the same time—in the sense that a start of some sort has been made. I get very tense working, so I often have to get up and wander around the house. It is very bad on my stomach. I have to be mad to be working well anyway, and then I am mad about the way things are going on the page in addition. My ulcer flourishes and I have to chew lots of pills. When my work is going well, I am usually sort of sick.

INTERVIEWER: Did Jethro Furber take over *Omensetter's Luck* because of this methodology?

GASS: He certainly did. Furber went through a lot of midwives being born. When I first wrote the book, Furber wasn't even in it. That was the version that was stolen. Then I rewrote it to get the stolen version back. Furber was still not there. I looked at what my memory had regained from the thief and concluded that the book, although it was now much better than the original, was really no good. It was then that Furber began to emerge. The book began to be the book I should have been writing all along. Now, a lot of people find that the Furber section is where the book goes to hell. As far as I am concerned, it is the only justification for that book.

INTERVIEWER: Is Furber the hero of *Omensetter's Luck* because he has the best rhetoric?

GASS: Yes. In my books, if anybody gets to be the hero, he's got the best passages. Hamlet has the best lines. Milton's Satan has the best lines. Furber is what the book turned out eventually to be all about. That's not quite right. It's rhetoric the book is about, and *The Tunnel* is about rhetoric too. It's more completely, more single-mindedly about rhetoric, about the movement of language and the beauty and terror of great speech. Omensetter is certainly not the major figure because he is basically a person without language. He is a wall everybody bounces a ball off. Now anybody who emerges in my work with any strength at all is somebody who has a language, and that's why he's there.

INTERVIEWER: Do you like the stories still?

GASS: As soon as I finish something, it's dead, so my writing a preface about it, as I've just done, is very hard. I rarely read things that are in print when I give a reading somewhere. I publish a piece in order to kill it, so that I won't have to fool around with it any longer. The best I can say is that when I have to look back on the stories, I am sometimes not too terribly ashamed. *Omensetter's* got more passages which make me blush. There is one story in the collection which still suits me in the sense that when writing it I did fundamentally what I wanted to do. That's "Order of Insects." I think that's the best thing I ever wrote.

INTERVIEWER: How have visual art and music influenced your practice of fiction?

GASS: The kind of aesthetic necessary to comprehend the modern movement in painting up through, let's say, abstract expressionism, is one which I find very congenial. In great part it preceded the development of a similar kind of theory for literature. I think the impact of formalism, constructivism, and so on, was very great in the visual arts, even though music had been free to go its independent way for some time. Painting, though, had seemed to be about things, had seemed to be mimetic in a basic way, and now it was possible to see how such vulgarizations might be abandoned and real purity achieved. There were great paintings which didn't get their artistic value from some sort of statement they were making about the world. Then we could begin to wonder whether it was Fra Angelico's piety or his genius as a painter that makes his painting so wonderful. For him, of course, piety and painting were one. Not for us, though. There's nothing new about nonrepresentationalism, of course, but it is still very much misunderstood, and very much opposed.

INTERVIEWER: There's a lot of theorizing now about silence. Are you ever tempted by silence?

GASS: Obviously not. No. I think I am perfectly aware of the dangers and limitations of language. But the people who are talking about language running out as if it were the oil supply, or of reaching beyond language, as if there were a better plate of peaches just beyond the pears—well, that's just cheap romanticism. Beckett likes to work with silences the way a musician works with rests, though he works within a linguistic context, and even if he lowers and restricts his vocabulary, it is all language nevertheless, and language is all he is basically interested in. Then this glorious emptiness is employed as a romantic cliché by people who persist in using language all the same. They say they are going beyond the limits of language toward something or other and this excuses their execrable style. No matter. They will pass away.

The fact remains that we are moving away, in terms of science and other communications systems, from what one ordinarily calls language. I remain interested in what we are going to use to talk to ourselves with. One of the fundamental problems with film is not simply its easy effects, and its conceptual poverty. That may in time be overcome. Film may be able to carry universals in a useful way. But you can't show films to yourself. There is no way of communicating inside your head but speech. And if you can't talk well to yourself, who can you talk to? You simply aren't anybody. I frequently imagine people who get bored with their own talk, who don't talk to themselves very much. Talk is essential to the human spirit. It *is* the human spirit. Speech. Not silence. That's also Beckett's point.

INTERVIEWER: Does the aggressive motive you mentioned earlier make you a crabby reviewer?

GASS: I've been crabby about a few books, but I'm not often very mean. In a way I regret the times I have been, because I am rarely angry with the author. Once in a while you run into work which is actually corrupt. But by and large, I get crabby with critics. What happens is that you don't write against the book, whatever it is, but against some asinine prevailing critical climate in which the book appears. All these writers who have been touted as great—it is not their fault that they are just poor writers like the rest of us, trying to do their best, and having the damn bad luck to be praised by fools because they write so badly fools think they understand them. And the clubhouse journalists, the critics, who fall first for traditional kitsch, then experimental kitsch, for the latest French fad, for obfuscation, sensationalism, who are eager to froth at the mouth with the latest rage, with a collection of biases as large as the unemployed, and no standards, no nose for quality . . . well, as you can tell, it makes me mad, and so sometimes I light into the book. Which isn't a bit fair to the author. I've sworn not to do that anymore. Then there are times when I bitch about a biographer because the biographer is not interested in precisely these qualities in the subject which caused, presumably, the biography to be written in the first place. Then there are other problems. How can you write well enough to write about Colette? Find the verve required for Henry Miller, the depth for Lowry, or for Borges the proper philosophical wit?

INTERVIEWER: Who are some living novelists you respect?

GASS: Well, the question leaves out so many dead ones who are more alive. I think Barth is one of the great writers. I have admired his work since I first encountered it. I think he is incredible. Several of his books, in particular *The Sot-Weed Factor,* are the works which stand to my generation as *Ulysses* did to its. His habits of work are wholly unlike mine, and the kind of thing which engages him is quite different too. He is a great narrator, one of the best who ever plied the pen, as they used to say. He has been accused of being cold, purely mental, but I find him full of passion and excitement. And what I like about his work in great part is the unifying squeeze which that great intellectual grasp of his gives to his work, and the combination of enormous knowledge with fine feeling and artistic pride and energy and total control. I really admire a master. He's one.

A lot of the work of Hawkes is extraordinary, breathtaking. Everybody likes Beckett. Now. It's silly to mention Bellow, Borges, Nabokov—so obvious. And of course Stanley Elkin's work I like enormously. Some of Coover's, too, I find extraordinarily interesting. Control again. Gaddis. Control. Also Barthelme—a poet. A great many South American writers write rings around us. Infante's *Three Trapped Tigers* is a great book. I taught *Hopscotch* once. I'll never get over it. Márquez, Fuentes, Lima, Llosa . . . it is always an exciting time to be a reader. Lots of European writers are overblown, especially some of the French experimentalists, but Italo Calvino is wonderful. Thomas Bernhard's *The Lime Works* is impressive. In general, I would think that at present prose writers are much in advance of the poets. In the old days, I read more poetry than prose, but now it is in prose where you find things being put together well, where there is great ambition, and equal talent. Poets have gotten so careless, it is a disgrace. You can't pick up a page. All the words slide off.

INTERVIEWER: Have you ever read anything about your work that interested you?

GASS: It all interests me when I start to read it, but soon the critic is explaining to me what I meant, and then I get bored (whether I agree with what's being said or not). I start to skip. But even a good critic isn't likely to tell me anything about my work I don't already know, since I'm pretty careful and self-conscious in what I do. I also don't take much pleasure in approval. I have been well treated by critics on the whole. I would like to be deeply pleased by what they say, but my pleasure doesn't last very long. A two-second rush of warmth to the head, that's all. I feel a certain sense of relief that I got away with it again—that the critic didn't dislike it. Once in a while a negative criticism will be perceptive. You protect yourself from critics, of course, by anticipating all their censures, so you can say, "Yes, of course, I saw that long ago."

INTERVIEWER: If you were going to write an essay on your own work, what would you concentrate on?

GASS: I think I would immediately start talking about the manipulation of language, and I'd end writing just another essay on style. If I am anything as a writer, that is what I am: a stylist. I am not a writer of short stories or novels or essays or whatever. I am a writer, in general. I am interested in how one writes anything. So if I were to write about my own work, I would write about writing sentences.

INTERVIEWER: Do you teach any creative-writing courses?

GASS: I resent spending a lot of time on lousy stuff. If somebody is reading a bad paper in a seminar, it is nevertheless on Plato, and it is Plato we can talk about. Whereas if somebody is writing about their hunting trip—well—where can one go for salvation or relief? Creative-writing teachers, poor souls, must immerse themselves in slop and even take it seriously. Since I can't bear it, resent it, I shouldn't teach it. It is probably impossible to teach anyone to be a good writer. You can teach people how to read, possibly.

I am also aware of how little I can tolerate other people telling me how to write. So why should I do it to my students? I do not invite or accept this sort of personal criticism. I usually have poor to absent relations with editors because they have a habit of desiring changes and I resist changes. So why should I tell students to make changes? I also remember how bad I was. I wrote far worse stuff than I see from students. What can I fairly say to them?

INTERVIEWER: You've said no decent sentence could come from a half-formed man.

GASS: I said that? I shouldn't have. Most writers are probably quarter-formed. Hopeless and helpless. One's complete sentences are attempts, as often as not, to complete an incomplete self with words. If you were a fully realized person—whatever the hell that would be—you wouldn't fool around writing books.

THOMAS LeCLAIR
Summer 1977

12. Gore Vidal

Gore Vidal was born on October 3, 1925, at the United States Military Academy in West Point, New York. He spent much of his childhood in Washington, D.C. with his scholarly and witty maternal grandfather, Senator Thomas Gore, and was graduated from Phillips Exeter Academy in 1943.

At the age of eighteen Vidal enlisted in the army, and later drew on that experience in his first two novels, *Williwaw* (1946) and *In a Yellow Wood* (1947), both of which helped establish Vidal as one of the leading young novelists of the postwar period. However, his third novel, *The City and the Pillar* (1948) was given a generally poor reception; it is nonetheless noteworthy for its forthright treatment of homosexuality, which was considered very daring at the time. The mixed reviews that met his next five novels—largely historical allegories and satires—discouraged Vidal, and he turned to the dramatic form, writing several television and film scripts in addition to plays for the stage, including *Visit to a Small Planet* (1955) and *The Best Man* (1960). At the same time that the latter work, a political drama, was prospering on Broadway, Vidal ran unsuccessfully for election to the House of Representatives.

In 1964 Vidal published *Julian*, his first novel in ten years, and followed this success with novels widely different in content and form: *Washington, D.C.* (1967), *Myra Breckinridge* (1968), *Two Sisters* (1970), *Burr* (1973), *Myron* (1975), *1876* (1976), *Kalki* (1978), and *Creation* (1981). Over the past thirty years Vidal has also shown himself to be an acute political, social, and literary observer, and is the author of four books of essays.

Vidal lives in Rome, Italy.

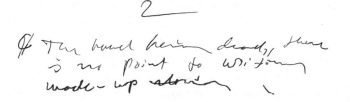

A manuscript page from *Myra Breckinridge*.

Drawing by Don Bachardy

Gore Vidal

Gore Vidal lives in a run-down penthouse above Rome's Largo Argentina: reconstructed temples from the pre-Augustan era are set incongruously in the middle of what looks to be Columbus Circle without the charm. It is August. Rome is deserted. The heat is breathtaking during the day, but at sundown a cool wind starts and the birds swarm in the blue-gold Tiepolo sky. He sits on a large terrace lined with plants in need of watering.

In photographs, or on television, Gore Vidal appears to be dark-haired and somewhat slight. He is neither. He stands six feet; his chest is broad and deep (a legacy of Alpine ancestors); despite constant attendance at a gymnasium, the once flat stomach is now reorganizing itself as a most definite paunch. He regards his own deterioration with fascination: "After all, in fifteen months I shall be fifty," he declares, apparently pleased and disturbed in equal parts.

His hair is light brown, evenly streaked with white. His teeth are meticulously capped. The agate-yellow eyes are myopic, and when he does not wear glasses he tends to squint. The voice . . . well, everyone knows the voice. He sits now in a broken wicker armchair; the baroque dome of San Andrea della Valle appears to float above his head. He wears a blue shirt, gray trousers, sandals. Although he talks naturally in complete sentences, he is not at ease talking about his own work . . . he prefers that others be the subject of his scrutiny. An accomplished debater, he tends to slip away from the personal, the inconvenient.

G. V.

INTERVIEWER: When did you first start writing?

VIDAL: I would suppose at five or six, whenever I learned how to read. Actually, I can't remember when I was *not* writing. I was taught to read by my grandmother. Central to her method was a tale of unnatural love called "The Duck and the Kangaroo." Then, because my grandfather Senator Gore was blind, I was required early on to read grown-up books to him, mostly constitutional law and, of course, the *Congressional Record.* The later continence of my style is a miracle, considering those years of piping the additional remarks of Mr. Borah of Idaho.

INTERVIEWER: When did you begin your first novel?

VIDAL: At about seven. A novel closely based on a mystery movie I had seen, something to do with "the blue room" or "hotel" (not Stephen Crane's). I recall, fondly, that there was one joke. The character based on my grandmother kept interrupting everybody because "she had not been listening." Merriment in the family during the first reading. It doesn't take much to launch a wit. Then I wrote a great deal of didactic poetry, all bad. With puberty the poetry came to resemble "Invictus," the novels *Of Human Bondage.* Between fourteen and nineteen I must have begun and abandoned six novels.

INTERVIEWER: How far did you get on these novels?

VIDAL: A few chapters, usually. I did get halfway through the one written before *Williwaw*. All about someone who deserted from the army—no doubt reflecting my state of mind, since I was in the army during the war (from seventeen to twenty). Unfortunately, my protagonist deserted to Mexico. Since I had never been to Mexico, I was obliged to stop.

INTERVIEWER: What were the other five about? School?

VIDAL: No. I began the first really ambitious one when I was fourteen or fifteen. I had gone to Europe in the summer of '39 and visited Rome. One night I saw Mussolini in the flesh at the Baths of Caracalla—no, he was not bathing but listening to *Turandot*. The baths are used for staging operas. I thought him splendid! That jaw, that splendid emptiness. After all, I had been brought up with politicians. He was an exotic variation on something quite familiar to me. So I started a novel about a dictator in Rome, filled with intrigue and passion, Machiavellian *combinazione*. But that didn't get finished either, despite my close study of the strategies of E. Phillips Oppenheim.

INTERVIEWER: Finishing *Williwaw* at nineteen broke the barrier; it was published and you wrote three novels in quick succession.

VIDAL: Yes. Every five minutes it seemed. Contrary to legend, I had no money. Since I lived on publishers' advances, it was fairly urgent that I keep on publishing every year. But of course I *wanted* to publish every year. I felt no strain, though looking back over the books I can detect a strain in the writing of them. Much of the thinness of those early novels is simply the pressure that I was under. Anyway, I've gone back and rewritten several of them. They are still less than marvelous but better than they were.

INTERVIEWER: What do you feel about going back and rewriting? Don't you think in a way that you're changing what another person, the younger Vidal, did?

VIDAL: No. You are stuck with that early self for good or ill, and you can't do anything about it even if you want to—short of total suppression. For me, revising is mostly a matter of language and selection. I don't try to change the narrative or the point of view, except perhaps toward the end of *The City and the Pillar.* I felt obligated to try a new kind of ending. But something like *Dark Green, Bright Red* needed a paring away of irrelevancies—the fault of all American naturalistic writing from Hawthorne to, well, name almost any American writer today. I noticed recently the same random accretion of details in William Dean Howells—a very good writer, yet since he is unable to select the *one* detail that will best express his meaning, he gives us everything that occurs to him and the result is often a shapeless daydream. Twain, too, rambles and rambles, hoping that something will turn up. In his best work it does rather often. In the rest—painful logorrhea.

INTERVIEWER: You once said that the test of a good work, or a perfect work, is whether the author can reread it without embarrassment. How did you feel when you reread your early books?

VIDAL: Sometimes less embarrassed than others. Rereading *Williwaw,* I was struck by the coolness of the prose. There is nothing in excess. I am still impressed by that young writer's control of his very small material. When I prepared the last edition, I don't suppose I cut away more than a dozen sentences. The next book, on the other hand, *In a Yellow Wood,* is in limbo forever. I can't rewrite it because it's so bad that I can't reread it. The effect, I fear, of meeting and being "ensorcelled" by Anaïs Nin. Or Jack London meets Elinor Glyn. Wow!

INTERVIEWER: What about your first "successful" novel, *The City and the Pillar*?

VIDAL: A strange book because it was, as they say, the first of its kind, without going into any great detail as to *what* its kind is. To tell such a story then was an act of considerable moral courage. Unfortunately, it was not an act of very great artistic courage, since I chose deliberately to write in the flat, gray, naturalistic style of James T. Farrell. Tactically if not aesthetically, this was for a good reason. Up until then homosexuality in literature was always exotic: Firbank, on the one hand; green carnations, on the other. I wanted to deal with an absolutely ordinary, all-American, lower-middle-class young man and his world. To show the dead-on "normality" of the homosexual experience. Unfortunately, I didn't know too many lower-middle-class, all-American young men—except for those years in the army when I spent a good deal of time blocking out my fellow soldiers. So I made it all up. But the result must have had a certain authenticity. Tennessee Williams read it in 1948 and said of the family scenes, "Our fathers were very much alike." He was surprised when I told him that Jim Willard and his family were all invented. Tennessee also said, "I don't like the ending. I don't think you realized what a good book you had written." At the time, of course, I thought the ending "powerful."

INTERVIEWER: Now you've changed the ending to have the young man—Bob—not killed by Jim, as he was originally.

VIDAL: Yes. Twenty years ago it was thought that I had written a tragic ending because the publishers felt that the public would not accept a happy resolution for my tale of Sodom, my Romeo and his Mercutio. But this wasn't true. The theme of the book which, as far as I know, no critic has ever noticed, is revealed in the title, *The City and the Pillar*. Essentially, I was writing about the romantic temperament. Jim Willard is so overwhelmed by a first love affair that he finds all other lovers wanting. He can only live in the past, as he imagined the past, or in the future as he hopes it will be when he finds Bob again. He has no present. So whether the first love object is a boy or girl is not really all that important. The novel was not about the city so much as about the pillar of salt, the looking back that destroys. Nabokov handled this same theme with infinitely greater elegance in *Lolita*. But I was only twenty when I made my attempt, while he was half as old as time. Anyway, my story could only have had a disastrous ending. Obviously, killing Bob was a bit much even though the original narrative was carefully vague on that point. Did he or didn't he kill him? Actually, what was being killed was the idea of perfect love that had existed only in the romantic's mind. The other person—the beloved object—had forgotten all about it.

INTERVIERWER: What is the procedure once a book is revised? Do publishers accept this with grace? Are the old books recalled from libraries?

VIDAL: *Williwaw* and *Messiah* were only slightly altered, *The City and the Pillar* was much revised. *The Judgment of Paris* was somewhat cut but otherwise not much altered. *Dark Green, Bright Red* was entirely rewritten. Except for *The City and the Pillar,* the new versions first appeared in paperback. Later the revised *Messiah* and *The Judgment of Paris* were also reissued in hardcover. I have no idea what the publishers thought of all this. It is not wise to solicit the opinions of publishers—they become proud if you do. As lovers of the environment, I suspect they were pleased that the new versions were so much shorter than the old, thus saving trees. The original editions can also be found in the libraries, margins filled with lewd commentaries, and the worms busy in the binding.

INTERVIEWER: Has anyone else done such a wholesale revision of his past work?

VIDAL: I shouldn't imagine that any American writer would want to do anything that reflected on the purity and the spontaneity of his genius at any phase of his sacred story. In the land of the free, one sentence must be as good as another because that is democracy. Only Henry James set out methodically to rewrite his early books for the New York edition. Some works he improved; others not. Tennessee, come to think of it, often rewrites old plays, stories . . . it's sort of a tic with him. Returning to an earlier time, different mood.

INTERVIEWER: You have said that *The Judgment of Paris* was your favorite of the early books.

VIDAL: It was the first book I wrote when I settled in on the banks of the Hudson River for what proved to be twenty years of writing, my *croisée.* . . . Certainly *The Judgment of Paris* was the novel in which I found my own voice. Up until then I was very much in the American realistic tradition, unadventurous, monochromatic, haphazard in my effects. My subjects were always considerably more interesting than what I was able to do with them. This is somewhat the reverse of most young writers, particularly young writers today.

INTERVIEWER: You mean they're proficient technically but don't have much to say?

VIDAL: They appear to rely on improvisation to get them to the end of journeys that tend to be circular.

INTERVIEWER: Which works and which authors are you thinking of?

VIDAL: Well, as I was talking I was thinking of a book—any book—by someone called Brautigan. I can never remember the titles. The last little book I looked at is about a librarian. Written in the see-Jane-run style. Very cheerful. Very dumb. Highly suitable for today's audience. But he's not exactly what I had in mind. There is one splendid new—to me—writer. Robert Coover. He, too, is circular, but the circles he draws enclose a genius of suggestion. Particularly that story in *Pricksongs and Descants* when the narrator creates an island for you *on the page.* No rude art his. Also *Omensetter's Luck* by William Gass. A case of language doing the work of the imagination, but doing it very well.

INTERVIEWER: What is there in writing except language?

VIDAL: In the writing of novels there is the problem of how to shape a narrative. And though the search for new ways of

telling goes on—I've written about this at terrible length*—
I don't think there are going to be any new discoveries. For one
thing, literature is not a science. There is no new formula.
Some of us write better than others; and genius is never forced.
There are signs that a number of writers—University or U-
writers, as I call them—are bored with the narrative, character,
prose. In turn they bore the dwindling public for novels. So
Beckett stammers into silence, and the rest is cinema. Why
not?

INTERVIEWER: But in the forties . . .

VIDAL: In the forties I was working in the American tradition
of straight narrative, not very different from John P. Marquand
or John Steinbeck or Ernest Hemingway. For me it was like
trying to fence in a straitjacket. In fact, my first years as a writer
were very difficult because I knew I wasn't doing what I should
be doing, and I didn't know how to do what I ought to be
doing. Even interestingly conceived novels like *Dark Green,
Bright Red* or *A Search for the King* came out sounding like
poor Jim Farrell on a bad day. Not until I was twenty-five, had
moved to my house in the country, was poor but content, and
started to write *The Judgment of Paris,* that suddenly I was all
there, writing in my own voice. I had always had a tendency
to rhetoric—Senator Borah, remember? But fearing its excess,
I was too inhibited to write full voice. I don't know what
happened. The influence of Anaïs Nin? The fact that I had
stopped trying to write poetry and so the poetic line fused with
the prose? Who knows? Anyway, it was a great release, that
book. Then came *Messiah.* Unfortunately, my reputation in
'54 was rock bottom. The book was ignored for a few years, to
be revived in the universities. Dead broke, I had to quit writing
novels for ten years—just as I was hitting my stride. I don't say
that with any bitterness because I had a very interesting ten

*"On the French New Novel," *Encounter* (December, 1967). Also, collected in *Homage to Daniel Shays* (Random House, 1972).

years. But it would have been nice to have gone on developing, uninterruptedly, from *Messiah.*

INTERVIEWER: What voice are you using now?

VIDAL: My own. But I confess to a gift for mimicry. The plangent cries of Mrya are very unlike the studied periods of Aaron Burr, but the same throat, as it were (deep, deep), sings the song of each. I envy writers like Graham Greene who, year in and year out, do the same kind of novel to the delight of the same kind of reader. I couldn't begin to do that sort of thing. I have thrown away a number of successful careers out of boredom. I could have gone on after *The City and the Pillar* writing shocking John Rechy novels, but chose not to. My first two Broadway plays were successful, and I could have continued for a time to be a popular year-in, year-out playwright. Chose not to. Chose not to keep on as a television playwright. Then once *Julian* did well, I could have gone on in *that* genre. The same with *Washington, D.C.,* when I, inadvertently, captured the mind and heart of the middle-class, middle-aged, middle-brow lady who buys hardcover novels—not to mention the book clubs. But then I let *Myra* spring from my brow, armed to the teeth, eager to lose me ladies, book clubs, book-chat writers—everything, in fact, except her unique self, the only great "woman" in American literature.

INTERVIEWER: And *Burr*? You seem to have got them all back again.

VIDAL: Doubtless a misunderstanding. I had assumed that *Burr* would be unpopular. My view of American history is much too realistic. Happily, Nixon, who made me a popular playwright (the worst man in *The Best Man* was based on him), again came to the rescue. Watergate so shook the three percent of our population who read books that they accepted *Burr,* a book that ordinarily they would have burned while reciting the pledge of allegiance to the flag.

INTERVIEWER: Is it true that you were thinking of putting out *Myra Breckinridge* under a pseudonym?

VIDAL: No. Oh, well, yes. I wanted to make an experiment. To publish a book without reviews or advertising or a well-known author's name. I wanted to prove that a book could do well simply because it was interesting—without the support of book-chat writers. Up to a point, the experiment worked. The book was widely read long before the first reviews appeared. But for the experiment to have been perfect my name shouldn't have been on the book. I didn't think of that till later. Curious. Twenty years ago, after *Messiah* was published, Harvey Breit of *The New York Times* said, "You know, Gore, anything you write will get a bad press in America. Use another name. Or do something else." So for ten years I did something else.

INTERVIEWER: Why will you always get a bad press?

VIDAL: That's more for you to determine than for me. I have my theories, no doubt wrong. I suspect that the range of my activity is unbearable to people who write about books. Lenny Bernstein is not reviewed in *The New York Times* by an unsuccessful composer or by a student at Julliard. He might be better off if he were, but he isn't. Writers are the only people who are reviewed by people of their own kind. And their own kind can often be reasonably generous—*if* you stay in your category. I don't. I do many different things rather better than most people do one thing. And envy is the central fact of American life. Then, of course, I am the Enemy to so many. I have attacked both Nixon and the Kennedys—as well as the American Empire. I've also made the case that American literature has been second-rate from the beginning. This caused distress in book-chat land. They *knew* I was wrong, but since they don't read foreign or old books, they were forced to write things like "Vidal thinks Victor Hugo is better than Faulkner." Well, Hugo *is* better than Faulkner, but to the residents of book-chat land Hugo is just a man with a funny name who wrote *Les Misérables,* a movie on the late show. Finally, I am proud to say that I am most disliked because for twenty-six years I have been in open rebellion against the heterosexual dictatorship in the United States. Fortunately, I have lived long enough to see the dictatorship start to collapse. I now hope to live long enough to see a sexual democracy in America. I deserve at least a statue in Du Pont Circle—along with Dr. Kinsey.

INTERVIEWER: You often refer to critics.

VIDAL: Reviewers . . . actually newspaper persons who chat about books in the press. They have been with us from the beginning and they will be with us at the end. They are interested in writers, not writing. In good morals, not good art. When they like something of mine, I grow suspicious and wonder.

INTERVIEWER: One of the comments sometimes made is that your real position—your greatest talent—is as an essayist. How would you answer that?

VIDAL: My novels are quite as good as my essays. Unfortunately, to find out if a novel is good or bad you must first read it, and that is not an easy thing to do nowadays. Essays, on the other hand, are short, and people do read them.

INTERVIEWER: You once said the novel is dead.

VIDAL: That was a joke. What I have said repeatedly is that the *audience* for the novel is demonstrably diminishing with each passing year. That is a fact. It is not the novel that is declining, but the audience for it. It's like saying poetry has been declining for fifty years. Poetry hasn't. But the audience has. The serious novel is now almost in the same situation as poetry. Eventually the novel will simply be an academic exercise, written by academics to be used in classrooms in order to test the ingenuity of students. A combination of Rorschach test and anagram. Hence, the popularity of John Barth, a perfect U-novelist whose books are written to be taught, not to be read.

INTERVIEWER: As long as we're on Barth, let me ask you what you think of your contemporaries, people in your generation, people in their forties?

VIDAL: You must realize that anything I *say* (as opposed to write) about other novelists is governed by my current mood of jaunty disgust—which is quite impartial, cheerful, even loving. But totally unreliable as criticism—putting me in the great tradition of American journalism, now that I think of it.

INTERVIEWER: Do you read your contemporaries? Do you read their new works as they come out?

VIDAL: I wouldn't say that I am fanatically attentive. There's only one living writer in English that I entirely admire, and that's William Golding. Lately I've been reading a lot of Italian and French writers. I particularly like Italo Calvino.

INTERVIEWER: Why do you think Golding good?

VIDAL: Well, his work is intensely felt. He holds you completely line by line, image by image. In *The Spire* you see the church that is being built, smell the dust. You are present at an event that exists only in his imagination. Very few writers have ever had this power. When the priest reveals his sores, you see them, feel the pain. I don't know how he does it.

INTERVIEWER: Have you ever met him?

VIDAL: Once, yes. We had dinner together in Rome. Oxford don type. I like his variety: each book is quite different from the one before it. This confuses critics and readers, but delights me. For that reason I like to read Fowles—though he is not in Golding's class. Who else do I read for pleasure? I always admire Isherwood. I am not given to mysticism—to understate wildly, but he makes me see something of what he would see. I read P. G. Wodehouse for pleasure. Much of Anthony Burgess. Brigid Brophy. Philip Roth when he is at his most demented. I like comic writers, obviously. I reread Evelyn Waugh. . . .

INTERVIEWER: Were you influenced by Waugh?

VIDAL: Perhaps. I was given *Scoop* in 1939 and I thought it the funniest book I'd ever read. I used to reread it every year. Of the American writers—well, I read Saul Bellow with admiration. He never quite pulls off a book for me, but he's interesting—which is more than you can say for so many of the other Jewish Giants, carving their endless Mount Rushmores out of halvah. Calder Willingham I've always liked—that frantic heterosexuality. There must be a place for his sort of thing in American literature. I've never understood why he was not an enormously popular writer.

INTERVIEWER: You have known a good many writers. Is there anything to be got from knowing other writers personally?

VIDAL: I don't think so. When I was young I wanted to meet the famous old writers that I admired. So I met Gide, Forster, Cocteau, and Santayana. I sent Thomas Mann a book. He sent me a polite letter with my name misspelled. I never expected to "learn" anything from looking at them. Rather it was a laying on of hands. A connection with the past. I am perhaps more conscious of the past than most American writers, and need the dead for comfort.

INTERVIEWER: Do you enjoy being with other writers? Henry James once said, for example, that Hawthorne was handicapped because he was isolated from other writers.

VIDAL: Yes, I like the company of other writers. Christopher Isherwood, Tennessee Williams, and Paul Bowles have been friends. But I am not so sure James meant that Hawthorne's isolation had to do with not knowing other writers. I think James meant that the American scene was culturally so thin that it was hard to develop intellectually if you had nobody to talk to. This explains the solipsistic note in the work of so many American writers. They think they are the only ones in the world to doubt the existence of God, say—like Mark Twain, for instance.

INTERVIEWER: Who was the first writer you ever met?

VIDAL: Well, growing up in Washington, a lot of journalists came to the house. Walter Lippmann, Arthur Krock, Drew Pearson . . . but I did not think much of journalists. I was more interested in Michael Arlen, who used to come and play bridge. A splendid, rather ornate, Beerbohmesque dandy. And by no means a bad writer. I was fascinated recently by *Exiles,* his son's book about him. One summer before the war we were all at the Homestead Hotel in Hot Springs, Virginia, where Michael and Atalanta Arlen were much admired by everyone, including my mother and her husband, Hugh Auchincloss. But to my astonishment, I now read that the boy was embarrassed by them—they were too dark, flashy, exotic, not pink and square like the American gentry. Like us, I suppose. Life is odd. Michael's son wanted for a father a stockbroker named Smith, while I would've given anything if his father had been my father—well, *step* father.

INTERVIEWER: But later, on your own, whom did you meet, know. . . .

VIDAL: I was still in uniform when I met Anaïs Nin in 1945. I refer you to the pages of her diary for that historic encounter. I thought she was marvelous but didn't much like her writing. Years later, reading her journals, I was horrified to discover that she felt the same about me. In '48 I met Tennessee in Rome, at the height of his fame. We traveled about in an old Jeep. I have never laughed more with anyone, but can't say that I learned anything from him or anyone else. That process is interior. Paradoxically, in the ten years that I wrote for television, theater, movies, I learned how to write novels. Also, writing three mystery novels in one year taught me that nothing must occur in narrative which is not of use. Ironic that the lesson of Flaubert—which I thought that I had absorbed—I did not really comprehend until I was potboiling.

INTERVIEWER: You have described meeting E. M. Forster at King's College. . . .

VIDAL: I met him first at a party for Isherwood. London '48. Forster was very excited at meeting Tennessee and not at all at meeting me—which I considered unfair, since I had read and admired all his books while Tennessee, I fear, thought that he was in the presence of the author of *Captain Horatio Hornblower.* Part of Tennessee's wisdom is to read nothing at all.

Anyway, Forster, looking like an old river rat, zeroed in on Tennessee and said how much he admired *Streetcar*. Tennessee gave him a beady look. Forster invited us to King's for lunch. Tennessee rolled his eyes and looked at me. Yes, I said quickly. The next day I dragged Tennessee to the railroad station. As usual with Tennessee, we missed the first train. The second train would arrive in half an hour. Tennessee refused to wait. "But we *have* to go," I said, "He's sitting on one of the lions in front of the college, waiting for us." Tennessee was not moved by this poignant tableau. "I can't," he said, gulping and clutching his heart—when Tennessee does not spit blood, he has heart spasms. "Besides," said Tennessee primly, wandering off in the wrong direction for the exit, "I cannot abide old men with urine stains on their trousers." I went on alone. I have described that grim day in *Two Sisters*.

INTERVIEWER: You seem to still see this scene vividly. Do you think of the writer as a constant observer and recorder?

VIDAL: Well, I am not a camera, no. I don't consciously watch anything and I don't take notes, though I briefly kept a diary. What I remember I remember—by no means the same thing as remembering what you would like to.

INTERVIEWER: How do you see yourself in an age of personality-writers, promoting themselves and their work? For instance, Capote says he is an expert at promoting books and gaining the attention of the media.

VIDAL: Every writer ought to have at least one thing that he does well, and I'll take Truman's word that a gift for publicity is the most glittering star in his diadem. I'm pretty good at promoting my views on television but a washout at charming the book-chatters. But then I don't really try. Years ago Mailer solemnly assured me that to be a "great" writer in America you had to be fairly regularly on the cover of the Sunday *New York Times* book section. Nothing else mattered. Anyway, he is now what he wanted to be: the patron saint of bad journalism, and I am exactly what I set out to be: a novelist.

INTERVIEWER: Where do you place Nabokov?

VIDAL: I admire him very much. I'm told he returns the compliment. We do exchange stately insults in the press. Shortly after I announced that I was contributing a hundred dollars to the Angela Davis defense fund in Nabokov's name —to improve his image—he responded by assuring an interviewer from *The New York Times* that I had become a Roman Catholic. It is curious that Russia's two greatest writers— Nabokov and Pushkin—should both have had Negro blood.

INTERVIEWER: Have you read *Ada*?

VIDAL: No one has read *Ada*. But I very much admired *Transparent Things*. It is sad that the dumb Swedes gave their merit badge to Solzhenitsyn instead of Nabokov. Perfect example, by the way, of the unimportance of a writer's books to his career.

INTERVIEWER: How about some of the younger writers? What do you think of John Updike, for example?

VIDAL: He writes so well that I wish he could attract my interest. I like his prose, and disagree with Mailer, who thinks it bad. Mailer said it was the kind of bad writing that people who don't know much about writing think is good. It is an observation that I understand, but don't think applies to Updike. With me the problem is that he doesn't write about anything that interests me. I am not concerned with middle-class suburban couples. On the other hand, I'm not concerned with adultery in the French provinces either. Yet Flaubert commands my attention. I don't know why Updike doesn't. Perhaps my fault.

INTERVIEWER: Are there others of the younger generation who are perhaps less well known whom you like?

VIDAL: Alison Lurie. Viva's autobiography . . .

INTERVIEWER: Andy Warhol's superstar?

VIDAL: Yes. And it's marvelous. Part fiction, part tape recording, part this, part that, gloriously obscene. Particularly interesting about her Catholic girlhood in upstate New York. Her father beating her up periodically beneath the bleeding heart of Jesus. And those great plaster Virgins that he had all over the lawn, lit up at night with three thousand candles. That kind of thing appeals to me more than stately, careful novels.

INTERVIEWER: You came out of the Second World War. What do you think of the writers of the previous generation —Hemingway, for example?

VIDAL: I detest him, but I was certainly under his spell when I was very young, as we all were. I thought his prose was perfect —until I read Stephen Crane and realized where he got it from. Yet Hemingway is still the master self-publicist, if Capote will forgive me. Hemingway managed to convince everybody that before Hemingway everyone wrote like—who?— Gene Stratton Porter. But not only was there Mark Twain before him, there was also Stephen Crane, who did everything that Hemingway did and rather better. Certainly *The Red Badge of Courage* is superior to *A Farewell to Arms*. But Hemingway did put together an hypnotic style whose rhythm haunted other writers. I liked some of the travel things—*Green Hills of Africa*. But he never wrote a good novel. I suppose, finally, the thing I most detest in him is the spontaneity of his cruelty. The way he treated Fitzgerald, described in *A Moveable Feast*. The way he condescended to Ford Madox Ford, one of the best novelists in our language.

INTERVIEWER: What are your feelings about the so-called great writers of the twentieth century, Hemingway aside? You didn't like Faulkner, I take it.

VIDAL: I like mind and fear rhetoric—I suppose because I have a tendency to rhetoric. I also come from a Southern family—back in Mississippi the Gores were friends of the Faulkners, all Snopeses together. In fact, when I read Faulkner I think of my grandfather's speeches in the Senate, of a floweriness that I have done my best to pluck from my own style— along with the weeds.

INTERVIEWER: How about Fitzgerald?

VIDAL: If you want to find a place for him, he's somewhere between Maurice Baring and Evelyn Waugh. I like best what he leaves out of *The Great Gatsby*. A unique book. Incidentally, I think screenwriting taught him a lot. But who cares what he wrote? It is his life that matters. Books will be written about him long after his own work has vanished—again and again we shall be told of the literary harvest god who was devoured at summer's end in the hollywoods.

INTERVIEWER: You said you thought you had been influenced by Waugh, but weren't quite sure how. Who else has influenced you? Either now or years ago.

VIDAL: Oh, God, it's so hard to list them. As I said, by the time I got to *The Judgment of Paris* I was myself. Yet I'm always conscious that literature is, primarily, a chain of connection from the past to the present. It is not reinvented every morning, as some bad writers like to believe. My own chain or literary genealogy would be something like this: Petronius, Juvenal, Apuleius—then Shakespeare—then Peacock, Meredith, James, Proust. Yet the writers I like the most influenced me the least. How can you be influenced by Proust? You can't. He's inimitable. At one point Thomas Mann fascinated me; thinking he was imitable, I used to compose Socratic dialogues in what I thought was his manner. One reason for rewriting *The City and the Pillar* was to get rid of those somber exchanges.

INTERVIEWER: How much do you think college English courses can influence a career? Or teach one about The Novel?

VIDAL: I don't know. I never went to college. But I have lectured on campuses for a quarter-century, and it is my impression that after taking a course in The Novel, it is an unusual student who would ever want to read a novel again. Those English courses are what have killed literature for the public. Books are made a duty. Imagine teaching novels! Novels used to be written simply to be read. It was assumed until recently that there was a direct connection between writer and reader.

Now that essential connection is being mediated—bugged?—
by English departments. Well, who needs the mediation?
Who needs to be taught how to read a contemporary novel?
Either you read it because you want to or you don't. Assuming,
of course, that you can read anything at all. But this business
of taking novels apart in order to show bored children how they
were put together—there's a madness to it. Only a literary
critic would benefit, and there are never more than ten good
critics in the United States at any given moment. So what is
the point to these desultory autopsies performed according to
that little set of instructions at the end of each text? Have you
seen one? What symbols to look for? What does the author
mean by the word "white"? I look at the notes appended to
my own pieces in anthologies and know despair.

INTERVIEWER: How would you "teach" the novel?

VIDAL: I would teach world civilization—East and West—
from the beginning to the present. This would occupy the
college years—would be the spine to my educational system.
Then literature, economics, art, science, philosophy, religion
would be dealt with naturally, sequentially, as they occurred.
After four years, the student would have at least a glimmering
of what our race is all about.

INTERVIEWER: If you were teaching one of those "desultory"
courses, how would you describe your style?

VIDAL: As a novelist I have a certain mimetic gift. I can
impersonate a number of characters. In *Myra Breckinridge*
there are two different voices. One for Buck Loner, one for
Myra—neither mine. On the other hand, when I write an
essay, the style is my own—whatever that is, for the subject
often imposes its own rhythm on my sentences. Yet I can
usually spot my own style, and tell if a word's been changed.

INTERVIEWER: *Two Sisters* is hard to categorize and put in
any tradition. You call it a memoir in the form of a novel, or
novel in the form of a memoir. What led you to write in that
form?

VIDAL: It created its own form as I went along. I didn't feel that a straightforward memoir would be interesting to do. On the other hand, I don't like romans à clef. They're usually a bit of a cheat. You notice I keep talking not about the effect my writing is going to have on others but the effect it has on me. I don't really care whether I find a form that enchants others as much as I care about finding something that can delight me from day to day as I work it out. I was constantly fascinated and perplexed while writing that book. It's done with mirrors. One thing reflects another thing. Each of the three sections is exactly the same story, no different, but each section *seems* to be different. Each section contains exactly the same characters, though not always in the same guise.

INTERVIEWER: It's typical of your newer novels that you make such use of interjected letters, tape recordings, and diaries. Do you find that technique easier, or better or preferable to a straight narrative?

VIDAL: It makes for immediacy. I know how difficult it is for the average American to read anything. And I'm speaking of the average "educated" person. It is not easy for him to cope with too dense a text on the page. I think the eye tires easily. After all, everyone under thirty-five was brought up not reading books but staring at television. So I am forced to be ingenious, to hold the reader's attention. I think I probably made an error using the screenplay form for part of *Two Sisters.*

INTERVIEWER: Why?

VIDAL: I'm told it was hard to read. Poor Anthony Burgess, following me, has just made the same mistake with *Clockwork Testament.* Also, I kept saying all through the book what a bad screenplay it was. Predictably, the reaction was, well, if *he* says it's a bad screenplay, why, it really must be a bad screenplay and so we better not read the bad screenplay. One must never attempt irony this side of the water.

INTERVIEWER: But you do in your work, on television . . .

VIDAL: Yes. And it has done me no good. In America the race

goes to the loud, the solemn, the hustler. If you think you're a great writer, you must say that you are. Some will disagree, of course, but at least everyone will know that you're serious about your work. Speak of yourself with the slightest irony, self-deprecation, and you will be thought frivolous—perhaps even a bad person. Anyway, the playing around with letters and tapes and so on is just . . . I keep coming back to the only thing that matters: interesting myself.

INTERVIEWER: What about writing in the third person?

VIDAL: I wonder if it is still possible—in the sense that Henry James used it. *Washington, D.C.* was my last attempt to write a book like that—and I rather admire *Washington, D.C.* After all, that was the time I got into the ring with Proust, and I knocked the little fag on his ass in the first round. Then I kneed old Leo T. the Great and on a technical KO got the championship. Funny thing, this being the best. . . . But even the world champ had a tough time licking *Washington, D.C.* The third person imposed a great strain on me, the constant maneuvering of so many consciousnesses through the various scenes while trying to keep the focus right. It was like directing a film on location with a huge cast in bad weather.

INTERVIEWER: Do you feel more at home with the first-person novel now? Do you think you'll continue with it?

VIDAL: Since I've done it recently in *Burr* and again in *Myron*, I'll probably *not* do it again, but who knows? The second person certainly holds few charms. Perhaps no pronouns at all!

INTERVIEWER: What sets you apart, do you think, from other American writers?

VIDAL: My interest in Western civilization. Except for Thornton Wilder, I can think of no contemporary American who has any interest in what happened before the long present he lives in, and records. Also, perhaps paradoxically, I value invention highly, and hardly anyone else does. I don't think I have ever met an American novelist who didn't, sooner or later,

say when discussing his own work, "Well, I really knew someone exactly like that. That was the way it happened, the way
I wrote it." He is terrified that you might think he actually
made up a character, that what he writes might not be literally
as opposed to imaginatively true. I think part of the bewilder-
ment American book-chat writers have with me is that they
realize that there's something strange going on that ought not
to be going on—that *Myra Breckinridge* might just possibly be
a work of the imagination. "You mean you never knew *anyone*
like that? Well, if you didn't, how could you write it?"

INTERVIEWER: *Two Sisters,* however, does invite that intense
search for clues you abhor. You meant for it to, didn't you? You
wonder who is who and what's what.

VIDAL: It would be unnatural if people didn't. After all, it is
a memoir as well as a novel. But mainly it is a study in vanity
and our attempts to conquer death through construction or
through destruction. Herostratus does it in one way, and I do
it in another—at least, the self that I use in the book. Erich
does it in yet another way. Those girls, each has her own view
of how she's going to evade death and achieve immortality.
And it's all a comedy from the point of view of a stoic writer
like myself.

INTERVIEWER: Can you tell me about your work habits? You
must be enormously disciplined to turn out so much in such
a relatively short time. Do you find writing easy? Do you enjoy it?

VIDAL: Oh, yes, of course I enjoy it. I wouldn't do it if I
didn't. Whenever I get up in the morning, I write for about
three hours. I write novels in longhand on yellow legal pads,
exactly like the First Criminal Nixon. For some reason I write
plays and essays on the typewriter. The first draft usually comes
rather fast. One oddity: I never reread a text until I have
finished the first draft. Otherwise it's too discouraging. Also,
when you have the whole thing in front of you for the first
time, you've forgotten most of it and see it fresh. Rewriting,

however, is a slow, grinding business. For me the main pleasure of having money is being able to afford as many completely retyped drafts as I like. When I was young and poor, I had to do my own typing, so I seldom did more than two drafts. Now I go through four, five, six. The more the better, since my style is very much one of afterthought. My line to Dwight Macdonald "You have nothing to say, only to add" really referred to me. Not until somebody did a parody of me did I realize how dependent I am on the parenthetic aside—the comment upon the comment, the ironic gloss upon the straight line, or the straight rendering of a comedic point. It is a style which must seem rather pointless to my contemporaries because they see no need for this kind of elaborateness. But, again, it's the only thing I find interesting to do.

Hungover or not, I write every day for three hours after I get up until I've finished whatever I'm doing. Although sometimes I take a break in the middle of the book, sometimes a break of several years. I began *Julian*—I don't remember—but I think some seven years passed between the beginning of the book and when I picked it up again. The same thing occurred with *Washington, D.C.* On the other hand, *Myra* I wrote practically at one sitting—in a few weeks. It wrote itself, as they say. But then it was much rewritten.

INTERVIEWER: Do you block out a story in advance? And do characters ever run away from you?

VIDAL: When I first started writing, I used to plan everything in advance, not only chapter to chapter but page to page. Terribly constricting . . . like doing a film from someone else's meticulous treatment. About the time of *The Judgment of Paris,* I started improvising. I began with a mood. A sentence. The first sentence is all-important. *Washington, D.C.* began with a dream, a summer storm at night in a garden above the Potomac—that was Merrywood, where I grew up. With *Julian* and with *Burr* I was held to historical facts. Still, I found places where I could breathe and make up new things. My Burr is not the real Burr any more than Henry Steele Commager's Jefferson is the real Jefferson. By and large history tends to be rather poor fiction—except at its best. The *Peloponnesian War* is a great novel about people who actually lived.

INTERVIEWER: In your novel *Messiah* . . .

VIDAL: I didn't know the end of the book when I started writing. Yet when I got to the last page I suddenly wrote, "I was he whom the world awaited," and it was all at once clear to me that the hidden meaning of the story was the true identity of the narrator, which had been hidden from him, too. *He* was the messiah who might have been. When I saw this coming out upon the page, I shuddered (usually I laugh as I write), knew awe, for I had knocked both Huxley and Orwell out of the ring. Incidentally, ninety percent of your readers will not detect the irony in my boxing metaphors. And there is nothing to be done about it.

INTERVIEWER: Except for me to interject that you are playing off the likes of Hemingway and Mailer in the use of them. Shall I go on? Do you keep notebooks?

VIDAL: I make a few pages of notes for each novel. Phrases. Names. Character descriptions. Then I seldom look again at the notes. At the end of each workday I do make notes on what the next day's work will be. I've a memory like a sieve. Under a pseudonym (Edgar Box) I wrote three mystery books in 1952 —I was very broke. Halfway through the last one I forgot who the murderer was and had to find a substitute.

INTERVIEWER: What do you start with? A character, a plot?

VIDAL: *Myra* began with a first sentence. I was so intrigued by that sentence that I had to go on. Who was she? What did she have to say? A lot, as it turned out. The unconscious mind certainly shaped that book.

INTERVIEWER: Do you find any difficulties in writing about America and Americans when you are out of the country so much?

VIDAL: Well, I think others would notice my lapses before

I did. Anyway, I come back quite often and my ears are pretty much attuned to the American . . . scream. But then I've been involved in one way or another with every election for nearly twenty years. And I spend at least two months each year lecturing across the country.

INTERVIEWER: Besides the pleasures of living, are there any advantages in terms of perspective for the writer who lives outside the country?

VIDAL: For me, every advantage. If I lived in America, I would be a politician twenty-four hours a day, minding everybody else's business and getting no work done. Also, there are pleasures to this sort of anonymity one has in a foreign city. And it's nice to be always coping with a language you don't speak very well. Occasionally I regret it when I'm with someone like Moravia, who speaks so rapidly and intricately in Italian that I can never follow him.

INTERVIEWER: What do you think generally about the writer engagé? Should a writer be involved in politics, as you are?

VIDAL: It depends on the writer. Most American writers are not much involved, beyond signing petitions. They are usually academics—and cautious. Or full-time *literary* politicians. Or both. The main line of our literature is quotidianal with a vengeance. Yes, many great novels have been written about the everyday—Jane Austen and so on. But you need a superb art to make that sort of thing interesting. So, failing superb art, you'd better have a good mind and you'd better be interested in the world outside yourself. D. H. Lawrence wrote something very interesting about the young Hemingway. Called him a brilliant writer. But he added he's essentially a photographer and it will be interesting to see how he ages because the photographer can only keep on taking pictures from the outside. One of the reasons that the gifted Hemingway never wrote a good novel was that nothing interested him except a few sensuous experiences like killing things and fucking—interesting things to do but not all that interesting to write about.

This sort of artist runs into trouble very early on because all he can really write about is himself and after youth that self— unengaged in the world—is of declining interest. Admittedly, Hemingway chased after wars, but he never had much of anything to say about war, unlike Tolstoy or even Malraux. I think that the more you know the world and the wider the net you cast in your society, the more interesting your books will be, certainly the more interested you will be.

INTERVIEWER: Do you think of your novels as *political* novels?

VIDAL: Of course not. I am a politician when I make a speech or write a piece to promote a political idea. In a novel like *Burr* I'm not composing a polemic about the founding fathers. Rather, I am describing the way men who want power respond to one another, to themselves. The other books, the inventions like *Myra,* are beyond politics, in the usual sense at least.

INTERVIEWER: Are you interested in the other arts at all? In painting, sculpture, music, opera, dance?

VIDAL: Architecture, for one. I'm fascinated by the ancient Roman Empire amongst whose ruins I live. I've been in every city and town of Italy, and I suppose I've been into nearly every Roman church. I particularly like mosaics. I am not musical. This means I very much like opera. And baroque organ music, very loud. I like ballet, but in Rome it's bad. In painting, I'm happiest with Piero della Francesca. I hate abstract painting. In sculpture, well, the Medici tombs—I had a small talent for sculpture when I was young.

INTERVIEWER: Does it help a writer to be in love? To be rich?

VIDAL: Love is not my bag. I was debagged at twenty-five and turned to sex and art, perfectly acceptable substitutes. Absence of money is a bad thing because you end up writing "The Telltale Clue" on television—which I did. Luckily, I was full of energy in those days. I used to write a seventy-thousand-word mystery novel in ten days. Money gives one time to rewrite books until they are "done"—or abandoned. Money also gave me the leisure to become an essayist. I spend more time on a piece for *The New York Review of Books* than I ever did on, let us say, a television play. If my essays are good it is because they are entirely voluntary. I write only what I want to . . . except, of course, in those money-making days at MGM —composing *Ben Hur.*

INTERVIEWER: But how about the movies? You're still writing for movies, aren't you?

VIDAL: Yes. I love movies, and I think a lot about movies. Recently I thought I would like to direct. More recently, I have decided it's too late. I am like the Walter Lippmanns. I saw them a few years ago. They were euphoric. Why? "Because," she said, "we have decided that we shall *never* go to Japan. Such a relief!"

INTERVIEWER: Why do you prefer movies to the theater?

VIDAL: I'm embarrassed by live actors. They're always having a much better time than I am. Also, few plays are very interesting, while almost any movie is interesting—if just to watch the pictures. But then I'm typically American. We weren't brought up with theater like the English or the Germans. On the other hand, I saw every movie I could in my youth. I once saw four movies in one day when I was fourteen. That was the happiest day of my life.

INTERVIEWER: Have you ever thought of acting, as Norman Mailer does?

VIDAL: Is *that* what he does? I have always been curious. Well, I appeared briefly in my own *The Best Man.* I also appeared in *Fellini Roma,* as myself. I made no sense, due to the cutting, but the movie was splendid anyway. I have been offered the lead in Ustinov's new play for New York. To play an American president. What else? I said no. For one thing, I cannot learn dialogue.

INTERVIEWER: Has your writing been influenced by films?

VIDAL: Every writer of my generation has been influenced by films. I think I've written that somewhere. Find out the movies a man saw between ten and fifteen, which ones he liked, disliked, and you would have a pretty good idea of what sort of mind and temperament he has. If he happened to be a writer, you would be able to find a good many influences, though not perhaps as many as Professor B. F. Dick comes up with in his recent study of me*—a brilliant job, all in all. Myra would've liked it.

INTERVIEWER: What did you see between ten and fifteen?

VIDAL: I saw everything. But I was most affected by George Arliss. Particularly his Disraeli. I liked all those historical fictions that were done in the thirties. Recently I saw my favorite, *Cardinal Richelieu,* for the first time in thirty years on the late show. Absolute chloroform.

INTERVIEWER: Well, you seem to have had an enormous knowledge of movies for *Myra.* Did you have to go back and research any of that?

VIDAL: I saw all those movies of the forties—in the forties. At school and in the army. They're seared on my memory. There wasn't anything in the book that I did not see first time around. Also—to help the Ph.D. thesis writers—almost every picture I mentioned can be found in Parker Tyler's *Magic and Myth of the Movies.* A work which has to be read to be believed.

INTERVIEWER: Have you ever had any trouble with writer's block?

VIDAL: No.

INTERVIEWER: When you get up in the morning to write, do you just sit down and start out with your pen? You don't have any devices you use to . . . ?

VIDAL: First coffee. Then a bowel movement. Then the muse joins me.

---

*The Apostate Angel: A Critical Study of Gore Vidal, by Bernard F. Dick (Random House, 1974).

INTERVIEWER: You don't sharpen pencils or anything like that?

VIDAL: No. But I often read for an hour or two. Clearing the mind. I'm always reluctant to start work, and reluctant to stop. The most interesting thing about writing is the way that it obliterates time. Three hours seem like three minutes. Then there is the business of surprise. I never know what is coming next. The phrase that sounds in the head changes when it appears on the page. Then I start probing it with a pen, finding new meanings. Sometimes I burst out laughing at what is happening as I twist and turn sentences. Strange business, all in all. One never gets to the end of it. That's why I go on, I suppose. To see what the next sentences I write will be.

GERALD CLARKE
Fall 1974

13. Jerzy Kosinski

Jerzy Kosinski was born in Lodz, Poland, on June 14, 1933. Six years later, at the outset of the war, he was separated from his parents and, until the war ended, wandered alone in war-torn Eastern Europe.

After the war, Kosinski studied social psychology and became the youngest associate professor and state grantee at the Polish Academy of Sciences in Warsaw. Kosinski soon began to plot his escape, for which purpose he invented four distinguished American "sponsors" to conduct a massive correspondence with Polish government agencies on his behalf and through whose "efforts" he eventually received his passport.

After arriving in the United States in 1957, he worked at odd jobs and taught himself English with the assistance of daily letters from his multilingual father. He began to write in English, and in 1960 published under the nom de plume Joseph Novak *The Future Is Ours, Comrade* and later *No Third Path* (1962), both of which were studies on the psychology of totalitarianism.

His first novel, *The Painted Bird* (1965), received Le Prix du Meilleur Livre Etranger in France. His next novel, *Steps,* received the 1969 National Book Award. Kosinski's other works include *Being There* (1971), which was adapted by him in 1979 into a popular film; *The Devil Tree* (1973); *Cockpit* (1975); *Blind Date* (1977); and *Passion Play* (1979).

In 1960 Kosinski met and soon after married Mary Hayward Weir of the Weirton Steel Company family. After her tragic death, he was a Guggenheim Fellow, then professor of English at Wesleyan, Princeton, and Yale universities. He has received the Award in Literature from the National Institute of Arts and Letters and served two terms as president of the American Center of P.E.N.

An avid skier, horseman, and photographer, Kosinski divides his time between New York City and Valais in Switzerland.

Third set of galley-proofs of _Passion Play_. Between the first and the third set, Kosinski managed to shorten the novel by one third (over 100 pages).

A professional polo player, Fabian was as fascinated by the animal as he was by the game. ~~In the beginning,~~ man had traveled on a horse, or his horse had pulled him in a carriage. Now, in the era of the automobile, Fabian reasoned, it was time for man to carry his horse with him in a motor home. ~~At this second thought, and fueled by a generous cash gift from the same friend, Fabian bought two disqualified show horses to train as his polo ponies.~~

[handwritten] Once s

[handwritten insertion] He fixed to each side of his VanHome a sign that read Quarantined. The sign shall proven useful: thieves kept away, and _[right margin handwritten]_ so did other drivers and pedestrians; but he needed help sometimes; he could more readily muster it.

[handwritten margin] small caps

Fabian reached the outskirts of a city. Acre on acre of cemeteries seemed to surround it; the dead watched the city like massed troops waiting for a fortress to submit. Against a smudged horizon, behind the giant ant hills of the city dumps, skyscrapers were strewn without pattern.

To Fabian, a city was always a place of deliverance. Nature opened between men the chasm of forest and river, but a city offered that solitude which was not only ⌐ freedom, but ⌐ refuge. Here in this enclosure of touch, of sidewalks, subways, buses, theaters, hospitals, morgues, cemeteries, where flesh was always only feet away from flesh, all streets led to his psychic home. _[handwritten]_ Fabian

[handwritten margin] ⁋/u.c./

~~To Fabian,~~ the city was a habitat of sex. ~~He~~ reasoned that if nature had given man, in proportion to his size, the largest and most developed organs of sex, it had done so because, of all mammals, only man could keep himself in a state of perpetual heat. Sexuality thus became the most human of instincts. Life gave man the fullness of time, to think and to do, to lust and to act. Because ~~feelings~~ those powers were suspended, were to be retrieved in sex, Fabian divided his life into the sphere of sleep and the sphere of sex.

[handwritten margin] in sleep and

Sleep was time's hostage, a prison which muted action, now inviting dreams, now forbidding them entry. Sex liberated, giving language to an urgent vocabulary of need, mood, signal, gesture, glance, a language truly human, universally available.

[handwritten margin] PR: run in — no ⁋

~~Sex was as natural as sleep, but as~~ sleep was the expression of his _[handwritten]_ u c. life's inner design, sex ~~was~~ its outward manifestation. In sleep, he existed for himself; in sex, for others. Thus, sleep imposed; sex proposed. He refused to think of "sleeping with somebody" as synonymous with having sex, the bed in which sleep and sex took place being often their only point of communion.

Sleep had always come easily to him, and his sexual urges came often, but their span was brief; he went about their fulfillment as _[handwritten]_ ultimately the crafting of ~~yet another~~ artwork, independent of the artist's own life. To be given sex was a favor, and he was always ready to return one favor with another—the gift of a meal in his VanHome or in a restaurant, a ride on his pony in some park, ~~even~~ money. ~~Yet~~ he never offered himself as a sexual reward ~~to strangers.~~ He saw the ~~spontaneous~~ play of sex ~~between lovers~~ as a consequence of a mutual inoculation ~~in the charge of feeling.~~ He did not need to be instructed in the natural.

[handwritten margin] an l.c.

[handwritten bottom] He did not see himself as sexually desirable ⊙

JERZY   KOSINSKI

A page from the third set of galley proofs of _Passion Play_. Between the first and third set, Kosinski shortened the novel by over 100 pages.

Jerzy Kosinski

Jerzy Kosinski

Editor's Note: *The following conversation with Jerzy Kosinski, which does not contain the customary interviewers' headnote, is a much expanded version of the one that appeared in* The Paris Review *in 1972. At that time Mr. Kosinski was traveling abroad and could not be reached when the transcribed text, prepared by interviewers Rocco Landesman and George Plimpton, was ready for his review. The preparation of this volume presented the author with an opportunity to edit his original interview.*

INTERVIEWERS: If you had continued to live in Eastern Europe and written in Polish or, as you were bilingual, in Russian, do you think your novels would have been published? And if so, would they have been popular?

KOSINSKI: It's not even a matter for speculation. I would never have written in Polish or in Russian. I never saw myself as a man willingly expressing opinions in a totalitarian State. Make no mistake about it: all my generation was perfectly aware of the political price paid for our existence in the total State. To be a writer was to become a spokesman for a particular philosophical dogma. I considered this a trap: I would not speak for it; nor could I publicly speak against it. That's why I slowly moved toward visual expression: while officially studying social psychology, I became a professional photographer. Of course, there were some other reasons for my apprehension about becoming a writer. Which language would I choose? I was split, like a child who belongs to two different families; studying in Polish at the university, but at home—my parents, even though Polish, were both Russian-born and -educated— all that mattered was Russian tradition and Russian literature.

INTERVIEWERS: Given the dimensions of the political trap could you express in photographs anything you felt?

KOSINSKI: Within the limits of photography, I could contrast collective behavior with individual destiny. Thus, my photographs often portrayed old age which knows no politics. They showed the solitude of a man alone in an empty field or on a crowded street, and the State buildings and Party memorials, ridiculously monumental, inhuman in their grandeur. My photographs pointed out an independent, naked human being who, even in the total State, was still willing to be photographed naked. I even produced some nudes of rather attractive nonsocialist female forms. It ended on a very unpleasant political note however; at one annual meeting of the Photographers' Union I was officially accused of being a cosmopolitan who sees the flesh, but not its social implications. My membership in the union and my right to have my photographs published or exhibited nationally or abroad was suspended for an indefinite period. For the same reason, I was also suspended at the university, but then reinstated thanks to my uniformly good grades—and the personal intervention by the dean and the rector, both scholars of "the old guard."

INTERVIEWERS: Who accused you?

KOSINSKI: First, the Party members of the Photographers' Union. The same politically oriented State setup as the Writers' Union, you know. These unions control work assignments and permits, exhibitions, grants, awards, etcetera. They are geared to policing; that is what they're there for. Then my case was picked up by the Party cell of the Students' Union at the university. By then it was all very serious. One's whole life depended on an outcome of such an accusation—and of the review of one's total conduct that followed.

INTERVIEWERS: Can one defend oneself?

KOSINSKI: Within the limits of the totalitarian doctrine; there is no defense against the supremacy of the Party that claims to be "the arm of the people." When I was growing up in a Stalinist society my guidelines were: Am I going to survive physically? Mentally? Am I going to remain a decent being? Will they, the Party, succeed in turning me into their pawn and unleash me against others like me? Since I could not avoid being in conflict with the Party, the unions, the whole totalitarian routine imposed on everyone, my real plight had to remain hidden. I avoided having close friends, men and women who would know too much about me and could be coerced into testifying against me. Still, the accusations, the reprimands, the attacks, continued. I was twice thrown out from the Students' Union and twice ordered back. From week to week, from meeting to meeting, it was a very perilous existence. Until I left for America I lived the life of an "inner emigré," as I called myself.

INTERVIEWERS: An inner emigré?

KOSINSKI: Yes. The photographic darkroom emerged as a perfect metaphor for my life. It was the one place I could lock myself in (rather than being locked in) and legally not admit anyone else. For me it became a kind of temple. There is an episode in *Steps* in which a young philosophy student at the State university selects the lavatories as the only temples of privacy available to him. Well, think how much more of such a temple a darkroom is in a police state. Inside, I would develop my own private images; instead of writing fiction I imagined myself as a fictional character. I identified very strongly with characters of both Eastern and Western literature. I saw myself as Petchorin, in Lermontov's novel, *A Hero of Our Time;* as Romashov, the hero of Kuprin's *The Duel;* as Julien Sorel, or Rastignac, and once in a while as Arthur of E. L. Voynich's *The Gadfly,* facing the oppressive society and being at war with it. I wrote my fiction emotionally; I would never commit it to paper.

INTERVIEWERS: Paddy Chayefsky said once that he felt these sort of oppressive strictures were really quite important in producing fine literature. He felt that a straitjacket was essential to a writer.

KOSINSKI: Easily said. One could as well argue the opposite and make a point for the Byronesque kind of expression with its abandonment, its freedom to collide with others, to express outrage—for Nabokov's kind of vitality. Or we can make a point for a man who chooses a self-imposed visionary straitjacket, perhaps the best one there is. Look at Stendhal, Proust, Melville, Faulkner, Flannery O'Connor. For every Solzhenitsyn who manages to have his first novel published officially *(One Day in the Life of Ivan Denisovitch),* there are probably hundreds of gifted writers in the Soviet bloc who create emotionally in their "darkrooms," and who will never write anything. Or those very desperate ones who do commit their vision to paper but hide their manuscripts somewhere under the floorboards.

INTERVIEWERS: What has been the reaction of the Soviet-bloc press to your achievements in English prose?

KOSINSKI: The reaction of the East European press towards, for example, *The Painted Bird* was hostile propaganda. They reinvented the content of the novel. Their major effort was to prove that any Pole who settled abroad, writes in English, and is published by various Western publishers had to do it by selling himself to the Library of Congress! According to the official Party journal, the most damaging proof of my collaboration with the White House was that the novel carried the Library of Congress number . . . which, of course, is automatically assigned to every book published in the U.S. There are a few things, however, which they can't quite cope with: my novels are warmly received by the progressive leftist press in the rest of Western Europe. To counteract it, the East European bureaucrats said that to achieve a "monetary success" in the West, I decided to abandon my "real" idiom, writing instead in English.

INTERVIEWERS: Who are the people in the Writers' Union in the Soviet bloc?

KOSINSKI: They are journalists, novelists, literary critics, poets. They have to pay their bills, and to pay their bills they have to earn income and be published from time to time by the State publishing houses. I think many of them are primarily concerned with survival in their profession. It's easy to attach labels, but we have to remember they have to function within a most threatening and unpredictable reality governed by the Party bureaucracy and the total State. Hence, many of them are extremely cautious, many tend to be dogmatic, many are just desperate, and some are servile agents of the State organs. The creative man in a police state has always been trapped in a cage where he can fly as long as he does not touch the wires. His predicament is how to spread his wings in the cage. I think the majority fight for sanity, and when one of them says I don't like this cage, I want out, and does something about it, the others descend on him because he is threatening the safety of all of them. Most often, the writer, poet, or playwright in the Soviet bloc feels that what he writes is the best thing that he can do for his nation, for his country; in good faith he delivers his manuscript to the publisher, and often is persecuted from the next day on—his case discussed by the Writers' Union because, apparently, according to the accusations, in his manuscript he reveals himself as an anti-Soviet character. This was the case of Pasternak, among many others. When he wrote *Dr. Zhivago* he thought it was about the fate of a man caught in the changing patterns of political upheavals. Well, the Party didn't see it that way. Instead, his official accusers declared it antisocialist, cosmopolitan, amoral, etcetera. He was condemned by the Writers' Union.

INTERVIEWERS: Given the unusual circumstances of your life, many people think of all your novels as a form of an extended autobiography, or autobiographical even.

KOSINSKI: I have argued against such views many times. To say that any novel is autobiographical may be convenient for classification, but it's not easily justified. What we remember lacks the hard edge of fact. To help us along we create little fictions, highly subtle and individual scenarios which clarify and shape our experience. The remembered event becomes an incident, a highly compressed dramatic unit that mixes memory and emotion, a structure made to accommodate certain feelings. If it weren't for these structures, art would be too personal for the artist to create, much less for the audience to grasp. Even film, the most literal of all the arts, is edited.

INTERVIEWERS: You wrote once that *The Painted Bird* is the result of a "slow unfreezing of a mind long gripped by fear." I assume this fear refers to the horrors of World War Two.

KOSINSKI: In terms of "a mind long gripped by fear," I see no essential difference between war and any other traumatic experience. For example, I know many people whose adolescence in the peaceful United States or Sweden was in its own way just as traumatic as was the war or Stalinist oppression for millions of Central and East Europeans.

INTERVIEWERS: Yes, but in this case a whole generation was affected by the Holocaust. A noted American critic spoke of a "brutalization of the imagination" produced in many writers by this one catastrophe.

KOSINSKI: I don't believe that human experience can be graded, from less brutal to extremely brutal. It depends on how it affects the mind. Among the East Europeans I know, I never saw myself as a victim; rather, as one of the multitude. I think I was no more, no less affected by the war than were millions of others.

INTERVIEWERS: You sound like Roman Polanski, who said that violence is horrible and traumatic only when you look at it from a particular point of view.

KOSINSKI: We both tend to perceive violence as human, and thus plausible. There is no objective yardstick to human imagination or emotion. A needle or the sight of blood may be as terrifying to a North Dakotan as a bomb is to the Vietnamese.

INTERVIEWERS: So in your view, subjective experience is arbitrary; X pretty much equals Y or Z?

KOSINSKI: Our judgment of our experience is arbitrary. It all depends on the perceiving mind.

INTERVIEWERS: But the experiences that you deal with, in *Steps,* for instance, are certainly not what we might call "ordinary" experiences. One episode takes place in an asylum, another in a rest home, another in a lavatory, another in the New York underworld. And you continually choose incidents that to other people, at least, seem unusual.

KOSINSKI: I don't know who those "other people" are. The asylum in itself is not a very unusual institution: one-half of all hospital beds in the United States are occupied by psychiatric patients. One in every ten North Americans develops some form of mental or emotional illness; soon one in five will be over sixty-five, and lavatories seem to me to be as common in our daily life as the underworld is in the life of our cities. When *Cockpit* was published, its imaginative scenario containing, among others, a secret agent in hiding, instances of radiation, mass subway poisoning, mysterious disease, kidnappings, food-color dye panic, etcetera; a well-known art critic reproached me for what he called my supposed freedom to ignore in my fiction all worldly plausibility. Well, years later, the American public learned to its horror from the pages of *The New York Times* that for the past fifteen years the unsuspecting staff of the U.S. Embassy in Moscow has been irradiated by microwaves, that a mysterious new disease—possibly army toxin—has spread in several states, that CIA scientists secretly spread simulated biological poison on Manhattan subway lines to test its vulnerability to a biological warfare attack, and that its agents have routinely kidnapped and tortured suspected foreign spies in U.S.; that the food-color dye was finally banned, etcetera, etcetera. Come to think, reality has always caught up with the novelist's imagination. . . . In any case, my novels are not about wars, credit cards, darkrooms, asylums, rest homes, lavatories, subways, or diseases. They are about people and their relationships with themselves and with each other. "I'm myself—it's the ultimate risk," says a character in *Blind Date.* My novels are about such characters—and about taking such risks. The greatest risks there are.

INTERVIEWERS: If all our institutions and experiences have for you an equal imaginary value, that is, if anything goes, isn't there a corresponding reduction in the immediacy or intensity of your response?

KOSINSKI: It depends, I think, primarily on one's outlook. *JAMA,* the *Journal of the American Medical Association,* recommended *Being There* as a supplement to scientific study of what they termed *unsaneness,* that awfully ambiguous line of demarcation between what is sane and what is insane in our lives. Most of my fiction takes place in this no-man's-land between sane and insane, common and uncommon, between collective norm and the individual schism, indeed in this realm of unsaneness of the self as well as of its environment. If such fiction makes one "less sensitive"—that conversely would mean that the least aware, the most provincial among us, is also the most sensitive.

INTERVIEWERS: It would seem then that no one thing would faze you more than anything else.

KOSINSKI: Well, on one level, that's true: humanity does not surprise me. By its very nature as art, fiction rises above the world of realities and stays within the realm of plausibility and perception. But I detest the dismissal of the true drama of our life by the emissaries of the popular culture—the videots of Disneyland, the fiddlers of Broadway's sentimentality, and so many other professional cultural propagandists whose moral tenet apparently demands that we should never appear as we really are.

INTERVIEWERS: Why did you choose the United States when you left the Soviet bloc?

KOSINSKI: I was not leaving for any specific place. Attempting to leave Eastern Europe, I had three priorities on my list, in alphabetical order as well as in the order of my intent: Argentina, Brazil, and the United States, all large multiethnic societies where I assumed I could find anonymity. I remember that first I carefully began collecting Spanish and Portuguese dictionaries. Only much later, English and American ones. In addition to Polish, Russian, and Ukrainian, I knew a bit of French and of Italian, of Latin and Esperanto. I assumed it would have been easier for me to pick up Spanish or Portuguese. But I was turned down by both Argentina and Brazil. Having studied at the Communist universities in Poland and in the Soviet Union made me potentially threatening to the strongly anti-Communist governments of Latin America. On December 20, 1957, I was admitted to the United States, and had to decide what to do next. I was twenty-four. I did not believe in cumulative riches, as I do not believe now, because while thinking they always win, the rich actually lose twice: once while they're alive, because with so much to lose they never really take chances; and once when they die, because being rich they lose so much. Hence my faith in "portable skills," originally photography, now writing, which leave me mobile, free to *exit—exiting* is for me very important. When I reached the United States, I decided that since photography unfortunately requires such expensive equipment, my exit would have to be the English language, writing prose.

INTERVIEWERS: How long did it take you to learn English?

KOSINSKI: Sufficiently to express myself in writing? About six months, when, in 1958, while studying for my Ph.D on a Ford Fellowship, I began writing in English my university term papers and essays. My father was a classical scholar, a philologist, fluent in English, and via air mail he kept sending me six times a week English lessons tailored to my needs. But, in fact, I am still learning. Doesn't every writer? Language is like a moody lover: she might take a leave at any time. In other words, I shouldn't leave her alone for too long. When I am abroad—I spend about half a year traveling—I fear that one day I might forget English. Do remember, I was in my mid-twenties when I began writing in English and ever since it has to be constantly pressed deeper and deeper, otherwise it might evaporate. It is my only true possession—and the possession possesses.

INTERVIEWERS: When did Joseph Conrad leave Poland?

KOSINSKI: He left for England when he was twenty-one. He wrote his first novel, *Almayer's Folly*, when he was thirty-eight, and he collaborated for a while with Ford Madox Ford. What is of interest is that he had difficulty expressing himself vocally; apparently, his accent was quite pronounced. Possibly, he considered speaking a nuisance—occasionally so do I: a writer's true calling is not about speaking, but about being "mute," about writing. Similarly, when in 1958 I sat down to write my first book in English, *The Future Is Ours, Comrade*, a nonfiction on collective behavior, I found that I could *write* the book, but I had great difficulty discussing its chapters with friends; even when it was published less than two years later, conversing in English did not interest me. I aimed at the written word, an expression which was articulate but abstract, a language without sound. I didn't want to meet or know my audience. In the act of writing in English, I extracted a part of myself, my preoccupation with the place of an individual in a collective society, hoping my American audience was eventually to be found. When it was, I followed two years later with another Novak book, *No Third Path: A Study of Collective Behavior.*

INTERVIEWERS: But listening to you telling stories on various TV and radio talk shows—Carson, Cavett, Long John Nebel, et al.—and then finding some of them in your novels, one wonders whether it is true that you test your stories on the listeners. If you do, how much do you change them according to audience reaction?

KOSINSKI: As a novelist, I am, first, a storyteller. I remember how in the Soviet Union I and several other students of social psychology were assigned by the university to lecture at a collective farm, traveling to and from the farm by train. There were always peasants taking the train to a farmers' market on the way, and they invariably listened in on the students' conversation. One of us would begin a tale; as the train approached the market station, the drama would increase, the narrator piling one dramatic incident upon another. The peasants, openmouthed, usually swallowed every word, laughing, crying, or gasping with terror. The train would stop at the market, but afraid to miss a word, they seldom moved. As the train pulled away from the platform and began to pick up speed, the story would end abruptly. Only then would they become aware that they had missed their stop. At the end of the week, the student whose storytelling had caused the largest number of peasants to miss the market stop won the game. Well, I use the talk shows as a trainful of passengers willing to listen to my story, even if they miss their stop. Mind you, not an easy task: commercials break any story more often than a train's stops. No wonder—in this country we watch the conversation, a TV host once reminded me graciously. But usually I don't use the

TV popular audience's reaction—mostly, an easily evokable laughter—as a yardstick, even though one of my novels, *Being There*, is about that very audience.

INTERVIEWERS: You are said to develop the suspense of your novels by first trying it out in life—sneaking about in disguise and employing yourself in various holy and unholy establishments, hiding in the apartments of your friends (after they assumed you had left them), bluffing your way with authorities with fictitious ID cards, etcetera. Is such turning what is real into fiction necessary for you?

KOSINSKI: It is from time to time. It reassures my belief that for a man or woman, who is often unsuspecting and unimaginative, the institutions of our daily, familiar environment entrap us more effectively than do all federal and state internal security agencies. Yet, it is in this very familiar setting that the actual and potential drama of our life unfolds. The purpose of a fictional protagonist who is sufficiently threatening and menacing is to enlist the reader on his side for the duration of the fictional ride of time, thus turning these overfamiliar conditions threatening and menacing, suddenly unfamiliar, inviting examination. Does my occasional impersonating of such a protagonist turn me into a writer engagé?

INTERVIEWERS: But your serving two terms as the president of the American Center of P.E.N. International, certainly does. Why are you so engagé?

KOSINSKI: Possibly because exclusion, persecution, censorship, and forced anonymity had been a fact of my daily life in Eastern Europe. I am now not only compelled to create a world of fiction to which all have access, but also to defend and fight for everyone's right to such creation and such access. I fear total State. I hate its spokesmen. If I were ever magically to turn into Tarden, the protagonist of *Cockpit*, or George Levanter of *Blind Date*, I would do to the oppressors what my protagonists have done to them. Meanwhile, I must employ other means—of remaining engagé: P.E.N., the International League for Human Rights, lecturing.

INTERVIEWERS: Could you see yourself starting as a writer all over again—in a new country, in a new language?

KOSINSKI: To leave America, to abandon English? It's a nightmare, but I do think about it. After all, most of the protagonists of my novels are often exposed to the fate of risk taking. Yes, I could. In French perhaps. But the French bureaucracy—the bureaucracy of the French mind as well as that of the state—threatens me a lot.

INTERVIEWERS: Do you ever think about abandoning writing altogether, be it in English, French, or whatever?

KOSINSKI: I do. What if I found myself again in a police state? Or, to be more exact, what if a police state found me? All my novels are about the self, the characters in the state of becoming, and they all are passionate enemies of totalitarian oppression—left, center, or right. I would be, clearly, among the writers whose voice would be stilled and declared subversive. I find it very indicative that I keep taking photographs and always have a completely equipped photographic darkroom available, not too far from my apartment. Photography as a profession remains even today my potential escape from a potential political terror.

INTERVIEWERS: Have you ever used it?

KOSINSKI: Occasionally I develop photographs for friends of mine who don't want to use the neighborhood's photo shop. I haven't done any creative photography. But as it turns out, the darkroom has another use. Recently I learnt that my eyesight was in danger. I took another look at my darkroom, and I thought, Oh my God, maybe it will become a metaphor for my American existence as well. I used the darkroom to practice dictating to a tape recorder just in case I would become blind. While dictating in darkness I noticed I developed a new kind of freedom—the tape-recorder prose seems to be looser, less controlled than the typewriter prose of *Steps,* for instance, or *Being There.* Afraid that I would lose my sight any minute, I prevented myself from editing: all I wanted to do was to develop the ability to be articulate while dictating. The rest I would somehow learn later. All I wanted to do was to permit my "vision," born in a darkroom, this inner vision, to reach the tape recorder.

INTERVIEWERS: Did you have it read back to you?

KOSINSKI: No, I didn't want to be stopped. I just wanted to pour it out.

INTERVIEWERS: What do you do with the various drafts of your manuscripts?

KOSINSKI: The last few of each novel I store in the bank vault where I also keep my negatives, letters, and the manuscripts and galleys of my novels (I collect or own not much else). The vault is almost as big as a one-room studio. I am always afraid that some oppressive societal force will go after me, and will try to penetrate not only my apartment—let them do it, there is nothing there—but also my inner life, which, they would claim, must be reflected in my writing, in my letters, and in photographs taken by me.

INTERVIEWERS: You said once that you rewrote your manuscripts dozens of times. Did you want to be sure that each word had exactly the power and meaning you intended, or was it more a general stylistic thing you were looking for?

KOSINSKI: I keep depressing my text, deescalating the language. I count words the way Western Union does; often, I'm afraid my prose tends to resemble a night letter. Every word is there for a reason, and if not, I cross it out. I do rewrite—often entirely—my galley pages, even page proofs. The publishers complain, but I argue that every new draft keeps improving my own as well as their book. Still, I am never certain whether my English prose is sufficiently clear. Also, I rarely allow myself to use English in an unchecked, spontaneous way.

I always have a sense of trembling—but so does a compass, after all.

INTERVIEWERS: So you are simply checking and rechecking your use of the language?

KOSINSKI: Rather, the impact of it. Whether my vision will ignite the reader's imagination I will never know. But I constantly attempt to make the language of my fiction as unobtrusive as possible, almost transparent, so that the reader would be drawn right away into each dramatic incident. What I have said carries no value judgment. It is the opposite, for example, of what Nabokov does. His language is made visible . . . like a veil or transparent curtain. You cannot help seeing the curtain as you peek into the intimate rooms behind. My aim, though, is to remove the veil, altogether if possible. It should come to the reader the way it does in life—in an impact during which one is not aware of the form but merely of its content. I think in *Steps* and in *The Devil Tree* I came closest to what I really wanted to do with English. The vision demanded a clear prose, a language as detached as the persona of the novel. For me, a novelist is not a displayer of stylistic bonfires; he is primarily conveying a vision. Of course, whether the vision will "ignite" the reader's mind is something the writer will never know.

INTERVIEWERS: What about your working habits? Are you Protestant and disciplined, or European and dissolute?

KOSINSKI: I guess both. I still wake up around 8 a.m. ready for the day, and sleep again for four hours in the afternoon, which allows me to remain mentally and physically active until the early dawn, when again I go to sleep. Being part of the Protestant ethos for less than one-third of my life, I acquired only some Protestant habits, while maintaining some of my former ones. Among the ones I acquired is the belief that I ought to answer my mail—a belief not shared by many happy intellectuals in Rome. In terms of my actual writing habits, I

am an old member of the Russian and Polish *inteligentzya*—
neither a professional intellectual nor a café-society hedonist.
I love writing more than anything else. Like the heartbeat,
each novel I write is inseparable from my life. I write when I
feel like it and wherever I feel like it, and I feel like it most
of the time: day, night, and during twilight. I write in a restaurant, on a plane, between skiing and horseback riding, when I
take my night walks in Manhattan, Paris, or in any other town.
I wake up in the middle of the night or the afternoon to make
notes and never know when I'll sit down at the typewriter.

INTERVIEWERS: How long is the time of actually putting
words to paper?

KOSINSKI: It varies. I think the longest uninterrupted stretch
I ever had was twenty-seven hours. I wrote nineteen pages of
The Painted Bird which in the drafts that followed shrank to
one page. On an average I probably "produce" about a page,
maybe a page and a half, in a sitting. I write very much the way
some of my poet friends do. I select from the novel's master
plan, from its topography, a fragment of a scene I find most
inspiring at the given time, and then write it moving either
"above it" or "below it." Since I start with an image, let's say,
of a man being driven in his car through the West Virginia
countryside—I might first write about the rain, or his car, or
what he felt at the end of the drive, and only then confront
the scene's dramatic center. I usually start a novel by writing
its opening and its end, which seem to survive relatively unchanged through all the following drafts and galley-proof
changes.

INTERVIEWERS: Have all your books had code words?

KOSINSKI: Yes: every book had a code name before I had a
title for it.

INTERVIEWERS: What was *The Painted Bird*'s?

KOSINSKI: It's code name was *The Jungle Book*. *Steps* was
The Two. And *Being There* was *Blank Page*, and sometimes

Dasein, a philosophical term, difficult to translate, which could mean the state in which one *is* and *is not* at the same time. One has to be careful with titles. If I had kept to that initial code name, it would have connected the book, possibly, with the philosophy of Heidegger. As a matter of fact, one of the American critics learned from my publisher that *Dasein* was the code name, and months later wrote a very negative review of *Being There* as a Heideggerian novel—a terribly unfair thing to do. Had the code name been *Kapital,* he probably would have considered the book a Marxist novel.

INTERVIEWERS: Unlike many writers, who are forever denying that they read their reviews, you seem to be rather interested in criticism.

KOSINSKI: I am attracted to literary criticism. In fact, as if to test this interest I wrote a series of critical comments on *The Painted Bird* and on *Steps.* They were initially letters I wrote in English to one of my foreign publishers, but when to please and surprise me he decided to translate them and have them published in his country, to secure my American copyright I was forced to have them published as two separate collections of short essays *(Notes of the Author* and *The Art of the Self).* I think that literary criticism can be just as creative as writing novels or poetry. It is unfortunate that in this country it has often been assumed that it is more glamorous to be a novelist than a critic because as a novelist you are assumed to have lived your novels. The Hollywood movies that at one time sentimentalized the novelist might have contributed to this notion. Conversely, being a literary critic is often considered "intellectual" and parasitic, living off the "hard gut" experiences of the novelist. One day I might be tempted to turn into a full-time literary critic.

INTERVIEWERS: Are you upset by adverse criticism of your work?

KOSINSKI: I am, but only when it is also bad art: poorly

written, unimaginative, ad hominem. When it chooses to denounce the author rather than to illuminate his vision. Among my favorite critics are also some who claimed all my work to be inferior, overrated, crude, amoral; but they wrote all this creatively, dissecting the philosophy and the character of my protagonists—not mine.

INTERVIEWERS: To what do you attribute the success of your books?

KOSINSKI: Let's call it their temporary survival. Judging by the reviews, letters, students' essays and term papers as well as by direct contact with my reading public at my public lectures, in schools and colleges where my novels are taught, the younger Americans seem to read *The Painted Bird* as a symbolic novel about their own lives: they are "the painted birds" in the hostile environment of industrial America. *Steps,* on the other hand, typifies to many the complexity of a man who has been a product of an indifferent, automatized society, a society in which hé is not only manipulated by others, but cannot help manipulating them. As for *Being There,* the reaction focuses on Chauncey Gardiner, a formidable tribute to corporate image making. There is more and more preoccupation with the visual aspects of American political life. Think of the priority given to the looks of our candidates. They all come across well on TV. Do we have have a hunchback? A man with a missing jaw? A man with a nervous tic? No, he simply wouldn't make it. Can you imagine an American politician, however bright, with a damaged face, or with one eye? Moshe Dayan, all right, he's up there; he's theirs, not ours. As for *The Devil Tree,* that is to many of them a reflection of what it takes to become "one's own event" even when, like Jonathan Whalen, one is American, young, handsome, and rich. *Cockpit* presents the dilemma of aging—even when, like Tarden, one is a former intelligence agent trained to survive at any cost. And *Blind Date* seems to be to them about life's various dichotomies, destiny and chance in the world of power abuse.

INTERVIEWERS: What has been the reaction to your books in England?

KOSINSKI: *The Future Is Ours, Comrade* was generally praised for its insights into collective mentality, but the British were upset by the cruelties of *The Painted Bird,* abhorred the coldness of *Steps,* accorded *Being There* the status of the best novel of the year, liked *The Devil Tree,* and highly praised *Cockpit* and *Blind Date.* So the reception seems to vary from book to book, from country to country, and from period to period. I like to think that at different times different people read books for different reasons. Or don't read them.

INTERVIEWERS: Doesn't it bother you that there are so many different reactions and interpretations?

KOSINSKI: It doesn't. After all, if the writer's imagination is free enough to crystallize his vision in a novel, why shouldn't the reader's imagination be equally free in decoding it? Like any other societal event or artifact, the novel confronts the reader arbitrarily, designed to involve and to manipulate him. My fiction portrays the self in a state of recoil against the all-pervasive, all-powerful, ever-present forces—State, other people, language, sexual mores, etcetera—that render man's existence dependent upon arbitrarily imposed notions of life and destiny. As my fiction does not impose itself on the reader in an easily detectable, predigested manner, it aims for the impact, for the ethical collision. By engaging my reader, on one hand, in the concrete, visible acts of cunning, violence, assault, and disguise (as opposed to the diluted, camouflaged violence of our total environment), my fiction is, on the other, purging his emotions, enraging him, polarizing his anger, his moral climate, turning him against such acts (and often against the author as well). In a word, it is generating a uniquely private moral judgment. To generate such judgment, to evoke affirmation of the man's unique moral stand, is for me the supreme —and supremely didactic—role of good art, of true art. And as for the writer, he is not superior to anyone: in his work he merely particularizes our collective ability to evoke, to create situations and images entirely via our language.

INTERVIEWERS: After the success of your "Joseph Novak" nonfiction, did you find it difficult to get your first novel, *The Painted Bird*, published?

KOSINSKI: Yes, I did. When I had the finished manuscript, I showed it to four friends of mine, all editors in very large, respectable publishing houses in New York. All four had an interest in my work because of my two nonfiction books, and all four told me in very plain language that in their view my first novel was simply not publishable in America.

INTERVIEWERS: What were their reasons?

KOSINSKI: That it was a novel about a reality which is alien to Americans, set in an environment that Americans cannot comprehend, and portraying situations, particularly the cruelty to animals, that Americans cannot bear. No work of fiction could possibly survive all this, they said, and certainly not *The Painted Bird*. The verdict was: go back to writing your best-selling nonfiction under the pen name of Joseph Novak. I asked them who, in their view, would be the *least* likely publisher for my novel. They said short of Vatican City, I should try the distinguished and venerable Houghton Mifflin in Boston. I sent the manuscript to Houghton Mifflin, and a few weeks later they called that they wanted to publish *The Painted Bird*. It appeared in the fall of 1965. Years later, I had similar difficulties finding a publisher for *Steps, Being There,* and *Cockpit.*

INTERVIEWERS: Since you often teach English, what is your feeling about the future of the written word?

KOSINSKI: I think its place has always been at the edge of popular culture. Indeed, it is the proper place for it. Reading novels—serious novels, anyhow—is an experience limited to a very small percentage of the so-called enlightened public. Increasingly, it's going to be a pursuit for those who seek unusual experiences, moral fetishists perhaps, people of heightened imagination, the troubled pursuers of the ambiguous self.

INTERVIEWERS: Why such a limited audience?

KOSINSKI: Today, people are absorbed in the most common denominator, the *visual.* It requires no education to watch TV. It knows no age limit. Your infant child can watch the same program you do. Witness its role in the homes of the old and incurably sick. Television is everywhere. It has the immediacy which the evocative medium of language doesn't. Language requires some inner triggering; television doesn't. The image is ultimately accessible, i e., extremely attractive. And, I think, ultimately deadly, because it turns the viewer into a bystander. Of course, that's a situation we have always dreamt of . . . the ultimate hope of religion was that it would release us from trauma. Television actually does so. It "proves" that you can always be an observer of the tragedies of others. The fact that one day you will die in front of the live show is irrelevant—you are reminded about it no more than you are reminded about real weather existing outside the TV weather program. You're not told to open your window and take a look; television will never say that. It says, instead, "The weather today is . . ." and so forth. The weatherman never says, "If you don't believe me, go find out."

From way back, our major development as a race of frightened beings has been towards how to avoid facing the discomfort of our existence, primarily the possibility of an accident, immediate death, ugliness, and the ultimate departure. In terms of all this, television is a very pleasing medium: one is always the observer. The life of discomfort is always accorded to others, and even *this* is disqualified, since one program immediately disqualifies the preceding one. Literature does not have this ability to soothe. You have to evoke, and by evoking, you yourself have to provide your own inner setting. When you read about a man who dies, part of you dies with him because you have to recreate his dying inside your head.

INTERVIEWERS: That doesn't happen with the visual?

KOSINSKI: No, because he dies on the screen in front of you, and at any time you can turn it off or select another program. The evocative power is torpedoed by the fact that this is another man; your eye somehow perceives him as a visual object. Thus, of course, television is my ultimate enemy and it will push reading matter—including *The Paris Review*—to the extreme margin of human experience. Ultimately it's going to be a pursuit for those who seek the unusual, masochists probably, who *want* sensations. They will all read *The Painted Bird*, I hope.

INTERVIEWERS: But couldn't the masochists get enormous pleasure out of watching *The Painted Bird* as a film?

KOSINSKI: No. At best they would become voyeurs, which is a low level of experience. No. The very fact that it is happening on the screen tells the viewer two things: one, it is *not* about him; and two, it is not real. It is already *there*, it is artificial, it is about someone else.

INTERVIEWERS: Doesn't one identify with Gary Cooper or John Wayne?

KOSINSKI: Very fleetingly. It's merely recognizing the symbol, saying, "This is John Wayne playing so and so." The optimum that the visual medium can aim at is the moment when the observer decodes what he sees on the screen. In a curious way, the better the film the more it reminds the observer that he is only observing; in the moment of ultimate terror on the screen the man in the audience says to himself, Come on, hang on, it's only a film. With the novel, you cannot escape the evoking which is done within you since the screen is inside—and that is a very real and often painful process. But I never considered literature to be as important as the public highway system, for instance. Reading fiction is an esoteric pursuit; it aims at the blind and at those who can evoke, and the majority today don't have to. They are all provided with TV sets. I don't think literature ought to compete with cinema or television, though indeed it performs the essential function of the highest art . . . to bring man closer to what he is. The old Aristotelian idea: to *purge* him of his emotion—not merely to *show* him the emotion.

INTERVIEWERS: You say that literature demands more involvement and more effort from the reader than the visual media. Is this why your last two novels have been so spare?

KOSINSKI: Yes. I do trust the reader. I think he is perfectly capable of filling in the blank spaces, of supplying what I purposefully withdrew. *Steps* attempts to involve the reader through nonuse of the clear and discernible plot. From the first sentence of the book, "I was traveling further south," when the reader starts traveling down the page, he is promised nothing, since there is no obvious plot to seduce him. He has to make the same decisions my protagonist is making: Will he continue? Is he interested in the next incident?

INTERVIEWERS: Your intent, then, is subversive. You want to involve, to implicate the reader via his own imagination.

KOSINSKI: I guess I do. Once he is implicated he is an accomplice, he is provoked, he is involved, he is purged. That's why my novels don't provide easy moral guidelines. Does life? The reader must ask himself questions about what is good or what is evil about my characters. Was it his curiosity that dragged him into the midst of my story? Was it recognition of his complicity? For me this is the ultimate purpose of literature.

INTERVIEWERS: Do you want to be remembered as . . .

KOSINSKI: No bookkeeper is as false and fraudulent as collective memory. It's best to be forgotten.

INTERVIEWERS: Yet you file things away; you're very meticulous about preserving your work.

KOSINSKI: I merely facilitate the work of executors of my last will. They will follow its text, and thanks to its clarity (a new draft written every year), they will know where to find what I asked them to destroy. Meanwhile, living my life, I take care of its prefaces, footnotes, postscripts, etcetera.

INTERVIEWERS: You always expect the worst?

KOSINSKI: No: the unexpected. I look forward to it.

INTERVIEWERS: But all the preparations against the future . . .

KOSINSKI: The future? So far all my plans have always turned out to be for yesterday.

GEORGE PLIMPTON
ROCCO LANDESMAN
Summer 1972

14. Joan Didion

Joan Didion, author of novels, essays, and screenplays, was born in Sacramento, California, on December 5, 1934. She majored in English literature at the University of California at Berkeley and edited its literary magazine. In 1956 her article on the architect William Wilson Wurster won *Vogue* magazine's Prix de Paris award for college seniors; as part of the prize she was invited to join *Vogue's* editorial staff. Didion also contributed on a free-lance basis to *Mademoiselle* and the *National Review* before taking a leave of absence to complete her first novel.

The publication in 1963 of that novel, *Run River,* earned her an immediate reputation. The next year she married the novelist John Gregory Dunne, with whom she has written such screenplays as *Panic in Needle Park* (1971) and *A Star Is Born* (1976), in addition to the "Points West" column for the *Saturday Evening Post* (1967–69). She has also been a columnist for *Life* and *Esquire.*

Her other works include two collections of essays, *Slouching Toward Bethlehem* (1968) and the best-selling *The White Album* (1979), as well as the novels *Play It As It Lays* (1970), which was nominated for a National Book Award, and *A Book of Common Prayer* (1977).

Didion and her husband live in Los Angeles, California, with their teenage daughter, Quintana.

¶ You were both wrong but it's all the same in the end.

As a matter of fact Charlotte had told me that she and Marin once modeled matching tennis dresses in a fashion show at the Burlingame Country Club and that because she did not play tennis she had needed to ask Marin how to hold the racquet correctly.

"I'm quite sure your mother didn't play tennis," I said.

"She always wore a tennis dress," Marin Bogart said.

"More than once?"

"Always."

"Didn't you play tennis?"

"Tennis," Marin Bogart said, "is *just one more* ⋀ mode of teaching an elitest strategy. If you subject it to a revolutionary analysis you'll see that. Not that I think you will."

We sat facing each other in the bleak room.

We all remember what we need to remember.

Marin remembered Charlotte in a tennis dress and Charlotte remembered Marin in a straw hat for Easter. I remembered Edgar~ *Edgar as* very clearly, but nothing I remembered would accommodate a meeting with Leonard Douglas in Bogota. Charlotte remembered *I did not remember the man who financed the Tupamaros.* she bled. I remembered the light in Boca Grande. I sat in this Why did you bother agreeing to see me," I said finally. room in Buffalo where I had no business being and I talked to this child who was not mine and I remembered the light in Boca Grande.

Another place I *have* had no business being.

In the end I had dreamed my life as Charlotte had. ¶ *It seems to me now.*

A manuscript page from *A Book of Common Prayer.*

Joan Didion

It is usual for the interviewer to write this paragraph about the circumstances in which the interview was conducted, but the interviewer in this case, Linda Kuehl, died not long after the tapes were transcribed. Linda and I talked on August 18 and August 24, 1977, from about ten in the morning until early afternoon. Both interviews took place in the living room of my husband's and my house on the sea north of Los Angeles, a house we no longer own. The walls in that room were white. The floors were of terra cotta tile, very highly polished. The glare off the sea was so pronounced in that room that corners of it seemed, by contrast, extremely dark, and everyone who sat in the room tended to gravitate toward these dark corners. Over the years the room had in fact evolved to the point where the only comfortable chairs were in the dark, away from the windows. I mention this because I remember my fears about being inter-

viewed, one of which was that I would be construed as the kind of loon who had maybe 300 degrees of sea view and kept all the chairs in a kind of sooty nook behind the fireplace. Linda's intelligence dispelled these fears immediately. Her interest in and acuity about the technical act of writing made me relaxed and even enthusiastic about talking, which I rarely am. As a matter of fact this enthusiasm for talking technically makes me seem to myself, as I read over the transcript, a kind of apprentice plumber of fiction, a Cluny Brown at the writer's trade, but there we were.

J.D.

INTERVIEWER: You have said that writing is a hostile act; I have always wanted to ask you why.

DIDION: It's hostile in that you're trying to make somebody see something the way you see it, trying to impose your idea, your picture. It's hostile to try to wrench around someone else's mind that way. Quite often you want to tell somebody your dream, your nightmare. Well, nobody wants to hear about someone else's dream, good or bad; nobody wants to walk around with it. The writer is always tricking the reader into listening to the dream.

INTERVIEWER: Are you conscious of the reader as you write? Do you write listening to the reader listening to you?

DIDION: Obviously I listen to a reader, but the only reader I hear is me. I am always writing to myself. So very possibly I'm committing an aggressive and hostile act toward myself.

INTERVIEWER: So when you ask, as you do in many nonfiction pieces, "Do you get the point?" you are really asking if you *yourself* get the point.

DIDION: Yes. Once in a while, when I first started to write pieces, I would try to write to a reader other than myself. I always failed. I would freeze up.

INTERVIEWER: When did you know you wanted to write?

DIDION: I wrote stories from the time I was a little girl, but

I didn't want to be a writer. I wanted to be an actress. I didn't realize then that it's the same impulse. It's make-believe. It's performance. The only difference being that a writer can do it all alone. I was struck a few years ago when a friend of ours —an actress—was having dinner here with us and a couple of other writers. It suddenly occurred to me that she was the only person in the room who couldn't plan what she was going to do. She had to wait for someone to ask her, which is a strange way to live.

INTERVIEWER: Did you ever have a writing teacher?

DIDION: Mark Schorer was teaching at Berkeley when I was an undergraduate there, and he helped me. I don't mean he helped me with sentences, or paragraphs—nobody has time for that with student papers; I mean that he gave me a sense of what writing was about, what it was for.

INTERVIEWER: Did any writer influence you more than others?

DIDION: I always say Hemingway, because he taught me how sentences worked. When I was fifteen or sixteen I would type out his stories to learn how the sentences worked. I taught myself to type at the same time. A few years ago when I was teaching a course at Berkeley I reread *A Farewell to Arms* and fell right back into those sentences. I mean they're perfect sentences. Very direct sentences, smooth rivers, clear water over granite, no sinkholes.

INTERVIEWER: You've called Henry James an influence.

DIDION: He wrote perfect sentences too, but very indirect, very complicated. Sentences *with* sinkholes. You could drown in them. I wouldn't dare to write one. I'm not even sure I'd dare to read James again. I loved those novels so much that I was paralyzed by them for a long time. All those possibilities. All that perfectly reconciled style. It made me afraid to put words down.

INTERVIEWER: I wonder if some of your nonfiction pieces aren't shaped as a single Jamesian sentence.

DIDION: That would be the ideal, wouldn't it. An entire piece —eight, ten, twenty pages—strung on a single sentence. Actually, the sentences in my nonfiction are far more complicated than the sentences in my fiction. More clauses. More semicolons. I don't seem to hear that many clauses when I'm writing a novel.

INTERVIEWER: You have said that once you have your first sentence you've got your piece. That's what Hemingway said. All he needed was his first sentence and he had his short story.

DIDION: What's so hard about that first sentence is that you're stuck with it. Everything else is going to flow out of that sentence. And by the time you've laid down the first *two* sentences, your options are all gone.

INTERVIEWER: The first is the gesture, the second is the commitment.

DIDION: Yes, and the last sentence in a piece is another adventure. It should open the piece up. It should make you go back and start reading from page one. That's how it *should* be, but it doesn't always work. I think of writing anything at all as a kind of high-wire act. The minute you start putting words on paper you're eliminating possibilities. Unless you're Henry James.

INTERVIEWER: I wonder if your ethic—what you call your "harsh Protestant ethic"—doesn't close things up for you, doesn't hinder your struggle to keep all the possibilities open.

DIDION: I suppose that's part of the dynamic. I start a book and I want to make it perfect, want it to turn every color, want it to *be the world.* Ten pages in, I've already blown it, limited it, made it less, marred it. That's very discouraging. I hate the book at that point. After a while I arrive at an accommodation: well, it's not the ideal, it's not the perfect object I wanted to make, but maybe—if I go ahead and finish it anyway—I can get it right next time. Maybe I can have another chance.

INTERVIEWER: Have any women writers been strong influences?

DIDION: I think only in the sense of being models for a life, not for a style. I think that the Brontës probably encouraged my own delusions of theatricality. Something about George Eliot attracted me a great deal. I think I was not temperamentally attuned to either Jane Austen or Virginia Woolf.

INTERVIEWER: What are the disadvantages, if any, of being a woman writer?

DIDION: When I was starting to write—in the late fifties, early sixties—there was a kind of social tradition in which male novelists could operate. Hard drinkers, bad livers. Wives, wars, big fish, Africa, Paris, no second acts. A man who wrote novels had a role in the world, and he could play that role and do whatever he wanted behind it. A woman who wrote novels had no particular role. Women who wrote novels were quite often perceived as invalids. Carson McCullers, Jane Bowles. Flannery O'Connor of course. Novels by women tended to be described, even by their publishers, as sensitive. I'm not sure this is so true anymore, but it certainly was at the time, and I didn't much like it. I dealt with it the same way I deal with everything. I just tended my own garden, didn't pay much attention, behaved—I suppose—deviously. I mean I didn't actually let too many people know what I was doing.

INTERVIEWER: Advantages?

DIDION: The advantages would probably be precisely the same as the disadvantages. A certain amount of resistance is good for anybody. It keeps you awake.

INTERVIEWER: Can you tell simply from the style of writing, or the sensibility, if the author is a woman?

DIDION: Well, if style is character—and I believe it is—then obviously your sexual identity is going to show up in your style. I don't want to differentiate between style and sensibility, by the way. Again, your style *is* your sensibility. But this whole question of sexual identity is very tricky. If I were to read, cold, something by Anaïs Nin, I would probably say that it was written by a man trying to write as a woman. I feel the same way about Colette, and yet both those women are generally regarded as intensely "feminine" writers. I don't seem to recognize "feminine." On the other hand, *Victory* seems to me a profoundly female novel. So does *Nostromo,* so does *The Secret Agent.*

INTERVIEWER: Do you find it easy to write in depth about the opposite sex?

DIDION: *Run River* was partly from a man's point of view. Everett McClellan. I don't remember those parts as being any harder than the other parts. A lot of people thought Everett was "shadowy," though. He's the most distinct person in the book to me. I loved him. I loved Lily and Martha but I loved Everett more.

INTERVIEWER: Was *Run River* your first novel? It seems so finished for a first that I thought you might have shelved earlier ones.

DIDION: I've put away nonfiction things, but I've never put away a novel. I might throw out forty pages and write forty new ones, but it's all part of the same novel. I wrote the first half of *Run River* at night over a period of years. I was working at *Vogue* during the day, and at night I would work on these scenes for a novel. In no particular sequence. When I finished a scene I would tape the pages together and pin the long strips of pages on the wall of my apartment. Maybe I wouldn't touch it for a month or two, then I'd pick a scene off the wall and rewrite it. When I had about a hundred and fifty pages done I showed them to twelve publishers, all of whom passed. The thirteenth, Ivan Obolensky, gave me an advance, and with that thousand dollars or whatever it was I took a two-month leave of absence and wrote the last half of the book. That's why the last half is better than the first half. I kept trying to run the first half through again, but it was intractable. It was set. I'd worked on it for too many years in too many moods. Not that the last half is perfect. It's smoother, it moves faster, but there are a great many unresolved problems. I didn't know how to do anything at all. I had wanted *Run River* to be very complicated chronologically, to somehow have the past and present operating simultaneously, but I wasn't accomplished enough to do that with any clarity. Everybody who read it said it wasn't working. So I straightened it out. Present time to flashback to present time. Very straight. I had no option, because I didn't know how to do it the other way. I just wasn't good enough.

INTERVIEWER: Did you or Jonathan Cape put the comma in the title of the English edition?

DIDION: It comes back to me that Cape put the comma in and Obolensky left the comma out, but it wasn't of very much interest to me because I hated it both ways. The working title was *In the Night Season,* which Obolensky didn't like. Actually, the working title during the first half was *Harvest Home,* which everybody dismissed out of hand as uncommercial, although later there was a big commercial book by Thomas Tryon called exactly that. Again, I was not very sure of myself then, or I never would have changed the title.

INTERVIEWER: Was the book autobiographical? I ask this for the obvious reason that first novels often are.

DIDION: It wasn't except that it took place in Sacramento. A lot of people there seemed to think that I had somehow maligned them and their families, but it was just a made-up story. The central incident came from a little one-inch story in *The New York Times* about a trial in the Carolinas. Someone was on trial for killing the foreman on his farm, that's all there was. I think I really put the novel in Sacramento because I was homesick. I wanted to remember the weather and the rivers.

INTERVIEWER: The heat on the rivers?

DIDION: The heat. I think that's the way the whole thing began. There's a lot of landscape which I never would have described if I hadn't been homesick. If I hadn't wanted to remember. The impulse was nostalgia. It's not an uncommon impulse among writers. I noticed it when I was reading *From Here to Eternity* in Honolulu just after James Jones died. I could see exactly that kind of nostalgia, that yearning for a place, overriding all narrative considerations. The incredible amount of description. When Prewitt tries to get from the part of town where he's been wounded out to Alma's house, every street is named. Every street is described. You could take that passage and draw a map of Honolulu. None of those descriptions have any narrative meaning. They're just remembering. Obsessive remembering. I could see the impulse.

INTERVIEWER: But doesn't the impulse of nostalgia produce the eloquence in *Run River?*

DIDION: It's got a lot of sloppy stuff. Extraneous stuff. Words that don't work. Awkwardnesses. Scenes that should have been brought up, scenes that should have been played down. But then *Play It As It Lays* has a lot of sloppy stuff. I haven't reread *Common Prayer,* but I'm sure that does too.

INTERVIEWER: How did you come to terms with point of view in *Play It As It Lays?* Did you ever question your authority to do it in both first and third person?

DIDION: I wanted to make it all first person, but I wasn't good enough to maintain a first. There were tricks I didn't know. So I began playing with a close third person, just to get something down. By a "close third" I mean not an omniscient third but a third very close to the mind of the character. Suddenly one night I realized that I had some first person and some third person and that I was going to have to go with both, or just not write a book at all. I was scared. Actually, I don't mind the way it worked out. The juxtaposition of first and third turned out to be very useful toward the ending, when I wanted to accelerate the whole thing. I don't think I'd do it again, but it was a solution to that particular set of problems. There's a point when you go with what you've got. Or you don't go.

INTERVIEWER: How long, in all, did *Play It As It Lays* take to write?

DIDION: I made notes and wrote pages over several years, but the actual physical writing—sitting down at the typewriter and working every day until it was finished—took me from January until November 1969. Then of course I had to run it through again—I never know quite what I'm doing when I'm writing a novel, and the actual line of it doesn't emerge until I'm finishing. Before I ran it through again I showed it to John and then I sent it to Henry Robbins, who was my editor then at Farrar, Straus. It was quite rough, with places marked "chapter to come." Henry was unalarmed by my working that way, and he and John and I sat down one night in New York and talked, for about an hour before dinner, about what it needed doing. We all knew what it needed. We all agreed. After that I took a couple of weeks and ran it through. It was just typing and pulling the line through.

INTERVIEWER: What do you mean exactly by "pulling through"?

DIDION: For example, I didn't know that BZ was an important character in *Play It As It Lays* until the last few weeks I was working on it. So those places I marked "chapter to come" were largely places where I was going to go back and pull BZ through, hit him harder, prepare for the way it finally went.

INTERVIEWER: How did you feel about BZ's suicide at the end?

DIDION: I didn't realize until after I'd written it that it was essentially the same ending as *Run River*. The women let the men commit suicide.

INTERVIEWER: I read that *Play It As It Lays* crystallized for you when you were sitting in the lobby of the Riviera Hotel in Las Vegas and saw a girl walk through.

DIDION: I had thought Maria lived in New York. Maybe she was a model. Anyway, she was getting a divorce, going through grief. When I saw this actress in the Riviera Hotel, it occurred to me that Maria could be an actress. In California.

INTERVIEWER: Was she always Maria Wyeth?

DIDION: She didn't even have a name. Sometimes I'll be fifty, sixty pages into something and I'll still be calling a character

"X." I don't have a very clear idea of who the characters are until they start talking. Then I start to love them. By the time I finish the book, I love them so much that I want to stay with them. I don't want to leave them ever.

INTERVIEWER: Do your characters talk to you?

DIDION: After a while. In a way. When I started *Common Prayer* all I knew about Charlotte was that she was a nervous talker and told pointless stories. A distracted kind of voice. Then one day I was writing the Christmas party at the American Embassy, and I had Charlotte telling these bizarre anecdotes with no point while Victor Strasser-Mendana keeps trying to find out who she is, what she's doing in Boca Grande, who her husband is, what her husband does. And suddenly Charlotte says, "He runs guns. I wish they had caviar." Well, when I heard Charlotte say this, I had a very clear fix on who she was. I went back and rewrote some early stuff.

INTERVIEWER: Did you reshuffle a lot and, if so, how? Did you use pins or tape or what?

DIDION: Toward the beginning of a novel I'll write a lot of sections that lead me nowhere. So I'll abandon them, pin them on a board with the idea of picking them up later. Quite early in *Common Prayer* I wrote a part about Charlotte Douglas going to airports, a couple of pages that I liked but couldn't seem to find a place for. I kept picking this part up and putting it in different places, but it kept stopping the narrative; it was wrong everywhere, but I was determined to use it. Finally I think I put it in the middle of the book. Sometimes you can get away with things in the middle of a book. The first hundred pages are very tricky, the first forty pages especially. You have to make sure you have the characters you want. That's really the most complicated part.

INTERVIEWER: Strategy would seem to be far more complicated in *Common Prayer* than in *Play It As It Lays* because it had so much more plot.

DIDION: *Common Prayer* had a lot of plot and an awful lot

of places and weather. I wanted a dense texture, and so I kept throwing stuff into it, making promises. For example, I promised a revolution. Finally, when I got within twenty pages of the end, I realized I still hadn't delivered this revolution. I had a lot of threads, and I'd overlooked this one. So then I had to go back and lay in the preparation for the revolution. Putting in that revolution was like setting in a sleeve. Do you know what I mean? Do you sew? I mean I had to work that revolution in on the bias, had to ease out the wrinkles with my fingers.

INTERVIEWER: So the process of writing the novel is for you the process of discovering the precise novel that you want to write.

DIDION: Exactly. At the beginning I don't have anything at all, don't have any people, any weather, any story. All I have is a technical sense of what I want to do. For example, I want sometime to write a very long novel, eight-hundred pages. I want to write an eight-hundred page novel precisely *because* I think a novel should be read at one sitting. If you read a novel over a period of days or weeks the threads get lost, the suspension breaks. So the problem is to write an eight-hundred-page novel in which all the filaments are so strong that nothing breaks or gets forgotten ever. I wonder if García Márquez didn't do that in *The Autumn of the Patriarch.* I don't want to read it because I'm afraid he might have done it, but I did look at it, and it seems to be written in a single paragraph. *One paragraph.* The whole novel. I love that idea.

INTERVIEWER: Do you have any writing rituals?

DIDION: The most important is that I need an hour alone before dinner, with a drink, to go over what I've done that day. I can't do it late in the afternoon because I'm too close to it. Also, the drink helps. It removes me from the pages. So I spend this hour taking things out and putting other things in. Then I start the next day by redoing all of what I did the day before, following these evening notes. When I'm really working I don't like to go out or have anybody to dinner, because then

I lose the hour. If I don't have the hour, and start the next day with just some bad pages and nowhere to go, I'm in low spirits. Another thing I need to do, when I'm near the end of the book, is sleep in the same room with it. That's one reason I go home to Sacramento to finish things. Somehow the book doesn't leave you when you're asleep right next to it. In Sacramento nobody cares if I appear or not. I can just get up and start typing.

INTERVIEWER: What's the main difference between the process of fiction and the process of nonfiction?

DIDION: The element of discovery takes place, in nonfiction, not during the writing but during the research. This makes writing a piece very tedious. You already know what it's about.

INTERVIEWER: Are the subject of pieces determined by editors or are you free to go your own way?

DIDION: I make them up. They reflect what I want to do at the time, where I want to be. When I worked for *Life* I did a great many Honolulu pieces—probably more than *Life* might have wanted—because that's where I wanted to be then. Last night I finished a piece for *Esquire* about the California Water Project. I had always wanted to see the room where they control the water, where they turn it on and off all over the state, and I also wanted to see my mother and father. The water and my mother and father were all in Sacramento, so I went to Sacramento. I like to do pieces because it forces me to make appointments and see people, but I never wanted to be a journalist or reporter. If I were doing a story and it turned into a big breaking story, all kinds of teams flying in from papers and magazines and the networks, I'd probably think of something else to do.

INTERVIEWER: You've said that when you were an editor at *Vogue*, Allene Talmey showed you how verbs worked.

DIDION: Every day I would go into her office with eight lines of copy or a caption or something. She would sit there and mark it up with a pencil and get very angry about extra words, about verbs not working. Nobody has time to do that except on a magazine like *Vogue*. Nobody, no teacher. I've taught and I've tried to do it, but I didn't have that much time and neither did the students. In an eight-line caption everything had to work, every word, every comma. It would end up being a *Vogue* caption, but on its own terms it had to work perfectly.

INTERVIEWER: You say you treasure privacy, that "being left alone and leaving others alone is regarded by members of my family as the highest form of human endeavor." How does this mesh with writing personal essays, particularly the first column you did for *Life* where you felt it imperative to inform the reader that you were at the Royal Hawaiian Hotel in lieu of getting a divorce?

DIDION: I don't know. I could say that I was writing to myself, and of course I was, but it's a little more complicated than that. I mean the fact that eleven million people were going to see that page didn't exactly escape my attention. There's a lot of mystery to me about writing and performing and showing off in general. I know a singer who throws up every time she has to go onstage. But she still goes on.

INTERVIEWER: How did the "fragility of Joan Didion" myth start?

DIDION: Because I'm small, I suppose, and because I don't talk a great deal to people I don't know. Most of my sentences drift off, don't end. It's a habit I've fallen into. I don't deal well with people. I would think that this appearance of not being very much in touch was probably one of the reasons I started writing.

INTERVIEWER: Do you think some reviewers and readers have mistaken you for your characters?

DIDION: There was a certain tendency to read *Play It As It Lays* as an autobiographical novel, I suppose because I lived out here and looked skinny in photographs and nobody knew anything else about me. Actually, the only thing Maria and I have in common is an occasional inflection, which I picked up from her—not vice versa—when I was writing the book. I like Maria a lot. Maria was very strong, very tough.

INTERVIEWER: That's where I have difficulty with what so many critics have said about your women. Your women hardly seem fragile to me.

DIDION: Did you read Diane Johnson's review of *Common Prayer* in *The New York Review of Books?* She suggested that the women were strong to the point of being figures in a ' romance, that they were romantic heroines rather than actual women in actual situations. I think that's probably true. I think I write romances.

INTERVIEWER: I'd like to ask you about things that recur in your work. There's the line about "dirty tulips" on Park Avenue in a short story and in a piece. Or how about the large, square emerald ring that Lily wears in *Run River* and Charlotte wears in *Common Prayer?*

DIDION: Does Lily wear one too? Maybe she does. I've always wanted one, but I'd never buy one. For one thing emeralds— when you look at them closely—are always disappointing. The green is never blue enough. Ideally, if the green were blue enough you could look into an emerald for the rest of your life. Sometimes I think about Katherine Anne Porter's emeralds, sometimes I wonder if they're blue enough. I hadn't planned that emerald in *Common Prayer* to recur the way it does. It was just something I thought Charlotte might have, but as I went along the emerald got very useful. I kept taking that emerald one step further. By the end of the novel the emerald is almost the narrative. I had a good time with that emerald.

INTERVIEWER: What about the death of a parent, which seems to recur as a motif?

DIDION: You know how doctors who work with children get the children to tell stories? And they figure out from the stories what's frightening the child, what's worrying the child, what the child thinks? Well, a novel is just a story. You work things out in the stories you tell.

INTERVIEWER: And the abortion or loss of a child?

DIDION: The death of children worries me all the time. It's on my mind. Even *I* know that, and I usually don't know what's on my mind. On the whole, I don't want to think too much about why I write what I write. If I know what I'm doing I don't do it, I can't do it. The abortion in *Play It As It Lays* didn't occur to me until I'd written quite a bit of the book. The book needed an active moment, a moment at which things changed for Maria, a moment in which—this was very, very important—Maria was center stage for a number of pages. Not at a party reacting to somebody else. Not just thinking about her lot in life, either. A long section in which she was the main player. The abortion was a narrative strategy.

INTERVIEWER: Was it a narrative strategy in *Run River?*

DIDION: Actually, it was the excuse for a digression, into landscape. Lily has an abortion in San Francisco and then she comes home on the Greyhound bus. I always think of the Greyhound bus and not the abortion. The bus part is very detailed about the look of the towns. It's something I wrote in New York; you can tell I was homesick.

INTERVIEWER: How about the freeways that reappear?

DIDION: Actually, I don't drive on the freeway. I'm afraid to. I freeze at the top of the entrance, at the instant when you have to let go and join it. Occasionally I *do* get on the freeway—usually because I'm shamed into it—and it's such an extraordinary experience that it sticks in my mind. So I use it.

INTERVIEWER: And the white space at the corner of Sunset and La Brea in Hollywood? You mention it in some piece and then in *Play It As It Lays.*

DIDION: I've never analyzed it, but one line of poetry I always have in mind is the line from *Four Quartets:* "at the still point of the turning world." I tend to move toward still points. I think of the equator as a still point. I suppose that's why I put Boca Grande on the equator.

INTERVIEWER: A narrative strategy.

DIDION: Well, this whole question of how you work out the narrative is very mysterious. It's a good deal more arbitrary than most people who don't do it would ever believe. When I started *Play It As It Lays* I gave Maria a child, a daughter, Kate, who was in kindergarten. I remember writing a passage in which Kate came home from school and showed Maria a lot of drawings, orange and blue crayon drawings, and when Maria asked her what they were, Kate said, "Pools on fire." You can see I wasn't having too much success writing this child. So I put her in a hospital. You never meet her. Now, it turned out to have a great deal of importance—Kate's being in the hospital is a very large element in *Play It As It Lays*—but it began because I couldn't write a child, no other reason. Again, in *Common Prayer*, Marin bombs the Transamerica Building because I *needed* her to. I needed a crisis in Charlotte's life. Well, at this very moment, right now, I can't think of the Transamerica Building without thinking of Marin and her pipe bomb and her gold bracelet, but it was all very arbitrary in the beginning.

INTERVIEWER: What misapprehensions, illusions and so forth have you had to struggle against in your life? In a commencement address you once said there were many.

DIDION: All kinds. I was one of those children who tended to perceive the world in terms of things read about it. I began with a literary idea of experience, and I still don't know where all the lies are. For example, it may not be true that people who try to fly always burst into flames and fall. That may not be true at all. In fact people *do fly,* and land safely. But I don't really believe that. I still see Icarus. I don't seem to have a set of physical facts at my disposal, don't seem to understand how things really work. I just have an *idea* of how they work, which is always trouble. As Henry James told us.

INTERVIEWER: You seem to live your life on the edge, or, at least, on the literary idea of the edge.

DIDION: Again, it's a literary idea, and it derives from what engaged me imaginatively as a child. I can recall disapproving of the golden mean, always thinking there was more to be learned from the dark journey. The dark journey engaged me more. I once had in mind a very light novel, all surface, all conversations and memories and recollections of some people in Honolulu who were getting along fine, one or two misapprehensions about the past notwithstanding. Well, I'm working on that book now, but it's not running that way at all. Not at all.

INTERVIEWER: It always turns into danger and apocalypse.

DIDION: Well, I grew up in a dangerous landscape. I think people are more affected than they know by landscapes and weather. Sacramento was a very extreme place. It was very flat, flatter than most people can imagine, and I still favor flat horizons. The weather in Sacramento was as extreme as the landscape. There were two rivers, and these rivers would flood in the winter and run dry in the summer. Winter was cold rain and tulle fog. Summer was 100 degrees, 105 degrees, 110 degrees. Those extremes affect the way you deal with the world. It so happens that if you're a writer the extremes show up. They don't if you sell insurance.

LINDA KUEHL
Fall/Winter 1978

15. Joyce Carol Oates

Joyce Carol Oates was born in Lockport, New York, on June 16, 1938. Interested in writing since childhood, she recalled later that her first stories were told through pictures. She attended Syracuse University, where she was elected to Phi Beta Kappa, and in 1960 was graduated first in her class; during her senior year she also won a *Mademoiselle* magazine college fiction award. Oates received her M.A. under a Knapp Fellowship at the University of Wisconsin in 1961 before accompanying her husband, Raymond J. Smith, a college professor, to Texas, where she abandoned her plans to pursue a doctorate in order to concentrate on her fiction. Thereafter Oates produced several impressive early works, publishing her first collection of short stories, *By the North Gate* in 1963; her first novel, *With Shuddering Fall,* the following year; and a second collection of stories, *Upon the Sweeping Flood,* in 1965.

Since then Oates has maintained an astonishing literary pace, publishing at least one book per year, including the 1970 winner of the National Book Award in fiction, *them,* and two National Book Award nominees, *A Garden of Earthly Delights* (1970) and *Expensive People* (1969), among the more than thirty novels, collections of short fiction, and books of poetry that she has written to date. Her most recent works of fiction are the short-story collections *Night-Side* (1977) and *All the Good People I've Left Behind* (1979), and the novels *Unholy Loves* (1979) and *Bellefleur* (1980).

Oates, who since 1978 has served as Writer-in-Residence at Princeton University, has also taught at the University of Windsor (Canada) and New York University, and was recently inducted into the American Academy of Arts and Letters and the National Institute of Arts and Letters. She lives with her husband in Princeton, New Jersey.

other customers in <u>Rinaldi's</u> to overhear. Voice shrill,
laughter shrill. Must guard against excitement. ...A true
gift, such women possess; "artistic arrangement of life" a
phrase I think I read somewhere. Can't remember. She wants
to understand me but will not invade me like the others.
Sunshine: her hair. (Though it is brown, not very unusual.
But always clean.) Sunshine: dispelling of demons. Intimacy
always a danger. Intimacy/hell/intimacy/hell. Could possibly
make love to her thinking of XXXXXXXXXXXXX or (say) the boy with
the kinky reddish hair on the bicycle...but sickening to think
of. What if. What if an attack of laughter. Hysterical gig-
gling. And. Afterward. Such shame, disgust. She would not
laugh of course but might be wounded for life: cannot exaggerate
the dangers of intimacy, on my side or hers. The Secret between
us. My secret, not hers. Our friendship--nearly a year now--
on my footing, never hers. Can't deny what others have known
before me, the pleasure of secrecy, taking of risks.

--With XXXXXXXXXXX etc. last night, unable to wake this morning
till after ten; already at work; sick headache, dryness of
mouth, throat. But no fever. Temperature normal. XXXXXXXXXXXXX
so bitter, speaks of having been blackmailed by some idiot,
but (in my opinion) it all happened years ago, not connected
with his position here in town. Teaches juniors, seniors.
Advises Drama Club. Tenure. I'm envious of him & impatient
with his continual bitterness. Rehashing of past. What's the
point of it? Of course, he is over forty (how much over forty
is his secret) and I am a decade younger, ■ maybe fifteen years
younger. Will never turn into that. Hag's face, lines around
mouth, eyes. Grotesque moustache: trying to be 25 years old
& misses by a ■ mile.... Yet my pen-and-ink portrait of him
is endearing. Delighted, that it should please even him. &
did not mind the CA$H. Of course I am talented & of course
misused at the agency but refuse to be bitter like the others.
XXXXXXXXXXX lavish, flattery and money. I deserve both but
don't expect everyone to recognize me...in no hurry...can't
demand fame overnight. Would I want fame anyway???? Maybe not.
With XXXXXXXXXXXXX's hundred dollars bought her that $35 book of
Toulouse-Lautrec's work, dear Henri, perhaps should not have
risked ■ it with her but genuinely thought she would like it.
Did not think, as usual. She seemed grateful enough, thanking
me, surprised, said she'd received only a few cards from home
& a predictable present from her mother, certainly did not
expect anything from me--"but aren't you saving for a trip to
Europe"--remembers so much about me, amazing--so sweet--unlike
XXXXXXXXXXXX who calls me by the names of strangers and is
vile. His image with me till early afternoon, tried to vomit
in the first-floor lavatory where no one from the office might _stomach._
drop in, dry heaving gasps, not so easy to do on an empty ~~stomach.~~
Mind over matter?????? Not with "Farrell van Buren"!

--A complete day was wasted. Idiotic trendy "collage" for
Mackenzie's Diary, if you please. Cherubs, grinning teenagers,
trophies. An "avant-garde" look to it. Haha. Looking forward
to lay-out for the Hilton & Trader Vic's, at least some precedent
to work from and resist. ...Could send out my Invisible Soldiers
to hack up a few of these bastards, smart-assed paunchy hags
bossing me around. Someday things will be different. (Of course

A manuscript page from a story by Joyce Carol Oates.

Joyce Carol Oates

Joyce Carol Oates is the rarest of commodities, an author modest about her work, though there is such a quantity of it that she has three publishers—one for fiction, one for poetry, and a "small press" for more experimental work, limited editions, and books her other publishers simply cannot schedule. And despite the added demands of teaching, she continues to devote much energy to The Ontario Review, *a literary quarterly which her husband edits and for which she serves as a contributing editor.*

Ms. Oates is striking-looking and slender, with straight dark hair and large, inquiring eyes. A highly attractive woman, she is not photogenic; no photo has ever done justice to her appearance, which conveys grace and high intelligence. If her manner is taken for aloofness—as it sometimes has been—it is, in fact, a shyness which the publication of thirty-three books, the pro-

duction of three plays, and the winning of the National Book Award has not displaced.

This interview began at her Windsor home in the summer of 1976 before she and her husband moved to Princeton. When interviewed her speaking voice was, as always, soft and reflective. One receives the impression that she never speaks in anything but perfectly formed sentences. Ms. Oates answered all questions openly while curled with her Persian cats upon a sofa. (She is a confirmed cat lover and recently took in two more kittens at the Princeton house.) Talk continued during a stroll by the banks of the Detroit River where she confessed to having sat for hours, watching the horizon and the boats, and dreaming her characters into existence. She sets these dreams physically onto paper on a writing table in her study, which faces the river.

Additional questions were asked in New York during the 1976 Christmas season, when Ms. Oates and her husband attended a seminar on her work which was part of that year's Modern Language Association convention. Many of the questions in this interview were answered via correspondence. She felt only by writing out her replies could she say precisely what she wished to, without possibility of misunderstanding or misquotation.

INTERVIEWER: We may as well get this one over with first: you're frequently charged with producing too much.

OATES: Productivity is a relative matter. And it's really insignificant: what is ultimately important is a writer's strongest books. It may be the case that we all must write many books in order to achieve a few lasting ones—just as a young writer or poet might have to write hundreds of poems before writing his first significant one. Each book as it is written, however, is a completely absorbing experience, and feels always as if it were *the* work I was born to write. Afterward, of course, as the years pass, it's possible to become more detached, more critical.

I really don't know what to say. I note and can to some
extent sympathize with the objurgatory tone of certain critics,
who feel that I write too much because, quite wrongly, they
believe they ought to have read most of my books before
attempting to criticize a recently published one. (At least I
think that's why they react a bit irritably.) Yet each book is a
world unto itself and must stand alone, and it should not
matter whether a book is a writer's first, or tenth, or fiftieth.

INTERVIEWER: About your critics—do you read them, usually? Have you ever learned anything from a book review or an
essay on your work?

OATES: Sometimes I read reviews, and without exception I
will read critical essays that are sent to me. The critical essays
are interesting on their own terms. Of course, it's a pleasure
simply to discover that someone has read and responded to
one's work; being understood, and being praised, is beyond
expectation most of the time. . . . The average review is a
quickly written piece not meant to be definitive. So it would
be misguided for a writer to read such reviews attentively. All
writers without exception find themselves clapperclawed from
time to time; I think the experience (provided one survives it)
is wonderfully liberating: after the first death there is no other.
. . . A writer who has published as many books as I have has
developed, of necessity, a hide like a rhino's, while inside there
dwells a frail, hopeful butterfly of a spirit.

INTERVIEWER: Returning to the matter of your "productivity": have you ever dictated into a machine?

OATES: No, oddly enough I've written my last several novels
in longhand first. I had an enormous, rather frightening stack
of pages and notes for *The Assassins,* probably eight hundred
pages—or was it closer to a thousand? It alarms me to remember. *Childwold* needed to be written in longhand, of course.
And now everything finds its initial expression in longhand and
the typewriter has become a rather alien thing—a thing of

formality and impersonality. My first novels were all written on a typewriter: first draft straight through, then revisions, then final draft. But I can't do that any longer.

The thought of dictating into a machine doesn't appeal to me at all. Henry James's later works would have been better had he resisted that curious sort of self-indulgence, dictating to a secretary. The roaming garrulousness of ordinary speech is usually corrected when it's transcribed into written prose.

INTERVIEWER: Do you ever worry—considering the vast body of your work—if you haven't written a particular scene before, or had characters say the same lines?

OATES: Evidently, there are writers (John Cheever, Mavis Gallant come immediately to mind) who never reread their work, and there are others who reread constantly. I suspect I am somewhere in the middle. If I thought I *had* written a scene before, or written the same lines before, I would simply look it up.

INTERVIEWER: What kind of work schedule do you follow?

OATES: I haven't any formal schedule, but I love to write in the morning, before breakfast. Sometimes the writing goes so smoothly that I don't take a break for many hours—and consequently have breakfast at two or three in the afternoon on good days. On school days, days that I teach, I usually write for an hour or forty-five minutes in the morning, before my first class. But I don't have any formal schedule, and at the moment I am feeling rather melancholy, or derailed, or simply lost, because I completed a novel some weeks ago and haven't begun another . . . except in scattered, stray notes.

INTERVIEWER: Do you find emotional stability is necessary in order to write? Or can you get to work whatever your state of mind? Is your mood reflected in what you write? How do you describe that perfect state in which you can write from early morning into the afternoon?

OATES: One must be pitiless about this matter of "mood." In a sense, the writing will *create* the mood. If art is, as I believe it to be, a genuinely transcendental function—a means by which we rise out of limited, parochial states of mind—then it should not matter very much what states of mind or emotion we are in. Generally I've found this to be true: I have forced myself to begin writing when I've been utterly exhausted, when I've felt my soul as thin as a playing card, when nothing has seemed worth enduring for another five minutes . . . and somehow the activity of writing changes everything. Or appears to do so. Joyce said of the underlying structure of *Ulysses* —the Odyssean parallel and parody—that he really didn't care whether it was plausible so long as it served as a bridge to get his "soldiers" across. Once they were across, what does it matter if the bridge collapses? One might say the same thing about the use of one's self as a means for the writing to get written. Once the soldiers are across the stream . . .

INTERVIEWER: What does happen when you finish a novel? Is the next project one that has been waiting in line? Or is the choice more spontaneous?

OATES: When I complete a novel I set it aside, and begin work on short stories, and eventually another long work. When I complete *that* novel I return to the earlier novel and rewrite much of it. In the meantime the second novel lies in a desk drawer. Sometimes I work on two novels simultaneously, though one usually forces the other into the background. The rhythm of writing, revising, writing, revising, etcetcra, seems to suit me. I am inclined to think that as I grow older I will come to be infatuated with the art of revision, and there may come a time when I will dread giving up a novel at all. My next novel, *Unholy Loves,* was written around the time of *Childwold,* for instance, and revised after the completion of that novel, and again revised this past spring and summer. My reputation for writing quickly and effortlessly notwithstanding, I am strongly in favor of intelligent, even fastidious revision, which is, or certainly should be, an art in itself.

INTERVIEWER: Do you keep a diary?

OATES: I began keeping a formal journal several years ago. It resembles a sort of ongoing letter to myself, mainly about literary matters. What interests me in the process of my own experience is the wide range of my feelings. For instance, after I finish a novel I tend to think of the experience of having written it as being largely pleasant and challenging. But in fact (for I keep careful records) the experience is various: I do suffer temporary bouts of frustration and inertia and depression. There are pages in recent novels that I've rewritten as many as seventeen times, and a story, "The Widows," which I revised both before and after publication in *The Hudson Review*, and then revised slightly again before I included it in my next collection of stories—a fastidiousness that could go on into infinity.

Afterward, however, I simply forget. My feelings crystallize (or are mythologized) into something much less complex. All of us who keep journals do so for different reasons, I suppose, but we must have in common a fascination with the surprising patterns that emerge over the years—a sort of arabesque in which certain elements appear and reappear, like the designs in a well-wrought novel. The voice of my journal is very much like the one I find myself using in these replies to you: the voice in which I think or meditate when I'm not writing fiction.

INTERVIEWER: Besides writing and teaching, what daily special activities are important to you? Travel, jogging, music? I hear you're an excellent pianist?

OATES: We travel a great deal, usually by car. We've driven slowly across the continent several times, and we've explored the South and New England and of course New York State with loving thoroughness. As a pianist I've defined myself as an "enthusiastic amateur," which is about the most merciful thing that can be said. I like to draw, I like to listen to music, and I spend an inordinate amount of time doing nothing. I don't even think it can be called daydreaming.

I also enjoy that much-maligned occupation of housewifery, but hardly dare say so, things being what they are today. I like to cook, to tend plants, to garden (minimally), to do simple domestic things, to stroll around shopping malls and observe the qualities of people, overhearing snatches of conversations, noting people's appearances, their clothes, and so forth. Walking and driving a car are part of my life as a writer, really. I can't imagine myself apart from these activities.

INTERVIEWER: Despite critical and financial success, you continue to teach. Why?

OATES: I teach a full load at the University of Windsor, which means three courses. One is creative writing, one is the graduate seminar (in the Modern Period), the third is an oversized (115 students) undergraduate course that is lively and stimulating but really too swollen to be satisfying to me. There is, generally, a closeness between students and faculty at Windsor that is very rewarding, however. Anyone who teaches knows that you don't *really* experience a text until you've taught it, in loving detail, with an intelligent and responsive class. At the present time I'm going through Joyce's work with nine graduate students and each seminar meeting is very exciting (and draining) and I can't think, frankly, of anything else I would rather do.

INTERVIEWER: It is a sometimes publicized fact that your professor-husband does not read most of your work. Is there any practical reason for this?

OATES: Ray has such a busy life of his own, preparing classes, editing *The Ontario Review* and so forth, that he really hasn't time to read my work. I do, occasionally, show him reviews, and he makes brief comments on them. I would have liked, I think, to have established an easygoing relationship with some other writers, but somehow that never came about. Two or three of us at Windsor do read one another's poems, but criticism as such is minimal. I've never been able to respond very fully to criticism, frankly, because I've usually been absorbed in another work by the time the criticism is available to me. Also, critics sometimes appear to be addressing themselves to works other than those I remember writing.

INTERVIEWER: Do you feel in any way an expatriate or an exile, living in Canada?

OATES: We are certainly exiles of a sort. But we would be, I think, exiles if we lived in Detroit as well. Fortunately, Windsor is really an international, cosmopolitan community, and our Canadian colleagues are not intensely and narrowly nationalistic.

But I wonder—doesn't everyone feel rather exiled? When I return home to Millerport, New York, and visit nearby Lockport, the extraordinary changes that have taken place make me feel like a stranger; the mere passage of time makes us all exiles. The situation is a comic one, perhaps, since it affirms the power of the evolving community over the individual, but I think we tend to feel it as tragic. Windsor is a relatively stable community, and my husband and I have come to feel, oddly, more at home here than we probably would anywhere else.

INTERVIEWER: Have you ever consciously changed your lifestyle to help your work as a writer?

OATES: Not really. My nature is orderly and observant and scrupulous, and deeply introverted, so life wherever I attempt it turns out to be claustral. Live like the bourgeois, Flaubert suggested, but I was living like that long before I came across Flaubert's remark.

INTERVIEWER: You wrote *Do With Me What You Will* during your year living in London. While there you met many writers such as Doris Lessing, Margaret Drabble, Colin Wilson, Iris Murdoch—writers you respect, as your reviews of their work indicate. Would you make any observations on the role of the writer in society in England versus that which you experience here?

OATES: The English novelist is almost without exception an

observer of society. (I suppose I mean "society" in its most immediate, limited sense.) Apart from writers like Lawrence (who doesn't seem altogether *English*, in fact) there hasn't been an intense interest in subjectivity, in the psychology of living, breathing human beings. Of course, there have been marvelous novels. And there *is* Doris Lessing, who writes books that can no longer be categorized: fictional parable, autobiography, allegory . . . ? And John Fowles. And Iris Murdoch.

But there is a feel to the American novel that is radically different. We are willing to risk being called "formless" by people whose ideas of form are rigidly limited, and we are wilder, more exploratory, more ambitious, perhaps less easily shamed, less easily discouraged. The intellectual life as such we tend to keep out of our novels, fearing the sort of highly readable but ultimately disappointing cerebral quality of Huxley's work . . . or, on a somewhat lower level, C. P. Snow's.

INTERVIEWER: The English edition of *Wonderland* has a different ending from the American. Why? Do you often rewrite published work?

OATES: I was forced to rewrite the ending of that particular novel because it struck me that the first ending was not the correct one. I have not rewritten any other published work (except of course for short stories, which sometimes get rewritten before inclusion in a book) and don't intend to if I can possibly help it.

INTERVIEWER: You've written novels on highly specialized fields, such as brain surgery. How do you research such backgrounds?

OATES: A great deal of reading, mainly. Some years ago I developed a few odd symptoms that necessitated my seeing a doctor, and since there was for a time talk of my being sent to a neurologist, I nervously and superstitiously began reading the relevant journals. What I came upon so chilled me that I must have gotten well as a result. . . .

INTERVIEWER: In addition to the novel about medicine,

you've written one each on law, politics, religion, spectator sports: Are you consciously filling out a "program" of novels about American life?

OATES: Not really consciously. The great concern with "medicine" really grew out of an experience of some duration that brought me into contact with certain thoughts of mortality: of hospitals, illnesses, doctors, the world of death and dying and our human defenses against such phenomena. (A member of my family to whom I was very close died rather slowly of cancer.) I attempted to deal with my own very inchoate feelings about these matters by dramatizing what I saw to be contemporary responses to "mortality." My effort to wed myself with a fictional character and our synthesis in turn with a larger, almost allegorical condition resulted in a novel that was difficult to write and also, I suspect, difficult to read.

A concern with law seemed to spring naturally out of the thinking many of us were doing in the sixties: What is the relationship between "law" and civilization, what hope has civilization without "law," and yet what hope has civilization *with* law as it has developed in our tradition? More personal matters blended with the larger issues of "crime" and "guilt," so that I felt I was able to transcend a purely private and purely local drama that might have had emotional significance for me, but very little beyond that; quite by accident I found myself writing about a woman conditioned to be unnaturally "passive" in a world of hearty masculine combat—an issue that became topical even as the novel *Do With Me What You Will* was published, and is topical still, to some extent.

The "political" novel, *The Assassins,* grew out of two experiences I had some years ago, at high-level conferences involving politicians, academic specialists, lawyers, and a scattering—no, hardly that—of literary people. (I won't be more specific at the moment.) A certain vertiginous fascination with work which I noted in my own nature I was able to objectify (and, I think, exaggerate) in terms of the various characters' fanaticism involving their own "work"—most obviously in Andrew Petrie's obsession with "transforming the consciousness of America." *The Assassins* is about megalomania and its inevitable consequences, and it seemed necessary that the assassins be involved in politics, given the peculiar conditions of our era.

The new "religious" novel, *Son of the Morning,* is rather painfully autobiographical, in part; but only in part. The religion it explores is not institutional but rather subjective, intensely personal, so as a novel it is perhaps not like the earlier three I have mentioned, or the racing novel, *With Shuddering Fall.* Rather, *Son of the Morning* is a novel that begins with wide ambitions and ends very, very humbly.

INTERVIEWER: Somewhere in print you called *The Assassins* the favorite of your novels. It received very mixed reviews. I've often thought that book was misread. For instance, I think the "martyr" in that novel arranged for his own assassination, true? And that his wife was never really attacked outside the country house; she never left it. Her maiming was all confined within her head.

OATES: What a fine surprise! You read the scene exactly as it was meant to be read. Even well-intentioned reviewers missed the point; so far as I know, only two or three people read Yvonne's scene as I had intended it to be read. Yet the hallucinatory nature of the "dismemberment" scene is explicit. And Andrew Petrie did, of course, arrange for his own assassination, as the novel makes clear in its concluding pages.

The novel has been misread, of course, partly because it's rather long and I think reviewers, who are usually pressed for time, simply treated it in a perfunctory way. I'm not certain that it is my favorite novel. But it is, or was, my most ambitious. It involved a great deal of effort, the collating of passages (and memories) that differ from or contradict one another. One becomes attached to such perverse, maddening ugly ducklings, but I can't really blame reviewers for being impatient with the novel. As my novels grow in complexity they please me more and please the "literary world" hardly at all—a sad situation, but not a paralyzing one.

INTERVIEWER: It's not merely a matter of complexity. One feels that your fiction has become more and more urgent, more subjective and less concerned with the outward details of this world—especially in *Childwold*. Was that novel a deliberate attempt to write a "poetic novel"? Or is it a long poem?

OATES: I don't see that *Childwold* is not concerned with the outward details of the world. In fact, it's made up almost entirely of visual details—of the natural world, of the farm the Bartletts own, and of the small city they gravitate to. But you are right, certainly, in suggesting that it is a "poetic novel." I had wanted to create a prose poem in the form of a novel, or a novel in the form of a prose poem: the exciting thing for me was to deal with the tension that arose between the image-centered structure of poetry and the narrative-centered and linear structure of the interplay of persons that constitutes a novel. In other words, poetry focuses upon the image, the particular thing, or emotion, or feeling, while prose fiction focuses upon motion through time and space. The one impulse is toward stasis, the other toward movement. Between the two impulses there arose a certain tension that made the writing of the novel quite challenging. I suppose it is an experimental work, but I shy away from thinking of my work in those terms: it seems to me there is a certain self-consciousness about anyone who sets himself up as an "experimental" writer. All writing is experimental.

But experimentation for its own sake doesn't much interest me; it seems to belong to the early sixties, when Dadaism was being rediscovered. In a sense we are all post-*Wake* writers and it's Joyce, and only Joyce, who casts a long terrifying shadow. . . . The problem is that virtuoso writing appeals to the intellect and tends to leave one's emotions untouched. When I read aloud to my students the last few pages of *Finnegans Wake*, and come to that glorious, and heartbreaking, final section

("But you're changing, acoolsha, you're changing from me, I can feel"), I think I'm able to communicate the almost overwhelmingly beautiful emotion behind it, and the experience certainly leaves *me* shaken, but it would be foolish to think that the average reader, even the average intelligent reader, would be willing to labor at the *Wake,* through those hundreds of dense pages, in order to attain an emotional and spiritual sense of the work's wholeness, as well as its genius. Joyce's *Ulysses* appeals to me more: that graceful synthesis of the "naturalistic" and the "symbolic" suits my temperament also. . . . I try to write books that can be read in one way by a literal-minded reader, and in quite another way by a reader alert to symbolic abbreviation and parodistic elements. And yet, it's the same book—or nearly. A trompe l'oeil, a work of "as if."

INTERVIEWER: Very little has been made of the humor in your work, the parody. Some of your books, like *Expensive People, The Hungry Ghosts,* and parts of *Wonderland,* seem almost Pinteresque in their absurd humor. Is Pinter an influence? Do you consider yourself a comedic writer?

OATES: There's been humor of a sort in my writing from the first; but it's understated, or deadpan. Pinter has never struck me as very funny. Doesn't he really write tragedy?

I liked Ionesco at one time. And Kafka. And Dickens (from whom Kafka learned certain effects, though he uses them, of course, for different ends). I respond to English satire, as I mentioned earlier. Absurdist or "dark" or "black" or whatever: what isn't tragic belongs to the comic spirit. The novel is nourished by both and swallows both up greedily.

INTERVIEWER: What have you learned from Kafka?

OATES: To make a jest of the horror. To take myself less seriously.

INTERVIEWER: John Updike has been accused of a lack of violence in his work. You're often accused of portraying too much. What is the function of violence in your work?

OATES: Given the number of pages I have written, and the

"violent" incidents dispersed throughout them, I rather doubt that I am a violent writer in any meaningful sense of the word. Certainly, the violence is minimal in a novel like *them,* which purported to be a naturalistic work set in Detroit in the sixties; real life is much more chaotic.

INTERVIEWER: Which of your books gave you the greatest trouble to write? And which gave the greatest pleasure or pride?

OATES: Both *Wonderland* and *The Assassins* were difficult to write. *Expensive People* was the least difficult. I am personally very fond of *Childwold,* since it represents, in a kind of diffracted way, a complete world made of memory and imagination, a blending together of different times. It always surprises me that other people find that novel admirable because, to me, it seems very private . . . the sort of thing a writer can do only once.

Aside from that, *Do With Me What You Will* gives me a fair amount of pleasure, and of course, I am closest to the novel I finished most recently, *Son of the Morning.* (In general, I think we are always fondest of the books we've just completed, aren't we? For obvious reasons.) But then I think of Jules and Maureen and Loretta of *them* and I wonder if perhaps that isn't my favorite novel, after all.

INTERVIEWER: For whom do you write—yourself, your friends, your "public"? Do you imagine an ideal reader for your work?

OATES: Well, there are certain stories, like those in *The Hungry Ghosts,* which I have written for an academic community and, in some cases, for specific people. But in general the writing writes itself—I mean a character determines his or her "voice" and I must follow along. Had I my own way the first section of *The Assassins* would be much abbreviated. But it was impossible to shut Hugh Petrie up once he got going and, long and painful and unwieldy as his section is, it's nevertheless been shortened. The problem with creating such highly conscious and intuitive characters is that they tend to perceive the contours of the literary landscape in which they dwell and, like Kasch of *Childwold,* try to guide or even to take over the direction of the narrative. Hugh did not want to die, and so his section went on and on, and it isn't an exaggeration to say that I felt real dismay in dealing with him.

Son of the Morning is a first-person narration by a man who is addressing himself throughout to God. Hence the whole novel is a prayer. Hence the ideal reader is, then, God. Everyone else, myself included, is secondary.

INTERVIEWER: Do you consider yourself religious? Do you feel there is a firm religious basis to your work?

OATES: I wish I knew how to answer this. Having completed a novel that is saturated with what Jung calls the God-experience, I find that I know less than ever about myself and my own beliefs. I have beliefs, of course, like everyone—but I don't always believe in them. Faith comes and goes. God diffracts into a bewildering plenitude of elements—the environment, love, friends and family, career, profession, "fate," biochemical harmony or disharmony, whether the sky is slate-gray or a bright mesmerizing blue. These elements then coalesce again into something seemingly unified. But it's a human predilection, isn't it?—our tendency to see, and to wish to see, what we've projected outward upon the universe from our own souls? I hope to continue to write about religious experience, but at the moment I feel quite drained, quite depleted. And as baffled as ever.

INTERVIEWER: You mention Jung. Is Freud also an influence? Laing?

OATES: Freud I have always found rather limited and biased; Jung and Laing I've read only in recent years. As an undergraduate at Syracuse University I discovered Nietzsche and it may be the Nietzschean influence (which is certainly far more provocative than Freud's) that characterizes some of my work. I don't really know, consciously. For me, stories usually begin

—or began, since I write so few of them now—out of some magical association between characters and their settings. There are some stories (I won't say which ones) which evolved almost entirely out of their settings, usually rural.

INTERVIEWER: Your earliest stories and novels seem influenced by Faulkner and by Flannery O'Connor. Are these influences you acknowledge? Are there others?

OATES: I've been reading for so many years, and my influences must be so vast—it would be very difficult to answer. An influence I rarely mention is Thoreau, whom I read at a very impressionable age (my early teens), and Henry James, O'Connor and Faulkner certainly, Katherine Anne Porter, and Dostoyevsky. An odd mixture.

INTERVIEWER: The title *Wonderland,* and frequent other allusions in your work, point toward a knowledge of, if not an affinity for, Lewis Carroll. What is the connection, and is it an important one?

OATES: Lewis Carroll's *Alice in Wonderland* and *Through the Looking Glass* were my very first books. Carroll's wonderful blend of illogic and humor and horror and justice has always appealed to me, and I had a marvelous time teaching the books last year in my undergraduate course.

INTERVIEWER: Was there anything you were particularly afraid of as a child?

OATES: Like most children, I was probably afraid of a variety of things. The unknown? The possibility of those queer fortuitous metamorphoses that seem to overtake certain of Carroll's characters? Physical pain? Getting lost? . . . My proclivity for the irreverent and the nonsensical was either inspired by Carroll or confirmed by him. I was always, and continue to be, an essentially mischievous child. This is one of my best-kept secrets.

INTERVIEWER: You began writing at a very early age. Was it encouraged by your family? Was yours a family of artistic ambitions?

OATES: In later years my parents have become "artistic," but when they were younger, and their children were younger, they had no time for anything much except work. I was always encouraged by my parents, my grandmother, and my teachers to be creative. I can't remember when I first began to tell stories—by drawing, it was then—but I must have been very young. It was an instinct I followed quite naturally.

INTERVIEWER: Much of your work is set in the 1930s, a period during which you were merely an infant at best. Why is that decade so important to your work or vision?

OATES: Since I was born in 1938, the decade is of great significance to me. This was the world of my parents, who were young adults at the time, the world I was born into. The thirties seem in an odd way still "living" to me, partly in terms of my parents' and grandparents' memories, and partly in terms of its treatment in books and films. But the twenties are too remote—lost to me entirely! I simply haven't had the imaginative power to get that far back.

I identify very closely with my parents in ways I can't satisfactorily explain. The lives they lived before I was born seem somehow accessible to me. Not directly, of course, but imaginatively. A memory belonging to my mother or father seems almost to "belong" to me. In studying old photographs I am struck sometimes by a sense of my being contemporary with my parents—as if I'd known them when they were, let's say, only teenagers. Is this odd? I wonder. I rather suspect others share in their family's experiences and memories without knowing quite how.

INTERVIEWER: When we were undergraduates together at Syracuse, you already were something of a legend. It was rumored you'd finish a novel, turn it over, and immediately begin writing another on the back side. When both sides were covered, you'd throw it all out, and reach for clean paper. Was it at Syracuse you first became aware you were going to be a writer?

OATES: I began writing in high school, consciously training myself by writing novel after novel and always throwing them out when I completed them. I remember a three-hundred-page book of interrelated stories that must have been modeled on Hemingway's *In Our Time* (I hadn't yet read *Dubliners*) though the subject matter was much more romantic than Hemingway's. I remember a bloated, trifurcated novel that had as its vague model *The Sound and the Fury.* . . . Fortunately, these experiments were thrown away and I haven't remembered them until this moment.

Syracuse was a very exciting place academically and intellectually for me. I doubt that I missed more than half a dozen classes in my four years there, and none of them in English.

INTERVIEWER: I remember you were in a sorority. It is incredible to contemplate you as "a sorority girl."

OATES: My experience in a sorority wasn't disastrous, but merely despairing. (I tried to resign but found out that upon joining I had signed some sort of legal contract.) However, I did make some close friends in the sorority, so the experience wasn't a total loss. I would never do it again, certainly. In fact, it's one of the three or four things in my entire life I would never do again.

INTERVIEWER: Why was life in a Syracuse sorority so despairing? Have you written about it?

OATES: The racial and religious bigotry; the asininity of "secret ceremonies"; the moronic emphasis upon "activities" totally unrelated to—in fact antithetical to—intellectual exploration; the bullying of the presumably weak by the presumably strong; the deliberate pursuit of an attractive "image" for the group as a whole, no matter how cynical the individuals might have been; the aping of the worst American traits—boosterism, God-fearing-ism, smug ignorance, a craven worship of conformity; the sheer *mess* of the place once one got beyond the downstairs. . . . I tried to escape in my junior year, but a connection between sororities and the Dean of Women and the university-housing office made escape all but impossible, and it seemed that, in my freshman naïveté, I had actually signed some sort of contract that had "legal" status . . . all of which quite cowed me. I remember a powdered and perfumed alum explaining the sorority's exclusion of Jews and blacks: "You see, we have conferences at the Lake Placid Club, and wouldn't it be a shame if *all* our members couldn't attend. . . . Why, it would be embarrassing for them, wouldn't it?" I was valedictorian of my class, the class of 1960. I fantasized beginning my address by saying, "I managed to do well academically at Syracuse despite the concerted efforts of my sorority to prevent me. . . ."

I haven't written about it, and never will. It's simply too stupid and trivial a subject. To even *care* about such adolescent nonsense one would have to have the sensitivity of a John O'Hara, who seems to have taken it all seriously.

INTERVIEWER: I recall you won the poetry contest at Syracuse in your senior year. But your books of poetry appeared relatively later than your fiction. Were you always writing poetry?

OATES: No, I really began to write poetry later. The poetry still comes with difficulty, I must admit. Tiny lyric asides, droll wry enigmatic statements: They aren't easy, are they? I'm assembling a book which I think will be my last—of poems, I mean. No one wants to read a novelist's poetry. It's enough— too much, in fact—to deal with the novels. Strangely enough, my fellow poets have been magnanimous indeed in accepting me as a poet. I would not have been surprised had they ignored me, but, in fact, they've been wonderfully supportive and encouraging. Which contradicts the general notion that poets are highly competitive and jealous of one another's accomplishments. . . .

INTERVIEWER: You say no one wants to read a novelist's

poetry. What about Robert Penn Warren? John Updike? Erica Jong? I suppose Allen Tate and James Dickey are poets who happened to write novels. . . .

OATES: I suppose I was thinking only of hypothetical reactions to my own poetry. Robert Penn Warren aside, however, there *is* a tendency on the part of critics to want very much to categorize writers. Hence one is either a writer of prose or of poetry. If Lawrence hadn't written those novels he would have been far more readily acclaimed as one of the greatest poets in the language. As it is, however, his poetry has been neglected. (At least until recently.)

INTERVIEWER: *By the North Gate,* your first book, is a collection of short stories, and you continue to publish them. Is the short story your greatest love? Do you hold with the old adage that it is more difficult to write a good story than a novel?

OATES: Brief subjects require brief treatments. There is *nothing* so difficult as a novel, as anyone knows who has attempted one; a short story is bliss to write set beside a novel of even ordinary proportions.

But in recent years I haven't been writing much short fiction. I don't quite know why. All my energies seem to be drawn into longer works. It's probably the case that my period of greatest productivity is behind me, and I'm becoming more interested in focusing upon a single work, usually a novel, and trying to "perfect" it section by section and page by page.

INTERVIEWER: Nevertheless, you've published more short stories, perhaps, than any other serious writer in America today. I remember that when you chose the twenty-one stories to compose *The Wheel of Love,* you picked from some ninety which had been in magazines the two years since your previous collection. What will become of the seventy or so stories you didn't include in that collection? Were some added to later collections? Will you ever get back and pick up uncollected work?

OATES: If I'm serious about a story, I preserve it in book form;

otherwise I intend it to be forgotten. This is true of course for poems and reviews and essays as well. I went back and selected a number of stories that for thematic reasons were not included in *The Wheel of Love,* and put them into a collection called *The Seduction And Other Stories.* Each of the story collections is organized around a central theme and is meant to be read as a whole—the arrangement of the stories being a rigorous one, not at all haphazard.

INTERVIEWER: You don't drink. Have you tried any consciousness-expanding drugs?

OATES: No. Even tea (because of caffeine) is too strong for me. I must have been born with a rather sensitive constitution.

INTERVIEWER: Earlier you mentioned Hugh Petrie in *The Assassins.* He is but one of many deranged characters in your books. Have you known any genuine madmen?

OATES: Unfortunately, I have been acquainted with a small number of persons who might be considered mentally disturbed. And others, strangers, are sometimes drawn my way; I don't know why.

Last week when I went to the university, I wasn't allowed to teach my large lecture class because, during the night, one of my graduate students had received a telephone call from a very angry, distraught man who announced that he intended to kill me. So I had to spend several hours sequestered away with the head of our department and the head of security at the university and two special investigators from the Windsor City Police. The situation was more embarrassing than disturbing. It's the first time anyone has so explicitly and publicly threatened my life—there have been sly, indirect threats made in the past, which I've known enough not to take seriously.

(The man who called my student is a stranger to us all, not even a resident of Windsor. I have no idea why he's so angry with me. But does a disturbed person really need a reason . . . ?)

INTERVIEWER: How about the less threatening, but nonetheless hurtful, reactions of friends and relatives—any reactions to conscious or unconscious portraits in your work?

OATES: My parents (and I, as a child) appear very briefly in *Wonderland,* glimpsed by the harassed young hero on his way to, or from, Buffalo. Otherwise there are no portraits of family or relatives in my writing. My mother and father both respond (rather touchingly at times) to the setting of my stories and novels, which they recognize. But since there is nothing of a personal nature in the writing, I have not experienced any difficulties along those lines.

INTERVIEWER: Aside from the singular incident at the university, what are the disadvantages of being famous?

OATES: I'm not aware of being famous, especially here in Windsor, where the two major bookstores, Coles', don't even stock my books. The number of people who are "aware" of me, let alone who read my writing, is very small. Consequently I enjoy a certain degree of invisibility and anonymity at the university, which I might not have at an American university —which is one of the reasons I am so much at home here.

INTERVIEWER: Are you aware of any personal limitations?

OATES: Shyness has prevented me from doing many things; also the amount of work and responsibility here at Windsor.

INTERVIEWER: Do you feel you have any conspicuous or secret flaw as a writer?

OATES: My most conspicuous flaw is . . . well, it's so conspicuous that anyone could discern it. And my secret flaw is happily secret.

INTERVIEWER: What are the advantages of being a woman writer?

OATES: Advantages! Too many to enumerate, probably. Since, being a woman, I can't be taken altogether *seriously* by the sort of male critics who rank writers 1, 2, 3 in the public press, I am free, I suppose, to do as I like. I haven't much sense of, or interest in, competition; I can't even grasp what Hemingway and the epigonic Mailer mean by battling it out with the

other talent in the ring. A work of art has never, to my knowledge, displaced another work of art. The living are no more in competition with the dead then they are with the living.
. . . Being a woman allows me a certain invisibility. Like Ellison's *Invisible Man.* (My long journal, which must be several hundred pages by now, has the title *Invisible Woman.* Because a woman, being so mechanically judged by her appearance, has the advantage of hiding within it—of being absolutely whatever she knows herself to be, in contrast with what others imagine her to be. I feel no connection at all with my physical appearance and have often wondered whether this was a freedom any man—writer or not—might enjoy.)

INTERVIEWER: Do you find it difficult to write from the point of view of the male?

OATES: Absolutely not. I am as sympathetic with any of my male characters as I am with any of my female characters. In many respects I am closest in temperament to certain of my male characters—Nathan Vickery of *Son of the Morning,* for instance—and feel an absolute kinship with them. The Kingdom of God *is* within.

INTERVIEWER: Can you tell the sex of a writer from the prose?

OATES: Never.

INTERVIEWER: What male writers have been especially effective, do you think, in their depiction of women?

OATES: Tolstoy, Lawrence, Shakespeare, Flaubert . . . Very few, really. But then very few women have been effective in their depiction of men.

INTERVIEWER: Do you enjoy writing?

OATES: I do enjoy writing, yes. A great deal. And I feel somewhat at a loss, aimless and foolishly sentimental, and disconnected, when I've finished one work and haven't yet become absorbed in another. All of us who write work out of a conviction that we are participating in some sort of communal activity. Whether my role is writing, or reading and responding, might not be very important. I take seriously Flaubert's statement that we must love one another in our art as the mystics love one another in God. By honoring one another's creation we honor something that deeply connects us all, and goes beyond us.

Of course, writing is only one activity out of a vast number of activities that constitute our lives. It seems to be the one that some of us have concentrated on, as if we were fated for it. Since I have a great deal of faith in the processes and the wisdom of the unconscious, and have learned from experience to take lightly the judgments of the ego and its inevitable doubts, I never find myself constrained to answer such questions. Life is energy, and energy is creativity. And even when we as individuals pass on, the energy is retained in the work of art, locked in it and awaiting release if only someone will take the time and the care to unlock it. . . .

ROBERT PHILLIPS
Fall 1978

Notes on the Contributors

FRANKLIN ASHLEY *(Interview with James Dickey)* teaches in the College of General Studies at the University of South Carolina in Columbia. He has published in *Harper's, The New Republic, New Times, People, Sport, Change, True,* and *Partisan Review.* His book of poems is entitled *Hard Shadows.*

MICHAEL BARBER *(Interview with Kingsley Amis)* is an English journalist and broadcaster who covers the literary scene. In addition to *The Paris Review,* he has written for *The New York Times Book Review* and *Quest/80.* In Britain, he regularly contributes to the BBC World Service.

GERALD CLARKE *(Interviews with Gore Vidal and P. G. Wodehouse)* is an associate editor of *Time* magazine specializing in show business and television. He is currently at work on a biography of Truman Capote.

BENJAMIN DEMOTT *(Interview with Archibald MacLeish)* teaches at Amherst and is a contributing editor of the *Atlantic.*

HAROLD FLENDER *(Interview with Isaac Bashevis Singer)* is the author of a novel, *Paris Blues,* and a work of nonfiction, *Rescue in Denmark.* He has contributed to *Saturday Review, The Nation,* and *The New Leader.*

ANNETTE GRANT *(Interview with John Cheever)* is editor of the Living Section of *The New York Times.*

RITA GUIBERT *(Interview with Pablo Neruda)* is the author of *Seven Voices,* published by Alfred A. Knopf in 1973, by Vintage in paperback in 1973, and in translation as *Siete Voces* by Editorial Novaro de Mexico in 1974. A former reporter for *Life En Espagnol,* she is currently engaged in creating and consulting on projects to build a better understanding of Latin America in the United States.

LINDA KUEHL *(Interview with Joan Didion),* an authority on jazz, published book reviews and interviews in *The New York Times Book Review, Saturday Review,* and *Playboy.* She was at work on a biography of Billie Holiday when she died in 1977 at the age of thirty-eight.

ROCCO LANDESMAN *(Interview with Jerzy Kosinski)* was born in St. Louis, has taught criticism at the Yale School of Drama, and now manages a mutual fund in New York.

THOMAS LECLAIR *(Interview with William Gass)* teaches at the University of Cincinnati. His essays on contemporary fiction have appeared in academic journals and in *The New Republic, The New York Times Book Review, Saturday Review,* and other magazines.

LUCAS MATTHIESSEN *(Interview with Irwin Shaw)* is an associate editor at Penguin Books and a contributing editor of *The Paris Review.*

WILLIE MORRIS *(Interview with Irwin Shaw)* is a former editor of *Harper's* and the author of *The Last of the Southern Girls, North Towards Home,* and other books. He writes: "As a onetime ten-flat halfback for the Yazoo City, Mississippi, Indians after the advent of the two-platoon system, he knew that Irwin Shaw was the quarterback and safetyman for Brooklyn College long before he started reading Shaw, but once he did, he became a lifelong admirer." Morris lives in Oxford, Mississippi.

JOHN PHILLIPS *(Interview with Irwin Shaw)* is the author of *The Second Happiest Day.* His articles and stories have appeared in a number of magazines.

ROBERT PHILLIPS *(Interview with Joyce Carol Oates)* is the author of nine books, including a short-story collection and a book of poetry. His work appears in a variety of publications, including *The New Yorker, The Hudson Review,* and *Partisan Review.* He is a contributing editor of *The Paris Review,* in which his interviews with both William Goyen and Joyce Carol Oates were published.

GEORGE PLIMPTON *(Interviews with Joseph Heller, Jerzy Kosinski, and Irwin Shaw)* is the author of *Out of My League, Paper Lion, Shadow Box,* and other books. He is the editor of *The Paris Review.*

TERRY SOUTHERN *(Interview with Henry Green)* is the author of *Flash and Filigree, Red Dirt Marijuana and Other Tastes, The Magic Christian,* and (with Mason Hoffenberg) *Candy.*